Uncoded Multimedia Transmission

Multimedia Computing, Communication and Intelligence

Series Editor

Chang Wen Chen & Shiguo Lian

PUBLISHED

Effective Surveillance for Homeland Security:

Balancing Technology and Social Issues

By Francesco Flammini, Roberto Setola, and Giorgio Franceschetti

ISBN: 9781138199705

Advances in Visual Data Compression and Communication:

Meeting the Requirements of New Applications

By Feng Wu

ISBN: 9781482234138

TV Content Analysis:

Techniques and Applications

By Yiannis Kompatsiaris, Bernard Merialdo, and Shiguo Lian

ISBN: 9780367900946

Music Emotion Recognition

By Yi-Hsuan and Homer H. Chen

ISBN: 9781439850466

Uncoded Multimedia Transmission

Feng Wu
Chong Luo
Hancheng Lu

CRC Press
Taylor & Francis Group
Boca Raton London New York

CRC Press is an imprint of the
Taylor & Francis Group, an **informa** business

First edition published 2021
by CRC Press
6000 Broken Sound Parkway NW, Suite 300, Boca Raton, FL 33487-2742

and by CRC Press
2 Park Square, Milton Park, Abingdon, Oxon, OX14 4RN

ISBN: 9780367632953 (hbk)
ISBN: 9780367632977 (pbk)
ISBN: 9781003118688 (ebk)

DOI: 10.1201/9781003118688

Typeset in Nimbus font
by KnowledgeWorks Global Ltd.

Contents

Part V Hybrid Digital and Analog Transmission

Preface

We learned about the work SoftCast very early when it appeared as an MIT technical report. We cannot remember who first mentioned this work to us. Since it was related to our research on video compression and transmission, and especially since it was quite different from the "conventional wisdom", we asked Chong Luo and our intern Xiaolin Liu to read it and find a time for detailed discussion. Soon after that, Chong took maternity leave. By then, we had been convinced that SoftCast did work but we were not able to determine its fundamental difference from existing approaches, which later inspired a series of excellent research.

When Chong was not in the lab, Feng Wu had to spend more time to consult with Liu on her research. When he read the SoftCast paper by himself, he was immediately attracted by the description "Compression and error correction reallocate bits in a data stream to maximize the information flow from sender to receiver. ... Each bit in a data stream effectively consumes equal transmission power on the medium, and hence, a reallocation of bits within a bitstream corresponds to a reallocation of power in the transmitted signal. Since SoftCast's data stream consists directly of real-valued numbers rather than bits, SoftCast can achieve the same goal of maximizing the information flow by directly controlling the power allocation for the different real values."

Anyone who has studied Shannon's information theory must know the data processing inequality, which states that no clever manipulation of the data can improve the inferences that can be made from the data. *Coded transmission* indirectly allocates transmission power through bit allocation, while *uncoded transmission* directly allocates transmission power. From this perspective, uncoded transmission should perform at least no worse than coded transmission (under certain channel conditions), although we did not see it at that time because technologies for coded transmission had been developed for decades and were very mature. Therefore, we made a decision to invest more in this research.

Our first work was *ParCast*. In uncoded transmission, every coefficient is transmitted independently and you can perform a per-coefficient channel allocation. It is widely recognized that low-frequency and high-frequency coefficients have very different levels of importance to the image reconstruction quality. In addition, orthogonal frequency division multiplexing (OFDM) technologies are broadly adopted in modern wireless communications, which decomposes a wideband channel into a set of mutually orthogonal subchannels. Different subchannels have different channel gains. We can better utilize the overall channel if important coefficients are transmitted in high-gain subchannels. In coded transmission, no one can allocate channels coefficient by coefficient. This work was submitted to ACM MobiCom 2012 and fortunately got accepted although the conference is highly competitive.

With better understanding of the uncoded transmission, we found more problems that have to be solved.

- The most important problem should be how to better utilize temporal correlation in video. 3D transform used in SoftCast can exploit temporal correlation, but temporal frames are not motion aligned. Motion compensation used in conventional video compression cannot be applied because the uncoded transmission cannot guarantee exactly the same references in the encoder and the decoder. When the references are different, motion compensation will result in serious drifting errors. The first part of our research in this book studies how to better utilize temporal and spatial correlations in the uncoded transmission.
- SoftCast provides an algorithm which can optimally allocate transmission power in additive white Gaussian noise (AWGN) Unicast channel and when the channel bandwidth matches the source bandwidth. However, real channel conditions are more complicated. In a multicast channel, diverse users may have different channel conditions or even screen resolutions. When the channel bandwidth is not known a priori, ad-hoc scheduling is needed. In the Rayleigh fading channel, discarding low-priority data and saving the channel uses for high-priority data can significantly improve the quality of the received video. The second part of our research in this book studies how to optimally allocate subchannel, bandwidth, and power among transmitted coefficients.
- By exploiting spatial dimension across multiple antennas at the sender and the receiver, multiple input multiple output (MIMO) could potentially improve a wireless system's capacity, range and reliability. It is an interesting topic to study the interaction between MIMO technologies and the uncoded transmission. One fundamental difference from the existing MIMO technologies is that coefficients transmitted through multiple antennas are correlated. It provides great flexibility in how to allocate and combine transmitted coefficients among antennas. This is the third part of our research in this book.
- Based on our research, we truly believe that uncoded transmission is not a replacement for coded transmission. Coded and uncoded transmissions have their respective advantages. On the one hand, uncoded transmission is good at channel adaptation, so it is very useful when the channel quality varies drastically, or in broadcast and multicast. On the other, coded transmission is more efficient in utilizing channel bandwidth when the channel quality is high. Therefore, the fourth part of our research in this book is hybrid coded and uncoded transmissions.

To our best knowledge, this is the first book that systematically studies uncoded multimedia transmission. Limited by the authors' ability and current knowledge, it is impossible to cover all the problems in uncoded transmission. This book is just a starting point for the research on uncoded transmission. With more experts working on this field, we believe that uncoded transmission will become more mature and can achieve higher transmission efficiency. In particular, more efforts are needed to find killer applications for uncoded transmission.

Feng Wu
Chong Luo
Hancheng Lu

Acknowledgments

We first would like to thank Dr. Hao Cui for his great technical contributions on multimedia correlation processing, resource allocation, and MIMO support. He played a key role in developing our uncoded multimedia transmission. When Cui started the research, he was a Ph.D. student in the University of Science and Technology of China, co-supervised by Prof. Chang Wen Chen and Prof. Feng Wu. He was an intern working with Dr. Chong Luo in Microsoft Research Asia. His contributions are included in Chapter 3, Chapter 6 and Chapter 12.

We would like to thank Dr. Xiaolin Liu for her technical contributions on channel allocation and MIMO support. When Liu started the research on uncoded multimedia transmission, she was a Ph.D. student in the University of Science and Technology of China, supervised by Prof. Feng Wu. She was an intern working with Dr. Chong Luo and Dr. Wenjun Hu in Microsoft Research Asia. Her contributions are included in Chapter 10 and Chapter 11.

We would like to thank Prof. Xiaopen Fan for his technical contributions on distributed uncoded video transmission. He is now a professor at Harbin Institute of Technology working on distributed video coding. When he visited MSRA for six months, Prof. Feng Wu mentored him and extended his research from compression to communications. DCast was done while he was at MSRA. His contributions are included in Chapter 4. After the visit, he went back to Harbin Institute of Technology and continued his research in this direction.

We would like to thank Dr. Xiulian Peng for her technical contributions on distributed line-based uncoded image transmission. When Peng started the research, she was a Ph.D. student in the University of Science and Technology China, supervised by Prof. Feng Wu. She was an intern working with Dr. Ji-zheng Xu in Microsoft Research Asia. Her contributions are included in Chapter 5. After graduation, she joined Microsoft Research Asia where she is now a researcher.

We would like to thank Dr. Xiaoda Jiang for his technical contributions on superposed transmission with NOMA. He was a Ph.D. candidate in the University of Science and Technology of China, supervised by Prof. Chang Wen Chen and co-supervised by Prof. Hancheng Lu. His contributions are included in Chapter 8.

We would like to thank Yongqiang Gui for his technical contributions on joint bandwidth and power allocation. He is currently a Ph.D. candidate in the University of Science and Technology of China, supervised by Prof. Chang Wen Chen and co-supervised by Prof. Hancheng Lu. His contributions are included in Chapter 9.

We would like to thank Prof. Wenjun Hu for her technical contributions on channel allocation and MIMO support. When she worked on the research, she was an associate researcher in the Wireless Networking Group of Microsoft Research Asia. Because of the common research interests on uncoded transmission, she collaborated with us and jointly mentored Xiaolin Liu. Her contributions are included in Chapter 10 and Chapter 11. She is currently an assistant professor at Yale University after leaving Microsoft Research Asia.

We would like to thank Prof. Ruiqin Xiong for his technical contributions in analyzing the performance of uncoded multimedia transmission. He is an associate professor at Beijing University working on multimedia compression and processing. When he visited MSRA for six months, Prof. Feng Wu mentored him and extended his research to communications. His contributions are included in Chapter 6. After the visit, he went back to Beijing University and continued his research in this direction.

We would like to thank Dongliang He for his technical contributions on progressive transmission and hybrid digital and analog transmission. He was a Ph.D. candidate in the University of Science and Technology of China, supervised by Prof. Feng Wu. He was an intern working with Dr. Chong Luo at MSRA. His contributions are included in Chapter 7 and Chapter 14.

We would like to thank Dr. Cuilin Lan for her technical contributions on progressive transmission and hybrid digital and analog transmission. She is an associate researcher in Microsoft Research Asia. Before that, she was a Ph.D. candidate in XIDIAN University, supervised by Prof. Feng Wu. She works with Dr. Chong Luo as a team. Her contributions are included in Chapter 7 and Chapter 13.

We would like to thank Dr. Fei Liang for his technical contributions on the resource allocation for hybrid digital-analog transmission. He was a Ph.D. candidate in the University of Science and Technology of China, supervised by Prof. Feng Wu. He was an intern working with Dr. Chong Luo at MSRA. His contributions are included in Chapter 15.

We would like to thank Xiao Zhao for his technical contributions on adaptive hybrid digital-analog video transmission in mobile networks with wireless fading channels. He was a master's student in the University of Science and Technology of China, supervised by Prof. Hancheng Lu. His contributions are included in Chapter 16.

We would like to thank Prof. Chang Wen Chen for his technical advice. Prof. Chen closely collaborated with us at MSRA. He visited us for two or three weeks every year under a consulting contract. We had many technical discussions on the uncoded multimedia transmission.

Acronyms

AWGN   Additive White Gaussian Noise
BL   Base Layer
BM3D   Block Matching and 3D Filtering
BPSK   Binary Phase Shift Keying
CFO   Carrier Frequency Offset
CIF   Common Intermediate Format
CMT   Coded Multimedia Transmission
CRC   Cyclic Redundancy Check
CS   Compressive Sensing
CSI   Channel State Information
CSNR   Channel Signal Noise Ratio
DCT   Discrete Cosine Transform
DWT   Discrete Wavelet Transform
DSC   Distributed Source Coding
DVB   Digital Video Broadcasting
DVC   Distributed Video Coding
EL   Enhancement Layer
FEC   Forward Error Correction
FFT   Fast Fourier Transform
FGS   Fine Granularity Scalability
FPGA   Field Programmable Gate Array
GOP   Group of Pictures
GPS   Global Positioning System
GPU   Graphic Processing Unit
HARQ   Hybrid Automatic Request
HD   High Definition
HDA   Hybrid Digital-Analog
HM   Hierarchical Modulation
HVS   Human Visual System
HP   High Priority
IFFT   Inverse Fast Fourier Transform

JPEG   Joint Photographic Experts Group
JSCC   Joint Source Channel Coding
KKT   Karush Kuhn Tucker
KLT   Karhunen-Loève Transform
LAN   Local Area Network
LDPC   Low-Density Parity-Check code
LLSE   Linear Least Square Estimator
LMMSE   Linear Minimum Mean Square Error
LMT   Linear Multimedia Transmission
LP   Low Priority
LRP   Long Range Prediction
LTE   Long Term Evolution
MBMS   Multimedia Broadcast Multicast Service
MC   Motion Compensation
MCE   Motion Compensated Extrapolation
MCI   Motion Compensated Interpolation
MCTF   Motion Compensated Temporal Filtering
MDC   Multiple Description Coding
MIMO   Multiple Input Multiple Output
MINLP   Mixed Integer Nonlinear Programming
MIT   Massachusetts Institute of Technology
MLQ   Modulo Lattice Quantization
MMSE   Minimum Mean Squared Error
MPEG   Moving Picture Experts Group
MRC   Maximum Ratio Combining
MSD   Multiple Similar Description
MSDC   Multiple Similar Description Coding
MSTBC   Multiplexed Space Time Block Coding
MSE   Mean Squared Error
MV   Motion Vector
NLM   Non-Local Mean
NOMA   Non-Orthogonal Multiple Access
OFDM   Orthogonal Frequency Division Multiplexing
OMA   Orthogonal Multiple Access
OSI   Open Systems Interconnection
PAT   Pseudo Analog Transmission
PDO   Power Distortion Optimization
PSNR   Peak Signal-to-Noise Ratio
QAM   Quadrature Amplitude Modulation
QPSK   Quadrature Phase Shift Keying
RA   Rate Adaptive
RIP   Restricted Isometry Property
RTP   Real-time Transport Protocol
SAD   Sum of Absolute Differences
SC   Superposition Coding

SDK	Software Development Kit
SDR	Signal to Distortion Ratio
SER	Symbol Error Rate
SIC	Successive Interference Cancellation
SINR	Signal to Interference and Noise Ratio
SM	Streaming Multiprocessor
SNF	SUSAN Noise Filter
SNR	Signal Noise Ratio
SORA	Software Radio
SSIM	Structural Similarity
STBC	Space Time Block Coding
SVC	Scalable Video Coding
SVD	Singular Value Decomposition
UEP	Unequal error protection
UMT	Uncoded Multimedia Transmission
VLC	Variable Length Coding
VNI	Visual Networking Index
WLAN	Wireless Local Area Network
WHDI	Wireless High Definition Interface

Part I
Video Transmission - Coded or Uncoded

In 2017, global IP traffic was 1.5 Zettabytes (ZB) per year and video traffic constitutes 75 percent of it [1]. It is estimated that by 2022 IP video traffic will be 82 percent of all consumer Internet traffic [1]. The importance of video transmission is evident.

Televisions and movies have long existed before the Internet emerged. Back then, videos were analog in their entire life cycle, including capturing, storage, transmission and playback. In an analog video transmission, such as television broadcast, the luminance and chrominance of the moving pictures are directly represented by the amplitude, frequency or phase of the signal. This is the traditional form of uncoded transmission. All broadcast television systems have used uncoded transmission before the digital television became a real possibility in 1990s.

In the digital era, videos are stored as binary data and transmitted in a digital form. The process of converting moving pictures to bit streams is called video coding. Generations of video coding/decoding (CODEC) standards have been established towards more concise binary representations of videos. During transmission, channel coding is commonly adopted to ensure faithful data recovery against channel noise and packet losses. The concatenation of source coding and channel coding is the canonical digital video transmission paradigm, which we refer to as coded transmission.

It is generally believed that digital (coded) video transmission is far more efficient than analog video transmission. This is true, and it is an unstoppable trend that analog video will eventually fade out. As a matter of fact, most governments around the world have started or finished shutting down the analog television system. However, the uncoded video transmission we are going to discuss in this book is not the conventional analog video transmission. The word *uncoded* simply means skipping the binarization process in video transmission. Sometimes, this new video transmission paradigm is also called pseudo analog video transmission.

An uncoded video transmission (UVT) system is one that skips quantization and entropy coding in compression and all subsequent binary operations including channel coding and bit-to-symbol mapping of modulation. By directly transmitting non-binary symbols with amplitude modulation, the uncoded system avoids the annoying cliff effect observed in the coded transmission system and provides graceful quality degradation of the transmitted content with the varying channel conditions. Because of this feature, uncoded transmission is more suited to both unicast and multicast in dynamic and heterogeneous channel settings.

A crucial problem we shall consider in uncoded transmission is its efficiency. If source coding and channel coding are removed, how can we keep the optimality of video communication according to the definition of Shannon's information theory? In fact, uncoded transmission has been proved to be optimal for any colored Gaussian source to any colored Gaussian noise channel. However, developing practical uncoded video systems still has a long way to go. In this part, we provide background information on video transmission systems. We will also overview our research on uncoded and hybrid video transmission to help the audience quickly get a full picture of the entire book.

Chapter 1
Uncoded Video Transmission

This book assumes that the audience already has basic knowledge of image/video compression and data communication. In image/video compression, the audience is expected to know the technologies of image coding (e.g., JPEG and JPEG 2000) and video coding (e.g., H.264 and HEVC standard). In data communication, the audience is expected to know the technologies of channel coding and modulation. In this section, we will briefly introduce the coded and uncoded video transmission.

1.1 Coded Video Transmission

All natural signals, including images and videos, are analog in nature, but they are usually digitized and compressed for storage and transmission. Most contemporary video transmission systems are coded ones, and a large portion of them adopt separate source-channel design. The theoretical ground is Shannon's source-channel separation theorem [2, 3], which states that we can achieve the optimal communication performance by separately optimizing the source code and the channel code. Owing to the simplicity of separate design, researchers have clustered into two camps, one focusing on source coding and the other working on channel coding.

In the past decades, image/video codecs do an excellent job of removing redundancy and compressing the data. However, they also make the compressed bit stream highly vulnerable to bit errors and packet losses. In particular, all multimedia codecs use entropy coding, after which a single bit flip may confuse symbol boundaries, producing arbitrary errors in the original content. Therefore, before transmission, channel coding has to be used to add back a certain level of redundancy in forms of forward error correction (FEC) codes. The objective is to eliminate bit errors and packet losses. An exemplified coded framework for image transmission is shown in Fig. 1.1. This coded framework has achieved great success for digital image/video transmission.

DOI: 10.1201/9781003118688-1

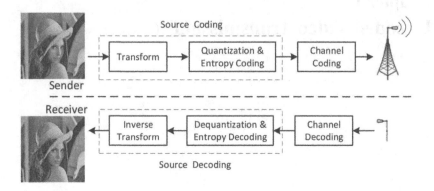

Fig. 1.1 The coded framework for image transmission.

Unfortunately, two conditions to achieve the optimality of this coded framework are often ignored.

First, the optimality of the separate design is only valid for point-to-point communications or unicast. In a broadcast or multicast system, separate design cannot be optimal for all receivers. In conventional broadcasting systems, the overall performance tends to tailor to the weakest receiver with the worst channel condition, since every user in the system needs the broadcasting content. This strategy leads to inefficient channel usage and is unfair to strong receivers. This problem is likely to be exacerbated in the systems featuring MIMO technologies, where receivers are equipped with different numbers of antennas (i.e., antenna heterogeneity). In such a system, the number of simultaneous streams is limited by the least number of receiver antennas again.

Second, even in the unicast, the channel capacity should be known to the source encoder to achieve optimality. However, wireless channel is time-varying. It is not possible to precisely estimate future channel conditions. When the actual channel is better than expected, no additional gain can be achieved. Specifically, the received video quality is a constant when the channel quality is above a certain threshold. The constant is decided by the quantization parameter in source coding. This is often referred to as the *saturation effect*. Moreover, when the actual channel is worse than expected, the entire message could be corrupted. This is known as the *cliff effect*. One main reason for such behavior is that FEC code is only capable of correcting a certain number of bit errors. When the number of errors exceeds the pre-allocated redundancy, decoding fails and errors spread in the entire data block.

Some results of coded video transmission are presented in Fig. 1.2, where video is compressed by H.264 [4] and a convolutional code with polynomials $\{133, 171\}$ is adopted as FEC code for channel protection. FEC rate and modulation are selected according to the channel signal-to-noise ratio (SNR). Both *saturation effect* and *cliff effect* can be clearly observed from the figure.

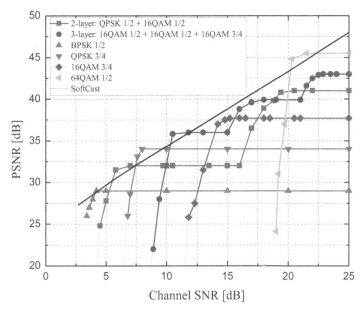

Fig. 1.2 The performance curves of coded and uncoded multimedia transmission.

Essentially, the receiver SNR heterogeneity in multicast and the varying channel condition in unicast present the same challenge to a video transmission system, which is the channel adaptation capability. This challenge can be addressed from either the source coding side or the channel coding side or both sides.

On the source side, *multi-resolution coding* is often used to successively refine the source rate-distortion trade-off, such as H.264/SVC [5] and JPEG2000 [6, 7]. The entropy coded bits are separated into layers with varying levels of importance. The base layer can be independently decoded and provides a basic quality, while joint decoding with enhancement layers leads to better quality. In a multicast scenario, the base layer should be received by all the users and strong users can enjoy a better quality by receiving and decoding the enhancement layers. In a unicast scenario, the base layer should be received at the worst possible channel condition, but when the actual channel condition is better, the receiver is able to receive more layers and decode the video with a better quality. We can combine layered source coding with UEP through channel coding or modulation. This approach has proven to be effective and popular for error resilient video transmission [8].

On the channel side, there are also layered channel code and layered modulation schemes. The layered channel code is known as rate-compatible channel code. Examples are rate-compatible LDPC code [9], rate-compatible Turbo code, and rateless code such as LT and Raptor code. They are usually used in conjunction with hybrid automatic request (HARQ) for unicasting single-layer video contents.

The layered modulation schemes are known as hierarchical modulation (HM), where low-priority symbols with lower transmission power are superimposed to high-priority symbols with higher transmission power. At the receiver, the high-priority symbols are first decoded treating the low-priority symbols as noise. Then, the decoded symbols are removed from the received symbols so that the low-priority symbols can be decoded. HM naturally combines with the multi-resolution coding at the source, such that layered source data with different priorities are mapped to different parts of the HM symbol. Such combination finds a perfect application in video multicast, and is adopted in several digital video broadcasting (DVB) systems [10, 11].

However, these layered source-channel schemes only alleviate the cliff effects of digital systems and introduce new design challenges. First, multi-resolution coding imposes a particular decoding order and dependency between layers, and the bandwidth of the weak receivers is reduced by the transmission of the enhancement layer data. Second, due to the power difference requirement between layers for successful decoding, only two or three levels can be embedded in an HM symbol, which constrains the granularity of code rates.

To summarize, the design space of video transmission systems includes source and channel coding, channel selection, modulation and power allocation.

1.2 Uncoded Video Transmission

1.2.1 Basic Concept

It is clear that quantization and entropy coding in source coding and channel coding result in the cliff effect and make the coded transmission inefficient in unicast in varying channels and in broadcast. Can they be removed from the coded framework? This question was first raised by Gastpar et al. in [12]. Intuitively, transmission without compression will be inefficient. However, in some simple cases (e.g., a Gaussian source over the additive white Gaussian noise channel), source coding and channel coding are not needed at all. Motivated by it, Gastpar's theoretic work derives a general condition for optimal communication, namely, source and channel have to be matched in a probabilistic sense [12]. Coding is one general way to match source and channel but definitely not the only way.

Except for the simplest cases, it is impossible to match source and channel without any processing. As proposed in [13], a theoretic uncoded scheme after removing quantization, entropy coding and channel coding is shown in Fig. 1.3. Instead, bandwidth allocation and power allocation are needed. First, transform is adopted to convert N-dimensional correlated data to N-dimensional independent coefficients. Second, if channel bandwidth is less than transmitting rate, some coefficients with small energy have to be dropped (i.e., *Bandwidth compression*). If channel bandwidth is more than the transmitting rate, some coefficients with large energy are transmitted multiple times (i.e., *bandwidth expansion*). Together they are called *bandwidth allocation*. Third, in order to optimally transmit a signal under the

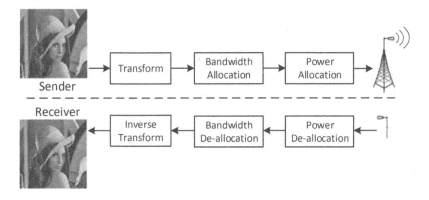

Fig. 1.3 The uncoded framework for image transmission.

MSE criterion in a power-constrained system, each coefficient should be scaled by a factor, which is inversely proportional to the fourth root of its variance. This is called *power allocation*.

More theoretic studies have been reported on matching complicated source and channel. Reznic et al. proposed using Wyner-Ziv coding and modulo-lattice modulation for bandwidth expansion [14]. Wilson et al. proposed the Costa and Wyner-Ziv coding scheme for the presence of interference known only to the transmitter and the presence of side information about the source known only to the receiver [15]. Kochman et al. proved that combining prediction and modulo-lattice operations is possible to match any colored Gaussian source to any colored Gaussian noise channel [16].

1.2.2 Theoretical Work

The early satellite image transmission and TV broadcasting are both analog communication systems. It is known that analog transmission is more robust than its digital counterpart and is not sensitive to exact channel knowledge at the sender. However, the conventional wisdom is that analog communication is not as efficient as digital communication. For TV broadcasting, the received video quality is generally not as high as that in current digital systems.

However, looking into the theoretical work on analog communication, we find that there are many cases in which analog communication is optimal. A famous example is to transmit a uniform-distributed binary source with a Hamming distance distortion metric over a binary symmetric channel. Another example is to transmit a Gaussian source with a squared-error distortion metric over an AWGN channel.

Further theoretical analyses by Gastpar et al. [12] have confirmed that channel coding is not necessary in some cases for optimal communication, but the source and the channel have to be matched in a probabilistic sense. Recently, Kochman and Zamir [16] showed that, by combining prediction and modulo-lattice arithmetic, one can match any stationary Gaussian source to any colored-noise Gaussian channel, and hence achieve Shannon's capacity limit. In other words, the AM scheme can asymptotically achieve optimal performance in point-to-point communication and becomes robust at high SNR ranges when the source and channel match each other.

Now we know that analog communication is not necessarily sub-optimal and certain processing needs to be performed to improve its performance. In fact, analog communication systems are mostly joint source-channel coding (JSCC) schemes. Among the large body of theoretical work on analog JSCC, linear coding and single-letter coding have attracted the most attention for their simplicity and low delay. At the intersection of these two coding schemes, there is a so-called uncoded transmission strategy in which no compression or channel coding is used and the source samples are transmitted by appropriately scaling according to the transmitter power constraint P. Surprisingly, such a simple strategy has been shown to achieve optimality in certain practical cases [17, 12].

The uncoded video transmission concerned in this book is slightly different from the above examples, because the source under consideration is not uni-variant Gaussian. Instead, video sources are modeled by a multi-variate Gaussian, or parallel Gaussian, after de-correlation transform. Source samples (i.e., coefficients) belonging to different Gaussian distributions should be scaled by different factors to achieve optimality. Lee and Petersen [13] carried out a comprehensive investigation on this optimal linear coding problem, and SoftCast [18, 19] is a straightforward implementation based on their results.

However, the bad news is that analog transmission of a parallel Gaussian source [20] over an AWGN channel is definitively suboptimal [21]. Let $S_i, i = 1, 2...M$ be the M sub-sources of a parallel Gaussian source. According to Lee and Peterson [13], the optimal energy allocation in analog transmission can be achieved by enforcing different scaling factors g_i over sources S_i with different variances $\sigma_i^2, i = 1, 2, \cdots, M$, under the average energy constraint. At the receiver, we observe that: (i) the average distortion d_{ai} for the signal from source S_i is proportional to its standard deviation, i.e., $d_{ai} \propto \sigma_i$; (ii) the average energy consumption P_{ai} for transmitting a signal from source S_i is proportional to the standard deviation of the source, i.e., $P_{ai} \propto \sigma_i$. Intuitively, the sources with large variances consume much more energy but result in larger distortion. Theoretically, the loss in performance of the analog approach with respect to the digital approach for sufficiently large transmission powers is

$$\frac{D_{analog}}{D_{digital}} = \left(\frac{(\sigma_1 + \sigma_2 + \cdots + \sigma_M)/M}{(\sigma_1 \sigma_2 \cdots \sigma_M)^{1/M}} \right)^2, \tag{1.1}$$

where σ_i^2 ($i = 1...M$) is the variance of the S_i and D_{analog} and $D_{digital}$ are the MSE distortions of the analog approach and the digital approach, respectively [20].

In a nutshell, the uncoded transmission we discuss in this book is not like the very basic analog TV broadcast system which almost does not do any processing over the video signal. In the transmission framework we considered, much better performance can be achieved by employing transform and power allocation techniques, while still maintaining a low complexity. The main advantage over digital systems is that a transmitter does not need to know users' channel conditions and receivers can naturally get a quality matching their channel conditions. The main drawback is that it is hard to achieve the optimal point-to-point performance as its digital counterpart does.

1.2.3 SoftCast

The first concrete scheme for uncoded video transmission is *SoftCast* [22]. The early version of SoftCast only considers the correlation of pixels in the same frame and ignores the correlation of frames. It operates on small blocks of pixels and thus each frame is divided into 8×8 blocks. An improved version of SoftCast de-correlates the spatial and temporal correlation through 3-dimensional (3D) transform [19]. For simplification, the SoftCast with 2D transform is discussed here as in [22].

1.2.3.1 Encoder

The first step in encoding a frame aims at removing correlation across pixels in the same block. SoftCast adopts a 2-dimensional Discrete Cosine Transform (DCT) of pixel luminance in each block. As shown in Fig. 1.4, DCT is a linear transform that takes as input an 8×8 image block, multiplies it by the known DCT matrix, and produces an 8×8 spatial frequency representation of the block. The spatial frequency representation is then traversed in a zig-zag order as in MPEG to produce a 64×1 column vector $\mathbf{x}$. The first row of $\mathbf{x}$ represents the DC component of the block, i.e., the average value of its pixels. The other rows refer to the projection of a block on some spatial frequency bands, with the low spatial frequencies in the top rows and the high spatial frequencies in the bottom rows. Since most images are smooth, most of the energy is in the low spatial frequency bands, i.e., the first few rows of vector $\mathbf{x}$. If a row of $\mathbf{x}$ is consistently zero across all blocks in a frame, it will be ignored.

It is important to generate a compact and resilient representation of $\mathbf{x}$ before transmission on the channel. Power allocation scales the magnitudes of $\mathbf{x}$ to provide the representation that minimizes reconstruction error. To find the optimal scaling factors, an image block is considered as a random vector derived from some distribution over all image blocks in the video frame. The covariance matrix of $\mathbf{x}$, $\Lambda_x = E[\mathbf{x}\mathbf{x}^T]$, is the average correlation between different rows in the random vector $\mathbf{x}$. An entry, λ_{ij} in this matrix, refers to the correlation between row i and j of $\mathbf{x}$, computed across all blocks in the frame. Since DCT is highly effective at

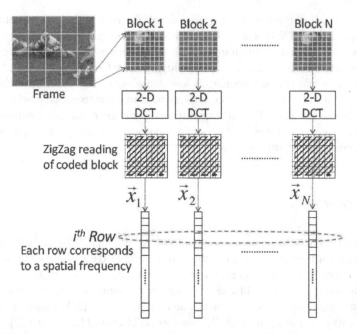

Fig. 1.4 The multimedia processing in the SoftCast scheme proposed in [22].

decorrelating most images, the correlation between different rows is effective zero in practice, and the only relevant elements of this covariance matrix are the diagonal elements.

Given these diagonal elements, SoftCast can compute the optimal scale as

$$g_i = \lambda_i^{-1/4} \left(\sqrt{\frac{P}{\sum_{j=1}^{64} \sqrt{\lambda_j}}} \right), \tag{1.2}$$

where P is the total power. The linear encoder that minimizes the mean square reconstruction error is

$$\mathbf{y} = G\mathbf{x}, \tag{1.3}$$

where G is a diagonal matrix with elements g_i. Observe that this scaling is analogous to traditional compression and error correction in the sense that it finds the representation that maximizes the information flow from sender to receiver, i.e., minimizes the error.

The scaled block vectors are assigned to packets. One might think that this could be addressed by assigning rows in blocks to packets. The problem, however, is that these rows differ significantly in their power, and hence some packets would have higher power than others. This unequal distribution is undesirable in the face of packet loss, because the loss of high-power packets would have far greater impact on the quality of the reconstructed signal than the loss of low-power packets. Thus, a linear transform is needed to change the representation of the vectors, $\mathbf{x}$'s, to a new representation, where all rows have equal average power. This transform must also maintain the power allocation done before. Typically, communication systems use the Hadamard matrix for this purpose. The Hadamard matrix is an orthogonal transform composed entirely of +1s and -1s. Multiplying by this matrix creates a whitening effect because it creates a new representation, where the original rows are smeared across all dimensions. Putting this together, the linear encoding can be described as

$$\mathbf{y} = H G \mathbf{x}, \tag{1.4}$$

where H is the Hadamard matrix. Thanks to this whitening, rows of $\mathbf{y}$'s can be assigned to packets now. These packets will have equal power and hence offer better packet loss protection.

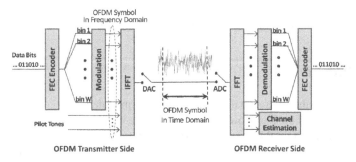

Fig. 1.5 The diagram of a typical OFDM system.

SoftCast's PHY layer directly transmits the real values of $\mathbf{y}$. This allows channel noise, which manifests as small perturbations of the transmitted signal, thus directly translating to small perturbations of the transmitted real value. The transmission of Orthogonal Frequency Division Multiplexing (OFDM) is adopted, which is already part of the 802.11 PHY layer. It divides the 802.11 spectrum into many independent narrow subcarriers, called *OFDM bins*. Fig. 1.5 shows a schematic of a typical OFDM channel. A data stream is FEC encoded and striped across the OFDM bins. The bits in each bin are modulated to generate a signal with in-phase and quadrature components. The signals across all bins are then converted to the time domain using an Inverse Fast Fourier Transform (IFFT) and sent on the medium by the transmitter.

SoftCast adds an option to the PHY interface to allow OFDM to bypass FEC and modulation, presenting a raw OFDM channel to higher layers. In this case, the OFDM channel will have the schematic in Fig. 1.6. It assigns a pair of values to each bin, mapping one to the in-phase, and the other to the quadrature component, of the signal. As before, these signals are then input to an IFFT module to generate a time-domain signal, which is transmitted across the channel.

In addition, the encoder sends a small amount of metadata, especially the diagonal elements, λ_i, of the covariance matrix to assist the decoder in inverting the received signal. The overhead of this metadata is low (0.005 bits per pixels

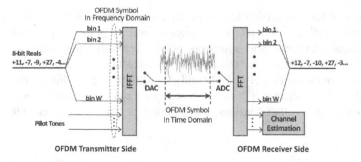

Fig. 1.6 The diagram of SoftCast's raw OFDM system.

in SoftCast, i.e., less than 2% overhead), and it can be sent using the traditional mechanism at the lowest 802.11 bit rate to allow reliable reception by all receivers. The matrix G can be computed directly from this covariance metadata.

1.2.3.2 Decoder

At the receiver, the time signal is sent to an FFT module to retrieve the values in each of the OFDM bits, as shown in Fig. 1.6. These values are scaled and calibrated using the standard OFDM processing. At this point, the traditional OFDM pipeline of demodulation and FEC is bypassed, and the raw values are transmitted to the receive socket. The end result is that for each value y_i that is sent, the received value is $y_i + n_i$, where n_i is a random noise. Hence, the received block $\widehat{\mathbf{y}}$ is

$$\widehat{\mathbf{y}} = \mathbf{y} + \mathbf{n}. \tag{1.5}$$

$\mathbf{n}$ is a noise vector whose entries are i.i.d Gaussian variables.

Let us assume that the receiver has received all packets. The received signal can be rewritten as

$$\widehat{\mathbf{y}} = HG\mathbf{x} + \mathbf{n} = C\mathbf{x} + \mathbf{n}, \tag{1.6}$$

where C is the encoder matrix that combines the effect of power allocation and whitening. Given the received signal and the encoding matrix C (which can be computed from the received metadata), the best estimate of $\mathbf{x}$ has to be computed.

The solution to this problem is widely known as the Linear Least Square Estimator (LLSE). Specifically, if the decoder knows the covariance matrix of the source signal Λ_x, and the covariance matrix of the channel noise, Σ, then the LLSE estimates the original signal as

$$\mathbf{x}_{LLSE} = \Lambda_x C^T (C\Lambda_x C^T + \Sigma)^{-1}\widehat{\mathbf{y}}, \tag{1.7}$$

where $\mathbf{x}_{LLSE}$ refers to the LLSE estimate of block $\mathbf{x}$, C^T is the transpose of the encoder matrix C. Note that the diagonal Σ_x matrix is transmitted as metadata by the encoder. The noise covariance matrix, Σ, is also a diagonal matrix, where each entry corresponds to the noise variance experienced by the packet in which the respective row was transmitted.

Consider how the LLSE estimator changes with SNR. At high SNR, the noise is small, (i.e., $\|\Sigma\|_2 \approx 0$), and Eq. (1.7) becomes

$$\mathbf{x}_{LLSE} \approx \Lambda_x C^T (C\Lambda_x C^T)^{-1} \widehat{\mathbf{y}} = C^{-1}\widehat{\mathbf{y}}. \tag{1.8}$$

Thus, at high SNR, the LLSE estimator becomes the inverse of the measurements. This is because at high SNR one can trust the measurements and we do not need the correlation of the blocks Λ_x. In contrast, at low SNR, when the noise power is high, one cannot fully trust the measurements and it is better to readjust the estimate according to the correlation statistics of the original blocks.

What if a receiver experiences packet loss? How can such a receiver decode? Recall that we spread an encoded block across multiple packets to ensure that the loss of a packet reduces the resolution of all blocks in a frame rather than create a patch on the screen. Let us assume that the lost packet contains the ith row of the blocks. Then this loss would eliminate row y_i for $i \in \{1, 2, \cdots, 64\}$. Define $\mathbf{y}_{*i}$ as $\mathbf{y}$ after removing the ith row, and similarly C_{*i} and $\mathbf{n}_{*i}$ as the encoder matrix and the noise vector after removing the ith row. Effectively:

$$\mathbf{y}_{*i} = C_{*i}\mathbf{x} + \mathbf{n}_{*i}. \tag{1.9}$$

The LLSE decoder becomes

$$\mathbf{x}_{LLSE} = \Lambda_x C_{*i}^T (C_{*i}\Lambda_x C_{*i}^T + \Sigma_{(*i,*i)})^{-1}\widehat{\mathbf{y}}_{*i}. \tag{1.10}$$

Note that a row and a column are removed from Σ. Eq. (1.10) gives the best approximation of the 64 elements in $\mathbf{x}$ using only 63 measurements, i.e., the approximation that minimizes the mean square errors.

The final steps are simple: reorganize $\mathbf{x}_{LLSE}$ into an 8×8 DCT block by undoing the zigzag traversal in Fig. 1.4, multiply by the inverse of the DCT matrix to generate the original video block, and tile the blocks into a video frame.

In SoftCast, we can clearly observe that real-valued data is directly transmitted with amplitude modulation. In this case, channel noise translates to a small perturbation in the received value. As a result, a receiver with high SNR (i.e., low noise) receives the wireless symbols that are close to the transmitted ones, and hence decodes the values that are close to the original values. A receiver with low SNR (i.e., high noise), on the other hand, receives wireless symbols that are away from the transmitted ones. To present a better performance, the results of SoftCast with 3D transform is shown in Fig. 1.2. Clearly, it can provide graceful degradation of the transmitted signal depending on the quality of the user's channel. It avoids the cliff effect in the coded transmission and can well serve multiple receivers with heterogeneous channels in broadcast.

1.3 Challenges in UVT

However, the research on the uncoded transmission is still in its infancy. Many key theoretical and technical problems are not fully addressed. Now it is not the right time to discuss whether or not the uncoded transmission can achieve better performance than the coded transmission in the end-to-end communication. At least in our opinion, three key issues have to be addressed in the current uncoded transmission.

Correlation processing - Natural visual signals have both temporal and spatial correlations. How to efficiently process these correlations is of paramount importance to both coded and uncoded schemes. In conventional coded schemes, the temporal correlation is exploited by motion estimation (ME) and motion compensation (MC) while the spatial correlation is exploited by block-based transform. In SoftCast, 3D-DCT transform is adopted to remove both the spatial and temporal correlations in video frames. Obviously, it is not as efficient as ME and MC in removing temporal redundancy. One of the most important problems we shall address in uncoded transmission is how to better compact visual signals.

Resource allocation - In wireless communications, power and bandwidth are precious resources. Previous research has shown that, when the source and channel bandwidths are matched, the optimal power allocation in an additive white Gaussian noise (AWGN) channel is to let the power of a source be inversely proportional to the square root of its standard deviation. However, in practical fading channels, how to allocate power for uncoded transmission is still an open problem. Besides, SoftCast assumes that the available bandwidth for a particular video stream is known a priori, so that source and channel bandwidth matching can be achieved by dropping low-energy source blocks. However, in practice, multiple users are in the same access point (AP) and competing for the bandwidth. How to allocate bandwidth in such an environment is also an open problem.

MIMO support - Multiple Input Multiple Output (MIMO) antenna technologies have become the default building blocks for wireless communication. MIMO can significantly improve the transmission rate by spatial multiplexing. However, in a multicast session, the maximum spatial multiplexing order is constrained by the use with the least number of antennas. It is not clear whether the uncoded transmission can support MIMO, especially the antenna heterogeneity, in a more flexible way.

Besides, it is natural to ask whether it is possible to combine coded and uncoded transmission so that we can take advantage of their respective strengths and avoid the shortcomings. Actually, hybrid digital-analog (HDA) transmission is not a new concept. In the context of HDA transmission for visual signals, we shall at least answer the following two questions: 1) what information is more efficiently represented by bits and what information should be left in the analog form; 2) how to share the power and bandwidth resources among digital (coded) and pseudo-analog (uncoded) contents.

Finally, we discussed some other names for the uncoded transmission. The first one is linear multimedia transmission (LMT) because, after removing quantization, entropy coding and channel coding, the rest of the processing such as transform and power allocation are all linear. The second one is pseudo analog transmission (PAT) because the transmission is carried out by amplitude modulation. It is similar to analog transmission but the implementation is still digital. The uncoded transmission, linear transmission and pseudo analog transmission characterize the same framework from different viewpoints.

Chapter 2
Advances in Uncoded and Hybrid Multimedia Transmission

2.1 Advances in Uncoded Multimedia Transmission

In this book, we focus on our recent research on developing the practical uncoded multimedia transmission. Three key problems, namely multimedia correlation processing, resource allocation, and MIMO support, will be addressed. An advanced scheme for uncoded multimedia transmission is presented in Fig. 2.1 according to our research. The scheme is divided into three parts. The first part is correlation processing, which handles temporal and spatial correlation in multimedia. The second part allocates subchannel, bandwidth and transmission power to the transmitted multimedia. The third part is how to process transmitted signal for supporting MIMO. The technical problems and proposed solutions in these parts are briefly discussed as follows.

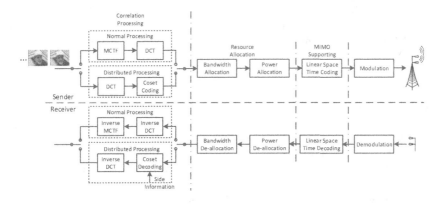

Fig. 2.1 Advances in the uncoded multimedia transmission.

DOI: 10.1201/9781003118688-2

2.1.1 Multimedia Correlation Processing

"Uncoded" does not mean unprocessed. If the redundancies in multimedia are not processed properly, it is impossible to achieve the optimal transmission performance. Similar to conventional compression, multimedia correlation can be processed at either the sender side or the receiver side. We refer to the former as normal processing and the latter as distributed processing, as shown in Fig. 2.1.

2.1.1.1 Normal Processing

For natural video sequences, motion compensation (MC) is an essential step in the coded framework to remove temporal redundancy. MC is a closed-loop prediction, i.e., the prediction is based on the reconstructed frame at the decoder not the original frame. In the coded framework, the transmission is assumed to be lossless if channel coding provides enough protection. Thus, the encoder could create the reconstruction from the bit stream it generated. However, in the uncoded framework, the encoder is not able to know the exact reconstructed frame at the receiver, not to mention that in a multicast session different receivers will receive different reconstructions. In this case, the closed-loop prediction will bring drifting errors. SoftCast [19] simply adopts 3D-DCT to get around the problem, but transform without motion alignment cannot fully exploit the temporal correlation.

We adopted an approach called *MCTF* (Motion Compensated Temporal Filtering) [23], which is an open-loop prediction, i.e., the prediction is based on original pixel values not the reconstructed ones. It has been shown that the drifting errors are much smaller than its closed-loop counterpart. Therefore, in the normal processing of Fig. 2.1, a video sequence is first divided into groups of pictures (GOPs). Assume that each GOP has M frames $\{I_m, m = 1, \cdots, M\}$. It is first de-correlated in the temporal axis via MCTF. The temporally filtered frames $\{I_m^T, m = 1, \cdots, M\}$ are then transformed into frequency domain by 2-dimensional (2D) DCT to get the transformed frames $\{I_m^D, m = 1, \cdots, M\}$. This part is included in Chapter 3.

2.1.1.2 Distributed Processing

The other way is to process the multimedia correlation at the receiver, like that in distributed video coding (DVC). As shown in the distributed processing of Fig. 2.1, temporal correlation can be exploited at receivers as side information [24]. Similar to MCTF, the distributed approach does not bring drifting errors and can align different temporal frames with motion information.

Chapter 4 gives an example of the distributed correlation processing in uncoded transmission. Each frame is first transformed into frequency domain by 2D DCT. After that, coset coding is adopted, which is a typical technique used in DVC. It partitions the set of possible coefficient values into several cosets and transmits coset indexes to the receiver. Coset coding achieves compression because the coset indexes have typically lower entropy than the coefficients. Unlike distributed coded transmission, syndrome coding is removed. Coset indexes are directly transmitted after bandwidth and power allocation. At the receiver, side information is generated from temporal neighboring frames. With the coset index and the side information, the receiver can recover the coefficient value by choosing the one in the coset closest to the side information.

In Chapter 5, a line-based distributed uncoded scheme is illustrated for transmitting high-resolution satellite images captured by line scanning cameras. At the sender, each captured line is immediately processed by 1D transform and coset coding. Without syndrome coding, transmission power is directly allocated to the coset indexes by scaling the indexes according to their distributions. Finally, the scaled indexes are transmitted over an amplitude modulation. At the receiver, the side information is generated from the previous received lines, which exploits the correlation among lines. The line-based distributed uncoded scheme is featured by low delay, low memory cost and low complexity.

2.1.2 Resource Allocation

Although the bandwidth and power allocation has been extensively studied in the coded transmission, the solution cannot be directly applied to the uncoded transmission. This is because, coded schemes couple power and bandwidth allocation problems through bit representation. In particular, entropy coding in compression allocates different numbers of bits to different coefficients according to their entropy or importance. Each encoded bit essentially carries the same amount of information. They are treated with equal importance during channel coding and modulation. As such, power and bandwidth allocations are both realized through bit allocation.

In uncoded transmission, there is no entropy coding. Each coefficient is directly transmitted with amplitude modulation, consuming a power which is proportional to its variance. The lack of bit representation couples power and bandwidth allocation problems and makes the joint optimization much more complicated. Especially in fast fading channels, if high-priority (HP) data (e.g., DC coefficients) unfortunately experiences a deep fade, the overall distortion would be dramatically increased. Simply allocating more power to the HP coefficients does not solve the problem. Experiences in the coded transmission have shown that diversity increases robustness and improves bit error rate (BER) performance in fading channels. This suggests that we may sacrifice the transmission opportunity of some low-priority (LP) data and save the channel bandwidths for HP data to secure their quality. While the optimal power allocation under AWGN channel has been addressed in prior work [13], the optimal joint bandwidth and power allocation in fading channels remains an open problem.

In Chapter 6, we first address the case where the PHY bandwidth provisioning is stable, but the channel SNR is dramatically varying. For resource allocation in Fig. 2.1, each transformed frame I_m^D is divided into N equal-sized chunks. Let λ_n denote the variance of the nth ($1 \leq n \leq N$) chunk. We consider the coefficients in the nth chunk as random variables drawn from a Gaussian distribution $\mathscr{D}_n = \mathscr{N}(0, \lambda_n)$. As all chunks have the same size, we could simply model the source as a random vector $(c_1...c_N)^T$ with $c_n \sim \mathscr{D}_n$. The objective of resource allocation is to find the power scaling factor g_n and the number of repeated transmissions k_n for random variable c_n. Once the two values are determined, each instance of c_n will be multiplied by g_n and be repeated for k_n times.

The joint optimization of g_n and k_n is a mixed integer nonlinear programming (MINLP) problem, which has been proved to be NP-hard. In [25], an algorithm was proposed to allocate bandwidth and power iteratively. At first, the chunks are sorted in descending order with their variances. In each iteration, the chunk with the least variance is dropped and the saved channel resource will be assigned to other chunks. The distortion under a given bandwidth allocation can be computed through the optimal power allocation. Dropping LP data increases distortion, while assigning more bandwidth to HP data can decrease more distortion. Therefore, the assignment can achieve the maximum net decrease in distortion. The iteration will be stopped until the distortion cannot decrease any more.

Then in Chapter 7, we further consider the case where multiple users or multiple applications share the bandwidth and the bandwidth provisioning for a particular video stream is not stable. In the original design of SoftCast, the coefficients to be transmitted are power scaled according to their variances and the total power budget. Since the coefficients with different variances need dramatically different transmission power, sometimes by several degrees of magnitude, they are mixed in order to form PHY packets of similar power. As a result, each packet contains both important and not-so-important coefficients. During the transmission, if the available bandwidth is smaller than expected, some of the packets may not have the transmission opportunity. When this happens, the important coefficients in these packets are discarded and the received video quality will be dramatically degraded.

We therefore investigate a progressive pseudo-analog video transmission scheme. The basic idea is as simple as to transmit the DCT coefficients successively according to their importance. However, the importance of a coefficient is determined by its variance, which is exactly the transmission power in amplitude modulation. If we group important coefficients together, we shall suppress their transmission power in any single transmission, but allow for re-transmission so that the power from multiple transmissions can be accumulated. At the receiver, video reconstruction can be performed at any moment, and preferably right before the playback deadline of a GOP. With this feature, the proposed progressive transmission scheme can operate in a "rebuffer-free" mode.

Next in Chapter 8, we further develop a superposed transmission scheme in NOMA systems. NOMA has shown potential for scalable multicast of video data. However, one key drawback for NOMA-based video multicast is the limited number of layers allowed by the embedded successive interference cancellation algorithm, failing to meet satisfaction of heterogeneous receivers. Therefore, we propose a novel receiver-driven superposed video multicast (Supcast) by integrating SoftCast into NOMA-based system, attempting to cater for multiple receivers with heterogeneous channel conditions as well as enhance performance in SoftCast in the case of insufficient bandwidth. In Supcast, coefficients are grouped into chunks, which are basic units for power allocation and superposition scheduling. These chunks are bisected into base layer (BL) and enhancement layer (EL), based on their chunk characteristics. One EL chunk and one BL chunk compose the superposed signal in a physical packet. Since decoding performance of each chunk is proportional to channel quality, each receiver can obtain satisfied video quality. Owing to superposition coding (SC), more information can be conveyed compared with SoftCast when bandwidth is limited.

In Chapter 9, joint subcarrier matching and power allocation is investigated for uncoded transmission, since the uncoded multimedia transmission is generally implemented through an orthogonal frequency-division multiplexing (OFDM)-based physical layer. In the OFDM-based physical layer, a large frequency band is divided into multiple narrow-band subcarriers with different channel fading factors. As significant wireless resources, subcarriers should be allocated properly. To further exploit this subcarrier gain, we propose a Spatial Scalability enabled Robust Video Broadcast (SSRVB) system, which can accommodate diverse users with heterogeneous resolutions as well as heterogeneous channel conditions. In SSRVB, a novel spatial decomposition method is first designed to fully exploit the performance gains from robust video transmission. Then a distortion optimization problem is formulated and solved through the joint subcarrier matching and power allocation scheme, with the goal to minimize the average distortion of multiple users.

2.1.3 MIMO Support

MIMO is a building block for high-capacity wireless link technologies, such as 802.11n, WiMAX and 3GPP LTE. In addition, the OFDM technology has become another building block for next generation wireless networks. It decomposes a wideband channel into a set of mutually orthogonal subchannels. The channel gains across these subchannels are usually different, sometimes by as much as 20 dB. Compared with coded multimedia transmission, uncoded multimedia transmission is more flexible in supporting MIMO and channel diversity.

2.1.3.1 Subchannel Allocation

The subchannel allocation problem is discussed in Chapter 10. The motivation is as follows. If we divide a frame into 8×8 blocks and perform a block DCT transform for each block, we can obtain the DCT coefficients in 64 different frequency bands. We compute the average energy for each frequency band and we can see very non-uniform distributions. The energy often spreads across 5 or 6 orders of magnitude, and the high-energy end drops very quickly. This non-uniform energy distribution is exacerbated when the inter-frame correlation is taken into account simultaneously through a temporal transform. Similarly, we also see a large spread between the strongest and weakest subchannels, though with a faster drop-off at the low gain end.

Therefore, it seems natural to match both sides, so that the high-energy DCT components are transmitted on the high-gain subchannels to avoid them acting against each other. Furthermore, power allocation between different subchannels can also affect the achieved channel rates, which would eventually translate to the reconstructed source distortion based on a suitable rate-distortion function. Therefore, a joint source-channel power allocation strategy can optimize the overall recovery performance. In [26], we present ParCast+, which tailors the video unicast quality to the MIMO-OFDM channel. It matches important source components to high-gain subchannels and scales the source data with power weights computed with joint source-channel considerations.

2.1.3.2 Compressive Sampling Code

In Chapter 11, compressive sampling code is introduced to handle antenna heterogeneity in video multicast. In the third part of Fig. 2.1, the transmitted signals $\hat{c}_n$ are generated after resource allocation. The CS sampling module generates measurements m_k from $\hat{c}_n$ through linear projections. However, the number of transmitted signals to represent a frame is usually on the order of hundreds of thousands. Performing CS sampling and decoding on such a large vector is impractical. Since the transmitted signals in the same chunk have the same statistical characteristics, we form short vectors with the same compressibility characteristic by taking the same number of elements from each chunk. The measurements are finally generated on the short vectors and sent out by multiple antennas through amplitude modulation.

A Hadamard sampling matrix is adopted in the sampling. It has been shown that a Hadamard sampling matrix has the same desirable properties and comparable recovery performance as the optimal random Gaussian matrix ensemble, but allows us to generate measurements at a lower complexity. CS theory makes the scheme feasible to decode under-determined systems at single-antenna users. On the other hand, multi-antenna receivers are able to benefit from additional antennas via higher rates, because the CS recovery quality scales with the number of received measurements. Furthermore, the lower the noise level in each measurement, the higher the CS decoding performance. With the antenna setting determining the number of received measurements, and the channel SNR governing the quality of each measurement, the overall recovery quality will then be simultaneously in line with antenna number and channel SNR.

2.1.3.3 Multiple Similar Description Code

Chapter 12 presents a video multicast system which naturally scales the video quality in the air according to the antenna settings. The basic idea is inspired by the multiple description (MD) coding [27]. In the simplest implementation, two $B/2$-Hz descriptions of a signal are generated from the odd and the even samples of a B-Hz description. In a $\{1,2\} \times 2$ system, if the sender transmits the adjacent odd and even samples, the symbol received by a 1-antenna user is a weighted average of the two samples and the weights are the corresponding channel parameters. A sequence of the received symbols can be looked on as another $B/2$-bits/s description of the original signal created in the air. Meanwhile, the 2-antenna user is able to decode both odd and even samples and reconstruct a B-bits/s signal with full quality.

However, the implementation of this idea is facing three main challenges. First, the channel parameters are not under control. In the worst case, signals from different antennas may cancel out each other. To solve this problem, we propose multiplexed space-time block coding (M-STBC), which ensures that all transmitted signals will be weighed by a positive factor in the received signal. Second, we discover that the key to the success of M-STBC is to construct similar streams to be concurrently transmitted on multiple antennas. We propose multiple similar description (MSD) coding, which produces highly similar streams through sub-sampling and pixel-shift prediction. Note that the conventional MD coding only ensures that any description alone is decodable, but the proposed MSD coding ensures that any linear combinations of the descriptions are decodable and more combinations lead to higher quality. However, the third challenge arises as similar streams contain too much redundancy which, if not removed, will greatly affect the power efficiency of the transmission. We tackle this problem by a two-phase transform. We create and transmit similar discrete cosine transform (DCT) coefficients but perform power allocation over Hadamard coefficients. With this design, we manage to transmit multiple similar streams with the same power efficiency as transmitting a single stream.

2.2 Advances in HDA Multimedia Transmission

Pseudo-analog video transmission not only realizes smooth adaptation but also achieves throughput comparable to the best digital scheme under certain conditions, among which the most important ones are: 1) the coefficients to be transmitted are completely decorrelated and are mixed-Gaussian; 2) the channel bandwidth matches the source bandwidth. However, these two conditions usually cannot be met in practice. First, 3D-DCT cannot fully remove the temporal correlations without motion alignment. Second, the available channel bandwidth could be much smaller than the source bandwidth, especially for high definition (HD) videos. For example, even the minimum-resolution HD video has 1280×720 pixels per frame and 27.648M coefficients per second when the frame rate is 30fps. Since every wireless symbol can only carry two coefficients in I and Q planes, transmitting a 720p video in pseudo-analog mode will demand a channel with roughly 13.824M bandwidth, which is unlikely to be satisfied. In these circumstances, the efficiency of pseudo-analog video transmission is seriously compromised.

The hybrid digital and analog (HDA) transmission is the combination of coded (digital) and uncoded (analog) transmission. The reason behind the combination of the coded and uncoded transmission is obvious. The coded transmission is bandwidth efficient and the uncoded transmission provides smooth quality adaptation to channel conditions. The key problem to solve in the HDA transmission is what data should be transmitted in a digital way and what data in a pseudo-analog way.

In Chapter 13, a practical HDA framework based on scalar quantization is proposed. Specifically, the 3D-DCT coefficients for a group of pictures are quantized to obtain the digital part, and the residuals become the analog part. Increasing the quantization step decreases the volume of the digital part and vice versa. The key challenge in this framework is how to allocate the constrained power and bandwidth resources between and among digital and analog components to achieve the minimal distortion at the receiver.

In Chapter 14, a structure-preserving HDA wireless video deliver scheme, named *SharpCast* is proposed, which simultaneously achieves continuous quality adaptation to varying wireless channel and high-quality visual experience of the reconstructed video. The basic approach of SharpCast is to decompose video into the content part (smooth image) and the structure part. The human visual system is sensitive to the structure part, so it is digitized, channel coded and reliably transmitted. The content part will be transmitted under the constraint of remaining bandwidth and power.

In Chapter 15, a hybrid digital-analog superimposed modulation (HDA-SIM) scheme is proposed for soft video delivery. In HDA-SIM, we treat the bandwidth of competing digital traffic as hidden resources for the video delivery system and the analog symbols are superimposed to the existing digital symbols. The key problem is how to allocate the bandwidth and power resources among various modulation symbols so that we can improve the performance of video delivery without sacrificing the throughput of existing digital traffic. We carry out both theoretical analysis and testbed evaluations for the proposed scheme.

In Chapter 16, an adaptive HDA video transmission scheme (A-HDAVT) is proposed, to achieve robust video streaming in mobile networks with realistic fading channel. In A-HDAVT, each GOP of video is first transformed into one Low-pass frame and several High-pass frames with MCTF. Then the critical Low-pass frame is reliably transmitted as base layer in a digital mode, while High-pass frames are transmitted as enhancement layers in an analog mode to achieve desired graceful degradation performance. To combat channel fading in mobile networks, the predicted channel status is exploited to perform power allocation. Extensive simulations show that A-HDAVT can achieve significant performance gains over competing schemes.

2.2.1 Theoretical Work

Naturally, one would like to have a system which has the advantages of both digital and analog systems while avoiding their drawbacks. The key research problem here is what information should be encoded into digital form and what information should be left in analog form. In addition, how should the digital and analog symbols be transmitted over a resource-constrained channel.

We again look into the theoretical work trying to find answers to these questions. In fact, there is quite a lot theoretical work on HDA. It is commented that HDA approaches can share some advantages with analog schemes and some with digital ones; but usually the design is complex [28]-[29].

Concretely, various HDA coding schemes are proposed to address the "leveling-off effect" of digital systems [30, 29]. They can asymptotically achieve good performance at the matched channel SNR while maintaining a "graceful change" characteristic at other channel SNRs. In [30, 29], hybrid digital-analog joint source-channel coding systems are proposed for a Gauss-Markov source and an independent and identically distributed (i.i.d.) Gaussian source based on vector quantization (VQ). Mittal et al. demonstrate the power of combining the digital code and analog linear code to achieve robust coding performance for transmitting a band-limited Gaussian source [31]. Wyner-Ziv coding [32, 15] has also been adopted in HDA transmissions to match source and channel.

Similar to the analog communications, most theoretical analyses on HDA are limited to a uni-variant Gaussian source, but there do exist a few works concerning the HDA transmission of parallel Gaussian sources. For example, Prabhakaran et al. [20] investigate the transmission of a parallel Gaussian source to a digital receiver and a linear-analog receiver. They design hybrid systems and theoretically analyze the trade-off between the distortion at the digital receiver and that at the analog receiver. In [21], the transmission of Gaussian sources to two users with smaller channel noise variance and larger channel noise variance is investigated. As Hamid Berhroozi et al. [33] commented, although the distortion is derived explicitly (in closed-form expression), the problem of finding an optimal power allocation policy among layers in order to optimize the overall end-to-end distortion pairs is still open.

Specifically for visual communications, Wang et al. [34] proposes a vector quantization based HDA scheme for image communication. However, it is not very flexible to optimize the allocation between digital coding and analog coding due to the high complexity in preparing codebooks of different dimensions. Kozintsev et al. propose a simple hybrid scheme in [28], which looks for an optimal partition position from the wavelet subbands. Divided by that optimized position, high frequency subbands are compressed in the digital approach, while the remaining subbands are coded using the analog approach. Such optimization is coarse, leaving a lot of space for improvement.

Efforts have also been made to explore the advantages of HDA coding in the video transmission scenarios. Some approaches take complicated video codecs as the digital coding tool [35]. Yu et al. present an HDA coding scheme [35] which uses wavelet transform to decompose a video segment to different frequency bands. The low frequency bands of the video coefficients are taken as a new video and coded using the state-of-the-art digital codec H.264/MPEG-4 AVC, in which complicated intra prediction and motion compensation are performed. Correspondingly, the coefficients in high frequency bands and the residuals are coded in analog.

2.3 Summary

What is the fundamental difference between the coded and uncoded transmissions? Both of them are on allocating transmission resources (power and bandwidth) to transmitted information. The coded transmission uses bits as its medium. It first allocates bits to transmitted information and then allocates power to coded bits. The uncoded transmission directly allocates transmission resources to transmitted information. Therefore it does not need entropy coding and channel coding any more.

The greatest advantage of the uncoded transmission is that it avoids the cliff effect and allows for graceful degradation of transmitted multimedia for different receivers depending on the quality of their channels. According to the experimental results reported in [19, 24, 36, 25], the performance of the uncoded transmission is comparable to that of the coded transmission in end-to-end communication. In broadcast, the performance of the uncoded transmission is significantly better than that of the coded transmission.

Furthermore, the uncoded transmission breaks the boundary of source coding and channel coding. In the PHY layer of the uncoded transmission, more high-level information about transmitted multimedia becomes known. It makes the design of multimedia transmission systems more flexible. The uncoded transmission also breaks the boundary of multimedia coding and processing. Some multimedia processing technologies, such as denoising and super-resolution, can be applied during multimedia transmission. It is the exact trend for multimedia communication to make digital and analog mixed, make source and channel mixed, and make coding and processing mixed.

In the uncoded transmission, received multimedia always contain channel noise unless the channel is noise-free. It may be not accepted for content archives. In this sense, the uncoded transmission will not replace the coded transmission. Instead, they will co-exist for different applications. The uncoded transmission is more suitable delivering content to large-scale audiences for browsing. Because of the noise in the received content, the uncoded transmission is inapplicable to multi-hop transmission because the noise in the first hop will be amplified by transmission power in the second hop. After several hops, the contents contain serious noise.

Part II
Correlation Processing

In this part, we discuss three technologies for multimedia correlation processing in uncoded transmission. It challenges the conventional wisdom that multimedia redundancy should be removed as much as possible for efficient communications. By keeping multimedia spatial redundancy at the sender and properly utilizing it at the receiver, it demonstrates the possibility to build a more robust and even more efficient wireless multimedia communication system than existing ones.

In Chapter 3, we present a video communication system which we call *Cactus* [37]. In this system, inter-frame (temporal) redundancy in video is removed at the encoder, but intra-frame (spatial) redundancy is retained. In doing so, pixel values after a transform-domain scaling are directly transmitted with amplitude modulation. At the receiver, spatial redundancy is utilized by image denoising. Note that denoising in our decoder is not a post-processing, but has to be immediately performed on channel output. Cactus is implemented on the SORA [38] platform and extensively evaluated in the 802.11a/g WLAN environment. On average, Cactus outperforms SoftCast by 4.7 dB in video peak signal-to-noise ratio (PSNR) and is robust to packet losses. In addition, Cactus is shown to be capable of transmitting high-definition videos in WLAN, and the performance is even better than an omniscient MPEG scheme.

Chapter 4 presents a novel framework called DCast [39] for distributed video coding and transmission over wireless networks, which is different from existing distributed schemes in three aspects. First, coset quantized DCT coefficients and motion data are directly delivered to the channel coding layer without syndrome or entropy coding. Second, transmission power is directly allocated to coset data and motion data according to their distributions and magnitudes without forward error correction (FEC). Third, these data are transformed by Hadamard and then directly mapped using a dense constellation (64K-QAM) for transmission without Gray coding. One of the most important properties in this framework is that the coding and transmission rate is fixed and distortion is minimized by allocating the transmission power. Thus we further propose a power distortion optimization algorithm to replace the traditional rate distortion optimization. This framework avoids the annoying cliff effect caused by the mismatch between transmission rate and channel condition. In multicast, each user can get almost the best quality matching its channel condition. Our experiment results show that the proposed DCast outperforms the typical solution using H.264 over 802.11 up to 8dB in video PSNR in video broadcast. Even in video unicast, the proposed DCast is still comparable to the typical solution.

Chapter 5 presents a novel coding and transmission scheme, called *LineCast* [40], for broadcasting satellite images to a large number of receivers. The proposed LineCast matches perfectly with the line scanning cameras that are widely adopted in orbit satellites to capture high-resolution images. On the sender side, each captured line is immediately compressed by a transform-domain scalar modulo quantization. Without syndrome coding, the transmission power is directly allocated to quantized coefficients by scaling the coefficients according to their distributions. Finally, the scaled coefficients are transmitted over a dense constellation. This line-based distributed scheme features low delay, low memory cost and low complexity. On the receiver side, our proposed line-based prediction is used to generate side information from previously decoded lines, which fully utilizes the correlation among lines. The quantized coefficients are decoded by the linear least square estimator (LLSE) from the received data. The image line is then reconstructed by the scalar modulo dequantization using the generated side information. Since there is neither syndrome coding nor channel coding, the proposed LineCast can make a large number of receivers reach the qualities matching their channel conditions. Our theoretical analysis shows that the proposed LineCast can achieve Shannon's optimum performance by using a high-dimensional modulo-lattice quantization (MLQ). Experiments on satellite images demonstrate that it achieves up to 1.9dB gain over the state-of-the-art 2D broadcasting scheme and a gain of more than 5dB over JPEG 2000 with forward error correction.

Chapter 3
Keeping Redundancy in Transmission

3.1 Introduction

Wireless video communications are facing a dilemma in achieving efficiency and robustness. On one hand, videos in their raw format are huge in size, and they need to be efficiently compressed for transmission. On the other, compressed video sequences have too little redundancy left, and therefore are susceptible to channel errors.

Direct application of Shannon's separation theorem [2] suggests that source redundancy should be completely removed and channel coding is responsible for adding redundancy against noise. However, joint source-channel coding (JSCC) suggests keeping a certain amount of source redundancy and has been shown to achieve better performance at limited complexity and delay. This inspires us to consider the following questions: how much source redundancy should be retained in wireless video communications in order to achieve both efficiency and robustness? Is it possible to skip channel coding and completely rely on source redundancy for channel protection?

Interestingly, the answer to the second question is a resounding YES, and the answer to the first question becomes clear after we carefully examine the two types of redundancy in video and their respective characteristics. Our research finds that: 1) Inter-frame (temporal) redundancy should be removed as much as possible at the encoder for high efficiency while intra-frame (spatial) redundancy should be retained to protect videos against channel noise. 2) Residual frames should be transmitted in spatial domain (e.g., scaled pixel values) instead of transform domain (i.e., coefficients) through amplitude modulation to combat losses and noises. 3) The key to fully utilizing the source redundancy is to perform image denoising at the decoder based on both source and channel characteristics.

Based on these findings, we present in this chapter an uncoded video communication system called *Cactus*. At the encoder, temporal redundancy is removed by motion-compensated temporal filtering (MCTF) [41]. Pixel values in residual frames are transmitted using amplitude modulation. Note that the sender

DOI: 10.1201/9781003118688-3

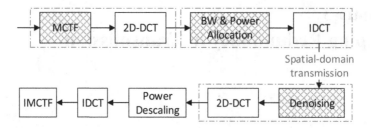

Fig. 3.1 Signal processing flowchart of the proposed system.

transmits scaled pixel values instead of transform-domain coefficients. This allows the receiver to fully utilize the source redundancy through applying image denoising techniques. In particular, Cactus employs median filter [42] to deal with packet losses and BM3D [43] to deal with additive noises.

We have implemented Cactus on SORA [38] platform and have evaluated it in 802.11a/g-based wireless LAN environments. It confirms that our design achieves high received video quality and is robust to channel variations. Besides, Cactus allows for graceful degradation in a wide range of receiver SNRs, and therefore can be readily used for multicasting.

3.2 Overview of the Proposed System

We aim to improve the transmission efficiency of the uncoded system through exploiting the correlations in video signals. Fig. 3.1 shows the signal processing flowchart of the proposed system. The three dashed-line boxes highlight the differences from previous work, which contribute to the significantly improved transmission efficiency.

First, we replace the 3D-DCT module in the existing uncoded framework with MCTF [41, 23] and 2D-DCT. The reason is that 3D-DCT without motion alignment cannot fully exploit temporal correlations. We do not use the popular motion estimation and compensation techniques in current video coding standards because they are based on closed-loop prediction, i.e., the prediction is based on the reconstruction of previous frames. In uncoded transmission, however, the encoder is unable to obtain the exact reconstruction at the decoder. This situation is similar to that in SVC, where part of the compressed data may be dropped. Therefore, we follow SVC to adopt MCTF to remove temporal redundancy. MCTF is based on an open-loop prediction model, i.e., the prediction is based on the original pixel values instead of the reconstructed ones. It has been shown that this leads to drifting errors that are much smaller than those of its closed-loop counterpart. As MCTF is a well-developed technique in source coding and is not challenging to integrate, we do not expand on its technical details here but instead refer readers to the paper [23].

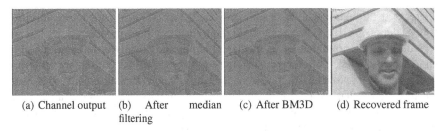

(a) Channel output   (b) After   median   (c) After BM3D   (d) Recovered frame
                      filtering

Fig. 3.2 Denoising processing at the receiver in the proposed framework.

Second, after 2D-DCT, the frequency-domain coefficients are truncated in order to match the source and channel bandwidths. The remaining coefficients are then power-scaled to minimize the MSE under given power budget. Of note in the proposed system is that we perform an inverse DCT (IDCT) over the power-scaled DCT coefficients and convert the signal back to the spatial domain for uncoded transmission. The reason is that denoising algorithms generally perform better if the signal impairments (including loss and additive noise) are presented in the spatial domain. If a pixel value is lost during transmission, the receiver can easily conceal the error through median filtering or interpolation, while in contrast, if a DCT coefficient is lost, the receiver will not have any clue about the original value and the best concealment is to set it to zero. However, we find that spatial domain transmission leads to non-trivial challenges in the resource allocation steps. In the next section, we will detail the proposed resource allocation algorithms which are well-suited for spatial-domain transmission.

Third, we propose to leverage image denoising techniques to fully exploit the spatial correlations at the receiver. We also emphasize that denoising should be immediately performed at the channel output. We will show later that performing denoising after power de-scaling or after the inverse MCTF is less effective than performing it at the channel output. We further propose cascaded denoising which adopts two or more denoising techniques to handle different unfavorable channel conditions. In particular, we first adopt the classic median filter [42] to handle losses. Under ideal interleaving, packet loss creates randomly dispersed pixel "holes" in the frame, as shown in Fig. 3.2(a). These holes are filled with the median of the surrounding eight pixel values. In the case of deep fading, the pixel values which experience deep fade can also be filled using the median filter. Fig. 3.2(b) shows the result after median filtering. The lost pixels become non-obvious. Then the state-of-the-art denoising algorithm BM3D [43] is adopted to reduce random noise.

The complete BM3D algorithm has two estimation steps: basic estimation and final estimation. Each estimation is also composed of two steps: block-wise estimation and aggregation. In block-wise estimation, similar blocks in a large neighborhood are found for each block and are stacked in a 3D array. Then, a 3D transformation, hard thresholding (Weiner filtering in the final estimation), and an inverse 3D transformation are consecutively performed to generate estimates for all the involved pixels. After all the blocks are processed, overlapping estimates are aggregated through a weighted sum operation. Fig. 3.2(c) shows the result after BM3D denoising. It can be seen that all the frames become smoother.

Note that the combination of median filtering and BM3D is just one possible choice in this step. Different denoising algorithms may be chosen for different devices according to their computational capability and end requirements. However, we discovered that using a more complex and effective algorithm than median filtering in the first denoising step does not bring much gain. This may be due to the fact that the subsequent BM3D algorithm is very powerful.

3.3 Resource Allocation for Spatial-Domain Transmission

In wireless communications, bandwidth and power are the major limiting resources. In the conventional coded framework, source bandwidth and channel bandwidth are matched through quantization. Transmission power is almost evenly distributed to each information bit. In uncoded transmission, however, the bandwidth expenditure is decided by the number of coefficients or pixels no matter whether they are quantized or not. Therefore, quantization becomes unnecessary and bandwidth matching has to be achieved through data truncation. In addition, the power used to transmit a symbol is proportional to the square of its value. When the total power is given, we shall fairly allocate the power to different variables in order to minimize the MSE.

3.3.1 Bandwidth Allocation

The source bandwidth of a video signal can be computed by $W \times H \times F$, where W and H are the width and height of a video frame and F is the frame rate. Without source compression, the source bandwidth is very large, especially for high-definition videos. The available channel bandwidth is usually smaller. Therefore, it is necessary to truncate the video data in a manner that fits the important information into the limited channel bandwidth.

It is known that data truncation should be performed in the frequency domain after the data are properly de-correlated. In a conventional digital video encoder, a video frame (either original or residual) is divided into blocks, and block-DCT is performed to transform pixel values into frequency coefficients. Then the coefficients are quantized. Using a larger quantization parameter (QP) will allow coefficients to be represented by fewer bits. In particular, small coefficients, usually appearing in the high frequency bands, may be quantized to zeros and exempted from subsequent encoding operations. In the uncoded transmission system SoftCast, frame-DCT is performed and the frequency coefficients are then divided into equal-sized chunks. The chunks with the minimal energy are discarded and the coefficients in the remaining chunks are kept completely intact.

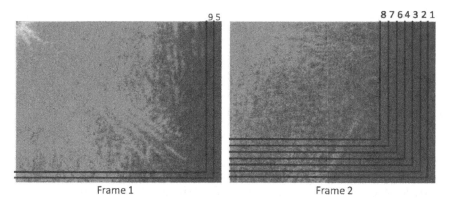

Fig. 3.3 L-shaped data truncation.

Algorithm 1 L-shaped data truncation

Input: $B_a, W, H, F^1, ...F^N, \Delta W$
Output: $W^1, ...W^N$
1: Initialization: $W^1 = W^2 = ... = W^N = W, B_s = W \times H \times N, \Delta H = \frac{H}{W}\Delta W$
2: Define $\mathscr{L}^n = \{c_{ij}^n | W^n - \Delta W < i \leq W^n, H^n - \Delta H < j \leq H^n\}$
3: **for** $n = 1$ to N **do**
4:    $\lambda^n = Var\{\mathscr{L}^n\}$
5: **end for**
6: **while** $B_s > B_a$ **do**
7:    $n = argmin\{\lambda^n\}$
8:    $B_s - = |\mathscr{L}^n|$
9:    $W^n - = \Delta W$
10:    $\lambda^n = Var\{\mathscr{L}^n\}$
11: **end while**

Unfortunately, neither of the previous approaches can be adopted in our system. This is because we will transmit the video signal in the spatial domain. In order to reduce source bandwidth, we have to reduce the number of pixels. However, neither quantization nor truncation of frequency-domain coefficients will change the number of pixels after the IDCT.

We tackle this problem through a novel L-shaped data truncation. In particular, we perform 2D-DCT for each frame in a GOP after MCTF. The high frequency bands, containing more low-energy coefficients, reside on the right and the bottom of each frame. Therefore, we truncate the L-shaped coefficients as shown in Fig. 3.3. Let $W' \times H'$ be the resolution of the remaining coefficients. Then the IDCT could use a $W' \times H'$ transform matrix. The resulting image is actually a down-sampled image of the original one. Transmitting the down-sampled image achieves bandwidth reduction.

Algorithm 3.3.1 gives the L-shaped data truncation algorithm. Since the wavelet transform is performed along the temporal axis, the low-pass and high-pass frames in a GOP have imbalanced energy. Therefore, bandwidth allocation should be

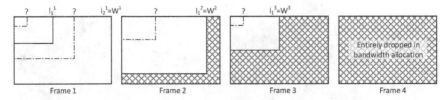

Fig. 3.4 Illustration of the greedy chunk division algorithm.

performed per GOP basis. The input of the algorithm is the available bandwidth per GOP (B_a), the video resolution ($W \times H$) and the coefficients within each frame of a GOP, denoted by $F^1, ... F^N$, where N is the GOP size and $F^n = \{c_{ij}^n\}$ ($i = 1...W, j = 1...H, n = 1...N$). The output is the new widths of each frame, denoted by $W^1...W^N$, in the GOP. For simplicity, we fix the aspect ratio of the remaining coefficients in each frame, so it is not necessary to output the heights. The parameters ΔW and ΔH are the horizontal and vertical truncation steps, respectively.

In this algorithm, lines 3-5 compute the variance of the bottom-right L-shaped chunk for each frame. Lines 6-10 repeatedly discard L-shaped chunks that have the minimal variance (or energy) until the bandwidth requirement is met. Fig. 3.3 gives an example of the data truncation process when only two frames are considered. The numbers above the L-shaped chunks indicate the order that each chunk is discarded. Normally, more chunks will be discarded among high-frequency frames than from low-frequency frames.

3.3.2 Power Allocation

Previous research has shown that in order to optimally transmit a signal under the MSE criterion in a power-constrained system, the signal should first be de-correlated and then each coefficient should be scaled by a factor which is inversely proportional to the fourth root of its variance [13]. In our proposed video transmission system, the video signal is de-correlated by MCTF and 2D-DCT. Ideally, each transform coefficient is scaled individually according to its variance. However, as the scaling factors are required at the receiver for signal recovery, there is a trade-off between power scaling efficiency and overhead. In our design, we adopt a compromise similar to SoftCast [19] that groups nearby coefficients into chunks and models the values in each chunk as random variables (RVs) from the same distribution. Then the coefficients in the same chunk will be scaled by the same factor and the overhead is only one scaling factor per chunk.

In contrast to SoftCast which divides coefficients into equal-sized rectangular chunks, we propose a new variable-size L-shaped chunk division method. The motivation for L-shaped chunk division is that transform coefficients decay rapidly from low-frequency to high-frequency and those belonging to a similar frequency band (constituting an L-shape) are more likely to have similar values. Grouping

Algorithm 2 Variable-size L-shaped chunk division

Input: $W^1, ... W^N, F^1 ... F^N, K$

Output: $\mathcal{B} = \left\{ \{ l_1^1 ... l_{K_1}^1 \} ... \{ l_1^N ... l_{K_N}^N \} \right\}$

1: Initialization: $\mathcal{B} = \emptyset$, $l_0^n = 0$
2: **if** $W^n > 0$ **then**
3: $\quad W^n \to \mathcal{B}$
4: **end if**
5: Greedy chunk division:
6: **for** each chunk k in each frame n ($1 \le k \le K_n$) **do**
7: $\quad$ Find $l_d(n,k)$ ($l_{k-1}^n < l_d(n,k) < l_k^n$) which minimizes $\Delta\Gamma$
8: $\quad$ Record $\Delta\Gamma_{min}(n,k)$
9: **end for**
10: **while** $|\mathcal{B}| < K$ **do**
11: $\quad$ Find $\Delta\Gamma_{min}$ among all the $\Delta\Gamma_{min}(n,k)$
12: $\quad$ Add corresponding position $l_d(n,k)$ to $\mathcal{B}$
13: $\quad$ Sort the boundary positions for frame n in $\mathcal{B}$
14: $\quad$ For the two new chunks, find $l_d(n,k)$ and $l_d(n,k+1)$ that minimizes $\Delta\Gamma$ within the respective chunk and record $\Delta\Gamma_{min}(n,k)$ and $\Delta\Gamma_{min}(n,k+1)$
15: **end while**

similar values in a chunk would allow an uncoded communication system to achieve higher power efficiency with a small overhead. An additional reason for using variable-size chunks is that the distribution of DCT coefficients differs frame by frame and video by video. While the initial idea of L-shaped chunk division has been mentioned in our earlier work [44], we present an algorithm with significantly reduced complexity in this work.

Similar to bandwidth allocation, power allocation should also be performed on a GOP basis. Suppose that a GOP has been divided into K L-shaped chunks, then the scaling factors for each chunk are given in the following Lemma. Proof of optimality is not given here as it can be easily derived from the conclusions drawn in [13] and [19].

Lemma 1 *Given K variable-size chunks, denoted by $C_1 ... C_K$, each with size $m_k = |C_k|$, assume that the coefficients in the kth chunk are drawn from the same distribution $\mathscr{D}_k$ with zero mean and variance λ_k. Given unit average transmission power, the scaling factor for each chunk, denoted by $g_1 ... g_K$, that minimizes MSE is:*

$$g_k = \lambda_k^{-\frac{1}{4}} \sqrt{\frac{M}{\sum_k \left(m_k \sqrt{\lambda_k} \right)}}, \quad k = 1 ... K \tag{3.1}$$

where $M = \sum_k m_k$ is the total number of coefficients or equivalently the total power budget for a GOP.

Now the problem is how to divide a GOP into a given number (K) of chunks. For simplicity and without loss of generality, we use linear decoding and assume an AWGN channel with noise power σ^2. Then the squared error at the decoder is:

$$\varepsilon = \sum_k m_k \cdot \frac{\sigma^2}{g_k^2} = \frac{\sigma^2}{M} \left(\sum_k m_k \sqrt{\lambda_k} \right)^2. \tag{3.2}$$

Minimizing the squared error is equivalent to minimizing

$$\Gamma = \sum_k m_k \sqrt{\lambda_k} = \sum_k \sqrt{m_k \sum_{c_{ij}^n \in C_k} (c_{ij}^n)^2}. \tag{3.3}$$

Based on this analysis, we propose a greedy algorithm for chunk division. In each iteration, the algorithm will split an existing chunk into two. Let C be an existing chunk in a particular frame. For clarity, we temporarily ignore the frame and chunk indices. If chunk C is to be divided into two L-shaped chunks denoted by C^i and C^o, the change of Γ, denoted by $\Delta\Gamma$, is computed as:

$$\Delta\Gamma = \sqrt{m^i \sum_{c_{ij} \in C^i} c_{ij}^2} + \sqrt{m^o \sum_{c_{ij} \in C^o} c_{ij}^2} - \sqrt{m \sum_{c_{ij} \in C} c_{ij}^2},$$

where $m = |C|$, $m^i = |C^i|$ and $m^o = |C^o|$. The dividing position (l_d, t_d) should be selected among all possible positions such that $\Delta\Gamma$ is minimized.

Algorithm 2 presents the proposed variable-size L-shaped chunk division algorithm. It is performed on a per GOP basis. The inputs are the dimensions of each frame after bandwidth allocation, all the remaining coefficients and the desired number of chunks K. The outputs are the chunk boundaries in each frame. K_n indicates the number of chunks in frame n. Again, we fix the aspect ratio of the horizontal and vertical coordinates of each L-shaped chunk boundary. Thus it is not necessary to include the vertical coordinates in the outputs.

Fig. 3.4 illustrates the greedy chunk division algorithm with a simple example. The shadowed areas indicate the coefficients dropped in the bandwidth allocation process. As frame 4 is entirely dropped, the initialization step between lines 2 to 4 only adds three boundaries to $\mathcal{B}$, indicating three initial chunks. In the first round of greedy chunk division, frame 1 is divided into two chunks: the new l_1^1 is added to $\mathcal{B}$ and the previous l_1^1 becomes l_2^1 after sorting. Now, the dotted lines in Fig.3.4 show four possible positions in the second round of greedy chunk division. These four positions are selected according to lines 10 to 15. The position corresponding to the minimum $\Delta\Gamma$ among the four will be added to $\mathcal{B}$ in line 12. Note that in each round of greedy selection between lines 10 to 15, we only need to find the minimum $\Delta\Gamma$ for the two new chunks. The worst case complexity is $O(KW)$.

3.4 Implementation

We implement the proposed uncoded video transmission system, named Cactus, through a compound approach. The application layer signal processing is

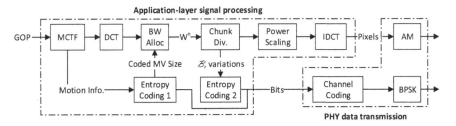

Application-layer signal processing

Fig. 3.5 Implementation of the Cactus sender is comprised of application-layer signal processing and PHY data transmission.

implemented in MATLAB® Compiler Runtime (MCR) and the PHY data transmission is built on a software radio platform called SORA [38].

3.4.1 Sender

Fig. 3.5 depicts the Cactus sender implementation. The GOP size is set to 16. We use a reference C code to implement the barbell-lifting based MCTF [23]. The motion information, including motion vectors and modes, is entropy coded and its coded size can be calculated. The bandwidth occupied by motion information will be deducted from the overall bandwidth provisioning. The bandwidth allocation module computes the remaining frame sizes, denoted by W^n ($n = 1...16$). Then, we divide the GOP into 160 L-shaped chunks (10 chunks per frame on average) and compute the variation for each chunk. We use a fixed number of bits (32 bits) to record chunk boundaries and variations. These metadata are also entropy coded. The power scaling module computes the scaling factors from each chunk, denoted by g_k ($k = 1...160$) assuming unit power for each symbol. Then variable-size IDCT is performed on each frame to generate spatial-domain pixel values.

Two application layer signal processing steps generate metadata, which should be faithfully received by receivers. They are transmitted using a robust digital scheme. We adopt the combination of 1/2-rate channel coding and binary phase shift keying (BPSK) modulation for transmitting metadata.

The scaled pixel values are transmitted through amplitude modulation (AM). Specifically, every two pixel values are mapped to the I and Q components of one wireless symbol. Note that AM can be implemented over digital hardware using a very dense discrete modulation constellation (the precision of today's A/D converter is about 12 bits per axis). This digital implementation allows our design to be easily integrated into an existing network stack. To resist packet loss, the adjacent symbols from a frame are pseudo-randomly shuffled across different physical layer convergence procedure (PLCP) frames. We further perform inter-frame shuffling to combat fading. We limit the shuffling within a GOP to reduce the decoding delay. The shuffled symbols are sequentially placed on each orthogonal frequency division multiplexing (OFDM) symbol. Therefore, when a PLCP frame is lost, it creates randomly dispersed "holes" in the video frame, which can be easily processed by median filtering.

3.4.2 Receiver

At the receiver, the digital and pseudo-analog transmissions can be separated from the packet header. The digital BPSK symbols are demodulated and grouped for channel decoding. If all information bits are correctly decoded, they will be entropy decoded to recover the motion information, chunk division boundaries and chunk variations. Otherwise, a receiver may request a retransmission.

The PHY at the receiver directly reads the amplitude values of pseudo-analog symbols and pieces together the 16 variable-size frames in a GOP. Each frame will be independently denoised. If packet loss is detected, we use the median function in MATLAB to perform the median filter denoising. Then, we use the MATLAB code published by the authors [45] to perform BM3D denoising. Then, DCT is performed and power de-scaling is applied over the frequency coefficients. The de-scaling factors can be computed from the chunk variations. For frames whose resolution is smaller than the standard resolution, we pad zeros in the high-frequency band and then perform a fixed-size IDCT. These recovered frames together with motion information can reconstruct the original frames through inverse MCTF.

3.5 Evaluation

3.5.1 Methodology

Evaluations are carried out using Sora [38] (equipped with a WARP radio board) over 802.11a/g-based WLAN. The 16 bit data representation in the Sora Tool Kit is fully utilized for amplitude modulation. The carrier frequency is 2.4GHz. The PHY is based on OFDM. Specifically, the channel is divided into 64 subcarriers and 48 of them are used to transmit modulation symbols. To reduce the overhead of the PLCP header, we use 100 OFDM symbols in each PLCP frame for data transmission. Overall, the channel bandwidth is 12MHz and the data bandwidth is about 11.4MHz. We have evaluated Cactus both for an exclusive stream and for two concurrent streams. The corresponding data bandwidth per stream is 11.4MHz and 5.7MHz, respectively. Traces are obtained at varying distances and reception power resulting in SNRs ranging from about 4dB to about 20dB. The SNR within each trace is fairly stable. Trace-driven evaluations ensure fairness among the comparison schemes.

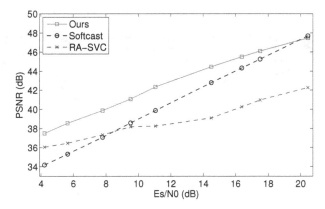

Fig. 3.6 Performance comparison between our system and reference systems, with a bandwidth ratio of 0.82.

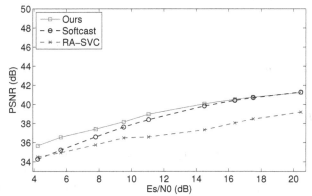

Fig. 3.7 Performance comparison between our system and reference systems, with a bandwidth ratio of 0.41.

We created a monochrome high-definition (HD) video sequence of resolution of 1280×720 for evaluation. It contains the first 32 frames (2 GOPs in our implementation) from 10 standard video test sequences, including *Intotree, Shields, Stockholm, City, Jets, Panslow, Parkrun, Sheriff, ShuttleStart, Spincalendar*. With a frame rate of 30 fps, the source bandwidth is 13.8MHz (assuming 2D source samples). In order to transmit the video in a 11.4MHz or 5.7MHz channel, bandwidth compaction is needed and the ratio of channel bandwidth to source bandwidth is about 0.82 or 0.41.

We evaluate video delivery quality with the standard peak signal-to-noise ratio (PSNR) in dB. The PSNR is averaged across frames.

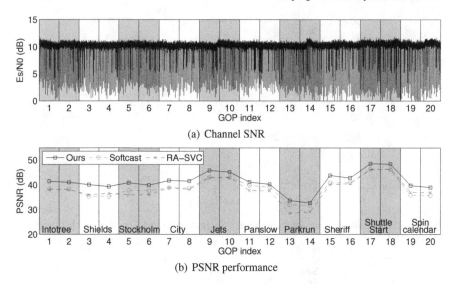

(a) Channel SNR

(b) PSNR performance

Fig. 3.8 Performance comparison between our system and reference systems under varying channel conditions, with a bandwidth ratio of 0.82.

3.5.2 System Comparison

We compare our system with two reference systems, namely SoftCast and RA-SVC. The pioneering uncoded video transmission system SoftCast is implemented exactly as described in the original paper [19]. In contrast to our system Cactus, the SoftCast encoder does not generate motion information and does not need to transmit the chunk boundaries since it adopts fixed-size rectangular chunks. However, the number of chunks is 64 per video frame, which is much larger than in Cactus. The metadata of SoftCast are also transmitted with robust digital methods and can be retransmitted when there are errors. Therefore, a receiver can always assume error-free metadata.

The other reference scheme, RA-SVC, is based on the Scalable Video Coding (SVC) extension of H.264/AVC and robust rate adaptation [46]. The combined test video sequence is encoded by the H.264 reference software JSVM [47] into three quality layers. The encoding parameters are selected and tuned for each GOP to ensure the best performance. The selection criterion is that a receiver which can successfully decode (BPSK, 1/2), (QPSK, 3/4) or (16QAM, 3/4) transmissions will obtain one, two or all three quality layers. These three coding and modulation choices are as defined in 802.11a/g. We adopt the RRAA rate adaptation algorithm [46] to handle varying channel conditions. In addition, we allow instantaneous retransmission when channel decoding fails, and the base layer data are always assigned the highest priority.

Overall performance under varying channel conditions: We evaluated the three systems over 36 traces with channel SNRs ranging from about 4dB to about

20dB. The SNR within each trace is fairly stable. After each transmission, the average video PSNR is computed at the receiver. We divide the receiver SNR range into 2dB bins, and average all the (receiver SNR, PSNR) pairs whose receiver SNR falls into the same bin.

Fig. 3.6 compares the performance of the three systems when the bandwidth ratio is 0.82. Results show that the proposed uncoded video transmission system significantly outperforms SoftCast and RA-SVC. The gain over SoftCast becomes more significant as the channel condition gets poorer. When the SNR is about 4dB, Cactus achieves a 3.3dB gain in received video PSNR. This is due to the fact that denoising is more helpful in poor channels. When the SNR is about 20dB, SoftCast starts to excel. This suggests that our system may turn off the denoising module when the channel SNR is above a certain threshold.

Comparing the performance of our system and RA-SVC, we find that the gain of our system increases as the channel condition improves. When the receiver SNR is between 14dB and 20dB, Cactus achieves about a 5dB gain in video PSNR over RA-SVC. This is due to the fact that when more encoding layers are involved in SVC, the source coding efficiency is more heavily affected. Even when the source coding is optimal (when the channel condition is poor, only the base layer will be transmitted), the performance of RA-SVC is still inferior to our system by about 2dB in video PSNR. The performance loss is due to the mismatched rate selection under varying channel conditions. We will give more details about this problem in the following experiment.

Fig. 3.7 shows the performance of the three systems when the bandwidth ratio is 0.41. This bandwidth setting is considered slightly less than adequate. In order to transmit a 120-minute 720p video with robust (BPSK, 1/2) modulation, the video has to be compressed into less than 2.57GB. In Fig. 3.7, the three performance curves show trends similar to Fig. 3.6. Cactus achieves up to a 3.3dB gain over SoftCast and up to a 5.3dB gain over RA-SVC.

Performance on a particular trace: We next zoom into a particular trace to compare the system performance. Fig. 3.8 shows the per-packet channel SNRs as well as the per-GOP performance of the three systems. From Fig. 3.8(a), we can find that although the channel SNR is about 10dB most of the time, there are many sudden drops to 0 to 5dB. When the SNR drops dramatically, the selected rate (according to the previous good channel condition) in RA-SVC would be too high and the receiver may completely fail in reception. Then when the channel recovers, the selected rate could be too conservative and the channel capacity is not fully utilized. On this trace, Cactus achieves an average of 3.1dB gain over RA-SVC.

Comparing the performance of Cactus and SoftCast in Fig. 3.8(b), we can find that the denoising gain greatly depends on the video characteristics. It can be seen that the denoising gain over *Shields* is significant but that over *Panslow* is small. On average, Cactus achieves a 2.6dB gain over SoftCast.

Fig. 3.10 compares the visual quality of the three schemes for frame 209, shown in Fig. 3.9. Frame 209 belongs to GOP 14. It was transmitted when the channel SNR was slightly above 10dB. The PSNRs achieved by SoftCast, RA-SVC and our scheme are 30.05dB, 31.15dB and 35.94dB, respectively. From the enlarged area,

Fig. 3.9 Original frame #209 in the test video.

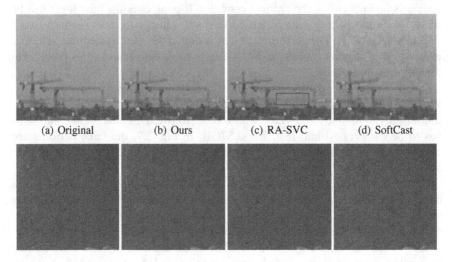

Fig. 3.10 Comparison of image details among our method, RA-SVC and SoftCast.

we can clearly see that RA-SVC tends to lose image details (see the highlighted area) and introduces some blocking effects, while the SoftCast result contains too much noise. In contrast, Cactus achieves a very clean image with details.

3.6 Summary

We have described in this chapter a novel uncoded video transmission system which has the potential to provide signal processing flexibility to wireless video communication. We show that by enabling denoising at the receiver, the efficiency of wireless video communication can be greatly improved. Trace-driven experiments show that our system outperforms the conventional digital system and the state-of-the-art uncoded video transmission system SoftCast in typical channel conditions of 802.11b/g. However, when the channel SNR is extremely low (such as 0dB), the digital scheme may outperform the proposed uncoded scheme because the former could use a high compression ratio for source coding and a very low rate channel coding for protection.

Chapter 4
Distributed Uncoded Video Transmission

4.1 Introduction

Distributed Video Coding [48, 49, 50, 51] is an attractive scheme for video compression that has been emerging for decades. Different from conventional video coding schemes, it utilizes cross-frame correlation only at decoder. This brings several unique advantages. First, DVC can shift intensive computation from encoder to decoder, which is appealing for low-complexity video encoding applications. Second, DVC framework is robust to transmission errors, which is desirable for wireless applications. Although it has been proven that the theoretical coding performance should be equivalent no matter what source correlation is utilized at encoder or decoder for some typical sources [52, 53], the actual coding performance of DVC is still far inferior to that of the conventional H.264 standard [4].

In DVC, quantized transform coefficients are converted to bit planes and compressed to bits by syndrome or entropy coding [49, 51, 54]. The syndrome coding is implemented via channel codes (e.g., low-density parity-check codes). These channel codes are also typically applied for error protection in the physical (PHY) layer. Therefore, Xu *et al.* propose the first work on designing the joint source-channel coding for distributed video transmission [55]. Except for this, the transmission of distributed coded video still looks like that of conventional coded video. All data from the PHY layer have been corrected by channel coding and thus are error-free. But it does not fully take the advantage that distributed coded video is robust to transmission errors.

In Softcast, 3D DCT is adopted to exploit cross-frame correlation. Many researches in scalable video coding have fully demonstrated that this is inefficient due to lack of motion alignment among frames [23, 41, 56]. However, motion compensation (MC) in H.264 is difficult to adopt in Softcast because the reconstructed frames are determined by channel noise and the encoder cannot obtain the same reconstructed frames as the decoder. Thus this chapter presents a novel framework called DCast, which cannot only utilize the cross-frame correlation by motion alignment but also keeps the nice properties provided by Softcast.

DOI: 10.1201/9781003118688-4

In the proposed DCast, transformed coefficients are first coset quantized and then are transmitted as Softcast. Similar to other DVC frameworks, DCast utilizes the cross-frame correlation at the decoder. The proposed DCast has two different approaches to process motion vectors (MVs). Like most traditional DVC schemes, in the first approach motion vectors are estimated at decoder. It does not need reference frames at encoder and greatly reduces encoding complexity. But the side information may be inaccurate, thus leading to low coding efficiency. Several DVC schemes also propose to estimate motion vectors at encoder and transmit them to decoder for improving the quality of side information [57, 58]. In the second approach, motion vectors are estimated at encoder and then transmitted to the decoder. The initial results of these two approaches have been reported in our conference papers [59, 39]. In this chapter we will focus our study on the second approach but both of them will be evaluated.

In the proposed DCast, each pair of quantized DCT coefficients or transformed motion vector is transmitted by a time slot and thus the transmission rate is fixed. The distortion is minimized by optimally allocating transmission power. This chapter evaluates the impact of channel noise on the distortion of motion vectors and then the impact of this distortion on the distortion of reconstructed video via the power spectrum approach [60]. Furthermore, a joint power optimization among coefficients and motion data is derived. Our experimental results show that the proposed DCast can outperform Softcast up to 2dB in video PSNR because it can better utilize the cross-frame correlation. Compared with the typical solution using H.264 over 802.11, the proposed DCast can gain up to 8dB in video PSNR in multicast. Even in unicast, it is still comparable to the typical solution of H.264 over 802.11.

4.2 Proposed DCast

DCast divides an input video sequence into groups of pictures (GOP). In each GOP, the first frame is intra coded, while the following frames are inter coded. The compression and transmission of intra frame in DCast is the same as in Softcast, which consists of DCT, power allocation and Hadamard transform. In the rest of this chapter, we will focus on the compression and transmission of inter frames. For simplicity, we mainly discuss the case with motion vectors estimated at encoder.

Fig. 4.1 depicts the server side of DCast. DCast first transforms the current frame into DCT domain. Meanwhile, DCast performs ME and MC on original video sequence to get predictions and MVs. Then DCast applies coset coding on the transform coefficients of the original frame to get, for each DCT coefficient, the coset data. The quantization step size of the coset coding is determined at encoder according to the estimated prediction noise of the decoder. The MVs of the current frame, in the form of a matrix, are also transformed by DCT. The coset data and the motion data are then scaled for power distortion optimization (PDO).

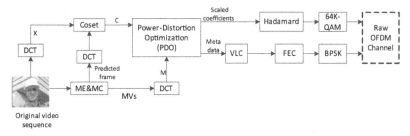

Fig. 4.1 DCast server for inter frames.

The scaling factors and other metadata are transmitted by using a conventional scheme consisting of variable length coding (VLC), forward error correction (FEC) and BPSK modulation. The scaled coefficients are transformed by Hadamard as pre-coding to make packets with equal power and equal importance. After that, the resulting coefficients are mapped to complex symbols directly by a dense constellation (64K-QAM): each coefficient is quantized into an 8-bit integer number and every two integers compose one complex number of 64k possible values. Finally, these complex numbers are passed into a raw OFDM module undergoing iFFT and D/A conversion for transmission.

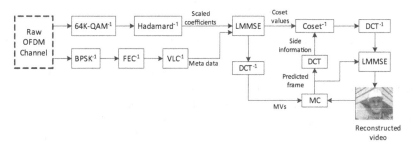

Fig. 4.2 DCast receiver for inter frames.

The receiver side of DCast is depicted in Fig. 4.2. The raw OFDM module performs A/D conversion and FFT to reconstruct modulated data including both scaled coefficients and metadata. The metadata is demodulated and decoded first. Then the scaled coefficients are reconstructed by inverse 64k-QAM and inverse Hadamard transform. The inverse 64k-QAM here does nothing but split each complex value back into two real values. Each real value here is actually the 8-bit integer number plus channel noise.

After inverse Hadamard transform, the Linear Minimum Mean Square Error (LMMSE) estimation of residual coefficients and MV coefficients is performed. Then the MVs are transformed back to spatial domain by inverse DCT. After this, the MC module generates the predicted frame by the MVs and the reference frame. The predicted frame is transformed into frequency domain by DCT. Then with the coset residues and the predictors, the coset decoding module recovers the DCT coefficients of the current frame. Finally, the signals are transformed back to spatial domain, and are linearly combined with the predicted signals by LMMSE to generate the final reconstruction.

4.2.1 Coset Coding

Coset coding is a typical technique used in DSC. It partitions the set of possible input source values into several cosets and transmits the coset index to the decoder. With the coset index and the predictor, the decoder can recover the source value by choosing the one in the coset closest to the predictor. Coset coding achieves compression because the coset index has typically lower entropy than the source value.

Let X be DCT coefficients of the original video frame. DCast encodes X to get coset values C. DCast divides the coefficients into 64 subbands according to the frequency. Let X_i be the ith subband of X, and C_i be the ith subband of C. For each i, DCast quantizes the ith subband of X by a uniform scaler quantizer $Q_i(\cdot)$ and gets the residual value [32] by

$$C_i = X_i - Q_i(X_i) = X_i - \lfloor \frac{X_i}{q_i} + \frac{1}{2} \rfloor q_i. \tag{4.1}$$

This coset coding is actually throwing away the main part of X. In some sense C represents the detail of X.

At the client side, with the side information S (i.e., the predicted DCT coefficients) and the received coset value $\hat{C}$, the receiver reconstructs the DCT coefficients by coset decoding. Let S_i be the ith subband of S, and $\hat{C}_i$ be the ith subband of $\hat{C}$. Since S_i is close to X_i, $S_i - \hat{C}_i$ is around $X_i - C_i$. Thus $S_i - \hat{C}_i$ is around $Q_i(X_i)$ from Eq. (4.1). The quantizers are carefully designed such that applying quantization $Q_i(\cdot)$ on $S_i - \hat{C}_i$ we could get $Q_i(X_i)$, i.e.,

$$Q_i(X_i) = Q_i(S_i - \hat{C}_i), \tag{4.2}$$

in high probability. Therefore, each subband of coefficients is decoded by

$$\hat{X}_i = Q_i(S_i - \hat{C}_i) + \hat{C}_i, \tag{4.3}$$

where $\hat{X}$ is the reconstruction of X, and each $\hat{X}_i$ is the ith subband of $\hat{X}$. When the coset decoding is successful, i.e., $Q_i(X_i) = Q_i(S_i - \hat{C}_i)$, the reconstruction noise is

$$\hat{X}_i - X_i = \hat{C}_i - C_i. \tag{4.4}$$

4.2.2 Coset Quantization

The value of each coset step q_i is crucial to the coding performance of DCast. If q_i is too small, the coset decoding may suffer failure. On the other side, if q_i is too large, the coset value C_i in Eq. (4.1) will be large and will consume a lot of transmission power to keep the distortion small. The value of each q_i is determined as follows. Injecting Eq. (4.1) into Eq. (4.2), we get

$$\begin{aligned} Q_i(X_i) &= Q_i(S_i - \hat{C}_i + C_i - X_i + Q_i(X_i)) \\ &= Q_i(X_i) + Q_i(S_i - \hat{C}_i + C_i - X_i). \end{aligned} \tag{4.5}$$

To guarantee successful coset decoding, the last item should be 0. This means the quantization step q_i should satisfy

$$\frac{q_i}{2} \geq |S_i - X_i + C_i - \hat{C}_i|. \tag{4.6}$$

In this equation, $S_i - X_i$ is the prediction noise at decoder and $C_i - \hat{C}_i$ is the reconstruction noise of coset value C_i due to transmission. In this work, we assume they are independent Gaussian sources. We let each q_i to be $2n$ times of the standard deviation of $S_i - X_i + C_i - \hat{C}_i$, i.e.,

$$q_i^2 = 4n^2 \sigma_{S_i - X_i + C_i - \hat{C}_i}^2, \tag{4.7}$$

and this guarantees the condition Eq. (4.6) is satisfied in probability

$$\text{Pr} = \text{erf}(n/\sqrt{2}). \tag{4.8}$$

Under the same assumption, the variance of $S_i - X_i + C_i - \hat{C}_i$ is the summation of the variance of $S_i - X_i$ and $C_i - \hat{C}_i$, i.e.,

$$\sigma_{S_i - X_i + C_i - \hat{C}_i}^2 = \sigma_{S_i - X_i}^2 + \sigma_{C_i - \hat{C}_i}^2, \tag{4.9}$$

and each q_i can be calculated by

$$q_i^2 = 4n^2 (\sigma_{S_i - X_i}^2 + \sigma_{C_i - \hat{C}_i}^2). \tag{4.10}$$

In our implementation, we let $n = 3$ such that the coset decoding is successful for more than 99.7% coefficients. In Eq. (4.10), $\sigma_{S_i - X_i}^2$ is the variance of the hypothetic residue between the source and the side information, and it is estimated by simulating at encoder a receiver with target channel SNR. $\sigma_{C_i - \hat{C}_i}^2$ is the distortion of coset value C_i due to transmission. It is also the distortion of the source X_i according to Eq. (4.5). $\sigma_{C_i - \hat{C}_i}^2$ is related to both the residue $\sigma_{S_i - X_i}^2$ and the channel SNR. The explicit expression of $\sigma_{C_i - \hat{C}_i}^2$ is given in Section 4.3.4.

4.2.3 Power Allocation

DCast transmits both coset values and motion information. Thus it has two levels of power allocation. The first allocation is between MV data and coset data. The second level means the allocation within MV coefficients or coset coefficients. The optimal power allocation between MV data and coset data is given in Section 4.3. The optimal power allocations within coset coefficients and MV coefficients are as follows.

Let P_{coset} be the total power for coset data, and g_{C_i} be the gain (scaling factor) of C_i. The problem is how to minimize the reconstruction distortion of X, by optimally allocating power among C_i. Under the assumption that the coset decoding is successful in high probability, the reconstruction distortion of X will be equal to the reconstruction distortion of C according to Eq. (4.10). This means the problem becomes how to minimize the reconstruction distortion of C, by optimally allocating power among C_i. Thus the solution has similar form as the one in Softcast [19], i.e.,

$$\tilde{C}_i = g_{C_i} C_i, \quad g_{C_i} = \left(\frac{P_{coset}}{\sigma_{C_i} \sum_j \sigma_{C_j}} \right)^{1/2}, \tag{4.11}$$

where $\tilde{C}$ is the coset value after power allocation, $\tilde{C}_i$ is the ith subband of $\tilde{C}$, and σ_{C_i} is the standard deviation of C_i. This power allocation tends to scale down large coefficients to get better performance under the constrained total power. The encoder calculates the variance $\sigma_{C_i}^2$ for each subband and transmits it to the decoder. With $\sigma_{C_i}^2$, both encoder and decoder calculate the gain g_{C_i} for each C_i by Eq. (4.11).

For MV data, DCast also performs power allocation. To apply power allocation, the encoder performs 2D DCT on MVs (the whole MV field) and gets transform coefficients M. Note that each MV contains horizontal and vertical components and the transform is actually applied to both components separately. Each coefficient M_i is then considered as a subband. The encoder applies a similar optimal power allocation over M, i.e.,

$$\tilde{M}_i = g_{M_i} M_i, \quad g_{M_i} = \left(\frac{P_{mv}}{\sigma_{M_i} \sum_j \sigma_{M_j}} \right)^{1/2}, \tag{4.12}$$

where $\tilde{M}$ is MV data after power allocation, $\tilde{M}_i$ is the ith subband of $\tilde{M}$, σ_{M_i} is the standard deviation of M_i and P_{mv} is the total power for motion data. Since each subband of M only contains one coefficient, it is not efficient to transmit the variance of each subband. In light of this, DCast only transmits the average variance $\sigma_M^2 = \frac{1}{n} \sum_i \sigma_{M_i}^2$ where n is the number of subbands. As shown in our previous work [39], the $\sigma_{M_i}^2$ and g_{M_i} are calculated by using σ_M^2. Under the assumption that the motion field is random Markov field, where the correlation coefficient between two neighboring MVs is ρ, each $\sigma_{M_i}^2$ can be calculated by

$$\sigma_{M_i}^2 = \sigma_M^2 V_{M_i}, \tag{4.13}$$

where V_{M_i} is the ith element of matrix V_M, and

$$V_M = \text{diag}(\text{2D\_DCT}(R^{(h)}))\text{diag}(\text{2D\_DCT}(R^{(w)}))^T \tag{4.14}$$

is a constant matrix for given ρ. Here function diag$(\cdot)$ produces the diagonal elements of the input matrix in the form of a column vector. 2D_DCT$(\cdot)$ means 2D DCT transform. w and h are the width and height of the motion field, respectively, and

$$R^{(k)} = \begin{bmatrix} 1 & \rho & \cdots & \rho^{k-1} \\ \rho & 1 & \cdots & \rho^{k-2} \\ \vdots & \vdots & \ddots & \vdots \\ \rho^{k-1} & \rho^{k-2} & \cdots & 1 \end{bmatrix}. \tag{4.15}$$

The value of σ_M^2 is calculated at the encoder and is transmitted to decoder as mentioned in the previous section. Both the encoder and the decoder calculate the value of each $\sigma_{M_i}^2$ by Eq. (4.13) - Eq. (4.15). In our experiments, we let $\rho = 0.7$ according to statistics over several different video sequences. With each $\sigma_{M_i}^2$, the optimal power allocation gain g_{M_i} for each subband is calculated at both encoder and decoder by Eq. (4.12). The decoder needs the value of g_{M_i} in Eq. (4.12) to reconstruct the signal.

4.2.4 Packaging and Transmission

Similar to Softcast [19], DCast transmits not only a small amount of binary symbols but also mainly real value symbols. The organization of the symbol stream is as follows. The symbol stream consists of a header and a following data stream

$$symbol\_stream = \{header\_bitstream, data\_stream\}. \tag{4.16}$$

The header bitstream contains coset variances $\sigma_{C_i}^2$, quantization steps q_i, average MV variance σ_M^2 and other useful parameters,

$$\begin{aligned} header\_bitstream \leftarrow \{ & coset\,variances, \\ & quantization\,steps, \\ & average\,MV\,variance, \\ & parameters \}. \end{aligned} \tag{4.17}$$

The header information is coded in a conventional way. The encoder applies 8-bits scalar quantization on σ_{C_i}, q_i and σ_M, respectively. Then the quantization results are compressed by variable length coding (VLC). The VLC is the universal one used for coding motion vectors in H.264 [4]. The compressed header bitstream is transmitted by the standard 802.11 PHY layer at the lowest speed, i.e., by using 1/2 convolutional code and BPSK modulation. This is to make sure that the header bits are decoded correctly when channel SNR is in typical working range (5-25dB) of 802.11. Note that the size of the header is very small with respect to the whole data of one frame. According to our experiments, the proportion of the bandwidth required by the header is less than 3%.

The data stream contains coset data $\tilde{C}$ and MV data $\tilde{M}$. Similar to Softcast [19], DCast applies Hadamard transform on the coset data $\tilde{C}$ and the MV data $\tilde{M}$ to create packets with equal energy. Coset data and MV data are mixed together and then every 64 numbers are grouped for Hadamard transform. This forms the data stream

$$data\_stream \overset{H}{\leftarrow} \{coset\,data, MV\,data\}. \qquad (4.18)$$

Note that the data stream consists of real values rather than binary values. In PHY layer, these real values are mapped to complex symbols directly by 64K-QAM constellation [19]. This constellation is a typical N-QAM constellation with N equal to 65536 (256 by 256). Each input real value is quantized into an 8-bit integer number by uniform scalar quantizer. The dynamic range of the quantizer is formed by the minimal and maximal input values. It is calculated for each frame at encoder and sent to decoder as a parameter in Eq. (4.17). After this quantization, every two integers compose one complex number as the output of the 64K-QAM constellation. An inverse FFT is computed on each packet of symbols, giving a set of complex time-domain samples. These samples are then quadrature-mixed to passband in the standard way. The real and imaginary components are first converted to the analogue domain using D/A converters; the analogue signals are then used to modulate cosine and sine waves at the carrier frequency, respectively. These signals are then summed to generate the transmission signal.

In DCast, both MV data and coset data are transmitted by the aforementioned direct source channel mapping. This makes the system adaptive to the fluctuation of the channel SNR. Given the same transmitter, high SNR users would receive accurate MVs and coset values, and reconstruct high quality video. Meanwhile, low SNR users would receive noisy MVs and coset values, and derive noisy prediction frame based on the noisy MVs. However, the coset decoding in DCast has good tolerance to the noise of the prediction. Thus the low SNR users would still reconstruct the video.

4.2.5 LMMSE Decoding

The proposed approach contains two linear minimal mean square error (LMMSE) estimators, operating in transform domain and spatial domain, respectively.

The first LMMSE estimator is to reconstruct coset data C and MV data M in transform domain with minimum distortion. Let Y be the received signal after inverse Hadamard transform. Y contains the noisy version of coset data and MV data. Y can be written as:

$$Y = \begin{bmatrix} \dot{C} \\ \dot{M} \end{bmatrix}, \tag{4.19}$$

where $\dot{C}$ is the noisy version of coset data, $\dot{M}$ is the noisy version of MV data. Let $W^{(C)}$ and $W^{(M)}$ be the channel noise in $\dot{C}$ and $\dot{M}$, respectively. Let $\dot{C}_i$, $\dot{M}_i$, $W_i^{(C)}$ and $W_i^{(M)}$ be the ith subband of $\dot{C}$, $\dot{M}$, $W^{(C)}$ and $W^{(M)}$, respectively. We model each element in $W^{(C)}$ and $W^{(M)}$ as i.i.d Gaussian source with variance N_0. Each subband of $\dot{C}$ and $\dot{M}$ can be expressed as

$$\dot{C}_i = g_{C_i} C_i + W_i^{(C)}, \quad \dot{M}_i = g_{M_i} M_i + W_i^{(M)}. \tag{4.20}$$

Therefore, the LMMSE reconstruction of original signals is

$$\hat{C}_i = \frac{\sigma_{C_i}^2}{\sigma_{C_i}^2 g_{C_i}^2 + N_0} \dot{C}_i, \quad \hat{M}_i = \frac{\sigma_{M_i}^2}{\sigma_{M_i}^2 g_{M_i}^2 + N_0} \dot{M}_i. \tag{4.21}$$

And the reconstruction distortion of each subband is

$$\mathbb{E}\{(\hat{C}_i - C_i)^2\} = \frac{\sigma_{C_i}^2 N_0}{\sigma_{C_i}^2 g_{C_i}^2 + N_0}, \tag{4.22}$$

$$\mathbb{E}\{(\hat{M}_i - M_i)^2\} = \frac{\sigma_{M_i}^2 N_0}{\sigma_{M_i}^2 g_{M_i}^2 + N_0}. \tag{4.23}$$

The purpose of the second LMMSE estimator is to reconstruct each pixel x in spatial domain with minimum distortion. DCast decoder applies inverse DCT transform on coset reconstruction $\hat{X}$ and gets a pixel-domain preliminary reconstruction $\hat{x}$. $\hat{x}$ is considered as the first noisy version of x. DCast also has the predicted pixel s as the second noisy version of x. With $\hat{x}$ and s, the optimal LMMSE estimation x^* is given by:

$$x^* = \theta s + (1 - \theta)\hat{x}, \tag{4.24}$$

where

$$\theta = \frac{\sigma_{\hat{x}-x}^2}{\sigma_{s-x}^2 + \sigma_{\hat{x}-x}^2}. \tag{4.25}$$

$\sigma_{\hat{x}-x}^2$ is the variance of $\hat{x} - x$, and σ_{s-x}^2 is the variance of $s - x$. In DCast, the prediction noise variance σ_{s-x}^2 is estimated at block level. Since $\hat{x}$ is close to x, σ_{s-x}^2 is estimated by calculating $\mathbb{E}\{(s - \hat{x})^2\}$. The variance $\sigma_{\hat{x}-x}^2$ is calculated as follows. According to the Parseval's theorem and Eq. (4.5), we have

$$\sigma_{\hat{x}-x}^2 = \mathbb{E}\{(\hat{x}-x)^2\} = \mathbb{E}\{(\hat{X}-X)^2\} = \mathbb{E}\{(\hat{C}-C)^2\}, \qquad (4.26)$$

where $\mathbb{E}\{(\hat{C}-C)^2\}$ is directly calculated by summation on Eq. (4.22).

4.3 Power-distortion Optimization

In DCast, both MVs and coset values require power to transmit. Thus it is necessary to investigate the optimal power allocation between MVs and coset values. Let D be the reconstruction distortion, and P be the transmission power. P_{coset} and P_{mv} be the transmission power for coset values and MVs, respectively. The optimal power allocation is the one minimizing the reconstruction distortion D for a given power P, i.e., the optimization problem is

$$\min \quad D, \qquad (4.27)$$
$$\text{s.t.} \quad P_{mv} + P_{coset} \leq P.$$

4.3.1 Relationship between Variables

The distortion D is directly related to both the decoder prediction noise variance σ_{S-X}^2, and the coset transmission power P_{coset}. Intuitively, using larger transmission power P_{coset} decreases the variance of the coset error $\hat{C}-C$ at decoder. This means smaller D because the reconstruction error $\hat{X}-X$ equals the coset error $\hat{C}-C$ according to Eq. (4.5). Meanwhile, larger σ_{S-X}^2 means lower quality of side information (SI), and lower quality SI leads to larger reconstruction distortion. Therefore, the distortion D should be a decreasing function of the coset power P_{coset} and an increasing function of the prediction noise variance σ_{S-X}^2.

Furthermore, the prediction noise variance σ_{S-X}^2 is related to the MV transmission power P_{mv}. We use two-dimensional random vector $\Delta \sim \mathcal{N}(0, \sigma_\Delta^2 \mathbf{I}_{2\times2})$ to model MV error, while $\sigma_\Delta^2 = \frac{1}{2}\mathbb{E}\{\Delta^T\Delta\}$ is the distortion of MV. Using larger transmission power P_{mv} decreases the MV distortion σ_Δ^2 and this means more accurate MVs. More accurate MVs produces higher quality SI S at decoder, and hence smaller prediction noise variance σ_{S-X}^2. Thus the prediction noise variance σ_{S-X}^2 should decrease with the increase of the MV transmission power P_{mv}.

However, due to the power constraint, allocating more power to coset (i.e., larger P_{coset}) means less power to MV (i.e., smaller P_{mv}), and vice versa. This is why we need power distortion optimization. In the following part of this section, before solving Eq. (4.19), we will derive the relationship between

- MV transmission power P_{mv} and MV distortion σ_Δ^2
- MV distortion σ_Δ^2 and prediction noise variance σ_{S-X}^2
- Distortion D, coset power P_{coset} and prediction noise variance σ_{S-X}^2

4.3.2 MV Transmission Power and Distortion

This subsection focuses on the relationship between MV transmission power P_{mv} and MV distortion σ_Δ^2. According to Parseval's theorem, the MV distortion σ_Δ^2 in spatial domain equals the MV distortion in DCT domain, i.e.,

$$\sigma_\Delta^2 = \frac{1}{n_{mv}} \sum_i \mathbb{E}\{(\hat{M}_i - M_i)^2\}, \tag{4.28}$$

where n_{mv} is the number of MV coefficients. From Eq. (4.22), we get

$$\sigma_\Delta^2 = \frac{1}{n_{mv}} \sum_i \frac{\sigma_{M_i}^2 N_0}{\sigma_{M_i}^2 g_{M_i}^2 + N_0} \approx \frac{1}{n_{mv}} \sum_i \frac{N_0}{g_{M_i}^2}, \tag{4.29}$$

where the approximation is accurate when $P_{mv} \gg N_0$. Substituting Eq. (4.12) into Eq. (4.29), we get

$$\sigma_\Delta^2 \approx \frac{N_0 (\sum_i \sigma_{M_i})^2}{n_{mv} P_{mv}}. \tag{4.30}$$

Then using Eq. (4.13) we get

$$\sigma_\Delta^2 \approx \frac{N_0 \sigma_M^2 (\sum_i V_{M_i}^{\frac{1}{2}})^2}{n_{mv} P_{mv}}. \tag{4.31}$$

By defining

$$\alpha_{mv} = (\frac{1}{n_{mv}} \sum_i V_{M_i}^{\frac{1}{2}})^2, \tag{4.32}$$

we can rewrite Eq. (4.31) as

$$\sigma_\Delta^2 \approx \frac{n_{mv} N_0 \sigma_M^2 \alpha_{mv}}{P_{mv}} = \alpha_{mv} \sigma_M^2 \left(\frac{P_{mv}}{n_{mv} N_0} \right)^{-1}. \tag{4.33}$$

In this equation, σ_M^2 is the variance of the MV signal to transmit, $\frac{P_{mv}}{n_{mv} N_0}$ is the SNR for MV signal. Thus α_{mv} can be considered as the extra gain owning to the power allocation in Eq. (4.12). From this equation, the MV distortion σ_Δ^2 is proportional to the inverse of the MV transmission power P_{mv}.

4.3.3 MV Distortion and Prediction Noise Variance

This subsection focuses on the relationship between MV distortion σ_Δ^2 and prediction noise variance σ_{S-X}^2. Let $\dot{S}$ be the original decoder prediction when the MVs are perfectly received. The practical decoder prediction noise $S - X$ consists of two components: the original prediction noise $\dot{S} - X$, and the additional prediction noise $S - \dot{S}$ caused by erroneous MVs. In this chapter, we assume they are independent of each other, and therefore

$$\sigma_{S-X}^2 = \sigma_{\dot{S}-X}^2 + \sigma_{S-\dot{S}}^2. \tag{4.34}$$

Given that the $\dot{S}$ is a phase-shift version of S, $\sigma_{S-\dot{S}}^2$ can be analyzed by using power density. Similar to the derivation in [60], we have

$$\sigma_{S-\dot{S}}^2 = \frac{1}{4\pi^2} \int_{-\pi}^{\pi} \int_{-\pi}^{\pi} 2\Phi_{ss}(\omega)(1 - \mathbb{E}\{cos(\omega^T \Delta)\})d\omega, \tag{4.35}$$

where $\Phi_{ss}(\cdot)$ is the power density function of side information, ω is two-dimensional frequency (in radians) and $\Delta \sim \mathcal{N}(0, \sigma_\Delta^2 \mathbf{I}_{2\times 2})$ is the MV error. For small σ_Δ^2, we have

$$1 - \mathbb{E}\{cos(\omega^T \Delta)\}) \approx \frac{1}{2}\mathbb{E}(\omega^T \Delta)^2 = \frac{1}{2}\sigma_\Delta^2 \omega^T \omega, \tag{4.36}$$

and thus

$$\sigma_{S-\dot{S}}^2 \approx \frac{1}{4\pi^2} \sigma_\Delta^2 \int_{-\pi}^{\pi} \int_{-\pi}^{\pi} \Phi_{ss}(\omega)\omega^T \omega d\omega. \tag{4.37}$$

We define

$$\gamma = \frac{1}{4\pi^2} \int_{-\pi}^{\pi} \int_{-\pi}^{\pi} \Phi_{ss}(\omega)\omega^T \omega d\omega, \tag{4.38}$$

and γ is a constant for a given video frame. Then we get

$$\sigma_{S-\dot{S}}^2 \approx \gamma \sigma_\Delta^2. \tag{4.39}$$

Substituting Eq. (4.39) into Eq. (4.34), we get

$$\sigma_{S-X}^2 = \sigma_{\dot{S}-X}^2 + \gamma \sigma_\Delta^2. \tag{4.40}$$

Therefore, the prediction noise variance σ_{S-X}^2 is linear to the MV distortion σ_Δ^2.

4.3.4 Distortion Formulation

The derivation of the distortion D is as follows. Firstly, from Eq. (4.5) we have $\hat{X} - X = \hat{C} - C$ in high probability. Thus the distortion D approximately equals the distortion of the coset value, i.e.,

$$D = \sigma^2_{\hat{X}-X} \approx \sigma^2_{\hat{C}-C}. \tag{4.41}$$

Similar to Section 4.3.2, we can derive and express the coset distortion as

$$\sigma^2_{\hat{C}-C} \approx \alpha_{coset} \sigma^2_C \left(\frac{P_{coset}}{n_{coset} N_0} \right)^{-1}, \tag{4.42}$$

where α_{coset} is the coding gain of power allocation, σ^2_C is the variance of C and n_{coset} is the number of coset subbands.

In general, our DCast transmits the coset values of the source X over Gaussian channel, with the side information S at the receiver side. Therefore, for each subband, it forms a typical Wyner-Ziv dirty-paper problem, in which transmitting the coset values has been proven to be as efficient as transmitting the residue $S - X$ over the same channel (assuming that $S - X$ is available to the encoder) [32]. Actually, according to the theorem in [32] (the existence of good lattice), the coset value C of each subband has the same variance with the prediction residue $S - X$ of each subband, i.e.,

$$\sigma^2_{C_i} = \mathbb{E}\{C_i^2\} = \mathbb{E}\{(S_i - X_i)^2\}. \tag{4.43}$$

Thus the coset value and the prediction residue have the same variance in frame level, i.e.,

$$\sigma^2_C = \mathbb{E}\{(S - X)^2\} = \sigma^2_{S-X}. \tag{4.44}$$

Therefore, Eq. (4.41), Eq. (4.42) and Eq. (4.44) implies

$$D = \sigma^2_{\hat{C}-C} \approx \alpha_{coset} \sigma^2_{S-X} \left(\frac{P_{coset}}{n_{coset} N_0} \right)^{-1}. \tag{4.45}$$

This means D is proportional to the prediction noise variance σ^2_{S-X} and the inverse of coset power P_{coset}.

4.3.5 Solution

Substituting Eq. (4.33) and Eq. (4.40) into Eq. (4.45), we get

$$D = (\sigma^2_{S-X} + \gamma \alpha_{mv} \sigma^2_M n_{mv} N_0 P^{-1}_{mv}) \alpha_{coset} n_{coset} N_0 P^{-1}_{coset}. \tag{4.46}$$

Then taking Eq. (4.46) into the problem Eq. (4.27), and solving the problem, we get

$$P_{mv} = [(A^2 + A)^{1/2} - A]P, \tag{4.47}$$

$$A = \frac{\gamma \alpha_{mv} \sigma_M^2 n_{mv} N_0 P^{-1}}{\sigma_{\dot{S}-X}^2}.$$

Although it seems A contains so many variables, there is actually a quite straightforward way to estimate A. In A, σ_M^2 is the variance of the MV signal to transmit, $\frac{P}{n_{mv} N_0}$ is the SNR when all power is allocated to MV and α_{mv} is the coding gain of the power allocation. This means that, if all power is allocated to MV, the MV distortion σ_Δ^2 will be $\alpha_{mv} \sigma_M^2 n_{mv} N_0 P^{-1}$ according to Eq. (4.33). Furthermore, Eq. (4.33) together with Eq. (4.39) implies that $\gamma \alpha_{mv} \sigma_M^2 n_{mv} N_0 P^{-1}$ is the variance of the additional prediction noise caused by erroneous MVs when all transmission power is allocated to MV. Therefore, the parameter A is estimated as follows. DCast simulates the transmission and decoding process to get a hypothetic side information S^*, which is the side information when all transmission power is allocated to MV data. DCast also calculates another hypothetical side information $\dot{S}$, which is the side information assuming the transmission of MVs are lossless. Since $S^* - \dot{S}$ is the additional prediction noise caused by erroneous MVs, we have

$$\sigma_{S^*-\dot{S}}^2 = \gamma \alpha_{mv} \sigma_M^2 n_{mv} N_0 P^{-1}. \tag{4.48}$$

With Eq. (4.48), the solution Eq. (4.47) is rewritten as

$$P_{mv} = [(A^2 + A)^{1/2} - A]P, \tag{4.49}$$

$$A = \frac{\sigma_{S^*-\dot{S}}^2}{\sigma_{\dot{S}-X}^2}.$$

Therefore, for optimal power distortion optimization, the encoder first estimates $\sigma_{S^*-\dot{S}}^2$ and $\sigma_{\dot{S}-X}^2$, and then calculates optimal MV transmission power P_{mv} by Eq. (4.49).

4.4 Experiments

In our experiments, we evaluate the performance of the proposed DCast in video streaming applications including both unicast and multicast. We compare DCast with Softcast [18], [19] and conventional frameworks. We have implemented two versions of Softcast based on 2D DCT, and 3D DCT, respectively, i.e., Softcast2D [18] and Softcast3D [19].

We have also implemented two conventional frameworks. One uses H.264 as video encoder and the other uses a DVC codec named Witsenhausen-Wyner Video Codec (WWVC) [58]. Both of the two frameworks use the standard 802.11 PHY layer with FEC and QAM modulations. We use JM14.2 software as H.264 codec.

For error resilience, the intra MB refresh rate is set to be 10%. Each video slice is packed into one RTP packet. We set the maximal slice size to be 1192 bytes such that the length of the RTP packet is no greater than 1200 bytes. The WWVC coded bitstream is also packed into an RTP packet of maximal length 1200 bytes. We append to each RTP packet a 32-bit CRC, and then encode each packet separately. Similar to the experiments in [19], for error protection we apply to each packet an outer Reed-Solomon code with the same parameters (188/204) used for digital TV. Each packet is individually interleaved between the outer Reed-Solomon code and the inner FEC in accordance with the same recommendation. For inner FEC, we generate the 1/2 convolutional code with polynomials {133, 171} and puncture it to get 2/3 and 3/4 convolutional codes. The FEC coded bits are mapped to the complex symbols by BPSK, QPSK, 16QAM or 64QAM. The complex symbols are then transmitted over OFDM. We assume the channel noise is Gaussian and the channel bandwidth is 1.15MHz. The FEC decoding is by soft Viterbi algorithm. After the FEC decoding and RS decoding, the decoder performs a CRC check for each RTP packet and forwards those error-free packets to video decoders. The WWVC decoder performs Wyner-Ziv decoding and is able to reconstruct the video frames when the reference frames have some error. The H.264 decoder can also tolerate a small percentage of RTP packet loss, by utilizing error concealment. In our test, we have configured the H.264 decoder to use the most complex error concealment method in JM14.2, the motion copy one, to get best reconstruction quality.

The test video sequences are standard CIF sequences (352×288, 30Hz), including "akiyo", "bus", "coastguard", "crew", "flower", "football", "foreman", "harbour", "husky", "ice", "news", "soccer", "stefan", "tempete", "tennis", and "waterfall". To evaluate average performance of each framework, we also create a monochrome 512-frame test video sequence, called "all_seq", by combining the first 32 frames of the above 16 test sequences.

For DCast, H.264 and WWVC, the GOP structure is "IPPP" and the GOP length is 32. In the following tests, all the PSNR results are for all the frames including both intra and inter frames. The number of reference frame for inter frame is 1. In DCast, the intra frame coding is exactly the same as Softcast with 2D DCT and the inter frame coding is by the proposed scheme. The transmission power allocated to an intra frame is set to be 4 times of the power of an inter frame. According to our experiments, this approximately makes intra and inter frames have similar video PSNR. The search range of ME is 32×32 and the MV precision is $1/4$ pixel. In ME, DCast uses only 8×8 block size, while H.264 and WWVC use all the 7 block size from 4×4 to 16×16. Table 4.1 gives a summary of the techniques and configurations of these frameworks.

Table 4.1 Summary of the four frameworks

Frameworks	Softcast2D	Softcast3D	DCast	H.264/WWVC
GOP	IIII...	-	IPPP...	IPPP...
Reference frames	0	-	1	1
ME	N	N	Y	Y
ME block size	-	-	fixed	variable
ME search range	-	-	32×32	32×32
MV precision	-	-	$1/4$	$1/4$
DCT	2D	3D	2D	2D
Coding delay	1 frame	4 frames	1 frame	1 frame
Modulation	OFDM	OFDM	OFDM	OFDM
Constellation	64k-QAM, BPSK	64k-QAM, BPSK	64k-QAM, BPSK	BPSK, QPSK, 16- or 64-QAM
FEC rate	1/2 (BPSK only)	1/2 (BPSK only)	1/2 (BPSK only)	1/2, 2/3, 3/4
RS rate	-	-	-	188/204

4.4.1 PDO Model Verification

This test is to verify the models of power distortion optimization (PDO) in Section 4.3. We use "all_seq" as test sequence. In the first test, we fix the coset transmission power P_{coset} and let the MV transmission power P_{MV} change. The channel noise power N_0 is set to 1. The results are given in Fig. 4.3. Fig. 4.3 (a) shows the relation between the MV transmission power P_{MV} and the MV distortion σ_{Δ}^2. According to the result, the inverse of P_{MV} is proportional to the MV distortion. This confirms Eq. (4.33). Fig. 4.3 (b) shows the linear relation between the MV distortion σ_{Δ}^2 and the prediction noise variance σ_{S-X}^2. This verifies the model of Eq. (4.40). Fig. 4.3 (c) shows the relation between the MV transmission power P_{MV} and the reconstruction distortion D. They are approximately in linear relation as shown in Eq. (4.46).

In the second test, we fix the MV transmission power P_{MV} and let the coset transmission power P_{coset} change. The channel noise power N_0 is set to 1. The result is given in Fig. 4.3 (d). The reconstruction distortion D is proportional to the inverse of the coset transmission power P_{coset}. This verifies the model in Eq. (4.45) and Eq. (4.46).

4.4.2 Unicast Performance

This test is to compare unicast performance among all the above frameworks. In this test the input video is "all_seq" and the channel SNR is $5 - 20$dB. Both encoder and decoder are assumed to know the channel SNR. For each channel SNR, the parameters of DCast are optimally tuned. The total transmission power is optimally allocated to coset data and motion data as explained in Section 4.3 The conventional framework is assumed to be able to choose the best combinations of the FEC and the QAM methods recommended by 802.11 according to the channel SNR, to get

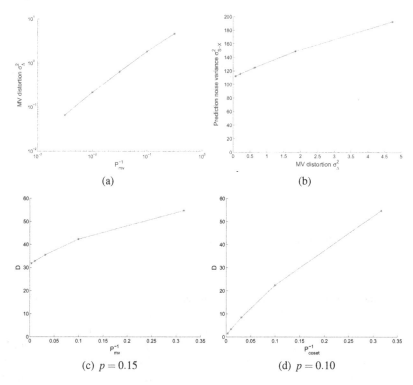

Fig. 4.3 Verification of the models of power distortion optimization in Section IV. P_{coset} and P_{MV} are transmission power of coset data and MV data, respectively. D is reconstruction distortion.

maximal bit-rate for source coding layer. The source coding layer, i.e., the H.264 codec, performs rate control to utilize the bit-rate as much as possible.

The experimental result is given in Fig. 4.4. This figure compares the reconstruction quality of all the five frameworks at different channel SNR. The reconstruction quality is measured by PSNR. DCast is uniformly 4dB better in video PSNR than Softcast2D at all channel SNR, mainly due to enabling inter frame prediction. DCast gains about 1.5dB in video PSNR over Softcast3D, which mainly comes from motion alignment. Compared with H.264 based framework, DCast is about 0.8dB worse in video PSNR at low channel SNR but is about 2.9dB better in video PSNR at high channel SNR. WWVC based framework performs slightly lower than H.264 based framework. In this test, we also implement another version of DCast in which the ME is performed at the decoder by motion compensated extrapolation [49]. Like most other DVC frameworks, the DCast with ME at decoder has low encoding complexity but high decoding complexity. Compared with conventional framework, the DCast with ME at decoder is about 1.6dB worse in video PSNR at low channel SNR but is 1.7dB better in video PSNR at high channel SNR.

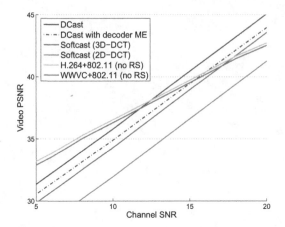

Fig. 4.4 Unicast performance comparison. Both encoder and decoder are assumed to know the channel SNR.

Note that the result in Fig. 4.4 does not mean that DCast can outperform H.264 in compression efficiency. H.264 is a video coding standard, while DCast is a wireless video transmission framework. H.264 has high compression efficiency but the coded stream is not robust to error. This is why H.264 coded stream needs additional FEC bits to protect. DCast may not be as efficient as H.264 in video compression, but is robust to channel noise. Thus it can skip FEC and can use a dense 64K-QAM modulation, and achieves high system efficiency.

4.4.3 Robustness Test

In practical wireless applications, the channel SNR may not be perfectly known to the encoder. In this test, we will evaluate the performance of DCast in this situation. The input video is "all_seq" and the channel SNR is 5 − 15dB. We let DCast optimize for target channel SNR of 5dB, 10dB and 15dB, respectively. The video PSNR are compared in Fig.4.5. According to the result, each of the three encoders performs best when the practical channel SNR matches its optimization target, but performs worse than the best one when the practical channel SNR does not match the target. The one optimized for 15dB channel performs 1dB lower in video PSNR than the other two when the practical channel SNR is 5dB, mainly due to unsuccessful coset decoding.

We then compare DCast with the conventional frameworks based on H.264 and WWVC. We still assume that only the decoder knows the channel SNR. DCast is optimized for a target channel SNR of 5dB in this test. For conventional framework, we implement all the eight recommended combinations of channel coding and modulation of 802.11. We calculate the corresponding bit-rates, respectively, according to the bandwidth, and set the bit-rates constraint to the H.264 encoder and

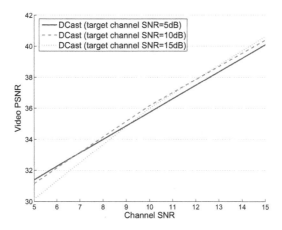

Fig. 4.5 Robustness test. DCast is configured to be optimized for target channel SNR of 5dB, 10dB and 15dB, respectively, and then tested under different channel SNR.

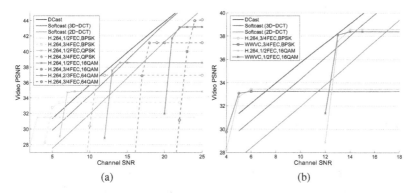

Fig. 4.6 Robustness comparison between DCast and (a) H.264 and (b) another DVC framework: WWVC. Channel SNR is unknown to all the encoders. DCast encoder is optimized for channel SNR of 5dB.

WWVC encoder for rate control. Both the video bit-rates and the channel bit-rates (the bit-rates after RS coding and FEC) under the eight transmission approaches are given in Table 4.2 (note that WWVC and H.264 have the same bit-rate constraints). For DCast, there is no bit-rate but only a channel symbol rate. Note that all the frameworks consume the same bandwidth and transmission power.

The video PSNR of each framework under different channel SNR is given in Fig. 4.6. In Fig. 4.6 (a), all eight conventional transmission approaches suffer a serious cliff effect. For example, the approach "H.264,1/2FEC,16QAM" performs well when channel SNR is between 13dB to 14dB, but is not good when channel SNR is out of this range. When the channel SNR becomes more than 14dB, the reconstruction quality does not increase. When the channel SNR becomes 12dB, the reconstruction quality drops quickly. When the channel SNR becomes even

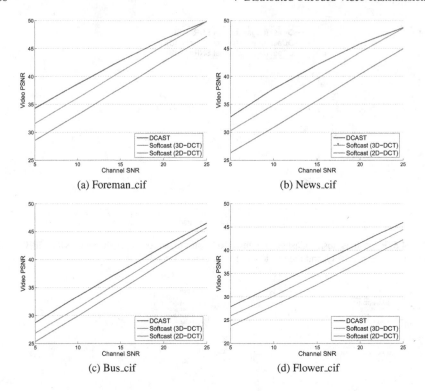

(a) Foreman_cif   (b) News_cif

(c) Bus_cif   (d) Flower_cif

Fig. 4.7 Multicast performance on different video sequences.

lower, the video decoder cannot work since almost all received RTP packets have bit errors. Note that the cliff effect can be partially mitigated in a layered approach [11], combining the scalable video extension of H.264 and a hierarchical modulation PHY layer. However, as shown in [19], the layered approach needs a higher channel SNR than the single layer approach to achieve the same PSNR. Fig.4.6 (b) shows the performance of WWVC based framework. Although WWVC can benefit from Wyner-Ziv decoding and achieves some gain over H.264 in erroneous situations, it still suffers a serious cliff effect.

In contrast, the three all-in-one frameworks do not suffer the cliff effect. When the channel SNR increases, the reconstruction PSNR increases accordingly, and vice versa. DCast is still the best one among the three all-in-one frameworks. At low channel SNR, DCast is 1.5dB and 4dB better in video PSNR than Softcast3D and Softcast2D, respectively. However, when the channel SNR increases, the gain of DCast decreases. When channel SNR is 25dB, DCast performs similar to Softcast3D and gains only about 2.5dB in video PSNR over Softcast2D. Compared with the unicast result in Fig. 4.4, the performance of DCast becomes 1.5dB worse in video PSNR at high channel SNR. This is mainly due to the fact that the optimization of DCast (including both the PDO and the coset quantization step) is for 5dB channel SNR in this test. Fig.4.7 gives the performance comparison on different video sequences.

4.4.4 Multicast Performance

We then let all the frameworks serve a group of three receivers with diverse channel SNRs. The channel SNR for each receiver is 6dB, 12dB and 18dB, respectively. The test result is shown in Fig. 4.8. In conventional frameworks based on H.264 and WWVC, the server transmits the video stream by using 3/4 FEC and BPSK. It cannot use a higher transmission rate because otherwise the 6dB user will not be able to decode the video. Due to this, although the other two receivers have better channel conditions, they will also only receive low speed 802.11 signal and reconstruct low quality video. In Softcast and DCast, the server can accommodate all the receivers simultaneously. Using DCast, the 6dB user can get slightly lower reconstruction quality than using H.264 or WWVC-based conventional frameworks. However, the 12dB and 18dB users get 4dB and 8dB better reconstruction quality, respectively, by using DCast than conventional frameworks.

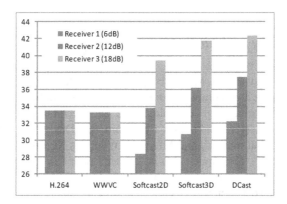

Fig. 4.8 Multicast to three receivers.

Fig. 4.9 compares the multicast performance of four frameworks, with respect to the range of receiver SNR. The range of receiver SNR is defined as the difference in the maximal and minimal channel SNR of the users in the group. The average channel SNR of the users in the group is 14dB. When the channel SNR range is 0dB, i.e., the channel SNR of all the users is equally 14dB, DCast, Softcast3D and H.264 framework perform similarly. However, when the users' channel SNRs become diverse, the performance of H.264 framework drops quickly.

The visual quality comparison is shown in Fig. 4.10. The channel SNR is set as 5dB. DCast has clearly better visual quality than both Softcast2D and Softcast3D. In all the tests including unicast and multicast, DCast performs better than both

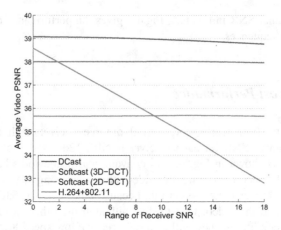

Fig. 4.9 Serving a group of receivers with diverse channel SNRs. The average channel SNR of each group is 14dB.

Softcast2D and Softcast3D. Moreover, DCast does not introduce frame delays as Softcast3D and is applicable for real-time video multicast like Softcast2D.

4.4.5 Complexity and Bit Rate

The proposed DCast allows ME to be performed at the encoder. Therefore the encoder would be in high complexity but the decoder would be in low complexity. Table 4.2 shows the average encoding time and decoding time per frame in milliseconds. The test machine has a Pentium (R) Dual-Core CPU E5300 @ 2.60GHz, 2G internal memory and Microsoft Windows XP Professional 5.1.2600, with Service Pack 3. The input video is "all_seq" with CIF size at 30 frames per second. DCast has less encoding time than H.264 codec (JM14.2) probably because DCast has no mode decision and no entropy coding. As to the decoding time, DCast is comparable to the H.264 codec.

Table 4.2 also shows the video bit-rate and channel bit-rate of H.264 solutions. For example, when the modulation is BPSK, the channel bit-rate is equal to the channel symbol rate, i.e., 1.15M/s. If the FEC is 1/2 convolutional code and the RS code is 188/204, then the video bit-rate is $1.15M \times \frac{1}{2} \times \frac{188}{204} = 530Kb/s$. When the modulation is QPSK and the FEC is 3/4 convolutional code, then the channel bit-rate is 2.3Mb/s and the video bit-rate is 1590Kb/s. The decoding time of H.264 codec depends on the video bit-rate. Basically, the decoding time becomes longer when the bit-rate increases. The DCast framework has no bit-rate but a universal channel symbol rate. Its decoding time is fixed and is similar to the decoding time of H.264 decoder at bit-rate 1590Kb/s.

| (a) Original | (b) Softcast2D | (c) Softcast3D | (d) DCast |

Fig. 4.10 Visual quality comparison with channel SNR as 5dB.

4.5 Summary

In this chapter, we have presented a novel framework called DCast for distributed video coding and transmission over wireless networks. DCast presents a new design on how to efficiently transmit distributed coded video data over Gaussian channel. The power distortion optimization for the proposed DCast is carefully investigated. DCast not only avoids the cliff effect in unicast transmission, it also allows a

Table 4.2 Comparison of complexity and bit-rate

Schemes	Encode time	Decode time	Video rate rate	Channel rate rate	Symbol rate rate
H.264+1/2FEC+BPSK	387ms	7ms	530Kb/s	1.15Mb/s	
H.264+3/4FEC+BPSK	387ms	8ms	795Kb/s		
H.264+1/2FEC+QPSK	406ms	9ms	1060Kb/s	2.3Mb/s	
H.264+3/4FEC+QPSK	389ms	10ms	1590Kb/s		
H.264+1/2FEC+16QAM	381ms	11ms	2120Kb/s	4.6Mb/s	1.15M/s
H.264+3/4FEC+16QAM	385ms	14ms	3180Kb/s		
H.264+2/3FEC+64QAM	371ms	15ms	4240Kb/s	6.9Mb/s	
H.264+3/4FEC+64QAM	427ms	16ms	4770Kb/s		
DCast	304ms	10ms	-	-	

single DCast server to accommodate multiple users with diverse channel SNRs in a multicast session. As shown in the experiments, DCast performs competitively with H.264 framework in unicast but gains up to 8dB in video PSNR in multicast.

DCast, as a unique DVC framework, does not utilize some sophisticated video coding tools such as variable block ME, intra mode, or mode decision. How to enable these tools to further improve the performance of DCast is one possible future work. In addition, the power distortion optimization in other wireless channels is also worthy of investigation.

Chapter 5
Line-based Uncoded Image Transmission

5.1 Introduction

Using satellites for navigation has become an indispensable part of modern life. Current global positioning systems (GPS) provide users free location and time information in all weather conditions, anywhere on Earth [61]. Recently, satellite services have been further developed. Google has announced that they can track ships at sea in real time through satellites and will provide this tracking as a public service on the Internet [62]. We are entering a new era, in which data from space-based and airborne commercial remote sensors are becoming available to the general public.

With the development of satellite imaging technologies, satellite systems can capture increasingly high-resolution geometric images. Nowadays a ground sample distance of 0.41 meters has become the reality using the latest GeoEye-1 satellite [63]. In current satellite systems (e.g., Google Earth), captured images are first transmitted to satellite ground receiving stations and then provided to users through ground networks (e.g., Internet). Such systems have two drawbacks that greatly hurt the advantages of using satellites. First, when the service is urgently required by people in a wild environment (e.g., desert and sea), it becomes unavailable because of the lack of a ground network. Second, it is difficult to provide users with captured images in real time because they are transmitted back only when the satellite flies over receiving stations.

It is desired to develop a new system that can broadcast captured images in real time from a satellite to mobile devices of subscribed users. With received satellite images, people are able to immediately see what they want to see tens of kilometers away. It is equivalent to breaking the physiological limitation of the human eye and greatly extends human vision into the distance. Therefore, we call this kind of satellite image service *Super Eyes*. However, developing such a satellite system faces two technical challenges with respect to data coding and transmission. First, captured images by a satellite cover a large area. Unlike the transmission from a satellite to its receiving stations, it is impossible to transmit all captured images to

DOI: 10.1201/9781003118688-5

all mobile devices. How can captured images at a region be transmitted only to the users in the region? Second, there may be a large number of users in a region with various channel conditions for receiving satellite images. How can the broadcast efficiently support such a broad range of channel conditions?

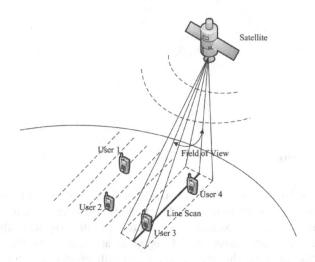

Fig. 5.1 Satellite line-based capturing and concentrated broadcasting.

For the first challenge, we propose a line-based coding and transmission framework. When a satellite camera captures a line of image, illustrated by the bold black line in Fig. 5.1, it is immediately coded and transmitted to the users in the corresponding dashed-line area in Fig. 5.1 because they are more interested in the content (e.g., User 3 and User 4). The area should not be too wide so that the transmission power can be concentrated on the area. Clearly, the proposed line-based framework provides a natural way to avoid broadcasting the whole area of images to all users. Furthermore, it does not need to wait for many lines of images to be captured before starting transmission. This will significantly reduce delay and memory cost.

For the second challenge, we propose an uncoded transmission of distributed coded digital coefficients. Specifically, every scanned line of an image is compressed by the transform-domain scalar modulo quantization without prediction, significantly reducing the computation in satellite. The correlation among lines is exploited in the receiver by side information. Furthermore, the quantized coefficients are directly transmitted without syndrome coding and channel coding, similar to the analog transmission proposed in [17] or uncoded transmission studied in [12]. Every user can receive the image with a quality matching its channel condition. It is exactly suited for broadcasting satellite images.

Based on these two technical contributions, we refer to the proposed scheme as *LineCast*. However, one major concern is whether the line-based coding and uncoded transmission can achieve an optimal system performance. Following the approach presented in [32] and [16], we analyze the theoretical performance of the proposed LineCast and prove that it can asymptotically achieve Shannon's optimum performance using a high-dimensional modulo-lattice quantization (MLQ). When the MLQ is degenerated as scalar modulo quantization in our implementation, the proposed LineCast is still comparably to or even better than the state-of-the-art 2D broadcasting scheme because of the high efficiency and flexibility of the proposed line prediction. Experimental results on satellite images demonstrate that the proposed LineCast can outperform JPEG 2000 [6] with a forward error correction (FEC) more than 5dB and the state-of-the-art 2D broadcasting scheme with up to 1.9dB gains in broadcast.

5.2 The Proposed LineCast

We first consider the case of the bandwidth of a channel B_c matching that of a source B_s, namely, one source sample uses one channel. More complicated cases that require bandwidth compression and expansion will be discussed in the next section. Fig. 5.2 shows the framework of our proposed LineCast scheme. Each signal in the figure is a vector signal corresponding to one line of an input image.

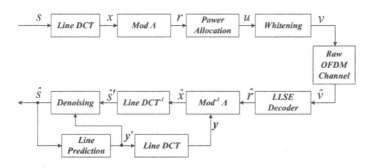

Fig. 5.2 The LineCast framework.

On the sender side, an image line **s** is first decorrelated by a 1D DCT. Then a scalar modulo quantization is performed on the transform coefficients **x**, resulting in the remainder signal **r**. It can exploit the correlations among lines by side information at the decoder. After the scalar modulo quantization, because different frequencies of **r** have different distributions, a power allocation technique is employed to these frequencies, which are scaled with different parameters at different frequencies. This process provides a kind of unequal error protection to different frequency coefficients against channel noises. Before transmission, the signal **u** is further input into a whitening module to get resilience against packet losses. Every two samples of the signal **v** are then mapped to a complex signal by a dense 64K-QAM constellation and transmitted through raw OFDM without digital forward error correction and modulation. This transmission simulating the analog process ensures that the received image qualities match channel conditions.

On the receiver side, after demapping from the 64K-QAM constellation, a linear-least-square estimator (LLSE) is first applied to each line to recover the remainder signal $\hat{\mathbf{r}}$ from the received signal $\hat{\mathbf{v}}$. To aid the modulo dequantization, a side information $\mathbf{y}'$ is generated by a prediction based on template matching from previous reconstructed lines. **y** is the transformed side information of $\mathbf{y}'$. With **y**, the transform coefficients $\hat{\mathbf{x}}$ are recovered from $\hat{\mathbf{r}}$ via scalar modulo dequantization. After an inverse transform and a denoising process, the current line is reconstructed as $\hat{\mathbf{s}}$.

The proposed LineCast can fully exploit source correlations with a low encoding complexity that is desired for satellite applications. The encoder only consists of 1D transform and scalar modulo quantization. Although we will show in Section V that a high-dimensional MLQ can greatly help the coding performance, we only use a scalar lattice in modulo quantization here for simplicity. By template matching at the decoder, the line-based prediction can fully exploit various kinds of intra correlations, including the anisotropic one commonly existing in natural images. This source correlation exploitation is even superior to 2D DCT, which only considers vertical and horizontal correlations. In the following subsections, we will elaborate each part of the proposed LineCast.

5.2.1 1D Transform

Before transformation, every sample in **s** is first shifted down 2^{b-1}, where b is the bit depth of samples. It is formulated as follows

$$\mathbf{x} = T \cdot (\mathbf{s} - 2^{b-1}I). \tag{5.1}$$

I is a vector with all elements as one. In this paper we use a 1D DCT to de-correlate each line. For high-resolution images, the DCT can be sped up using fast Fourier transform (FFT). T in Eq. (5.1) denotes the transform matrix.

5.2.2 Scalar Modulo Quantization

The scalar modulo quantization is similar to the coset coding used in DSC, which partitions source space into several cosets and transmits only coset indices to the decoder [64]. With signals in the same coset away from each other under some criterion, at the decoder it is possible to hypothesize which one in the coset is the source signal with the help of the side information. The scalar modulo quantization differs from traditional coset coding in that the signal takes a real value, i.e., the set of coset indices is infinite. After this quantization, the transmitted signal falls within a basic Voronoi cell of the lattice, which has a lower energy level than the original. Thus under the same power constraint, it can achieve a higher reconstruction quality at the decoder than directly transmitting original signals.

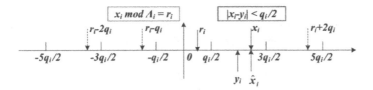

(a) Correct reconstruction

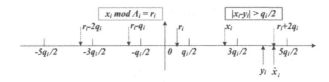

(b) Incorrect reconstruction

Fig. 5.3 Scalar modulo quantization without channel noises.

The basic idea of the scalar lattice quantization is shown in Fig. 5.3. Let the unbold symbols x_i, y_i and r_i denote the original signal, side information and remainder signal at the i-th frequency, respectively. $\Lambda_i = \{l | l = kq_i, k \in \mathbb{Z}\}$ denotes the scalar lattice at this frequency. As shown in Fig. 5.3, it has a basic Voronoi cell $\mathcal{V}_{0,i} = \{x_i | x_i \bmod \Lambda_i = x_i\} = (-\frac{q_i}{2}, \frac{q_i}{2})$. The lattice conforms to the following "distributive law" [32]

$$(x_i \bmod \Lambda_i - y_i) \bmod \Lambda_i = (x_i - y_i) \bmod \Lambda_i,$$

where $x_i \bmod \Lambda_i = x_i - Q_{\Lambda_i}(x_i)$. $Q_{\Lambda_i}(x_i)$ is the nearest neighbor quantization of x_i given by

$$Q_{\Lambda_i}(x_i) = \min_{l \in \Lambda_i} \| x_i - l \| = [\frac{x_i}{q_i}] \cdot q_i.$$

$\| \cdot \|$ denotes the Euclidian norm and $[x]$ denotes rounding x to the nearest integer.

On the sender side, the transmitted remainder signal is generated by

$$r_i = x_i \bmod \Lambda_i. \tag{5.2}$$

Let $\hat{r}_i$ denote the reconstructed remainder signal on the receiver side. The original signal is recovered by lattice decoding, i.e.,

$$\hat{x}_i = \min_{x_i \bmod \Lambda_i = \hat{r}_i} \| y_i - x_i \| = \hat{r}_i + Q_{\Lambda_i}(y_i - \hat{r}_i). \tag{5.3}$$

It finds the signal with a remainder $\hat{r}_i$ that is the nearest to y_i.

We define two noises

$$n'_i = \hat{r}_i - r_i,$$
$$z_i = x_i - y_i,$$

where n'_i is the transmission error on r_i and z_i is the correlation noise between x_i and y_i. The average reconstruction distortion is then given by

$$\begin{aligned}
d_i &= E[(x_i - \hat{r}_i - Q_{\Lambda_i}(y_i - \hat{r}_i))^2] \\
&= E[(n'_i - Q_{\Lambda_i}(z_i + n'_i))^2].
\end{aligned} \tag{5.4}$$

We can see that the average distortion depends on the choice of the lattice and the distributions of two noises, n'_i and z_i. It consists of two terms. One is the transmission error n'_i and the other is the lattice decoding error $Q_{\Lambda_i}(z_i + n'_i)$.

When there is no channel noise, i.e., $n'_i = 0$, the distortion reduces to only the lattice decoding error, i.e.,

$$d_i = E[(Q_{\Lambda_i}(z_i))^2]. \tag{5.5}$$

Let $d_i = 0$, we can get the condition $z_i \in \mathcal{V}_{0,i}$, i.e., $|z_i| < q_i/2$ (see Fig. 5.3). This condition imposes the constraint on lattice coarseness for correct lattice decoding. When considering the channel noise, Eq. (5.4) can be rewritten as

$$\begin{aligned}
d_i =& (1 - P_e) \cdot E[(n'_i)^2 | z_i + n'_i \in \mathcal{V}_{0,i}] \\
& + P_e \cdot E[(n'_i - Q_{\Lambda_i}(z_i + n'_i))^2 | z_i + n'_i \notin \mathcal{V}_{0,i}],
\end{aligned} \tag{5.6}$$

where P_e is the probability of incorrect lattice decoding. In order to get a distortion matching the channel SNR, we need to suppress the second term in Eq. (5.6), i.e., $P_e \approx 0$. Therefore, it is required that

$$q_i > 2\tau\sigma_{z_i + n'_i}, \tag{5.7}$$

where τ is a scalar factor depending on the distribution of $z_i + n'_i$. $\sigma_{z_i + n'_i}$ is the standard deviation of $z_i + n'_i$.

To find an appropriate parameter q_i at the i-th frequency, we need to estimate $\sigma_{z_i + n'_i}$. Since z_i is unknown at the sender, we need to estimate its statistics first. For this purpose, a side information $\tilde{y}_i$ is generated at the sender side by a prediction from previous original lines and a transform on the prediction. To reduce encoding complexity and memory requirements, we use only one previous line as the prediction. Given that $z_i = x_i - \tilde{y}_i + \tilde{y}_i - y_i$, the statistics of z_i can then be estimated from the two noises: $x_i - \tilde{y}_i$ and $\tilde{y}_i - y_i$. The lattice parameter q_i is finally set as

$$q_i = 2(\mu\sigma_{n'_i} + \mu\sigma_{\tilde{y}_i - y_i} + \max_j |x_j - \tilde{y}_j|). \tag{5.8}$$

$\sigma_{n'_i}$ can be estimated from the channel SNR. For broadcasting channels, we use the lowest channel SNR as 5dB in our consideration. $\sigma_{\tilde{y}_i - y_i}$ can be estimated by the reconstruction noise at this frequency, which equals $\sigma_{n'_i}$ if there is no lattice decoding error. The scalar value $\max_j |x_j - \tilde{y}_j|$ is the maximum element difference between $\mathbf{x}$ and $\tilde{\mathbf{y}}$ for the current line, which needs to be transmitted to the receivers as metadata. μ is an empirical value, which is set to 3.0 in our implementation.

5.2.3 Power Allocation and Transmission

The power allocation provides a sort of unequal protection to different frequencies of the signal $\mathbf{r}$ against channel errors. It scales each frequency of the remainder signal r_i by a different factor g_i so that the total distortion on $\mathbf{r}$ is minimized. According to [19], g_i is given by

$$g_i = \sqrt{\frac{P}{\sqrt{\lambda_i} \sum_{i=1}^{K} \sqrt{\lambda_i}}}, \tag{5.9}$$

where λ_i is the variance of r_i and K is the number of frequencies. If the diagonal matrix $G = \text{diag}\{g_1, g_2, \ldots, g_K\}$, the signal after power allocation is

$$\mathbf{u} = G \cdot \mathbf{r}. \tag{5.10}$$

For each line, the variances $\{\lambda_i\}$ need to be transmitted to the receiver as metadata so that $\mathbf{r}$ can be well recovered. To reduce such overhead, several neighboring frequencies are grouped into one band and thus only one parameter is transmitted. Besides, for high-resolution satellite images, the statistics for neighboring lines don't vary much. Therefore, several neighboring lines can share a set of $\{g_i\}$ and each line only transmits one scalar factor ρ that matches the variance of $\rho G \cdot \mathbf{r}$ per element to the power P.

After power allocation, the whitening module protects $\mathbf{u}$ against packet losses. It redistributes energy among different frequencies so that all packets are equally important. This is achieved by multiplying $\mathbf{u}$ by a Hadamard matrix H, i.e.,

$$\mathbf{v} = H \cdot \mathbf{u} = HG \cdot \mathbf{r}. \tag{5.11}$$

In the PHY layer, the signal $\mathbf{v}$ and the metadata $\max_j |x_j - \tilde{y}_j|$ and $\{\lambda_i\}$ are transmitted in different ways. For the signal $\mathbf{v}$, it is first mapped to complex signals through a dense 64K-QAM constellation, i.e., every two neighboring real samples are quantized by an 8-bit quantizer and combined into one complex symbol. The complex symbols are then transmitted using raw OFDM. Unlike traditional OFDM in 802.11 PHY layer, the raw OFDM skips the FEC and modulation steps and directly performs inverse FFT and D/A conversion. With such a transmission, it is able to achieve a reconstructed quality matching the channel conditions in the proposed LineCast.

Unlike **v**, the metadata is transmitted in the traditional way. Each transmitted sample is quantized by an 8-bit quantizer and coded using variable-length codes (VLC). The binary bits are then transmitted through OFDM in 802.11 PHY layer with FEC and modulation. To well protect the metadata part against poor channel conditions, a $1/2$ convolutional code is used for FEC and the BPSK is used for modulation.

5.2.4 LLSE Decoder

Let us define **n** as channel noise; the received signal is denoted by

$$\hat{\mathbf{v}} = \mathbf{v} + \mathbf{n} = HG \cdot \mathbf{r} + \mathbf{n}. \tag{5.12}$$

The remainder signal is recovered from the received signal $\hat{\mathbf{v}}$ by a linear-least-square estimator. Let $C = HG$; the recovered signal $\hat{\mathbf{r}}$ is given by

$$\hat{\mathbf{r}} = \Sigma_{\mathbf{r}} C^T (C \Sigma_{\mathbf{r}} C^T + \Sigma_{\mathbf{n}})^{-1} \hat{\mathbf{v}}, \tag{5.13}$$

where $\Sigma_{\mathbf{r}}$ and $\Sigma_{\mathbf{n}}$ are the covariance matrices of **r** and **n**, respectively.

5.2.5 Side Information Generation

The side information is generated at the receiver to aid the recovery of transform coefficients in scalar modulo dequantization. It exploits the correlation among neighboring lines by a line-based prediction using template matching, similar to our previous work in [65]. Each line is divided into segments with a size of 4×1 and the prediction is performed segment by segment. Let SG_c denote one segment of the current line to be predicted (see Fig. 5.4). Several neighboring reconstructed pixels constitute the template TP_c of SG_c. The template matching is to match TP_c against the templates of other line segments in the reconstructed area within a search range. M segments with their templates best matching TP_c under the mean-square-error (MSE) criterion will be averaged to get the prediction for SG_c. To remove bad candidates, M is dynamically set by thresholding. In our implementation, a maximum of 8 predictors is allowed. The template size is 6×2 and the search range is 32×8. After the prediction, a 1D DCT is performed on the prediction signal with DC level shifting to get the side information **y**.

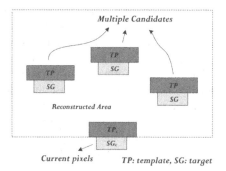

Fig. 5.4 Line-based template matching.

5.2.6 MMSE Denoising

The denoising process reconstructs the signal $\hat{s}$ in the spatial domain with minimum distortion based on two observations. One is the prediction signal y' and the other is the reconstructed signal $\hat{s}'$ (see Fig. 5.2). The final reconstruction is a weighted sum of y' and $\hat{s}'$ with the minimum mean square error (MMSE), i.e.,

$$\hat{s} = \alpha\hat{s}' + (1 - \alpha)y', \tag{5.14}$$

where

$$\alpha = \frac{\sigma^2_{s-y'}}{\sigma^2_{s-\hat{s}'} + \sigma^2_{s-y'}}.$$

The variances $\sigma^2_{s-y'}$ and $\sigma^2_{s-\hat{s}'}$ correspond to the correlation and reconstruction noises, respectively. Since, at the receiver, s is unknown, $\sigma^2_{s-y'}$ can be estimated by $\sigma^2_{\hat{s}'-y'}$ instead and $\sigma^2_{s-\hat{s}'}$ can be estimated by the actual channel SNR.

5.3 Bandwidth Expansion and Compression

In the previous section, we describe the details of the proposed LineCast under the bandwidth matched case, i.e., $B_c = B_s$. For bandwidth compression, i.e., $B_c < B_s$, the proposed LineCast discards some high-frequency subbands for each line because the human visual system is less sensitive to high-frequency components. At the receiver, the discarded subbands use corresponding subbands of the side information for their reconstruction.

For bandwidth expansion, i.e., $B_c > B_s$, SoftCast simply re-transmits the image and averages multiple samples at the receiver. This can only achieve 3dB gain in PSNR when the channel bandwidth is doubled. Its performance is restricted by the

linear processing. But in the proposed LineCast, we can transmit remainder signals
with progressively decreasing step sizes $\mathbf{q}$ of the scalar lattices. Let $B_c = \chi B_s, \chi \in \mathbb{N}$.
For each line, χ remainder signals $\mathbf{r}_1, \mathbf{r}_2, \ldots, \mathbf{r}_\chi$ are transmitted with decreasing step
sizes $\mathbf{q}_1, \mathbf{q}_2, \ldots, \mathbf{q}_\chi, \mathbf{q}_{i+1} < \mathbf{q}_i, i = 1, 2, \ldots, \chi - 1$. At the receiver, the reconstructed
line with $\mathbf{q}_i$ can be used as the side information of the subsequent transmission of
the same line with a smaller step size $\mathbf{q}_{i+1}$. Because the side information quality
is progressively improved, the remainder signal with a small step size can also be
decoded correctly. On the other hand, since a small step size results in a remainder
signal with a lower energy level, under the same power constraint it has a higher
SNR; thus the reconstruction quality is improved. In our implementation, the step
size decays exponentially, i.e.,

$$\mathbf{q}_i = \gamma^{(i-1)/2} \mathbf{q}_1, \tag{5.15}$$

where γ is the decaying factor. Therefore, the reconstruction PSNR increases
linearly with the bandwidth, which outperforms SoftCast with the $\log(B_c)$ law.

5.4 Experimental Results

To evaluate the performance of the LineCast scheme, we have implemented it using
MATLAB R2009a. In LineCast, the first line is transmitted similar to Softcast since
it cannot get an accurate prediction for scalar modulo quantization. Other lines
adopt the LineCast approach as described. The metadata in LineCast includes one
scalar value $\max_j |x_j - \tilde{y}_j|$ for each line, variances $\{\lambda_i\}$ for a group of lines and one
scalar ρ for each line. They are transmitted similar to that in [19], occupying less
than 4% bandwidth. For simplicity, we assume an AWGN channel for broadcasting
scenarios. Several satellite images (see Fig. 5.5) are used as the test data with a
resolution of 1024×1024, 1024×960 and 1024×1024, respectively. Among them,
"Image 1" and "Image 3" are from the Aerials volume of the USC-SIPI image
database [66] and "Image 2" is from Google Earth, showing part of Beijing, China.

(a) Image 1   (b) Image 2   (c) Image 3

Fig. 5.5 Test satellite images.

5.4.1 *LineCast Performance*

First we evaluate the performances of different parts of LineCast under broadcasting channels. In Fig. 5.6, two other schemes are compared here, LineCast without scalar modulo quantization and side information and LineCast without MMSE denoising, denoted by "LineCast wo SI" and "LineCast wo denoising", respectively. It is shown that without scalar modulo quantization and side information, there is a 3.1dB loss. By removing the denoising process, there is 0.6dB loss at low SNRs. We can see that scalar modulo quantization with side information plays an important part in LineCast, which fully exploits the anisotropic correlations among lines by flexible line-based prediction. The denoising process enhances the reconstructed quality especially at low channel SNRs because at high SNRs the decoded quality is good enough and much better than the quality of side information.

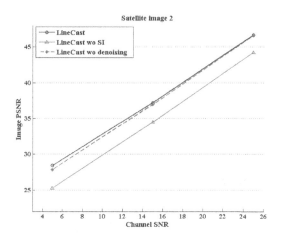

Fig. 5.6 LineCast performance.

5.4.2 *Broadcast Results*

In this subsection, we evaluate the performance of LineCast under broadcasting channels, compared with the other two schemes, Softcast and JPEG 2000. For Softcast, a whole frame DCT is employed for source decorrelation as that in [19]. For JPEG 2000, the reference software VM9.0 is used. Different combinations of FEC rates and modulation methods are tested and their corresponding source rates are listed in Table 5.1. Each image is decomposed by 5 levels using CDF 9/7. Fig. 5.7 shows the average results of five runs.

We can see that the digital separable source channel coding exhibits an obvious cliff effect, where below a certain SNR, the reconstructed quality drops dramatically

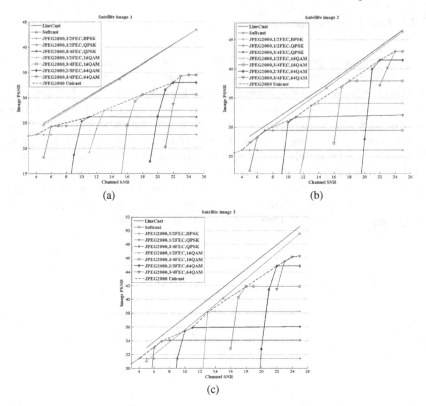

Fig. 5.7 Broadcasting performance comparison.

Table 5.1 Combinations of source rates, FEC rates and modulation in JPEG 2000

FEC&Modulation	Source Rate (bpp)	Reconstruction PSNR without channel noises (dB)		
		image 1	image 2	image 3
1/2 FEC+BPSK	0.25	22.70	26.06	31.40
1/2 FEC+QPSK	0.5	24.45	29.43	34.07
3/4 FEC+QPSK	0.75	26.18	32.05	36.04
1/2 FEC+16QAM	1.0	27.46	34.05	38.26
3/4 FEC+16QAM	1.5	30.60	37.92	41.87
2/3 FEC+64QAM	2.0	33.00	41.48	44.84
3/4 FEC+64QAM	2.25	34.50	42.97	46.29

while above it the quality maintains a constant value. However, the LineCast and Softcast schemes show a graceful degradation, owing to the analog-like transmission. The PSNR scales with the channel SNR. One can see that compared with Softcast, LineCast not only achieves low delay and low memory but also performs comparable or even better than Softcast in broadcasting for better source correlation exploration. An up to 1.9dB gain is achieved for image 3. Moreover, at

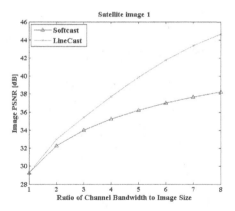

Fig. 5.8 Bandwidth expansion.

high SNRs, the superiority of LineCast over Softcast is lower than low SNRs. This is because the scalar modulo quantization parameters $\{q_i\}$ are set to be constant for broadcasting channels while at high SNRs a lower q_i is favored. It can also be seen that LineCast performs much better than the envelope of all digital schemes (see the dashed curve in Fig. 5.7), which can be considered as the unicast performance by JPEG 2000. These results validate the effectiveness of LineCast.

5.4.3 Bandwidth Expansion

This subsection shows the performance of LineCast when the channel bandwidth is larger than the source bandwidth. The decaying factor γ in Eq. (5.15) is set to 0.5 in our experiment. Fig. 5.8 shows the results of LineCast and Softcast when the channel SNR is 10dB. The horizontal axis denotes the bandwidth expansion ratio χ and the vertical denotes the reconstruction quality in dB. We can see that when χ is large, LineCast performs much better than Softcast. With LineCast, the reconstructed quality scales almost linearly with the channel bandwidth, which validates our analysis in Section IV.

5.4.4 Visual Quality

The visual quality comparison among JPEG 2000, Softcast and LineCast is shown in Fig. 5.9. The channel SNR is 5dB. We can see that LineCast shows a much better visual quality than the others. For JPEG 2000, the 1/2 FEC with BPSK is adopted to ensure that receivers with various channel conditions can decode correctly. The reconstructed quality is very poor, losing many details by quantization. The edges are severely smoothed and textures are missing. For Softcast, there are severe

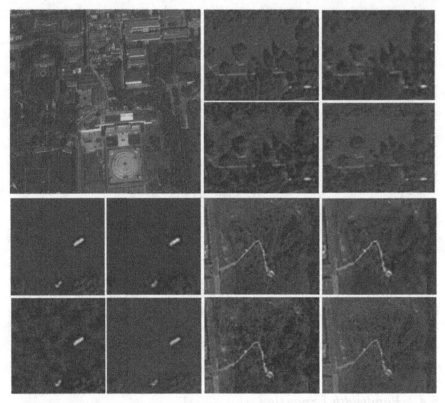

Fig. 5.9 Visual quality comparison at SNR=5dB. The image at the top-left corner is the satellite image 2. Other results are cropped images at the three rectangular regions denoted by dashed lines. For each cropped image, the four results from left to right, top to bottom are: original, JPEG 2000 at 0.25bpp with 1/2 FEC and BPSK, Softcast and LineCast, respectively. The received image PSNRs by JPEG 2000, Softcast and LineCast are 26.0557dB, 27.6133dB and 28.4106dB.

snow-like artifacts. In the water area, one cannot even recognize it as water. For LineCast, although there are slight "line" artifacts, most edges and textures are well preserved. Moreover, through some sophisticated line-wise denoising processes, the quality of LineCast can be further improved, which will be investigated in the future.

5.5 Summary

This chapter presents the LineCast scheme for high-resolution satellite image broadcasting. Due to line-by-line coding and transmission, it achieves low delay and bandwidth efficient transmission, low encoder complexity and low memory requirement. Moreover, owing to the uncoded transmission by scalar modulo quantization, it is able to achieve good broadcasting performance both theoretically and in experiments. These results show us the possibilities of satellite image broadcasting services in the future.

Part III
Resource Allocation

Resource allocation is a crucial problem in uncoded multimedia transmission. While all previous sections have considered power allocation among transmitted coefficients, we dedicate this part to the resource allocation problem in some more complicated situations, such as in Rayleigh fading channels, in non-orthogonal multiple access (NOMA) channels, and when there are bandwidth or resolution mismatches.

In Chapter 6, we address the problem of robust linear video transmission over the Rayleigh fading channel, where only statistical channel state information (CSI) is available to the sender [67]. We observe that discarding low-priority (LP) data and saving the channel uses for high-priority (HP) data can significantly improve the quality of the received video. We formulate an optimization problem that aims to minimize the total squared error of a multi-variant Gaussian random vector under the given bandwidth and power resources. To tame the complexity of this NP-hard problem, we analyze two sub-problems, namely, power allocation and bandwidth allocation, and propose an iterative algorithm to approximate the solution. Subsequently, we propose a one-pass two-step fast algorithm that further reduces both algorithmic and computational complexity. We implement a linear video transmission scheme based on the proposed algorithm. Simulations show that our scheme significantly outperforms Softcast, and the PSNR gain at the 5th percentile of 1000 test runs is between 4.0dB and 7.5dB under varying noise levels.

In Chapter 7, we propose a progressive uncoded video transmission scheme [68] which simultaneously handles SNR and bandwidth variations with graceful quality degradation for mobile video streaming. With the inherited SNR-adaptability from pseudo-analog transmission, the proposed progressive solution acquires the bandwidth-adaptability through an innovative scheduling algorithm with optimal power allocation. The basic idea is to aggressively transmit or re-transmit important coefficients such that the distortion is minimized at the receiver after each received packet. We derive the closed-form expression of reduced distortion for each packet under given transmission power and known channel conditions, and show that the optimal solution can be obtained by the water-filling algorithm. We also illustrate through analyses and simulations that a near-optimal solution can be found through approximation when only statistical channel information is available. Simulations show that our solution approaches the performance upper bound of pseudo-analog transmission in an AWGN channel and significantly outperforms existing pseudo-analog solutions in a fast Rayleigh fading channel.

In Chapter 8, we propose a novel receiver-driven superposed video multicast (Supcast) scheme [69] by integrating SoftCast into the NOMA-based system to achieve high bandwidth efficiency and gradual decoding quality proportional to channel conditions at receivers. Although SoftCast allows gradual performance by directly transmitting power-scaled transformation coefficients of frames, it suffers performance degradation due to discarding coefficients under insufficient bandwidth. Meanwhile, the power allocation strategy in SoftCast cannot be directly applied in NOMA due to interference. In Supcast, coefficients are grouped into chunks, which are basic units for power allocation and superposition scheduling. By bisecting chunks into base-layer chunks and enhanced-layer chunks, the joint power allocation and chunk scheduling problem is formulated as a distortion minimization problem. A two-stage power allocation strategy and a near-optimal low-complexity algorithm for chunk scheduling based on the matching theory are proposed. Simulation results have shown the advantage of Supcast against Softcast as well as the reference scheme in NOMA under various practical scenarios.

In Chapter 9, we propose a Spatial Scalability enabled Robust Video Broadcast (SSRVB) system [70], aiming at accommodating diverse users with both heterogeneous resolutions and heterogeneous channel conditions. In SSRVB, a novel spatial decomposition method based on linear projection is first designed for uncoded video transmission. Then the transmission distortion minimization problem with joint subcarrier matching and power allocation is formulated. A near-optimal low-complexity subcarrier matching algorithm based on auction theory and an optimal power allocation strategy are also proposed. Furthermore, an iterative algorithm is designed to solve the problem of joint resource allocation. Simulation results demonstrate that SSRVB can achieve an average of 3dB gain when compared with the reference schemes in terms of average PSNR under heterogeneous scenarios.

Chapter 6
Joint Bandwidth and Power Allocation

6.1 Introduction

In AWGN channels, SoftCast achieves similar end-to-end distortion to conventional digital methods while maintaining robustness to channel variations. However, the robustness of uncoded video communication under fast fading channels has not been studied before. If high-priority (HP) data (e.g., DC coefficient after DCT transform) unfortunately experience a deep fade, the overall distortion would be dramatically increased. Simply allocating more power to the HP coefficients does not solve the problem if only statistical channel state information (CSI), and not the precise CSI, is available to the sender. Experience in digital communications has shown that diversity increases robustness and improves the symbol error rate (SER) performance in fading channels [71, 72]. This suggests that we may sacrifice the transmission opportunity of some low-priority (LP) data and save the channel bandwidth for HP data to ensure the quality. While the optimal power allocation for the AWGN channel has already been addressed in previous work, the optimal joint bandwidth and power allocation for fading channels remains an open problem.

Although conventional digital communication is also constrained by limited bandwidth and power, the resource allocation problem does not appear to create hardships. This is because conventional digital methods are built upon Shannon's source-channel separation principle [2] and the entropy coding in the source encoder elegantly resolves the difficulties. In particular, entropy coding allocates a different number of bits to different coefficients according to their entropy or importance. Each encoded bit essentially carries the same amount of information. They are treated with equal importance during channel coding and modulation. As such, power and bandwidth allocations are coupled through bit allocation. In uncoded video communication, however, each coefficient is directly transmitted with amplitude modulation, consuming a power that is proportional to its variance. The absence of bit representation makes joint power and bandwidth optimization much more complicated.

DOI: 10.1201/9781003118688-6

In this chapter, we examine the optimal resource allocation problem under the Rayleigh fading channel. Previously, Kashyap et al. [73] derived the performance of the linear coding (uncoded) scheme under the assumption that the receiver has perfect CSI while the transmitter has only statistical information about the channel state. They found that for the Rayleigh fading channel, while linear coding is suboptimal in general, it is close to optimal in the low SNR regime. Xiao et al. [74] also considered the linear coding of a discrete memoryless Gaussian source transmitted through a discrete memoryless fading channel with AWGN. They showed that among all single-letter codes, linear coding achieves the smallest MSE. However, these works do not consider the multi-variate Gaussian source. The linear coding schemes mentioned in these works do not use quantization or entropy coding, so they are the same as the uncoded transmission scheme discussed in this book.

Video sources, after the de-correlating transform, can be modeled as a multi-variant Gaussian random vector. Although the joint optimization of bandwidth and power is a mixed integer nonlinear programming (MINLP) problem, which is in general NP-hard [75], we can tame the complexity by dividing it into two sub-problems. One sub-problem, the optimal power allocation under given bandwidth allocation, is proven to be a convex optimization problem and therefore can be solved via the gradient method. The joint optimization problem can be approximated through an iterative algorithm that allocates bandwidth in a greedy and progressive manner and evaluates each bandwidth allocation choice by executing the optimal power allocation algorithm.

This chapter makes two additional contributions. First, we provide theoretical analysis of the optimal resource allocation problem. In particular, we derive a necessary condition for the optimal power allocation sub-problem and two properties for the bandwidth allocation sub-problem. For the latter, we show that: 1) in Rayleigh fading channels, transmitting a Gaussian random variable (R.V.) repeatedly in $k + 1$ time slots results in smaller expected distortion than transmitting it in k time slots, under the same total power constraint; 2) when considering two Gaussian R.V.'s with different variances, both repeatedly transmitted in k time slots, the R.V. with the larger variance has a larger expected distortion reduction if additional channel use is granted. Second, we propose a one-pass two-step fast algorithm that greatly reduces the complexity of the iterative algorithm. Evaluations show that the performance gap to the iterative algorithm is within 0.4% of the achieved video PSNR.

6.2 Problem

6.2.1 System Model

Source: A video sequence is divided into GOPs. GOP size can vary from 8, 16, to 32. Usually, each GOP independently allocates resources, such as bandwidth and

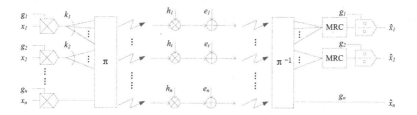

Fig. 6.1 Linear transmission paradigm.

power, to avoid delay. In uncoded video transmission, 3D-DCT is performed over each GOP, and the DCT coefficients are divided into N equal-sized chunks. Let λ_n denote the variance of the nth ($1 \leq n \leq N$) chunk. We consider the coefficients in the nth chunk to be random variables drawn from a Gaussian distribution $\mathscr{D}_n = \mathscr{N}(0, \lambda_n)$. Because all the chunks have the same size, we can simply model the source as a random vector $(c_1...c_N)^T$ with $c_n \sim \mathscr{D}_n$.

The objective of resource allocation is to find the power scaling factor g_n and the number of repeated transmissions k_n for random variable c_n. Once the two values are determined, each instance of c_n will be multiplied by g_n and be repeated for k_n times. Let s_{n_i} and s_{n_j} be two scaled coefficients from the same chunk (i.e., the same distribution $\mathscr{D}_n$); they form one wireless complex symbol:

$$x_m = (s_{n_i} + i \cdot s_{n_j})/\sqrt{2}.$$

Then all complex symbols within a GOP are interleaved to ensure that they experience independent fading during transmission.

Channel: We consider a fast Rayleigh fading channel with AWGN. In particular, for each transmitted symbol x_m, the received symbol y_m can be written as:

$$y_m = h_m \cdot x_m + e_m,$$

where $h_m \sim \mathscr{CN}(0, \sigma_h^2)$ is the fading parameter, and $e_m \sim \mathscr{CN}(0, \sigma^2)$ is the additive noise. It is assumed that only the CSI statistics, i.e., σ_h and σ, are known to the sender. Without changing the nature of the problem, we can normalize σ_h^2 to 1 for simplicity. The value of h_m can be estimated at the receiver, through pilot symbols, based on common coherence time assumptions. However, the exact value of e_m cannot be known by either sender or receiver.

Destination: Let $\mathbf{k} = (k_1, k_2, \ldots, k_N)^T$ be a bandwidth allocation solution, where k_n is the number of transmission opportunities for c_n. The fading parameters of the k_n transmissions can be stacked into a vector $\mathbf{H}_n$. We use x_n to denote a complex wireless symbol formed by two instances of c_n. The receiver would obtain k_n noisy versions of x_n, and they can be stacked into a vector:

$$\mathbf{Y}_n = \mathbf{H}_n x_n + \mathbf{E}_n,$$

where $\mathbf{E}_n = (e'_1, e'_2, \ldots, e'_{k_n})^T$ is the additive noise on the corresponding channel. The receiver performs the standard maximum ratio combining (MRC) to obtain an estimation of the transmitted symbol:

$$\hat{x}_n = \frac{\mathbf{H}_n^*}{\|\mathbf{H}_n\|^2} \mathbf{Y}_n = x_n + \hat{e}_n,$$

where $\hat{e}_n \sim \mathcal{N}(0, \sigma^2/\|\mathbf{H}_n\|^2)$.

Through minimum mean squared error (MMSE) detection, the corresponding DCT coefficients are recovered from the real and imaginary parts of $\hat{x}_n$

$$\hat{s}_{n_i} + i\hat{s}_{n_j} = \frac{g_n \lambda_n}{g_n^2 \lambda_n + \sigma^2/\|\mathbf{H}_n\|^2} \cdot \hat{x}_n.$$

6.2.2 Problem Statement

Define the distortion as the Euclidean norm $\varepsilon_n = \|\hat{s}_n - s_n\|^2$. The expected distortion under known fading gain and noise power is

$$\mathbb{E}[\varepsilon_n | \mathbf{H}_n, \sigma^2] = \frac{\lambda_n \sigma^2}{\|\mathbf{H}_n\|^2 g_n^2 \lambda_n + \sigma^2} = \frac{\lambda_n}{\|\mathbf{H}_n\|^2 \rho_n + 1}, \tag{6.1}$$

where $\rho_n = g_n^2 \lambda_n / \sigma^2$ is the signal-to-noise power ratio for the nth chunk.

Given the total bandwidth M and the total transmission power P, we find the bandwidth allocation, i.e., $\mathbf{k}$ and the power allocation, i.e., ρ, to minimize the total mean distortion. Mathematically,

$$\begin{aligned} &\min \sum_{n=1}^{N} \mathbb{E}\left[\varepsilon_n | \sigma^2\right], \\ &\text{s.t. } \sum_{n=1}^{N} k_n = M, \\ &\quad k_n \geq 0, \ k_n \in \mathbb{Z}, \\ &\quad \sum_{n=1}^{N} k_n \rho_n = \frac{P}{\sigma^2}, \\ &\quad \rho_n \geq 0, \ \rho_n \in \mathbb{R}. \end{aligned} \tag{6.2}$$

Note that $\varepsilon_n = f(\lambda_n, \rho_n, \mathbf{H}_n)$ is a multi-variable function and $\mathbf{H}_n$ depends on the channel use allocation k_n. $\mathbb{E}[\varepsilon_n | \sigma^2]$ is computed by taking expectation of (6.1) over the channel fading gain $\mathbf{H}_n$.

6.3 Analysis

The optimization problem as defined in (6.2) is a mixed integer nonlinear programming (MINLP) problem, which has been proven to be NP-hard [75]. To tame the complexity, we divide the optimization problem into two sub-problems, namely power allocation and bandwidth allocation, and perform a detailed analysis.

The objective function of problem (6.2) can be rewritten into:

$$\min_{\mathbf{k}} \left\{ \min_{\rho} \sum_{n=1}^{N} \mathbb{E}\left[\varepsilon_n | \mathbf{k}, \sigma^2\right] \middle| \sum_{n=1}^{N} k_n = M \right\}. \tag{6.3}$$

With this expression, it is clear that one sub-problem is to find the optimal power allocation under a given bandwidth allocation, and the other sub-problem is to find the optimal bandwidth allocation given that the first sub-problem can be solved.

6.3.1 Power Allocation Problem

Under a given bandwidth allocation $\mathbf{k}$, the power allocation problem is:

$$\begin{array}{l} \min \sum_{n=1}^{N} \mathbb{E}[\varepsilon_n | \mathbf{k}, \sigma^2], \\ \text{s.t. } \sum_{n=1}^{N} k_n \rho_n = \frac{P}{\sigma^2}, \\ \rho_n \geq 0, \ \rho \in \mathbb{R}, \end{array} \tag{6.4}$$

where the expectation is taken over the channel fading gains.

Theorem 1 *The power allocation problem as defined in (6.4) is a constrained convex optimization problem.*

Proof. $\mathbb{E}[\varepsilon_n | \mathbf{k}, \sigma^2]$ is a piecewise function:

$$\mathbb{E}[\varepsilon_n | \mathbf{k}, \sigma^2] = \begin{cases} \int \mathbb{E}[\varepsilon_n | \mathbf{H}_n, \sigma^2] d(\mathbb{P}(\mathbf{H}_n)) & k_n \geq 1 \\ \lambda_n & k_n = 0 \end{cases}. \tag{6.5}$$

When $k_n = 0$, the coefficients in the nth chunk are not transmitted. Thus, the expected distortion is simply the variance of the chunk. Next, we will focus on cases when $k_n \geq 1$.

Based on the Leibniz integral rule, we can derive the first order and second order partial derivative of $\mathbb{E}[\varepsilon_n | \mathbf{k}, \sigma^2]$ for $k_n \geq 1$. According to (6.1) and let $t = \|\mathbf{H}_n\|^2$,

$$\frac{\partial \mathbb{E}[\varepsilon_n | \mathbf{k}, \sigma^2]}{\partial \rho_n} = -\lambda_n \int \frac{t}{(\rho_n t + 1)^2} d(\mathbb{P}(t)), \tag{6.6}$$

$$\frac{\partial^2 \mathbb{E}[\varepsilon_n | \mathbf{k}, \sigma^2]}{\partial \rho_n^2} = \lambda_n \int \frac{2t^2}{(\rho_n t + 1)^3} d(\mathbb{P}(t)). \tag{6.7}$$

By definition, $t \geq 0$ and $\rho_n \geq 0$, therefore $\frac{2t^2}{(\rho_n t + 1)^3} \geq 0$. Unless $\mathbb{P}(t = 0) = 1$ which is impossible in practice, $\frac{\partial^2 \mathbb{E}[\varepsilon_n | \mathbf{k}, \sigma^2]}{\partial \rho_n^2} > 0$, i.e., $\mathbb{E}[\varepsilon_n | \mathbf{k}, \sigma^2]$ is a strict convex function of ρ_n. Therefore, (6.4) is a convex optimization problem.

Simplification of notations: Under independent Rayleigh fading channel, $t = \|\mathbf{H}_n\|^2$ is the sum of k_n i.i.d. Chi-square random variables, and therefore obeys the Gamma distribution $t \sim \Gamma(k_n, 1)$. The probability density function of t is:

$$d(\mathbb{P}(t)) = \frac{1}{\Gamma(k_n)} t^{k_n-1} e^{-t} dt. \tag{6.8}$$

Now let's define

$$\Phi(k, x) = \int_0^\infty \frac{1}{\Gamma(k)} \frac{x}{t+x} t^{k-1} e^{-t} dt, \tag{6.9}$$

$$\Omega(k, x) = \int_0^\infty \frac{1}{\Gamma(k+1)} \left(\frac{x}{t+x}\right)^2 t^k e^{-t} dt. \tag{6.10}$$

It is easy to derive that $0 \leq \Phi(k, x) \leq 1$ and $0 \leq \Omega(k, x) \leq 1$. By substituting (6.9) into (6.5) and (6.10) into (6.6), we can simplify the expressions into:

$$\mathbb{E}[\varepsilon_n | \mathbf{k}, \sigma^2] = \lambda_n \cdot \Phi\left(k_n, \frac{1}{\rho_n}\right), \tag{6.11}$$

$$\frac{\partial \mathbb{E}[\varepsilon_n | \mathbf{k}, \sigma^2]}{\partial \rho_n} = -\lambda_n \cdot k_n \cdot \Omega\left(k_n, \frac{1}{\rho_n}\right). \tag{6.12}$$

Next, we derive a necessary condition for the optimal power allocation through the analysis of the Karush-Kuhn-Tucker (KKT) condition of (6.4).

Theorem 2 *Let* $\mathbf{k}$ *be a given bandwidth allocation and* $\rho^+ = (\rho_1^+...\rho_N^+)^T$ *be a power allocation scheme. A necessary condition for* ρ^+ *being the optimal power allocation is that* $\forall k_n \geq 1$ *the following constraint holds, where* C *is a real number.*

$$\lambda_n \cdot \Omega\left(k_n, \frac{1}{\rho_n^+}\right) = C. \tag{6.13}$$

Proof. The Lagrangian $L : \mathbf{R}^N \times \mathbf{R} \times \mathbf{R}^N \to \mathbf{R}$ associated with (6.4) is

$$L(\rho, \gamma_0, \gamma_1, \ldots, \gamma_N) = \sum_{n=1}^N \mathbb{E}[\varepsilon_n | \mathbf{k}, \sigma^2]$$
$$+ \gamma_0 \left(\sum_{n=1}^N k_n \rho_n - \frac{P}{\sigma^2}\right) - \sum_{n=1}^N \gamma_n \rho_n. \tag{6.14}$$

The KKT conditions are

$$\left\{ \begin{array}{rl} \dfrac{\partial \mathbb{E}[\varepsilon_n | \mathbf{k}, \sigma^2]}{\partial \rho_n} + \gamma_0 k_n - \gamma_n = 0 & \text{(6.15a)} \\[2ex] \displaystyle\sum_{n=1}^{N} k_n \rho_n - \dfrac{P}{\sigma^2} = 0 & \text{(6.15b)} \\[2ex] \gamma_n \rho_n = 0 & \text{(6.15c)} \\[1ex] \gamma_n \geq 0 & \text{(6.15d)} \\[1ex] \rho_n \geq 0 & \text{(6.15e)} \end{array} \right.$$

Substituting (6.15a) into (6.15c), we have

$$\left(\frac{\partial \mathbb{E}[\varepsilon_n | \mathbf{k}, \sigma^2]}{\partial \rho_n} + \gamma_0 k_n \right) \rho_n = 0. \tag{6.16}$$

For the data that will be transmitted, $\rho_n > 0$. Hence,

$$\frac{\partial \mathbb{E}[\varepsilon_n | \mathbf{k}, \sigma^2]}{\partial \rho_n} + \gamma_0 k_n = 0. \tag{6.17}$$

Substituting (6.17) into (6.15b), we can derive that

$$\frac{\partial \mathbb{E}[\varepsilon_n | \mathbf{k}, \sigma^2]}{\partial \rho_n} = k_n \sum_{i=1}^{N} \frac{\rho_i}{P/\sigma^2} \frac{\partial \mathbb{E}[\varepsilon_i | \mathbf{k}, \sigma^2]}{\partial \rho_i}. \tag{6.18}$$

Therefore, by (6.18) and (6.12), the conclusion (6.13) holds.

The above analyses suggest that there are at least two ways to solve the power allocation problem. One is through solving equations (6.13), and another is through gradient descent based on the convexity of the problem. The latter is considered a tractable solution in practice.

6.3.2 Bandwidth Allocation Problem

Now that we have a tractable algorithm to solve the power allocation problem, the optimal bandwidth allocation problem can be written as:

$$\begin{array}{ll} \min_{\mathbf{k}} \min_{\rho} \sum_{n=1}^{N} \mathbb{E}\left[\varepsilon_n | \mathbf{k}, \sigma^2\right], & \\ \text{s.t.} \ \sum_{n=1}^{N} k_n = M, & \\ k_n \geq 0, \ k_n \in \mathbb{Z}. & \end{array} \tag{6.19}$$

In order to find the optimal bandwidth allocation scheme $\mathbf{k}^+$, we shall test all the possible combinations of $(k_1 \ldots k_N)$ by running the optimal power allocation algorithm and comparing the achieved minimum distortion. The computational complexity is apparently too high. Therefore, we shall look for some guidelines for bandwidth allocation to reduce the complexity. Intuitively, transmitting a variable with more channel uses will result in a smaller distortion even when the overall transmission power is the same. The distortion reduction could be significant for variables with large variance. If this is true, we may sacrifice the transmission opportunities of some LP data (with small variances) and allow the HP data to use more channel uses so that the overall distortion could be reduced. Next, we will present two theorems that confirm our conjecture.

Theorem 3 *Consider the repeated transmission of a Gaussian variable over a Rayleigh fading channel. Let $\rho\sigma^2$ be the total power budget. Transmitting the R.V. in $k+1$ time slots results in a smaller distortion than transmitting it in k time slots, where $k \geq 1$.*

Proof. It has been shown in [74] that, under the total power constraint, equal power division over k available channel uses minimizes the distortion. When there are k time slots, $\rho\sigma^2/k$ is allocated to each transmission. When there is an additional channel use, the power of each transmission is $\rho\sigma^2/(k+1)$. According to the relationship between the distortion and the Φ function as given in (6.11), and letting $x = 1/\rho$, we prove

$$\Phi(k, kx) > \Phi(k+1, (k+1)x).$$

Let's define

$$\Delta_1 = \Phi(k, (k+1)x) - \Phi(k, x)$$
$$= \int_0^\infty \frac{1}{\Gamma(k)} \left(\frac{(k+1)x}{t+(k+1)x} - \frac{kx}{t+kx} \right) t^{k-1} e^{-t} dt$$
$$= \int_0^\infty \frac{1}{\Gamma(k+1)} \frac{kx}{(t+(k+1)x)(t+kx)} t^k e^{-t} dt,$$

and

$$\Delta_2 = \Phi(k, (k+1)x) - \Phi(k+1, (k+1)x)$$
$$= \frac{1}{(k+1)x} \Omega(k, (k+1)x)$$
$$= \int_0^\infty \frac{1}{\Gamma(k+1)} \frac{(k+1)x}{(t+(k+1)x)^2} t^k e^{-t} dt.$$

Since $\forall t > 0$ and $x > 0$, we have

$$\frac{(k+1)x}{t+(k+1)x} - \frac{kx}{t+kx} = \frac{xt}{(t+(k+1)x)(t+kx)} > 0.$$

Therefore, $\Delta_2 > \Delta_1$, i.e., $\Phi(k, kx) > \Phi(k+1, (k+1)x)$.

Theorem 4 *Consider the repeated transmission of multiple Gaussian random variables and assume that we have an optimal power allocation scheme under a given bandwidth allocation. If L variables are allocated with the same number of* *channel uses, i.e., $k_1 = k_2... = k_L$, then the one with the largest variance has the maximum distortion reduction when it is allocated with an additional channel use while keeping its total power budget unchanged.*

Proof. Let $\lambda_1...\lambda_L$ denote the variances of the L Gaussian random variables. Without loss of generality, we assume $\lambda_1 \geq \lambda_2 \geq ... \geq \lambda_L$. From the distortion analysis, we know that the total distortion of the L random variables is

$$\sum_{i=1}^{L} \lambda_i \Phi(k_i, \frac{1}{\rho_i}).$$

In order to minimize the above distortion, the values of the Φ functions should be in descending order, i.e.,

$$\Phi(k_1, \frac{1}{\rho_1}) \leq \Phi(k_2, \frac{1}{\rho_2}) \leq ... \leq \Phi(k_L, \frac{1}{\rho_L}).$$

Hence, we have $\rho_1 \geq \rho_2 \geq ... \geq \rho_L$.

If an additional channel use is assigned to λ_i and ρ_i is unchanged, the distortion reduction, denoted by ΔD_i, will be

$$\Delta D_i = \lambda_i \left(\Phi(k_i, \frac{1}{\rho_i}) - \Phi(k_i + 1, \frac{k_i + 1}{k_i \rho_i}) \right).$$

We allocate the additional channel use to the R.V. with the maximum ΔD_i.

According to Theorem 2, the following equations hold for an optimal resource allocation scheme:

$$\lambda_1 \Omega(k_1, \frac{1}{\rho_1}) = \lambda_2 \Omega(k_2, \frac{1}{\rho_2}) = ... = \lambda_L \Omega(k_L, \frac{1}{\rho_L}) = C.$$

Divide the distortion reduction by C, and define:

$$f(x) = \frac{\Phi(k, kx) - \Phi(k+1, (k+1)x)}{\Omega(k, kx)}.$$

According to the definitions of $\Phi(\cdot)$ and $\Omega(\cdot)$, we have:

$$\Phi(k, kx) - \Phi(k+1, (k+1)x)$$
$$= \int_0^\infty \frac{xt}{(t+(k+1)x)^2(t+kx)} \frac{t^k e^{-t}}{\Gamma(k+1)} dt,$$

$$\Omega(k, kx) = \int_0^\infty \left(\frac{kx}{(t+kx)} \right)^2 \frac{t^k e^{-t}}{\Gamma(k+1)} dt.$$

Let's define

$$g(x) = \frac{xt}{(t+(k+1)x)^2(t+kx)} \Big/ \left(\frac{kx}{(t+kx)} \right)^2,$$

$\forall t > 0$, $g'(x) < 0$. Hence, $g(x)$ is a decreasing function of x. Since the integral is operated on t, therefore, $f(x)$ is a decreasing function of x.

Therefore, ΔD_1 has the maximum value among all ΔD_i's, meaning that the additional channel use should be assigned to the R.V. with largest variance λ_1.

6.4 Solution

Based on the above analyses, we first came out with an iterative solution that has tractable complexity. Then, both algorithmic and computational complexity are further reduced with marginal performance loss. The proposed fast algorithm allows a video source to be processed in real time.

6.4.1 An Iterative Algorithm

We first approximate the optimal solution through an iterative algorithm. The algorithm inputs are the variances of the R.V., denoted by $\lambda = (\lambda_1...\lambda_N)^T$, the total power constraint P, the number of available channel uses M, and the noise power σ^2. We assume that λ's have been sorted in descending order. The expected outputs are the bandwidth allocation scheme $\mathbf{k}^+ = (k_1...k_N)$ and the power allocation scheme $\rho^+ = (\rho_1...\rho_N)$.

In initialization, all the R.V.'s are allocated with the same number of channel uses. If M cannot be divided by N, then the first $M \mod N$ R.V.'s with larger variances are allocated with one more channel use. Then, the power allocation algorithm is applied to initialize ρ^+, and the minimum distortion is computed.

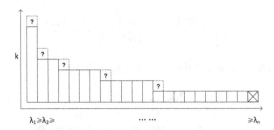

Fig. 6.2 An illustrative example of iterative bandwidth allocation.

In each iteration, we take one allocated channel use from the R.V. with the smallest variance and try to assign it to other R.V.'s. According to Theorem 4, among the R.V.'s that are allocated with the same number of channel uses in the previous iteration, the one with the largest variance will have the largest distortion reduction. Therefore, only a few candidates need be considered. In the algorithm description, this set is denoted by $\mathscr{S}_t$. Fig. 6.2 gives an illustrative example. The variables are sorted in descending order according to their variances. We try to take the channel use of the last variable (marked with a cross) and allocate it to higher priority variables. Only five positions marked with question marks should be considered for getting the additional channel use.

For each possible bandwidth reallocation k, we perform power allocation and compute the minimum total distortion. Then, we select the bandwidth reallocation option that results in the minimum total distortion. The iterative process ends if the reallocation does not reduce total distortion.

In Algorithm 3, we call function *PowerAlloc($\cdot$)* twice. Algorithm 4 presents the detailed gradient descent algorithm *PowerAlloc($\cdot$)*, which solves the optimal bandwidth allocation problem.

Algorithm 3 Iterative Algorithm

Input: λ, P, M, σ^2
Output: k^+, ρ^+
1: **for** $n = 1...N$ **do** $\triangleright$ Initialize $k^+, \rho^+, D^{(0)}$
2:      $k_n^+ = \lfloor \frac{M}{N} \rfloor$
3:      **if** $n \leq M \mod N$ **then**
4:          $k_n^+ \leftarrow k_n^+ + 1$
5:      **end if**
6: **end for**
7: $(\rho^+, D^{(0)}) \leftarrow$ *PowerAlloc$(\lambda, k^+, P, \sigma^2)$*
8: $t = 0$
9: **repeat** $\triangleright$ Iterative Processing
10:      $t \leftarrow t + 1$
11:      $\mathscr{S}_t = \{1\} \cup \{n | k_n^+ < k_{n-1}^+, n \geq 2\}$
12:      $n_d \leftarrow$ the largest index n that $k_n^+ \geq 1$
13:      **for all** n_t in $\mathscr{S}_t$ **do**
14:          $k = k^+$, except $k_{n_d} = k_{n_d}^+ - 1, k_{n_t} = k_{n_t}^+ + 1$
15:          $(\rho, D) \leftarrow$ *PowerAlloc$(\lambda, k, P, \sigma^2)$*
16:      **end for**
17:      $D^{(t)} = \min\{D\}$
18:      **if** $D^{(t)} < D^{(t-1)}$ **then**
19:          $\rho^+ \leftarrow \rho$ corresponding to the min D
20:          $k^+ \leftarrow k$ corresponding to the min D
21:      **end if**
22: **until** $D^{(t)} \geq D^{(t-1)}$

In Algorithm 4, the power allocation scheme ρ^+ is initialized by the optimal power allocation for AWGN channel as described in [13, 19]. $sgn(k_n)$ is a sign function that equals one when $k_n \geq 1$ and zero when $k_n = 0$. During iterations, the power allocation should be evolved along the direction θ that has the largest projection on the gradient descent direction ω [76].

Algorithm 4 Power Allocation Algorithm

Input: λ, k, P, σ^2
Output: ρ^+, D
1: **for** $n = 1...N$ **do**   ▷ Initialize ρ^+
2:     $\rho_n^+ = sgn(k_n) \cdot \sqrt{\lambda_n} \cdot \dfrac{P}{\sigma^2 \sum_{i=1}^{N} k_i \sqrt{\lambda_i}}$
3: **end for**
4: $t = 0$ ▷ Gradient descent approximation
5: $D^{(0)} = +\infty$
6: **repeat**
7:     $t \leftarrow t+1$
8:     $\kappa = k * sgn(\rho^+)$
9:     $\omega = -\dfrac{\partial \mathbb{E}[\varepsilon_n | \kappa, \sigma^2]}{\partial \rho} |_{\rho=\rho^+}$
10:    $\theta = \alpha_1 (\omega - \dfrac{\kappa \cdot \omega}{\|\kappa\|^2} \kappa)$
11:    $\rho^+ = \alpha_2 \max\{\rho^+ + \delta\theta, \mathbf{0}\}$
12:    $D^{(t)} = \sum_{n=1}^{N} \mathbb{E}[\varepsilon_n | \kappa, \sigma^2]$
13: **until** $\|D^{(t)} - D^{(t-1)}\| < \xi$
14: $D = D^{(t)}$
15: PowerAlloc($\cdot$)

$$
\begin{aligned}
\max \ & \sum_{i=1}^{N} \omega_i \theta_i, \\
\text{s.t.} \ & \sum_{i=1}^{N} \kappa_i \theta_i = 0, \\
& \sum_{i=1}^{N} \theta_i^2 = 1.
\end{aligned}
\tag{6.20}
$$

Through the Lagrangian method, we can derive a closed form of the direction.

$$
\theta_n = \alpha_1 \left(\omega_n - \kappa_n \frac{\sum_{i=1}^{N} \kappa_i \omega_i}{\sum_{i=1}^{N} \kappa_i^2} \right),
\tag{6.21}
$$

where $\alpha_1 > 0$ is the normalization factor that $\sum_{i=1}^{N} \theta_i^2 = 1$.

In line 9, the notation $*$ denotes element-wise multiplication. We force the bandwidth allocation to zero if the power allocation evolves to zero. We perform this operation because power is a non-negative scalar and should be bounded by zero if it evolves to a negative value. α_2 is a normalization factor that ensures $\alpha_2 \sum_{i=1}^{N} \kappa_i \rho_i = \frac{P}{\sigma^2}$.

6.4.2 Proposed Fast Algorithm

We propose a fast algorithm that reduces both the algorithmic and computational complexity of the proposed iterative algorithm. First, we find that the iterative process can be simplified into a one-pass two-step process with marginal performance loss. Second, we observe that the computation of the distortion and the first order derivative of the distortion consume a great deal of resources because both terms contain integral components that are hard to precisely compute. We

---

Algorithm 5 Fast Algorithm

Input: λ, P, M, σ^2
Output: k^+, ρ^+
1: Initialize $k^+, \rho^+, D^{(0)}$ Same as line 2-8 in Algorithm 3.
2:
3: **repeat**   ▷ Bandwidth allocation
4:     $t \leftarrow t+1$
5:     $\mathscr{S}_t = \{1\} \cup \{n | k_n^+ < k_{n-1}^+, n \geq 2\}$
6:     $n_d \leftarrow$ the largest index n that $k_n^+ \geq 1$
7:     **for all** n_t in $\mathscr{S}_t$ **do**
8:         $k = k^+$, except $k_{n_d} = k_{n_d}^+ - 1$, $k_{n_t} = k_{n_t}^+ + 1$
9:         $\rho = \rho^+$, except $\rho_{n_t} = \dfrac{\rho_{n_t}^+ \cdot k_{n_t}^+ + \rho_{n_d}^+}{k_{n_t}}$
10:        $D \leftarrow \mathbb{E}[\varepsilon_n | k, \rho, \sigma^2]$
11:    **end for**
12:    $D^{(t)} = \min\{D\}$
13:    **if** $D^{(t)} < D^{(t-1)}$ **then**
14:        $\rho^+ \leftarrow \rho$ corresponding to the min D
15:        $k^+ \leftarrow k$ corresponding to the min D
16:    **end if**
17: **until** $D^{(t)} \geq D^{(t-1)}$
18: $(\rho^+, D) \leftarrow PowerAlloc(\lambda, k^+, P, \sigma^2)$ ▷ Power allocation

---

propose a method to compute both terms through recursion that greatly reduces the computational complexity.

Reducing algorithmic complexity: Algorithm 5 gives the details of the proposed fast algorithm. Comparing it with the iterative algorithm (Algorithm 3), we find that the computationally costly function $PowerAlloc(\cdot)$ is only called twice in initialization and line 20 (final decision). Actually, we can simplify the power initialization step by using only line 3 in Algorithm 4 to further reduce the complexity. Although the bandwidth allocation is still an iterative process, we decouple power allocation from it by replacing line 16 in Algorithm 3 with lines 10 and 11 in Algorithm 5. In particular, we do not seek the optimal power allocation for the tested new bandwidth allocation, but simply reallocate the power of the dropped coefficient (n_d) to coefficient n_t, and compute the distortion under bandwidth allocation k and power allocation ρ. Note that $\rho_{n_t}^+ \cdot k_{n_t}^+ + \rho_{n_d}^+$ in line 10 is the new total power for coefficient n_t, and it is evenly divided among k_{n_t} time slots. After the bandwidth allocation is decided, $PowerAlloc(\cdot)$ is called in line 20 to make the final power allocation decision. We will show through evaluation that this fast algorithm incurs marginal performance loss compared to the iterative algorithm.

Reducing computational complexity: In both the bandwidth allocation and power allocation processes, we need to compute the expectation of distortion and its partial derivative as defined in (6.11) and (6.12). However, we need to compute integrals in evaluating Φ and Ω functions according to their definitions in (6.9) and (6.10). Next, we propose an efficient way to compute the integrals based on recursion.

When $k = 1$,

$$\Phi(1,x) = \int_0^\infty \frac{x}{t+x} e^{-t} dt = x e^x \int_x^\infty \frac{1}{t} e^{-t} dt$$
$$= x(-e^x Ei(-x)),$$

(6.22)

where $Ei(-x)$ is the exponential integral function.

$\forall k > 1$, we have the following recursion

$$\Phi(k,x) = \int_0^\infty \frac{1}{\Gamma(k)} \frac{x}{t+x} t^{k-1} e^{-t} dt$$
$$= \frac{x}{\Gamma(k)} \int_0^\infty \frac{t}{t+x} t^{k-2} e^{-t} dt$$
$$= \frac{x}{\Gamma(k)} \left(\int_0^\infty t^{k-2} e^{-t} dt - \int_0^\infty \frac{x}{t+x} t^{k-2} e^{-t} dt \right)$$
$$= \frac{x}{k-1} (1 - \Phi(k-1,x)).$$

(6.23)

In addition,

$$\Omega(k,x) = \int_0^\infty \frac{1}{\Gamma(k+1)} \left(\frac{x}{t+x} \right)^2 t^k e^{-t} dt$$
$$= \frac{1}{\Gamma(k+1)} \frac{-x^2}{t+x} t^k e^{-t} \Big|_0^\infty + \int_0^\infty \frac{1}{\Gamma(k)} \frac{x^2}{t+x} t^{k-1} e^{-t} dt$$
$$- \int_0^\infty \frac{1}{\Gamma(k+1)} \frac{x^2}{t+x} t^k e^{-t} dt$$
$$= x(\Phi(k,x) - \Phi(k+1,x)).$$

(6.24)

The exponential integral function $-e^x Ei(-x)$ can be implemented by a lookup table. Therefore, by recursion, the integral can be very efficiently computed. In addition, when there is enough memory, e.g., 1MB, the function $\Phi(k,x)$ for $k = 1,2,\ldots,100$ can also be implemented by a lookup table which further reduces the computation cost.

6.5 Evaluation

6.5.1 Implementation

Fig. 6.3 shows the source processing of the uncoded video transmission scheme. The processing unit is a group of pictures (GOP). The GOP size is 8 in our implementation. We perform 3D-DCT over a GOP after subtracting 128 from each pixel value. Then, DCT coefficients in each transformed picture are divided into equal-size rectangular chunks as shown in Fig. 6.3. The coefficients in a chunk are considered i.i.d. zero mean Gaussian distributed random variables and the variance is the average energy of the chunk. Using more chunks would produce better performance, but incurs higher overhead as well. Usually, 64 equal chunks per picture (or 512 chunks per GOP) introduces negligible overhead with little harm to performance [77]. Then, the resource allocation algorithm is performed based on the chunk variances and the coefficients in each chunk are scaled and duplicated accordingly. The scaled coefficients are pair wisely mapped to the amplitude of in-phase and quadrature-phase transmission signals.

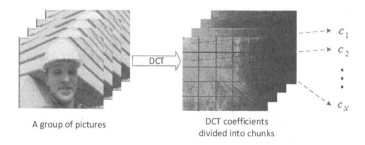

A group of pictures   DCT coefficients
                                                       divided into chunks

Fig. 6.3 Source processing in an uncoded video transmission scheme.

Note that the variances of the chunks should be faithfully transmitted to receivers as metadata. Therefore, they are encoded and transmitted in a digital manner. We adopt BPSK and 1/2 channel coding to ensure reliable transmission. At the receiver, with the correct variance information, both the scaling factors and the channel use assignment can be computed. If multiple channel uses are allocated to any single chunk, maximum ratio combining (MRC) is performed. Based on the estimated CSI and the refined noise power by MRC, the coefficients can be obtained with the minimum distortion by MMSE detection. Finally, the video can be reconstructed through inverse 3D-DCT and adding 128 to the pixel value.

Since this chapter focuses on the transmission for linear video, SoftCast is considered a reference scheme. We follow all the implementation details of SoftCast as outlined in [19], including the whitening step using the Hadamard matrix. For a fair comparison, all schemes use GOP size 8 and equal chunk division with 8×8 chunks per frame. Note that our scheme transmits the same amount of metadata as SoftCast. According to [19], the overhead is only 0.014 bpp (bits per pixel).

6.5.2 Settings

Video source: We use monochrome video sequences for our evaluation. In particular, only the luma (Y') components in the Y'UV video signals are transmitted. If color videos are of interest, the chrominance (U and V) components can be processed and transmitted in the same way as the luma components. Chunks from different color components will not be discriminated in resource allocation, as resource allocation decisions are made solely based on chunk variations.

In most evaluations, we use CIF sequences with resolution of 352×288 and frame rate of 30 fps (frame per second). Hence, the source bandwidth is 1.52 MHz (in complex symbols). The 12 standard video test sequences used are "akiyo," "bus," "coastguard," "container," "flower," "football," "foreman," "husky," "mobile," "news," "soccer" and "stefan".

Physical layer configurations: After power allocation, the scaled coefficients are directly used to modulate the amplitude of in-phase and quadrature-phase signals. Therefore, one complex symbol can be generated by two coefficients. The complex symbols are transmitted through OFDM so that the channel fading gain can be considered as a complex scalar. At the receiver end, different versions of a transmitted symbol from multiple channel use are combined by Maximum Ratio Combining (MRC).

Channel configurations: We use Rayleigh fading channel with the fading parameter $h_m \sim \mathscr{C} \mathscr{N}(0, 1)$. We change h_m every $40\mu s$ to simulate a fast fading channel. The random noise is generated based on the AWGN model. In most of the simulations, E_s/N_0 equal to 5dB, 10dB, 20dB and 30dB are considered. Except for the bandwidth compaction evaluation, the total bandwidth, i.e., the number of available channel use, is in default equal to the number of coefficients.

Evaluation metrics: We use PSNR as the evaluation metric. The PSNR of a sequence is the averaged PSNR over all frames. In order to evaluate the robustness of the transmission scheme, we conduct 1000 test runs for each test video for each target channel SNR. The tested video sequences are different in their data energy distribution. The average PSNR and its 5th and 95th percentiles are recorded.

6.5.3 Results

Comparison against reference scheme Softcast: We first compare the performance of our scheme with Softcast. Table 6.1 lists the average PSNR achieved for the 12 test videos. Our scheme consistently outperforms Softcast, and the average gain is between 1.7dB to 2.4dB under varying channel conditions. Table 6.2 gives the 5th percentile of the achieved PSNR, i.e., in 95% of all the 1000 test runs, this PSNR can be achieved. This metric indicates the robustness of a transmission scheme. We find that our scheme achieves an enormous gain over Softcast, ranging from 4.0dB to 7.5dB under varying channel conditions. Besides, comparing the average PSNR and the 5th percentile of our scheme, we find that the gap is very small. The results confirm that we have achieved our design goal to build a robust uncoded video transmission scheme.

We have also tested our scheme for videos with different resolutions and under different evaluation metrics. Fig. 6.4 shows the comparison between our scheme and SoftCast for a high-definition (1280×720) video "City" under both PSNR and SSIM (structural similarity) measures. Results show that we achieve similar

Table 6.1 Average PSNR (in dB) achieved by our scheme and Softcast

E_s/N_0 Sequence	5dB		10dB		20dB		30dB	
	Ours	Softcast	Ours	Softcast	Ours	Softcast	Ours	Softcast
Akiyo	38.53	36.28	42.78	40.12	50.90	48.18	61.74	57.60
Bus	27.27	25.52	30.93	28.82	38.82	36.46	46.44	44.95
Coastguard	32.82	30.92	36.44	34.29	44.26	41.94	51.33	50.08
Container	34.27	31.22	38.41	34.94	46.52	43.10	53.89	51.41
Flower	25.69	24.45	28.91	27.54	36.20	34.79	43.89	43.17
Football	28.48	26.47	32.21	29.77	40.25	37.43	47.66	45.93
Foreman	33.38	31.38	37.02	34.86	44.77	42.61	52.17	50.71
Husky	23.39	22.13	26.60	25.20	33.86	32.55	41.58	40.98
Mobile	25.94	24.10	29.41	27.33	36.95	34.88	44.46	43.39
News	33.41	30.85	37.44	34.56	45.83	42.67	53.50	51.00
Soccer	30.58	28.71	34.13	32.04	41.77	39.67	49.06	48.00
Stefan	27.87	25.72	31.65	29.02	39.72	36.72	47.40	45.27
Average	**30.14**	**28.15**	**33.83**	**31.54**	**41.65**	**39.25**	**49.43**	**47.71**

Table 6.2 5th percentile PSNR (in dB) of our scheme and Softcast

E_s/N_0 Sequence	5dB		10dB		20dB		30dB	
	Ours	Softcast	Ours	Softcast	Ours	Softcast	Ours	Softcast
Akiyo	37.67	32.42	41.92	34.17	50.07	39.69	58.88	47.18
Bus	26.79	23.8	30.41	25.91	38.03	31.2	44.02	38.53
Coastguard	32.26	28.38	35.9	30.25	43.55	35.56	48.86	41.94
Container	33.6	27.2	37.79	28.95	45.69	33.32	51.98	40.49
Flower	25.34	23.03	28.47	25.62	34.52	30.47	41.58	36.33
Football	28.04	24.57	31.74	26.96	39.32	32.31	45.32	38.93
Foreman	32.81	27.8	36.49	29.45	43.77	34.83	50.01	42.11
Husky	23.1	21.24	26.05	23.63	31.98	29.12	39.16	35.31
Mobile	25.57	22.73	28.82	24.96	35.00	30.33	41.56	36.76
News	32.73	27.3	36.83	29.01	45.08	34.55	52.40	41.68
Soccer	30.09	25.54	33.49	27.49	39.71	32.79	46.76	40.04
Stefan	27.41	23.77	31.13	25.8	38.75	31.15	45.31	38.09
Average	**29.62**	**25.65**	**33.25**	**27.68**	**40.46**	**32.94**	**47.15**	**39.78**

(slightly larger) PSNR gain over SoftCast for high-definition videos as for CIF videos. The improvement over SSIM measure is also significant.

Impact of inaccurate CSI and multicast: The proposed resource allocation algorithm needs the noise level at the receiver (denoted by σ^2) as an input. The provided σ^2 may be inaccurate under three situations. First, when σ^2 itself is not precisely measured. Second, when the estimated channel fading parameter h is larger or smaller than the actual value, it is equivalent to reducing or amplifying the additive noise. Third, when a multicast session is considered, multiple receivers may have varying CSI.

In order to evaluate the impact of inaccurate CSI, we run our scheme at typical target SNRs and evaluate the receiver PSNR when the actual noise power ranged

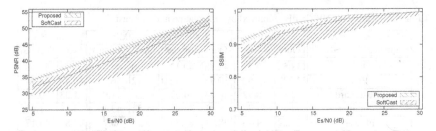

Fig. 6.4 Comparison between the proposed method and SoftCast for 720p video "City" under PSNR and SSIM measures. The shadowed regions are bounded by the 5th and 95th percentiles and the lines in the region indicate the average performance.

from 5dB to 30dB. Table 6.3 lists the average PSNR and the standard deviation (SD) averaged over all 12 test sequences.

Table 6.3 The mean and variance of the achieved PSNR when the CSI may be inaccurate

Scheme	Actual E_s/N_0			
(input E_s/N_0)	5dB	10dB	20dB	30dB
Ours(5dB)	30.14, 0.18	33.39, 0.17	37.65, 0.12	38.84, 0.05
Ours(10dB)	30.05, 0.25	33.83, 0.23	40.19, 0.18	42.88, 0.10
Ours(20dB)	29.45, 0.38	33.45, 0.37	41.65, 0.37	48.16, 0.32
Ours(30dB)	29.18, 0.45	33.05, 0.45	41.26, 0.52	49.43, 0.73
Softcast	28.15, 0.83	31.54, 1.01	39.25, 1.54	47.71, 2.01

We observe that underestimating E_s/N_0 will decrease the achieved PSNR, but the variation decreases as well. When the actual channel condition is poor or moderate (E_s/N_0 equals 5dB and 10dB in the table), inaccurate CSI has little impact on the achieved PSNR. However, when the channel condition is good, significantly underestimating the channel may incur a large loss. In the extreme case that the actual E_s/N_0 is 30dB but the algorithm input is 5dB, the loss in average PSNR could be as large as 10.7dB. In contrast, overestimating the channel is not so harmful. The loss in average PSNR is below 1dB under varying conditions.

The table also gives the performance of Softcast. As Softcast does not need CSI input, it only has one row of results. The PSNR variation of Softcast is significantly larger than our scheme. In addition, when a multicast session is considered, we shall use the CSI of strong receivers as the algorithm input. As an example, when we use 30dB as the input E_s/N_0, our scheme would consistently outperform Softcast with receiver E_s/N_0 ranging from 5dB to 30dB.

Performance under bandwidth compaction: In practice, the channel bandwidth is often smaller than the source bandwidth. The ratio between them is called bandwidth compaction ratio denoted by r. In this experiment, we evaluate the impact of bandwidth compaction ($r = 0.5$) on the average performance and robustness of our scheme, through the comparison with the $r = 1$ case and with the reference scheme Softcast. When $r = 1/2$, Softcast simply discards the less important half of the coefficient chunks (with smaller variances). The representative video test sequence Foreman is used, and the power constraint is unit power per channel use on average.

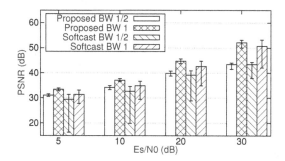

Fig. 6.5 Performance of our scheme and Softcast under bandwidth compaction ratio 1/2 and 1 (Video source: Foreman).

Fig. 6.5 shows the performance of our scheme and Softcast under bandwidth compaction ratio $r = 1/2$ and $r = 1$ (no compaction) at varying channel noise levels. Both average PSNR and the 5th and the 95th percentiles are shown in the figure. We find that our scheme is very robust under bandwidth compaction. The gap between the 5th and 95th percentiles when $r = 0.5$ remains very small as in the $r = 1$ case. In contrast, the 5th percentile of Softcast drops to 16.32dB, which is more than 11dB lower than when $r = 1$, when the channel E_s/N_0 is 5dB.

Performance and complexity evaluation of the fast algorithm: The proposed fast algorithm dramatically reduces the complexity of the iterative algorithm. In this experiment, we first evaluate the changes in bandwidth allocation as well as the performance loss of the fast algorithm. Fig. 6.6 compares the bandwidth allocation results (k_f denotes the fast algorithm and k_s denotes the iterative algorithm) for the first GOP of Foreman, with the two algorithms under typical channel conditions. We notice that the fast algorithm tends to allocate more time slots to the first few high-priority R.V.'s, but the overall allocation does not differ much. We also run evaluations for the iterative algorithm over all 12 test sequences. The achieved results by the fast algorithm and iterative algorithm are very close, and the differences in average PSNR, 5th and 95th percentiles are all within 0.4%.

We next evaluate the computational complexity of the proposed fast algorithm. We run the algorithm for the first GOP (8 frames) of 12 test sequences, and record the time taken by bandwidth allocation and power allocation, respectively. The desktop PC has an Intel core i7-3770 @ 3.4GHz. We run the algorithm in a single thread to provide a benchmark. The average times taken by the bandwidth and power allocation are 0.358s and 1.414s, respectively, so the total encoding time is 1.772s per GOP on average. The longest encoding time is 2.08s for the 9th sequence. If one considers a video sequence with a frame rate of 30fps, parallel processing using eight threads can ensure real-time encoding for all sequences.

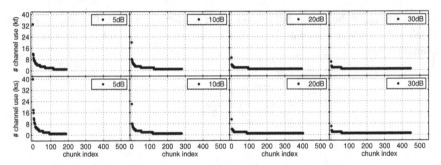

Fig. 6.6 Bandwidth allocation results by the iterative and the fast algorithm for the first GOP of Foreman.

6.6 Summary

We have considered robust uncoded video transmission over fast fading channels in this chapter. We have found that, similar to conventional digital communications, diversity increases robustness and reduces distortion under the total power constraint. We have carried out theoretical analysis on the problem of optimal power and bandwidth allocation for the minimum MSE of a Gaussian random vector. Practical algorithms have been derived and an uncoded video transmission scheme has been implemented. Evaluations have shown that our scheme achieves significant gains over Softcast, demonstrating the effectiveness of the proposed algorithm.

Chapter 7
Progressive Transmission

7.1 Introduction

The two greatest challenges facing a mobile streaming application are the dramatically varying channel conditions and the stringent latency requirement. When a mobile device is downloading and playing a video, each video frame has a playback deadline. Failing to transmit a decodable bit stream of a frame before its playback deadline not only creates an unpleasant user experience, but wastes precious network bandwidth resources. When a mobile device is recording and uploading a video, the transmission delay should also be kept small to avoid local buffer overflow. Under such a stringent latency requirement, it is very challenging to provide a high quality of experience (QoE) under the time-varying wireless channel.

The time-varying characteristic of wireless channels is reflected in both SNR and bandwidth variations. Fig. 7.1 shows the SNR trace we collected in a real wireless environment in around a 160ms time frame (where five video frames are collected and to be transmitted) and a possible bandwidth allocation. Note that the bandwidth variation is prominent in a multi-user system due to the shared nature of wireless medium. While uncoded video transmission is inherently SNR-adaptable, how does it perform in a bandwidth-varying environment?

Unfortunately, the current design of uncoded video transmission cannot gracefully handle bandwidth variation, especially in a low-latency setting. Specifically, the current design requires that the available bandwidth for each group of pictures (GOP) is known in advance. When the channel bandwidth is smaller than the source bandwidth, the sender discards the DCT coefficients with the least importance (or the smallest variances). Then, the remaining coefficients are power scaled according to their variances and the total power budget. Since the coefficients with different variances need dramatically different transmission power, sometimes by several degrees of magnitude, they need to be mixed in order to form PHY packets of the same power. As a result, each packet contains both important and not-so-important coefficients. During transmission, if the available bandwidth is smaller than expected, some of the packets may not have the opportunity to be

DOI: 10.1201/9781003118688-7

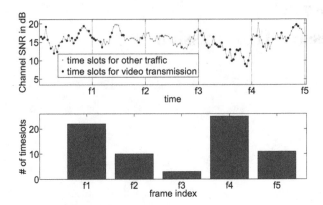

Fig. 7.1 Illustrating the challenges facing a mobile video streaming application: varying channel SNR and varying bandwidth share.

transmitted. When this happens, the important coefficients in these packets are discarded and the received video quality will be dramatically degraded.

In this chapter, we propose a progressive uncoded video transmission scheme, with the objective to simultaneously handle SNR and bandwidth variations in a timely and graceful manner. The basic idea is as simple as to transmit the DCT coefficients successively according to their importance in the digital systems. However, the importance of a coefficient is determined by its variance, which is exactly the transmission power in amplitude modulation. Grouping important coefficients together will create extremely high-power packets which is impossible for a practical system to transmit. To address this challenge, we suppress the transmission power of important coefficients in any single transmission, but allow for re-transmission of these coefficients so that the power from multiple transmissions can be accumulated.

At the receiver, video reconstruction can be performed at any moment, and preferably right before the playback deadline of a GOP. This is in contrast to the digital transmission in which the receiver has to wait for all the packets belonging to a specific GOP before it starts decoding. With this feature, the proposed progressive transmission scheme can operate in a "rebuffer-free" mode with a much smaller start-up delay than conventional digital schemes. Now the problem is, whenever there is a transmission opportunity, to determine the coefficients (or chunks) to be included in the packet and their transmission powers so that the overall distortion is minimized at the receiver when this packet is received. A scheduling algorithm and a power allocation algorithm need to be designed to solve this problem.

Simulations validate that, in AWGN channel, our progressive transmission scheme outperforms SoftCast by a notable margin. It closely approaches the performance upper bound of an uncoded scheme in which the actual bandwidth is assumed to be known in advance. Simulations also show that the proposed scheme achieves the design goal in fast fading channels, allowing a receiver to recover the

Fig. 7.2 The sender-side flowchart of a uncoded video transmission system named SoftCast [19]. IFFT stands for inverse fast Fourier transform which is used to perform the Orthogonal Frequency Division Multiplexing (OFDM) process and DAC stands for digital-to-analog converter.

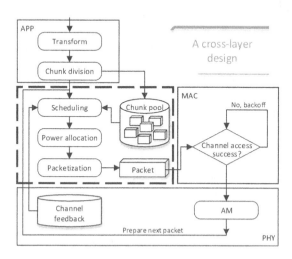

Fig. 7.3 The progressive uncoded video transmission framework.

video at a quality that is commensurate with its instantaneous SNR and bandwidth share. Trace-driven evaluations are also performed based on a software defined radio platform SORA [38]. Results show that in a realistic wireless environment, the proposed scheme outperforms SoftCast and the state-of-the-art digital solution (scalable video coding + 802.11PHY) in terms of both average and worst-case performance.

7.2 Progressive Uncoded Video Transmission

7.2.1 Framework Overview

The progressive uncoded video transmission is designed to be both SNR-adaptable and bandwidth-adaptable. While the SNR-adaptability is an inborn trait of uncoded transmission, the bandwidth-adaptability is achieved through the proposed greedy scheduling algorithm that allows retransmission of important chunks. Fig. 7.3 illustrates the proposed framework at the sender. It is a cross-layer design involving the application layer (APP), the medium access control (MAC) and the physical layer (PHY). Our unique designs are highlighted in the bold dashed box.

In APP, a decorrelation transform (e.g., 3D-DCT) is performed over the input video frames and the transform coefficients are divided into chunks. Coefficients in one chunk are treated as instances drawn from the same zero-mean Gaussian distribution. For simplicity and without loss of generality, we consider equal-sized rectangular-shape chunk division. All the chunks are put into a chunk pool and the variance of each chunk is computed. Generally speaking, the variance of a chunk reflects its importance.

The scheduling module is the key module in our design. It picks K chunks out of the total N chunks to compose a *tile*. The size of K is determined such that each tile can fit into one single PHY packet. The power allocation module serves two purposes. First, it ensures that the average symbol power of the packet does not exceed the given power budget. Second, it allocates the power among different chunks to minimize the distortion. Both the scheduling and the power allocation decisions are made with the objective of minimizing the total mean squared error (MSE) at the receiver after this packet is received, and by taking the previous channel feedback into consideration. At the MAC, the sender waits to access the wireless medium. Once a packet is successfully sent out, the scheduling model will prepare for the next packet. If the playback deadline for the current GOP is about to pass (in the case of downlink streaming) or the next GOP has been recorded in the buffer (in the case of uplink uploading), the sender will move to process the next GOP.

Note that, in the proposed framework, an important chunk can be transmitted multiple times. This never happens in the original SoftCast system. This is because SoftCast is optimized for an AWGN channel only. In an AWGN channel model, transmitting a signal n times using power P_1, P_2, ... P_n results in the same MSE as transmitting it once using power $\sum_{i=1}^{n} P_i$. Although the allocated power for different chunks is dramatically different, SoftCast mixes the instances from different chunks into one packet to ensure that the average power of each packet satisfies a given constraint. However, if a sender is not sure whether it has a chance to transmit one more entire packet for a given GOP, it should aggressively transmit the important chunks, under the power budget of each packet. If later there are more transmission opportunities, these important chunks should be re-transmitted so that the power can be accumulated to approach the optimal power allocation. If there are even more transmission opportunities, some less important chunks can also be transmitted. This is the basic idea behind our progressive design.

The receiver collects as many copies of each coefficient as possible for a GOP before its playback deadline or the sender stops transmitting it. Then, multiple copies of the same coefficient are merged by maximum ratio combining (MRC) before the minimum mean squared error (MMSE) decoding is performed. Finally, the inverse transform reconstructs the video frames.

7.2.2 System Model and Problem Formulation

Let us consider a video sequence with frame resolution $W \times H$, where W and H indicate the width and the height, respectively. Assume that a GOP has F frames (F can be as small as 1 when the application does not tolerate any delay). After the decorrelation transform, the transform coefficients of each frame are partitioned into M chunks, so that a GOP has $N = M \times F$ chunks in total. The size of each chunk is denoted by L, which equals $(W \times H)/M$. We sort these chunks in descending order according to their variances and re-index them from 1 to N. The source chunks are denoted by S_i, $i = 1...N$. Usually, chunks located in the lower frequency band have larger variances. Let λ_i denote the variance of the ith chunk and we have $\lambda_{i_1} \geq \lambda_{i_2}$, $\forall i_1 \leq i_2$.

Let K be the number of chunks which can fit into one PHY packet, and let Γ be the maximum number of packets that can be transmitted for a particular GOP. Without loss of generality, we consider the situation where $\Gamma = N/K$. We use $S_{c,i}$ to denote the complex source chunk and it is formed by combining the odd part $S_{i,o}$ and even part $S_{i,e}$ of S_i:

$$S_{c,i} = \frac{S_{i,o} + jS_{i,e}}{\sqrt{2}}, i = 1, 2, ...N \qquad (7.1)$$

Suppose after the scheduling process, the ith tile T_i is composed of K chunks whose indexes are $\Omega(i) = [i_1, i_2, ..., i_K]$. The corresponding power scaling factor of T_i is denoted by $G_i = diag\{g_{i_1,R_{i_1}}, g_{i_2,R_{i_2}}, ..., g_{i_K,R_{i_K}}\}$, where R_{i_k} denotes the total number of times that the i_k^{th} chunk has been transmitted. The whitening matrix, denoted by W_i, is a $K \times K$ unitary Hadamard matrix. Since these K chunks are transmitted in the same packet, we could simply assume that they have the identical channel gain. Let h_i denote the complex channel parameter that tile T_i experiences. Given the above notations, when there are $\Gamma_0 \leq \Gamma$ tiles transmitted, we can write the received signals Y in the following matrix form:

$$Y = HMGQX + V \triangleq AX + V \qquad (7.2)$$

where $X = [S_{c,1}, S_{c,2}..., S_{c,N}]^T$ denotes the source signal and V is the additive Gaussian channel noise with power σ_n^2. $M = blkdiag\{W_1, W_2, ..., W_{\Gamma_0}\}$ is a block diagonal matrix which performs tile-wise whitening, and $G = blkdiag\{G_1, G_2, ..., G_{\Gamma_0}\}$ is the diagonal power scaling matrix. $H = blkdiag\{H_1, H_2, ..., H_{\Gamma_0}\}$ denotes the channel parameters, where $H_i = h_i I_{K \times K}$ and $I_{K \times K}$ is the identical matrix. Q is the scheduling matrix composed of zeros and ones. For example, if $K = 2, N = 8$ and the scheduling results are $\Omega(1) = [1, 2], \Omega(2) = [1, 3], \Omega(3) = [2, 4]$, then

$$Q = \begin{bmatrix} 1 & 0 & 0 & 0 & 0 & 0 & 0 & 0 \\ 0 & 1 & 0 & 0 & 0 & 0 & 0 & 0 \\ 1 & 0 & 0 & 0 & 0 & 0 & 0 & 0 \\ 0 & 0 & 1 & 0 & 0 & 0 & 0 & 0 \\ 0 & 1 & 0 & 0 & 0 & 0 & 0 & 0 \\ 0 & 0 & 0 & 1 & 0 & 0 & 0 & 0 \end{bmatrix},$$

and $G = diag\{g_{1,1}, g_{2,1}, g_{1,2}, g_{3,1}, g_{2,2}, g_{4,1}\}$.

The MMSE decoder C reconstructs the source with minimum mean square error:

$$\hat{X} = CY = \Lambda A^H (A\Lambda A^H + \sigma_n^2 I)^{-1} Y, \tag{7.3}$$

where $\Lambda = diag\{\lambda_1, \lambda_2, ..., \lambda_N\}$ and $(\cdot)^H$ denotes Hermitian transpose.

In our progressive transmission framework, the scheduling algorithm picks K chunks at a time to form a tile (packet). For any integer i in $\{1, 2, ..., \Gamma\}$, in the ith round, the scheduling task is to find $\Omega(i)$ and G_i to minimize the expected MSE after T_i is received, given the entire sender-side information and available receiver-side information of the previous $i - 1$ tiles. Mathematically, the scheduling objective in the ith round can be expressed as:

$$\min_{G,Q} E\{(\hat{X}_i - X)^T (\hat{X}_i - X)\}$$

$$s.t. \sum_{k=1}^{K} g_{i_k, R_{i_k}}^2 \lambda_{i_k} \times L \leq K \times E_s \times L, \tag{7.4}$$

where $\hat{X}_i$ is the reconstruction of X after tile T_i is received. Notation $E\{\cdot\}$ denotes the expectation. The constraint in (7.4) means that each tile (packet) is energy constrained, and E_s is the average symbol energy.

7.3 The Proposed Solution

In the proposed progressive framework, chunk scheduling and power allocation are two coupled problems. In this section, we first derive the optimal power allocation within a tile when the chunks have been determined, and then present the scheduling algorithm which decides what chunks should be included in a tile. In addition, when only partial receiver-side information is known, we discuss the necessary approximations in implementing our algorithm.

7.3.1 Power Allocation

Each PHY packet contains one and only one tile, so all tiles have the same power budget. For each of the K chunks scheduled to tile T_i, the power scaling factors

$g_{i_k,R_{i_k}}$ should be determined in order to minimize the expected total distortion of all the N chunks at the receiver. Note that some of the chunks in tile T_i may have been transmitted in previous packets. Therefore, the quality of previous transmissions, if available, should be taken into account.

First of all, we derive the distortion of transmitting source $S_{c,i}$ with variance $\lambda_i R_i$ times when the additive channel noise power is σ_n^2. Suppose the channel parameter it experiences is $\bar{H}_i = diag\{h_{i,1}, h_{i,2}, ..., h_{i,R_i}\}$; the received signals are R_i noisy versions of $S_{c,i}$:

$$Y_i = \bar{H}_i \bar{G}_i S_{c,i} + V_i, \tag{7.5}$$

where $V_i = [v_{i,1}, v_{i,2}, ..., v_{i,R_i}]^T$ denotes the additive noise and $\bar{G}_i = [g_{i,1}, g_{i,2}, ..., g_{i,R_i}]^T$ denotes the power scaling factors. To leverage the channel diversity and improve the channel quality, maximum ratio combining (MRC) is applied before decoding the source, thus,

$$\tilde{S}_{c,i} = \frac{(\bar{H}_i\bar{G}_i)^H}{\|\bar{H}_i\bar{G}_i\|^2} Y_i = S_{i_k} + \tilde{V}_i, \tag{7.6}$$

where $\tilde{V}_i = \frac{(\bar{H}_i\bar{G}_i)^H}{\|\bar{H}_i\bar{G}_i\|^2} V$ and its variance equals $\sigma_n^2/\|\bar{H}_i\bar{G}_i\|^2$. $(\cdot)^H$ denotes the Hermitian transpose. MMSE estimation is used to detect the transmitted signal, as has been derived in [25], the distortion (or MSE) of transmitting $S_{c,i}$ R_i times becomes:

$$\zeta(S_{c,i}, R_i) = \frac{\lambda_i \sigma_n^2}{\sum_{l=1}^{R_i} \|h_{i,l}\|^2 g_{i,l}^2 \lambda_i + \sigma_n^2}. \tag{7.7}$$

Now we consider the case of transmitting a tile T_i which consists of chunks $S_{c,i_1}, S_{c,i_2}, ..., S_{c,i_K}$. Assume that chunk S_{c,i_k} has already been transmitted R_{i_k} times in the previous transmission opportunities, and its previous transmission state information ($PTSI$), i.e., $g_{i_k,1}, g_{i_k,2}, ..., g_{i_k,R_{i_k}}$ and $h_{i_k,1}, h_{i_k,2}, ..., h_{i_k,R_{i_k}}$ are available, according to (7.7), the distortion of tile T_i can then be derived as:

$$\begin{aligned}
\zeta(T_i) &= \sum_{k=1}^{K} \zeta(S_{c,i_k}, R_{i_k}+1) \\
&= \sum_{k=1}^{K} \frac{\lambda_{i_k} \sigma_n^2}{\left(\sum_{l=1}^{R_{i_k}} \|h_{i_k,l}\|^2 g_{i_k,l}^2 \lambda_{i_k}\right) + \sigma_n^2 + \|h\|^2 g_{i_k}^2 \lambda_{i_k}},
\end{aligned} \tag{7.8}$$

where h is the channel gain that the transmitted tile is to experience and g_{i_k} is the power scaling factor of chunk S_{c,i_k} which is to be optimized.

Note that our goal is to minimize the total distortion of all the N chunks such that at the transmission of tile T_i, the receiver can gain optimal performance. When the $PTSI$ is given and the K chunks are fixed for composing tile T_i, to minimize the distortion of the K chunks is equivalent to minimizing the total distortion. Therefore, to solve the optimal power allocation problem when K chunks and their $PTSI$ are given, the objective can be formulated as follows:

$$\min_{g_{i_k}} \sum_{k=1}^{K} \frac{\lambda_{i_k} \sigma_n^2}{\left(\sum_{l=1}^{R_{i_k}} \|h_{i_k,l}\|^2 g_{i_k,l}^2 \lambda_{i_k}\right) + \sigma_n^2 + \|h\|^2 g_{i_k}^2 \lambda_{i_k}} \qquad (7.9)$$

$$s.t. \sum_{k=1}^{K} g_{i_k}^2 \lambda_{i_k} \leq K * E_s.$$

The solution of this optimization problem can be obtained by the method of Lagrange multiplier and the water-filling algorithm. The closed-form expression can be derived as:

$$\begin{cases} g_{i_k} = \left(\sqrt{\frac{\sigma_n}{\sqrt{v\|h\|^2 \lambda_{i_k}}} - \frac{A_{i_k}}{\|h\|^2 \lambda_{i_k}}}\right)^+ \\ s.t. \sum_{k=1}^{K} g_{i_k}^2 \lambda_{i_k} \leq K * E_s, \end{cases} \qquad (7.10)$$

where v is some constant and is chosen to meet the total energy constraint as shown in (7.10), A_{i_k} equals $\sum_{l=1}^{R_{i_k}} \|h_{i_k,l}\|^2 g_{i_k,l}^2 \lambda_{i_k} + \sigma_n^2$, and the operator $(a)^+$ is defined as $\max\{0, a\}$.

In this subsection, in order to derive the power allocation strategy, we have assumed the availability of channel state information (CSI), including the channel gain $\|h\|^2$ and the noise power σ_n^2, of each previous packet. Both parameters can be estimated at the receiving station and be feedback to the sending station through the reverse channel. In practice, both parameters can be attached to the end of the acknowledgment (ACK) frame which is sent from the receiving station to the sending station after each data frame is received. For example, if each channel parameter is represented by 16 bits, the overhead on the reverse channel is around 15Kbps, which is quite small. This overhead can be further reduced if the CSI is reported once every few packets or the background noise power is approximated by the noise of the reverse channel.

7.3.2 Scheduling

In the proposed progressive transmission framework, the transform coefficients of a GOP are divided into equal-sized chunks which are put into a chunk pool. The scheduling task is to pick K chunks from the pool to form a tile (packet) for the next transmission opportunity. We consider a highly dynamic environment where the sender does not know how many more packets can be transmitted for the current GOP. Therefore, the scheduling algorithm adopts a greedy approach. Specifically, it tries to minimize the receiver-side distortion after the scheduled packet is received. In other words, the scheduling problem can be defined so as to determine what K chunks should be included in the current tile such that the largest distortion reduction can be achieved given the past and current channel conditions.

A straightforward way to solve the scheduling problem is to exhaustively search all the possible combinations of K chunks and compare their expected distortions

---

Algorithm 6 The proposed scheduling algorithm for progressive transmission

---

Input: $\Lambda = \{\lambda_i\}, i = 1,2,\cdots,N; E_s, \sigma_n^2; K$
Output: Tile compositions: $\Omega(1), \Omega(2), \cdots, \Omega(\Gamma)$;
$\qquad$ Power allocations: $\mathscr{G}_R$
Initialization: $U = 0; R = [0,0,...,0]$;
$\mathscr{G}_R = \Phi$
$\mathscr{U} = \Phi$ $\qquad\qquad\qquad\qquad\qquad\qquad\qquad$ ▷ the set of non-selected chunk IDs
for $i = 1$ to Γ **do**
$\qquad \Omega(i) = [U+1, U+2, ..., U+K]$ $\qquad\qquad\qquad$ ▷ initiate the K chunk ids
$\qquad \mathscr{U} = \{1,2,...,U\}$ $\qquad\qquad\qquad\qquad\qquad\qquad$ ▷ if $U = 0, \mathscr{U} = \Phi$
$\qquad R_{tmp} = R; R_{tmp}[\Omega(i)] = R_{tmp}[\Omega(i)] + 1$;
$\qquad \mathscr{G}_{R_{tmp}} = \mathscr{G}_R$;
$\qquad$ Calculate $g_{\Omega(i)}$ according to (7.10) and update $\mathscr{G}_{R_{tmp}}$
$\qquad D_{min} = \varepsilon_t(\mathscr{G}_{R_{tmp}}, R_{tmp}); \mathscr{G}_0 = \mathscr{G}_{R_{tmp}}; R_0 = R_{tmp}$
$\qquad$ **if** $\mathscr{U} \neq \Phi$ **then**
$\qquad\qquad$ **for** $v = U+K; v > U; v--$ **do**
$\qquad\qquad\qquad$ **for** each u in $\mathscr{U}$ **do**
$\qquad\qquad\qquad\qquad \widetilde{\Omega(i)} = \Omega(i)$
$\qquad\qquad\qquad\qquad$ Replace v in $\widetilde{\Omega(i)}$ by u
$\qquad\qquad\qquad\qquad R_{tmp} = R; R_{tmp}[\widetilde{\Omega(i)}] = R_{tmp}[\widetilde{\Omega(i)}] + 1$;
$\qquad\qquad\qquad\qquad \mathscr{G}_{R_{tmp}} = \mathscr{G}_R$;
$\qquad\qquad\qquad\qquad$ Calculate $g_{\widetilde{\Omega(i)}}$ according to (7.10) and update $\mathscr{G}_{R_{tmp}}$
$\qquad\qquad\qquad\qquad D_t = \varepsilon_t(\mathscr{G}_{R_{tmp}}, R_{tmp})$
$\qquad\qquad\qquad\qquad$ **if** $D_t < D_{min}$ **then**
$\qquad\qquad\qquad\qquad\qquad D_{min} = D_t; \Omega(i) = \widetilde{\Omega(i)}$
$\qquad\qquad\qquad\qquad\qquad \mathscr{G}_0 = \mathscr{G}_{R_{tmp}}; R_0 = R_{tmp}$
$\qquad\qquad\qquad\qquad$ **end if**
$\qquad\qquad\qquad$ **end for**
$\qquad\qquad\qquad \mathscr{U} = \{1,2,...,U,U+1,...,U+K\} - \{u_0|u_0 \text{ is in } \Omega(i)\}$
$\qquad\qquad$ **end for**
$\qquad$ **end if**
$\qquad \mathscr{G}_R = \mathscr{G}_0; R = R_0$;
$\qquad U = \max[\Omega(1),\Omega(2),...,\Omega(i)]$
end for

---

under the corresponding optimal power allocation. However, the total number of possible combinations is C_N^K. It is inefficient to perform power allocation for each of the combinations, so the challenge is how to reduce the computational complexity of the scheduling algorithm without breaching its optimality. To address this challenge, we first present a proposition.

Proposition 1: Let $S^{(1)}, S^{(2)}, ..., S^{(M)}, K \leq M \leq N$ be the collection of chunks which have never been transmitted in the chunk pool and their variances satisfy $\lambda^{(1)} \geq \lambda^{(2)} \geq, ..., \lambda^{(M)}$. If K chunks are to be chosen from these M chunks to form a tile, the optimal selection that minimizes the overall distortion of all the N chunks is to choose $S^{(1)}, S^{(2)}, ..., S^{(K)}$.

The proof of Proposition 1 can be found in [68]. The Proposition indicates that we do not need to search all the N chunks to compose a tile. If chunks $S_1, ...S_U$ have been transmitted at least once in the previous transmission opportunities, we only need to consider chunks $S_1, S_2, ..., S_{U+K}$ in the current transmission opportunity and pick K chunks from them.

The fast algorithm is described as follows. First, we initiate the current tile with the K chunks $S_{U+1}, S_{U+2}, ..., S_{U+K}$, which have not been transmitted before. Then, we look among $S_1, S_2, ..., S_U$ for a chunk to replace S_{U+K}, if the replacement could further reduce the total distortion. If such a chunk cannot be found, the process stops. Otherwise, look for a chunk among $S_1, S_2, ..., S_U$ to replace S_{U+K-1}. Continue this process until a replacement cannot be found or all the chunks in the initial set have been replaced. In the worst case, this fast algorithm needs to evaluate UK combinations to schedule a tile. The computational complexity is greatly reduced.

Algorithm 6 presents the proposed fast scheduling algorithm. Based on the variances λ_i of the chunks, the target noise power σ_n^2, and the average transmission power E_s, the algorithm determines the tile composition for transmission opportunity i, denoted as $\Omega(i), i = 1, 2, ..., \Gamma$, and the power allocation factors. Here, $\Omega(i) = [i_1, i_2, ..., i_K]$ is the array of chunk identifiers for tile T_i. The total distortion of N chunks, denoted by $\varepsilon_t(\mathscr{G}_R, R)$ is calculated by the following equation:

$$\varepsilon_t(\mathscr{G}_R, R) = \sum_{i=1}^{N} \frac{\lambda_i \sigma_n^2}{\left(\sum_{l=1}^{R_i} \|h_{i,l}\|^2 g_{i,l}^2 \lambda_i\right) + \sigma_n^2}, \tag{7.11}$$

where $\mathscr{G}_R$ is the set that contains all the $g_{i,l}, i = 1, 2, ..., N; \ l = 1, 2, ..., R_i$, and $\mathbf{R} = [R_1, R_2, ..., R_N]$ records the transmission times of each chunk. $h_{i,l}$ is the channel parameter the ith chunk experiences in its lth transmission.

7.3.3 Approximation

The general progressive solution described in the previous subsection is derived under the assumption that the *PTSI*, including the power scaling factors and the channel parameters are all available. While the power scaling factors are determined by the sender, the channel parameters need to be measured at the receiver and the feedback usually has delay. This should not create a big problem in an AWGN channel or a slow fading channel, because $\|h\|^2$ and all $\|h_{i_k,l}\|^2$ can be treated as constants in (7.9) and (7.10). However, in a fast fading channel, $\|h\|^2$ is almost impossible to estimate, while $\|h_{i_k,l}\|^2$ can be obtained from channel feedback of the measured channel state information.

In order to allocate the power under unknown variables, the objective function of the optimal power allocation problem is changed from $\zeta(T_i)$ to the expectation of $\zeta(T_i)$, denoted by $E\{\zeta(T_i)\}$:

$$\min_{g_{i_k}} \ E\{\zeta(T_i)\}$$
$$s.t. \ \sum_{k=1}^{K} g_{i_k}^2 \lambda_{i_k} \leq K * E_s \tag{7.12}$$

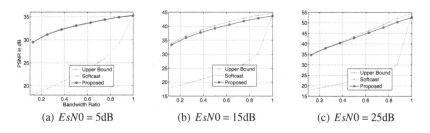

(a) $EsN0 = 5dB$ (b) $EsN0 = 15dB$ (c) $EsN0 = 25dB$

Fig. 7.4 The average reconstructed video PSNR of different schemes under different channel SNR and bandwidth settings.

In the expression of $\zeta(T_i)$ as given in (7.8), $\|h\|^2$ is the unknown variable. To explicitly show this, we write $\zeta(T_i)$ as $\zeta(T_i)(\|h\|^2)$. It is extremely difficult to obtain a closed-form expression of $E\{\zeta(T_i)\}$, so we propose to make the following approximation:

$$E\{\zeta(T_i)(\|h\|^2)\} \approx \zeta(T_i)(E\{\|h\|^2\}).\tag{7.13}$$

To demonstrate that (7.13) is a reasonable and close approximation, we carry out some experiments for the most challenging fast Rayleigh fading channel by simulation in MATLAB® 2014a. We consider the case where h differs for each packet. The only information we have is the statistical distribution of the fading parameter $h \sim \mathscr{CN}(0,1)$. Now that $\|h\|^2$ is a random variable following the Chi-squared distribution, and the probability density function (PDF) of $t = \|h\|^2$ is:

$$f(t) = \frac{e^{-t/2}}{2}, t \geq 0.\tag{7.14}$$

From (7.9), the distortion of tile T_i can be written as:

$$\zeta(T_i) = \sum_{k=1}^{K} \frac{1}{a_{i_k} + b_{i_k}t},\tag{7.15}$$

where $a_{i_k} = \sum_{l=1}^{R_{i_k}} \frac{\|h_{i_k,l}\|^2 g_{i_k,l}^2}{\sigma_n^2} + \frac{1}{\lambda_{i_k}}$ and $b_{i_k} = \frac{g_{i_k}^2}{\sigma_n^2}$. Next, we define

$$\Psi(a,b) = \int_0^{+\infty} \frac{1}{a+bt} f(t)dt,\tag{7.16}$$

$$\widehat{\Psi}(a,b) = \frac{1}{a+b\int_0^{+\infty} tf(t)dt} = \frac{1}{a+2b}, a,b > 0,$$

$$\Delta(a,b) = \Psi - \widehat{\Psi}.$$

If $\Delta(a,b)$ is small, we may conclude that (7.13) provides a close approximation.

When a and b are larger, the value of $\Psi(a,b)$ gets very small. It is obvious that $\Delta(a,b)$ is quite small in both absolute value and relative value to $\Psi(a,b)$. Therefore, if we replace $\|h\|^2$ by its mean value which is 2 in (7.8), it results in a close approximation of $E\{\zeta(T_i)\}$. Therefore, we can obtain the power scaling factors by substituting $\|h\|^2$ by 2 in (7.10). In the next section, we will show that the optimization results obtained with this approximation are very satisfactory. Until now, we have assumed the accessibility to the channel feedback of *PTSI* to obtain $\|h_{i_k,l}\|^2$. It is possible that the channel feedback delays for some time and part of $\|h_{i_k,l}\|^2$ is left unknown. We tackle this issue by replacing the unknown parameters by their mean values 2. In the next section, we will also evaluate the impact of feedback delay or even no feedback.

7.4 Evaluation

7.4.1 Settings

We implement the proposed scheme with AWGN channel model and fast fading channel mode, respectively, in MATLAB 2014a. In our implementation, the tile size K is set to 8 and the DCT coefficients of each frame are divided into 256 chunks. In the physical layer (PHY) of the OFDM system, the spectrum band is divided into 64 subcarriers and 48 of them are used to transmit complex analog symbols. After tile scheduling, power allocation and whitening within the tile, we pack all analog coefficients of each tile into one PLCP frame (packet), and then transmit one packet in one transmission opportunity. Besides, we perform trace-driven testbed experiments based on the software-defined radio platform SORA [38] to evaluate the progressive transmission scheme.

Test video source: In order to perform a comprehensive evaluation over videos of various contents, we use nine monochrome standard test videos as the source. The resolution of these video sequences is 720p (1280×720) and their frame rate is 30fps. These test videos are *stockholm, parkrun, city, spincalendar, sheriff, shuttlestart, in-to-tree, shields and jets* and they are available at Xiph test media [78]. For 720p video at frame rate of 30fps, there are $1280 \times 720 \times 30$ real valued coefficients per second to be transmitted, in transmission systems, every (I,Q) complex symbol can transmit 2 coefficients, therefore the full source bandwidth is 13.824MHz. In our evaluation, we describe bandwidth consumption as *bandwidth ratio*, which is defined as the actual channel bandwidth over full source bandwidth.

Reference schemes: In our simulation and trace-driven emulation, we choose SoftCast [19] as one of the reference schemes. However, SoftCast is originally designed for AWGN wireless channel. To compare the performance in fast fading channel, we choose Cui's solution presented in the previous chapter [67] as a reference scheme because it is an uncoded transmission scheme tailored for fast fading channels. As for digital solutions, considering that standard H.264 and HEVC-based solutions cannot offer scalability over neither channel bandwidth nor channel noise level, we use a state-of-the-art digital solution based on the scalable video coding (SVC) extension of H.264 [5]. Given that both SoftCast and Cui's solution require bandwidth ratio for their power and bandwidth allocation, we implement these reference schemes by assuming a known bandwidth ratio. For the SVC digital solution, the publicly available JSVM SVC reference software version 9.19.14 [47] is used.

7.4.2 Results in Simulated Environment

7.4.2.1 AWGN channel

We first evaluate our progressive solution against SoftCast in the AWGN channel. The signal-noise-ratio (SNR) is assumed to be known. We vary the bandwidth ratio, which is defined as the ratio of channel bandwidth to source bandwidth, from 0.125 to 1, but this information is not known to the sender in both SoftCast and our solution. SoftCast simply drops packets when the bandwidth ratio is smaller than 1. We also implement an omniscient scheme based on SoftCast, which knows the exact bandwidth ratio before the transmission so that the optimal power allocation and packetization can be achieved. This omniscient scheme provides the performance upper bound for uncoded video transmission. In this experiment, the GOP size is set to 8.

Fig. 7.4 shows the average received video PSNR on the nine test video sequences when the channel SNR equals to $5dB$, $15dB$ and $25dB$, respectively. It is clear that SoftCast performs very poorly when the bandwidth is unknown to the sender. When the channel bandwidth is much lower than the source bandwidth, the PSNR drops dramatically. From this experiment, we may conclude that the bandwidth adaptation capability of SoftCast is very weak.

In contrast, our proposed solution achieves graceful quality degradation with the reduced bandwidth ratio, and the performance is very close to the upper bound. As shown in Fig. 7.4(a), when the channel SNR is $5dB$, the proposed scheme achieves almost identical performance as the upper bound. We can also find from Fig. 7.4(b)(c) that when the channel SNR is higher, say $15dB$ and $25dB$, the performance gap between the proposed solution and the upper bound is very small. The gap is more noticeable when the channel condition is good and the bandwidth ratio is high. This is because our progressive solution ensures the reception quality of important chunks by sacrificing the transmission opportunity of not-so-important chunks. Nevertheless, the gap to the upper bound is only $0.96dB$ when the bandwidth ratio is 1 and SNR is $15dB$.

7.4.2.2 Fast Rayleigh Fading Channel

Next we perform the evaluation in a fast Rayleigh fading channel. For every transmission opportunity (or packet), the fading parameter $\|h\|$ is independently and randomly generated. There are two reference schemes used for comparison.

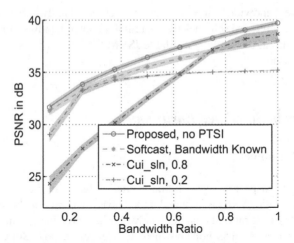

Fig. 7.5 Performance comparisons of difference schemes when channel SNR E_s/σ_n^2 equals $10dB$. The performance metrics are averaged over test video sequences; GOP size is set to 8.

One is omniscient SoftCast, to which the bandwidth ratio is known a priori, so that it can always perform optimal bandwidth and power allocation accordingly. The other is Cui's scheme [67], denoted as *Cui_sln*. The original design of Cui's scheme cannot adapt to bandwidth variations, so we implement two variations, assuming the bandwidth ratio to be 0.2 and 0.8 and the transmitter optimally allocates power and bandwidth accordingly. If the actual bandwidth ratio is lower than assumed, the sender randomly drops packet; if the actual bandwidth ratio is higher, the sender retransmits randomly selected packets to make full use of the network resource.

For fairness, we do not assume channel feedback in the implementation of our solution, because both *Cui_sln* and SoftCast do not use the channel state information (CSI) at the sender. We ran 100 tests using the test video sequences and averaged the PSNR metric over all the test runs. Fig. 7.5 shows the performance of all three schemes. The shadows denote the dynamic ranges from 10 to 90 percentile performance for every scheme. It can be observed that our scheme achieves the highest average PSNR among the three schemes and the PSNR variations are quite small. Interestingly, our progressive scheme outperforms the omniscient SoftCast at all bandwidth ratio settings, and the PSNR gain is up to 1.68dB. This is because, although the SoftCast sender knows the exact bandwidth information, the power allocation is optimized for AWGN channels. In a fast fading channel, if an important coefficient experiences deep fade, the overall performance will be greatly degraded.

Fig. 7.5 also shows that the bandwidth adaptation capability of Cui's solution is not as good as ours. When the target bandwidth ratio is 0.2, *Cui_sln* performs well when the bandwidth ratio is relatively low, but it tends to level-off when the actual bandwidth gets larger. When the target bandwidth is 0.8, *Cui_sln* performs well at the high end, but the performance drops dramatically at the low end. This experiment clearly shows that the proposed progressive solution (even

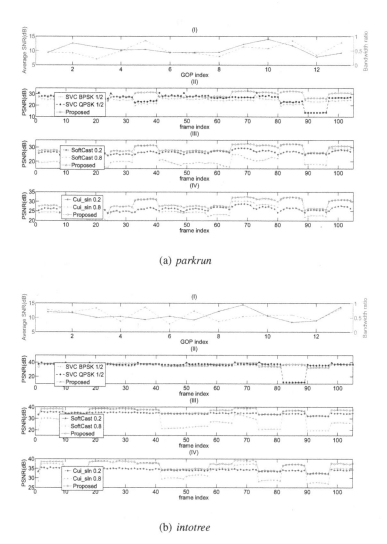

(a) *parkrun*

(b) *intotree*

Fig. 7.6 Performance comparisons in dynamic environments.

without channel feedback) outperforms state-of-the-art pseudo analog solutions in a bandwidth-varying fading channel.

7.4.3 Trace-Driven Emulation

We next evaluate the proposed scheme under real wireless environment. Evaluations are carried out using the channel fading and noise trace obtained from the software radio platform SORA [38] in a mobile setting. The bandwidth ratio is simulated by uniformly varying between 0.2 and 0.9. Fig. 7.6(a)(I) and Fig. 7.6(b)(I) shows the bandwidth ratio and average channel SNR for each GOP. Three reference schemes are evaluated along with the proposed scheme. In this experiment, the GOP size is set to 8. The PSNR of each frame is calculated to assess the channel SNR and bandwidth adaptation ability as well as the received video quality of different schemes. As examples, we show the results for sequences *parkrun* and *intotree* in Fig. 7.6.

We implement the digital transmission schemes with four-layer SVC [5] and two modulation and coding combinations. JSVM reference software [47] is used as source codec and the encoder is configured to enable inter-layer prediction and the intra period (GOP size) is set to 8 for fairness. Considering that SVC can provide finer scalability with the increment of number of layers at the cost of degradation of the coding efficiency, we implement a four-layer SVC scheme. Each source layer is encoded using up to 20% of the full bandwidth, and all four layers would take up to 80% of the full bandwidth. With this scalable source encoder, coarse-grained bandwidth-adaptability can be achieved. Rate-1/2 convolutional code is adopted as the channel code. The source coding rate per layer when QPSK (BPSK) modulation is used is roughly 2.76Mbps (1.38Mbps).

From subfigure (II) in Fig. 7.6(a)/(b), we can find that scheme *SVC QPSK 1/2* performs better than *SVC BPSK 1/2* most of the time. This is obvious since using (QPSK 1/2) allows the sender to transmit the video stream at twice the bit rate of that using (BPSK 1/2). However, notice that in the 12th GOP in the *parkrun* sequence and the 11th GOP in the *intotree* sequence, the performance of *SVC QPSK 1/2* degrades dramatically as the instantaneous channel SNR drops around 8dB. This is the typical *cliff effect* we often encounter in digital transmissions. If we had used an even higher coding and modulation rate (e.g., (16QAM 3/4)), such effect would have happened more often. There is always a trade-off in digital video streaming between high quality (high bit rate) and smooth experience (no sudden quality drop). Besides, there is also a trade-off between coding efficiency and scalability, so the coding efficiency of SVC is not as high as the standard H.264. In comparison, the *proposed* scheme smoothly adapts to both SNR and bandwidth variations and consistently achieves relatively high performance.

However, we can see from Fig. 7.6(b) that, in the 6th, 7th, 10th and 12th GOP, the performance of the proposed scheme is slightly inferior to the SVC-based digital scheme. In the 6th GOP, the bandwidth ratio is only 0.27. Such a low bandwidth ratio does not favor uncoded transmission, because too many coefficients have to be discarded. The digital scheme, on the other hand, utilizes motion estimation and compensation for source de-correlation and achieves a high coding efficiency, so its performance under low bandwidth ratio does not degrade too much. In fact, there exist approaches to improve the energy compaction efficiency of uncoded transmission and in turn improve its performance under low bandwidth ratio. Examples include the motion-compensated temporal filtering (MCTF) [26, 36] and HDA coding [79, 35]. We will leave the adoption of these techniques to our future work.

In the 7th GOP, the average channel SNR is slightly higher than 8dB, which is the threshold SNR for (QPSK 1/2) to achieve error-free transmission. In the 10th and 12th GOP, the bandwidth is just enough to support 3 and 2 layers of the SVC stream. We can find that the digital scheme performs quite well when the (source and channel) coding and modulation scheme is matched to the channel condition. Therefore, in a stable wireless environment where both channel SNR and bandwidth provisioning can be precisely estimated, the digital solution is superior to the analog solution. However, if the channel changes dynamically and violently, analog solution has its unprecedented advantage over its digital counterpart.

We implement two variations for both uncoded schemes (SoftCast and Cui_sln), with the target bandwidth ratios of 0.2 and 0.8 and the GOP size of 8. In the previous subsections, simulations have shown that these two uncoded schemes have inherent SNR-adaptability, but cannot gracefully handle bandwidth variations. We can draw similar conclusions in the emulated environment, as shown in subfigures (III) and (IV) in Fig. 7.6(a)/(b). For both schemes, the implementation with bandwidth ratio of 0.8 performs better when the bandwidth is sufficient, but degrades dramatically otherwise. The proposed progressive solution consistently outperforms SoftCast and Cui's solution for various channel conditions.

7.5 Summary

In this chapter, we propose a progressive uncoded solution for bandwidth-adaptive and SNR-adaptive mobile video streaming. Through solving an optimization problem, we ensure that the receiver-side distortion is minimized after each packet is received. The solution to the optimal power allocation problem is derived and a low-complexity scheduling algorithm is presented. Evaluations in both simulated and real wireless environments show that the proposed scheme successfully achieves the design goal and outperforms state-of-the-art digital and uncoded schemes by a notable margin in a dramatically varying wireless environment.

Chapter 8
Superposed Transmission with NOMA

8.1 Introduction

Non-orthogonal multiple access (NOMA) has been considered as a promising technology to improve bandwidth efficiency in the 5G systems [80], [81], [82], by leveraging superposition coding (SC) and successive interference cancellation (SIC). Considering that video traffic will be dominant in growing mobile traffic [1], it is desirable to exploit NOMA for high-volume video services. For video unicast, it has shown that NOMA can provide improved visual satisfaction compared with orthogonal multiple access (OMA) [83]. Meanwhile, multicast is an effective way to enhance bandwidth efficiency for high-volume video services. With SC, NOMA has the potential to enable scalable data multicast [84], [85]. In the NOMA-based multicast schemes, data is encoded into base-layer (BL) signal and enhanced-layer (EL) signal, which are transmitted simultaneously through SC. With SIC, near users with strong channel gains can decode both BL and EL signals, while far users with weak channel gains may only decode BL signals.

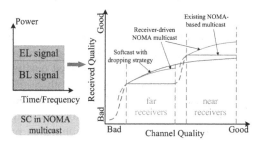

Fig. 8.1 Multicast performance to heterogeneous receivers in NOMA systems under insufficient bandwidth.

However, these NOMA-based multicast schemes cannot easily meet the satisfaction of all receivers with heterogeneous channel conditions. Since SIC implies that all other superposed signals have to be decoded in order before decoding the required signal, the complexity of SIC scales with the number of superposed signals and severe error propagation would occur in incorrect SIC decoding. Thus, existing NOMA-based multicast schemes generally cluster users to allow only two layer signals to be superposed; as Fig. 8.1 shows, the BL signal is pessimistically encoded at a bit rate decided by the decoding ability of the far user with worst channel quality [86]. It means other far users cannot receive better video quality proportional to their channel quality. Similar drawbacks would also occur when encoding the EL signal for near users.

In this chapter, we develop a receiver-driven scheme called Supcast (**Sup**erposed video multi**cast**) in NOMA systems, attempting to cater for all receivers with heterogeneous channel conditions as well as enhance performance in SoftCast in the case of insufficient bandwidth. In Supcast, BL and EL signals are distinguished across DCT chunks, which are generated by grouping nearby DCT coefficients. Specifically, DCT chunks are bisected into EL chunks and BL chunks, based on chunk characteristics. One EL chunk and one BL chunk compose the superposed signal in a physical packet. Since decoding performance of each chunk is proportional to channel quality, each receiver can obtain satisfied video quality. Owing to SC, more information can be conveyed compared with SoftCast when bandwidth is limited.

It should be emphasized that there exist two critical challenges in the design of Supcast. First, existing power allocation principles in SoftCast cannot be directly adopted for Supcast due to interference caused by SC. Second, existing NOMA optimization focuses on user scheduling to decide which users are to be superposed [87], [88], [89]. However, in Supcast, user scheduling has been handled by grouping users requesting the same video contents. In Supcast, DCT chunks are basic units for signal scheduling. With SIC, superposed chunks would be regarded as noise when decoding other chunks. In this case, decoding performance would be determined by assigned superposed chunks, whose allocated power reflects interference strength. Therefore, chunk scheduling, coupled with power allocation, will be the key to ensure the desired video reception quality proportional to channel quality. The solutions to these challenges constitute the main contributions of this research, which are summarized as follows.

- In Supcast, we combine the linear video processing of SoftCast and the SC operation of NOMA into one framework. By doing so, Supcast can implement receiver-driven video transmission, where received quality is scalable to the heterogeneous channel conditions. Compared with SoftCast developed for OMA systems, Supcast can achieve better bandwidth efficiency due to SC.
- In Supcast, we investigate the joint power allocation and chunk scheduling problem, and formulate it as a distortion minimization problem taking into account the characteristics of video contents in these chunks. This formulated problem is a mixed integer non-linear programming (MINLP) problem, which is an intractable NP-hard problem.
- To tackle the MINLP problem, we decompose it into two subproblems. For power allocation, a two-stage strategy is developed. For chunk scheduling, we reformulate it as a one-to-one two-sided matching game. EL chunks and BL

chunks are viewed as two disjoint player sets, which are matched with each other. A near-optimal and low-complexity matching algorithm is proposed. The stability, convergence, complexity and optimality of the proposed algorithm are analyzed thoroughly.

Extensive simulations have been carried out to validate the advantages of the proposed Supcast. The results demonstrate that Supcast outperforms SoftCast as well as the reference scheme in NOMA under different scenarios. Considering the complexity of the practical NOMA implementation, only two layers are used in Supcast, the same as that in existing NOMA-based multicast schemes. However, Supcast can be easily extended to one BL and multiple fine-grained ELs, by modeling the chunk scheduling as a one-to-many matching or multi-step two-sided one-to-one matching.

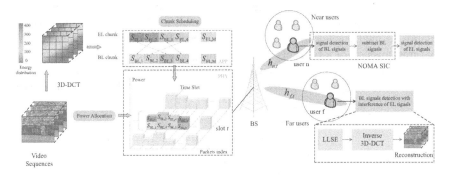

Fig. 8.2 Framework of the proposed Supcast over NOMA networks.

8.2 System Description

The framework of the proposed Supcast over NOMA system is introduced in this section, as shown in Fig. 8.2. Meanwhile, the video encoding process as well as the reconstruction process shall be elaborated, in which SoftCast and NOMA are integrated.

As illustrated in Fig. 8.2, a downlink scenario is considered, where video is transmitted from a base station (BS) to multiple users in a single cell. For practical system implementation, complexity should be carefully considered. For this reason, multicast users are divided into near users and far users according to their distances to the BS, similar to that in existing NOMA-based multicast schemes. Since Supcast can achieve graceful performance degradation, only one near user n and one far user f are considered in Supcast. Specifically, user n and user f are with the worst channel quality among near and far users, respectively, thus the optimized signals can be decoded by other users. Let $h_{n,t}$ and $h_{f,t}$ denote the channel gains from the BS to user n and user f, respectively, where t represents the index of time slot.

Particularly, $h_{n,t} = r_{n,t}/\sqrt{1+d_n^\eta}$ and $h_{f,t} = r_{f,t}/\sqrt{1+d_f^\eta}$, where d_n and d_f are the distance from the BS to user n and user f, respectively, η is the path-loss exponent, and $r_{n,t}, r_{f,t} \sim \mathscr{CN}(0,1)$ are the Rayleigh fading coefficient at the time slot t. In this chapter, we assume that the channel state information (CSI) is available at the BS, and the channel does not vary within a time slot.

In Supcast, video sequence is encoded into two types of signals, i.e., BL signals and EL signals with different transmission priorities. BL and EL signals can be simultaneously transmitted with SC for each physical packet in the downlink NOMA system. With the acquired CSI, the BS assigns different power levels to the superposed BL and EL signals, respectively, thus they can be distinguished in the power domain. According to the NOMA principle [80], [84], BL signals should be allocated more power. In this case, user f can only decode the BL signals, while regarding the EL signals as interference. For user n, the BL signals can be correctly decoded and subtracted by the deployed SIC algorithm before decoding the EL signals. Thus, it can decode both BL and EL signals to achieve better reconstruction quality. As the basic unit for video coding is a group of pictures (GOP), we assume that transmission of a GOP occupies one time slot. Therefore, the processing and transmission of video sequences are considered within the GOP interval. The details of how these BL and EL signals are generated and processed are presented in the following subsections.

8.2.1 SoftCast-based Video Encoding with SC

In Supcast, video sequences are first encoded based on the linear processing, similar to that in SoftCast. Specifically, a video sequence is divided into GOPs, and then 3D-DCT (three-dimensional DCT) is performed over each GOP. Next, these DCT coefficients are grouped into equal-sized rectangular-shaped chunks. Coefficients in each chunk are treated as random variables with zero-mean Gaussian distribution. As shown in Fig. 8.2, DCT can remove redundancy and thus make the energy distribution much more compact. As the energy of chunk reflects its importance, we partition each chunk into BL or EL according to its variance, which represents the mean energy of its contained coefficients. Particularly, these chunks are first sorted in descending order according to their variances, and then the sorted chunks are bisected into two sets. M chunks, denoted by $S_B = \{S_{BL,1}, \cdots, S_{BL,M}\}$, form the BL signal with larger variances $[\lambda_{BL,1}, \lambda_{BL,2}, \cdots, \lambda_{BL,M}]$. The other M chunks, denoted by $S_E = \{S_{EL,1}, \cdots, S_{EL,M}\}$, form the EL signal with smaller variances $[\lambda_{EL,1}, \lambda_{EL,2}, \cdots, \lambda_{EL,M}]$.

Without loss of generality, one BL chunk and one EL chunk are grouped into one physical packet via the SC operation. Besides, the bandwidth of a time slot is assumed to be enough for the transmission of a GOP. If the bandwidth is insufficient, Supcast would take the dropping strategy, similar to that in SoftCast. Specifically, first the least important chunks would be dropped to achieve bandwidth compaction, and then the remaining chunks are bisected into M' BL chunks and M' EL chunks, where $M' < M$. Before transmission, the BS selects one BL chunk and one EL chunk, e.g., $S_{BL,i}$ and $S_{EL,j}$, for superposition to form a NOMA packet, where $\forall i, j = \{1\cdots M\}$. This process is called chunk scheduling, and is implemented by the BS according to the available CSI.

Note that each modulated symbol in physical layer contains the I (in-phase) component and Q (quadrature) component. We use $S_{BL,i}^c$ and $S_{EL,j}^c$ to denote the complex source of $S_{BL,i}$ and $S_{EL,j}$, respectively

$$S_{BL,i}^c = \frac{S_{BL,i}^o + i_z \cdot S_{BL,i}^e}{\sqrt{2}}, \; S_{EL,j}^c = \frac{S_{EL,j}^o + i_z \cdot S_{EL,j}^e}{\sqrt{2}}, \tag{8.1}$$

where $S_{BL,i}^o$, $S_{EL,j}^o$ are the odd-index part of $S_{BL,i}$, $S_{EL,j}$, and $S_{BL,i}^e$, $S_{EL,j}^e$ are the even-index part of $S_{BL,i}$, $S_{EL,j}$, respectively. i_z is the imaginary unit.

Before transmission, coefficients in each BL chunk or EL chunk are scaled by the same scaling factor, denoted by $g_{BL,i}$ or $g_{EL,j}$, $\forall i, j = \{1\cdots M\}$. In Supcast, according to the principle of NOMA [80], [84], BL chunks should be allocated more power than EL chunks, thus to guarantee decoding performance of user f with the interference of EL signal. Fortunately, such a power allocation principle is coincident with the principle of optimal power allocation in SoftCast, which suggests chunks with larger variances should be allocated more power. However, in Supcast, the interference between BL and EL chunks and coupled relationship with chunk scheduling, make it unrealistic to directly adopt the power allocation results of SoftCast.

8.2.2 Video Reconstruction with SIC and LLSE

As mentioned above, the processing of video sequences and optimization are carried out within each GOP duration, corresponding to each time slot in the practical system. Thus, the index of time slot t is omitted for brevity in this chapter. For a pair of coefficients $S_{BL,i}$ and $S_{EL,j}$ in the transmitted packet, the received signals at user n and user f can be expressed as

$$\begin{aligned} Y_{n,i,j} &= h_n(g_{BL,i}S_{BL,i}^c + g_{EL,j}S_{EL,j}^c) + W_n, \\ Y_{f,i,j} &= h_f(g_{BL,i}S_{BL,i}^c + g_{EL,j}S_{EL,j}^c) + W_f, \end{aligned} \tag{8.2}$$

where $W_n, W_f \sim \mathscr{CN}(0, \sigma_w^2)$ are additive white Gaussian noise (AWGN) for user n and f, respectively, and σ_w^2 is the noise variance.

At the receiver side, user n first adopts SIC to decode the superposed signals. With perfect SIC, user n can eliminate the interference of BL signals [82], [84], [88], which are allocated more power. Specifically, user n first correctly decodes the BL signals with perfect SIC, then it subtracts this signal from the received signals and decodes the EL signals without interference. After that, linear least square estimator (LLSE) is used for the signal decoding. Then inverse 3D-DCT is performed on the

decoded BL and EL chunks to obtain an improved video reconstruction. In the case
with perfect SIC, distortion of user n comes from decoding errors of the LLSE of
EL chunks. As derived in [19], such distortion in terms of mean square error (MSE)
can be expressed as

$$d_{n,j} = \frac{\lambda_{EL,j}\sigma_w^2}{|h_n|^2 g_{EL,j}^2 \lambda_{EL,j} + \sigma_w^2}. \tag{8.3}$$

For user f, according to NOMA, it directly decodes BL chunks by regarding EL
chunks as interference. Therefore, its decoding distortion is

$$d_{f,i,j} = \frac{\lambda_{BL,i}(|h_f|^2 g_{EL,j}^2 \lambda_{EL,j} + \sigma_w^2)}{|h_f|^2 g_{BL,i}^2 \lambda_{BL,i} + |h_f|^2 g_{EL,j}^2 \lambda_{EL,j} + \sigma_w^2}. \tag{8.4}$$

Thus, overall distortion of transmitting $S_{BL,i}$ and $S_{EL,j}$ is

$$D_{i,j} = d_{n,j} + d_{f,i,j} + \sum_{j=1}^{M} \lambda_{EL,j}, \tag{8.5}$$

where $\sum_{j=1}^{M} \lambda_{EL,j}$ is the MSE distortion caused by user f completely failing to
decode EL chunks. Since this part of distortion is constant, it need not be considered
in the following optimization.

8.3 Problem Formulation and Analysis

In this section, a joint power allocation and chunk scheduling problem is first
formulated to minimize the overall system distortion, which is NP-hard. To develop
low-complexity and near-optimal solution, we decompose it into two subproblems.
For power allocation, a two-stage strategy is proposed with consideration of chunk
diversity and interference. For chunk scheduling, we reformulate it by utilizing the
one-to-one two-sided matching theory.

8.3.1 Problem Statement and Formulation

The objective of the joint power allocation and chunk scheduling problem is to
minimize overall transmission distortion, which is measured by the MSE. Define
the binary variable $\mu_{i,j}$ as the indicator for chunk scheduling

$$\mu_{i,j} = \begin{cases} 1, & S_{BL,i} \text{ is paired with } S_{EL,j}, \\ 0, & \text{otherwise.} \end{cases} \tag{8.6}$$

Variable $\mu_{i,j} = 1$ indicates that $S_{BL,i}$ and $S_{EL,j}$ are simultaneously transmitted via SC, while the distortion can be calculated via Eq. (8.5). Then the distortion minimization problem can be formulated as

$$\min_{\mu, \text{g}_{BL}, \text{g}_{EL}} \sum_{i=1}^{M} \sum_{j=1}^{M} \mu_{i,j} D_{i,j} \tag{8.7a}$$

$$\text{s.t.} \quad \sum_{i=1}^{M} \sum_{j=1}^{M} \mu_{i,j}(g_{BL,i}^2 \lambda_{BL,i} + g_{EL,j}^2 \lambda_{EL,j}) \leq P^t, \tag{8.7b}$$

$$g_{EL,j}^2 \lambda_{EL,j} \leq g_{BL,i}^2 \lambda_{BL,i}, \text{ if } \mu_{i,j} = 1, \tag{8.7c}$$

$$\sum_{i=1}^{M} \mu_{i,j} = 1, \sum_{j=1}^{M} \mu_{i,j} = 1, \ \forall i,j = \{1 \cdots M\}, \tag{8.7d}$$

$$\mu_{i,j} \in \{0,1\}, \ \forall i,j = \{1 \cdots M\}. \tag{8.7e}$$

Note that the optimization variable μ is the chunk scheduling matrix with entries $\mu_{i,j}$. The optimization variables g_{BL} and g_{EL} are the M-dimensional power scaling vectors for BL and EL chunks, respectively. Constraint (8.7b) ensures that the total transmitted power for a GOP does not exceed the budget P^t. Constraint (8.7c) guarantees the SIC decoding according to the NOMA power allocation principle. Constraint (8.7d) and (8.7e) indicate that each BL chunk can only be superposed with one EL chunk and vice versa.

It can be seen that problem (8.7) involves both continuous variables g_{BL}, g_{EL} and binary variable μ. Therefore, it is an NP-hard MINLP problem [90]. Finding global optimal solution is unrealistic for this type of problem. To tackle this coupled problem with low-complexity yet near-optimal solution, we divide it into two subproblems. One is the power allocation problem, which can be handled in two stages. The other is the chunk scheduling problem, which can be reformulated as a one-to-one two-sided matching problem.

8.3.2 Two-stage Power Allocation

Given the result of chunk scheduling, the two-tuple set of chunk superposition is given as T_c. Then problem (8.7) can be rewritten as

$$\min_{\text{g}_{BL}, \text{g}_{EL}} \sum_{\{i,j\} \in T_c} D_{i,j} \tag{8.8a}$$

$$\text{s.t.} \quad \sum_{\{i,j\} \in T_c} (g_{BL,i}^2 \lambda_{BL,i} + g_{EL,j}^2 \lambda_{EL,j}) \leq P^t, \tag{8.8b}$$

$$g_{EL,j}^2 \lambda_{EL,j} \leq g_{BL,i}^2 \lambda_{BL,i}, \ \forall \{i,j\} \in T_c. \tag{8.8c}$$

However, due to the existence of interference in the objective function in (8.8a), it is not trivial to convert such a nonlinear optimization problem into a convex optimization problem.

Actually, problem (8.8) belongs to the class of sum of generalized polynomial fractional functions (SGPFF) problem. As shown in [91], the global optimal solution of this problem can be obtained with the branch and bound algorithm. This algorithm works by solving an equivalent problem, which is further systematically converted into a series of linear programming (LP) problems. However, the number of converted LP problems depends on the dimension of optimization variables. In Supcast, the dimension of variables is $2M$, which is always large for DCT chunk division. Therefore, it is not practical to implement this algorithm to obtain the global optimal solution of problem (8.8). To handle this problem with high tractability, we propose a two-stage power allocation strategy to solve it.

At the first stage, we pre-allocate power across chunks according to their importance for reconstruction, without considering the channel gain diversity and interference. In this case, power shall be pre-allocated between BL-EL chunk pairs, which can be solved by the Lagrange multiplier method. Particularly, power allocated to BL and EL chunks at this stage can be derived as

$$
\begin{cases}
P_{BL,i} = \dfrac{\sqrt{\lambda_{BL,i}}}{\sum_{k \in M}(\sqrt{\lambda_{BL,k}} + \sqrt{\lambda_{EL,k}})} P^t, \\
P_{EL,j} = \dfrac{\sqrt{\lambda_{EL,j}}}{\sum_{k \in M}(\sqrt{\lambda_{BL,k}} + \sqrt{\lambda_{EL,k}})} P^t.
\end{cases}
\tag{8.9}
$$

The derivation process of such power distortion optimization can be traced from [19]. As Eq. (8.9) shows, power allocated to the BL (EL) chunk is proportional to its energy $\lambda_{BL,i}$ ($\lambda_{EL,j}$), which reflects the chunk importance.

At the second stage, with the power pre-allocation results obtained from Eq. (8.9), we re-allocate power within each superposed BL-EL chunk pair. If $\{i, j\} \in T_c$, the power re-allocation problem for a pair of $S_{BL,i}$ and $S_{EL,j}$ can be expressed as

$$
\min_{g_{BL,i}, g_{EL,j}} D_{i,j}
\tag{8.10a}
$$

$$
\text{s.t.} \quad g_{BL,i}^2 \lambda_{BL,i} + g_{EL,j}^2 \lambda_{EL,j} \leq P_{i,j}^t,
\tag{8.10b}
$$

$$
g_{EL,j}^2 \lambda_{EL,j} \leq g_{BL,i}^2 \lambda_{BL,i},
\tag{8.10c}
$$

where $P_{i,j}^t = P_{BL,i} + P_{EL,j}$. Since $g_{BL,i}$ and $g_{EL,i}$ are non-negative, it can be proven that problem (8.10) has unique solution. Substituting Eq. (8.3)-(8.5) and Eq. (8.9) into the objective (8.10a), we can derive the optimal solution as

$$
\begin{cases}
g_{EL,j}^* = \min([g_{EL,j}^v]^+, \ \dfrac{1}{2} \dfrac{\sqrt{\lambda_{BL,i}} + \sqrt{\lambda_{EL,j}}}{\sum_{k \in M}(\sqrt{\lambda_{BL,k}} + \sqrt{\lambda_{EL,k}})} P^t), \\
g_{BL,i}^* = (\dfrac{(\sqrt{\lambda_{BL,i}} + \sqrt{\lambda_{EL,j}}) P^t}{\sum_{k \in M}(\sqrt{\lambda_{BL,k}} + \sqrt{\lambda_{EL,k}})} - (g_{EL,j}^*)^2 \lambda_{EL,j})^{\frac{1}{2}} \dfrac{1}{\sqrt{\lambda_{BL,i}}},
\end{cases}
\tag{8.11}
$$

where $g_{EL,j}^v = (\frac{\sigma_w}{h_n h_f} \sqrt{\frac{h_f^2 P_{i,j}^t + \sigma_w^2}{\lambda_{BL,i} \lambda_{EL,j}}} - \frac{\sigma_w^2}{h_n^2 \lambda_{EL,j}})^{\frac{1}{2}}$, and $[x]^+$ means $\max(x, 0)$. The solution is generated by finding the stationary point. Due to space limits, the detailed derivation is omitted.

8.3.3 *Two-sided Matching Formulation for Chunk Scheduling*

Then with given power allocation, we formulate the chunk scheduling problem in (8.7) by utilizing the match theory. For convenience, we first give some definitions and notations.

8.3.3.1 Definition

To characterize the mutual relationship between BL and EL chunks, we model the chunk scheduling as a one-to-one two-sided matching process between the set of M BL chunks and the set of M EL chunks. At the BS, the chunks in these two disjoint sets are considered as selfish and rational players. Since perfect CSI is available at the BS, these players have complete information of each other when matching. We say $S_{BL,i}$ and $S_{EL,j}$ are matched together and form a *matching pair*, if $S_{BL,i}$ and $S_{EL,j}$ are superposed for transmission through a NOMA physical packet. In this case, we can formulate the chunk scheduling problem as a typical matching problem, presented as

Definition 1 (One-to-One Two-sided Matching): *Consider BL chunks and EL chunks as two disjoint sets, $S_B = \{S_{BL,1}, \cdots, S_{BL,M}\}$ and $S_E = \{S_{EL,1}, \cdots, S_{EL,M}\}$, respectively. A one-to-one, two-sided matching Φ is a mapping from the set of BL chunks S_B into the EL chunks set S_E, such that for every $S_{BL,i} \in S_B$ and $S_{EL,j} \in S_E$ satisfying*

1) $\Phi(S_{BL,i}) \in S_E$,
2) $\Phi(S_{EL,j}) \in S_B$,
3) $|\Phi(S_{BL,i})| = 1$, $|\Phi(S_{EL,j})| = 1$,
4) $S_{EL,j} = \Phi(S_{BL,i}) \Leftrightarrow S_{BL,i} = \Phi(S_{EL,j})$,

where $\Phi(S_{BL,i})$ represents $S_{BL,i}$'s partner in Φ and $\Phi(S_{EL,j})$ represents $S_{EL,j}$'s partner in Φ. Conditions 1), 2) and 3) state that each BL chunk is matched with one EL chunk, and vice versa. Such one-to-one setting is due to the complexity of SIC decoding in NOMA. Condition 4) implies $S_{BL,i}$ and $S_{EL,j}$ are matched with each other.

8.3.3.2 Preference Lists

According to [92], the competition and decision process among players have great influence on the result of such matching games. To better characterize these dynamic interactions, each player has its own *preferences* over the players in the other set. It has been studied that different settings of preferences would have various properties, which may lead to different designs of matching algorithms [93], [94]. In this chapter, the sum-distortion calculated in Eq. (8.5) is used to directly decide the order of preferences.

The BS can set the preference list for each player, which is ranked in a descending order by the value calculated in Eq. (8.5) paired with the player in the other set. For example, for any $S_{BL,i} \in S_B$ and $S_{EL,j}, S_{EL,k} \in S_E$

$$S_{EL,j} \succ_{S_{BL,i}} S_{EL,k} \Leftrightarrow D_{i,j} < D_{i,k} \qquad (8.12)$$

implies that $S_{BL,i}$ prefers $S_{EL,j}$ to $S_{EL,k}$ since the former can provide lower sum-distortion, i.e., higher utility.

With the above matching model and preference lists formulation, we propose an algorithm to solve the formulated matching problem in the next section.

8.4 Matching Algorithm for Chunk Scheduling

In this section, a near-optimal algorithm is proposed for chunk scheduling by utilizing the matching theory to reduce computational complexity. Furthermore, we also provide thorough analysis of the proposed algorithm.

8.4.1 Design and Description of Algorithm

Inspired by the matching theory [93], [94], [95], we propose the BL-EL chunk matching algorithm (BECMA) for chunk scheduling. Considering the competition behavior as mentioned in Sec. 8.3.3, the basic idea of BECMA is allowing the BL chunk to make a *proposal* to an EL chunk selected from its preference list, and the proposed EL chunk has the right to accept or reject the proposal.

Obviously, the conflict would occur when an EL chunk is so "popular" that it receives more than one proposal. Since this is a one-to-one matching, an intuitive question would arise that it should accept this proposal and reject others. To answer it, we first introduce the concept of *blocking pair* as follows.

Definition 2 (Blocking Pair): *A BL-EL chunk pair $(S_{BL,i}, S_{EL,j})$ is a blocking pair in Φ if it satisfies $S_{EL,j} \succ_{S_{BL,i}} \Phi(S_{BL,i})$ and $S_{BL,i} \succ_{S_{EL,j}} \Phi(S_{EL,j})$, where $\Phi(S_{BL,i})$ represents $S_{BL,i}$'s partner in Φ and $\Phi(S_{EL,j})$ represents $S_{EL,j}$'s partner in Φ.*

According to the above definition and Eq. (8.12), a blocking pair implies higher utility than the original matching pair. Thus, if a matched EL chunk receives another proposal, it will accept the proposing BL chunk only when they can form a blocking pair.

Now we can elaborate on the matching process in BECMA, as presented in Algorithm 1. Each BL chunk makes proposals to the EL chunk in the order of its preference list. The BL chunk would pause the process if an EL chunk temporarily accepts its proposal, but continue proposing if it is rejected. Meanwhile, for the proposed EL chunk, it will reject the BL chunk if they cannot form a blocking pair, otherwise it will accept the proposal for consideration. This process ends when no BL chunk needs to propose.

Algorithm 7 BL-EL Chunk Matching Algorithm (BECMA)

Input: Set of BL chunks S_B and set of EL chunks S_E.
Output: Stable matching Φ
1: Set up BL chunks' preference lists.
2: Set up EL chunks' preference lists.
3: Set up a set of unmatched BL chunks S_B^U to record BL chunks who have not been paired with any EL chunk.
4: **while** S_B^U is not empty **do**
5:    $S_{BL,i}$ proposes to its currently most preferred available EL chunk $S_{EL,j}$.
6:    **if** $S_{EL,j}$ already has a partner $S_{BL,k}$ and $(S_{BL,i}, S_{EL,j})$ is not a blocking pair **then**
7:       $S_{EL,j}$ rejects $S_{BL,i}$ and continues holding $S_{BL,k}$.
8:       $S_{BL,i}$ removes $S_{EL,j}$ from its preference lists.
9:    **else**
10:      $S_{EL,j}$ accepts $S_{BL,i}$ and rejects $S_{BL,k}$.
11:      $S_{BL,k}$ removes $S_{EL,j}$ from its preference lists.
12:      $S_{BL,i}$ is removed from S_B^U and $S_{BL,k}$ is added into S_B^U.
13:    **end if**
14: **end while**
15: Output the matching Φ.

8.4.2 Analysis of Algorithm

8.4.2.1 Complexity

For BECMA, the computational complexity comes from two aspects. One is the sorting operation to establish preference lists, which requires complexity of $O(2M^2)$. The other is the matching operation, where each BL chunk will propose at most M times. In the worst case, the complexity of matching is $O(M^2)$. Therefore, the complexity of BECMA is $O(3M^2)$.

For comparison, the computational complexity of two other matching schemes is analyzed as follows.

- Optimal Exhaustive Matching: It generates the optimal result by searching all possible $M!$ combinations, where ! denotes factorial operation. Thus, its complexity is $O(M!)$.
- Random Matching: BL chunks and EL chunks are randomly matched with each other. Therefore, its complexity is $O(M)$.

With the above analysis, it can be seen that the complexity of BECMA is much less than the optimal exhaustive scheme. However, according to the simulation comparison, as shown in Sec. 8.5.1, the performance degradation of BECMA is negligible comparing with the optimal scheme.

8.4.2.2 Stability and Convergence

To analyze the stability and convergence performance of BECMA, we first give the definition as below.

Definition 3 (Stable Matching): *A matching Φ is stable, if there exists no blocking pair $(S_{BL,i}, S_{EL,j})$ in Φ.*

With Definition 2 and 3, we now can prove the stability and convergence of BECMA.

Theorem 8.1. *The proposed BECMA converges to a stable matching Φ^* with limited iterations.*

Proof. First we prove the convergence. In each iteration in Algorithm 1 (Lines 5-13), each $S_{BL,i} \in S_B$ makes a proposal to its currently most preferred EL chunk, which has not rejected it in previous iterations. Since the total number of EL chunks is M, each BL chunk cannot make more than M proposals. In other words, the total number of iterations is less than M. Besides, the iteration would end until every BL chunk has been matched. Therefore, BECMA can converge to a final matching Φ^* after a limited number of iterations.

Next we prove that Φ^* is stable. With the detail in Algorithm 1, in the final matching Φ^*, for any chunk $S_{BL,i}$ in S_B, we cannot find a chunk $S_{EL,j}$ in S_E to form a blocking pair. Thus, according to Definition 3, Φ^* is a stable matching.

8.4.2.3 Optimality

Here, we give a Theorem to state whether an optimal matching can be achieved by Algorithm 1.

Theorem 8.2. *The stable matching Φ^* converged in BECMA is Pareto optimal for BL chunks.*

The proof can be completed similar to that in [95]. Since BL chunks are allowed to make proposals in Algorithm 1, we can refer it as a BL-driven matching algorithm. If we allow EL chunks to propose, we can similarly form an EL-driven matching algorithm, which generally produces different performance. According to [95], proposing players would be better off than proposed players, and achieve Pareto optimality. However, in the proposed BECMA, we can conclude the following remark.

Remark 8.1. The BL-chunk optimal BL-driven matching algorithm can have quite similar distortion performance, compared with the EL-chunk optimal EL-driven matching algorithm.

This property as described above is due to the fact that the formulated preference list in Sec. 8.3.3.2 is *mutual*, since the preferences of BL chunks and EL chunks are consistent in terms of sum-distortion. In Sec. 8.5.1, we will conduct a performance comparison between these two algorithms and validate our conclusion.

8.5 Performance Evaluation

Simulations are carried out to evaluate performance of the proposed Supcast under various scenarios. For a comprehensive evaluation, multiple standard video sequences [78] with different spatial-temporal content complexities are taken as test sequences, including *Bus, Coastguard, Crew, Foreman, Harbour, Husky* and *Ice*. In simulations, we extract the luminance component to generate monochrome video content for testing, and the chrominance component can be tested in the same way. These test sequences are with common intermediate format (CIF) resolution and frame rate of 30 fps (frames per second). In this case, the source bandwidth is $BW_s = 1.52$ MHz (in complex symbols). The GOP size is set as 4 and the default equal chunk division after 3D-DCT is set as 8×8 chunks. The performance metric we adopt in Supcast is peak signal-to-noise ratio (PSNR), which is an objective video quality assessment and can be expressed as

$$PSNR = 10\log_{10}(255^2/MSE), \tag{8.13}$$

where the distortion MSE is averaged over all pixels in a frame. Besides, the PSNR of each video sequence is the average PSNR of frames.

In simulations, a single-cell NOMA system is considered, with one BS located in the center, and ten heterogeneous multicast users equally partitioned into two distinct zones. Five near users are deployed within a ring between radius 100 meters and 500 meters, while another five far users are deployed within a ring between radius 500 meters and 900 meters. In each zone, all users are uniformly and randomly distributed. The average power budget for transmitting each chunk is set as $P = 1$ W. The path-loss exponent is set as $\eta = 2$. As discussed in Sec. 8.2.2, the AWGN of the fading channel for each user has the variance σ_w^2. Hence, the average channel signal-to-noise ratio (SNR) is defined as $10\log_{10}(P/\sigma_w^2)$. I-Q modulation is adopted in the physical layer, which means each channel use can convey one symbol as I component and one symbol as Q component. These two symbols compose a complex symbol. We define the bandwidth compression ratio as $\beta = BW_c/BW_s$, where BW_c is the channel bandwidth (in complex symbols), i.e., the number of available channel use. Unless otherwise specified, β is defaulted set as 0.5 in this chapter.

8.5.1 Performance Comparison

Two reference schemes are considered for performance comparison against the proposed Supcast. One is SoftCast developed in OMA, which discards these least important chunks once the bandwidth is insufficient. In this case, half of the chunks will not be transmitted when bandwidth compression ratio is at $\beta = 0.5$. The other reference scheme is referred to as NOMA-RA, where BL chunks and EL chunks are randomly scheduled for superposition in NOMA. In NOMA-RA, power allocation is the same as that in SoftCast.

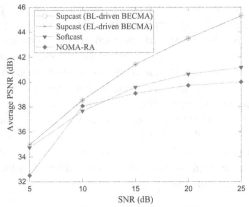

Fig. 8.3 Performance comparison of different schemes under different channel SNR, with $\beta = 0.5$, GOP = 4, 64 chunks/frame.

As we have described in Sec. 8.4.2, Algorithm 1 actually adopts a BL-driven chunk scheduling scheme, where BL chunks make the proposal. On the other hand, by setting EL chunks as the proposer, an EL-driven algorithm can be generated. Therefore, in simulations, we implement Supcast with these two types of BECMA algorithms. Their system performance is evaluated by averaging PSNR over all test sequences, as shown in Fig. 8.3. It can be seen that the performance of BL-driven BECMA is similar to that of EL-driven BECMA, which is in-consistent with the conclusion in Remark 1. The reason is that the formulated preferences of BL chunks and EL chunks are consistent in terms of sum-distortion.

As shown in Fig. 8.3, Supcast outperforms SoftCast and NOMA-RA over the entire range of SNR, and achieves gains up to 3dB in terms of average PSNR. When SNR is low at 5dB, performance of Supcast is similar to SoftCast. This is due to the fact that the poor channel condition can only support transmission of all BL chunks and very few EL chunks with SC. In this case, most EL chunks are allocated with no power in the power re-allocation stage according to Eq. (8.11). In contrast, without two-stage power allocation, NOMA-RA has poor performance, since reconstruction performance of BL chunks degrades with severe interference of randomly superposed EL chunks. At medium and high SNR, performance gains of Supcast enlarge accordingly, while both NOMA-RA and SoftCast start the effect of performance saturation. However, the saturation reasons of two schemes are totally different. The former is because severe interference of SC cannot be well alleviated in NOMA-RA with random scheduling and simple power allocation strategy. The latter is because distortion of discarding half chunks in SoftCast is nonrecoverable.

For the integrity of evaluation, comparison between the proposed BECMA scheduling and the optimal user scheduling through exhaustive search is also provided, as shown in Fig. 8.4. As the computational complexity of the optimal exhaustive search is $O(M!)$, the simulation is performed by setting the GOP size as

1 and the coefficients are divided into 16 chunks. Fig. 8.4 illustrates the results; we can see the performance of BECMA approaches the upper bound generated from exhaustive search.

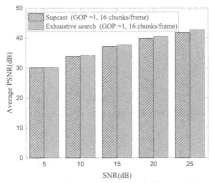

Fig. 8.4 PSNR comparison between the BECMA scheduling and the optimal exhaustive search scheduling, $\beta = 0.5$, GOP $= 1$, 16 chunks/frame.

8.5.2 Impacts of Bandwidth Compression Ratio β

Although Supcast has the ability to delivery twice the chunks compared to SoftCast owing to SC in NOMA, it has to discard some least important chunks before bisecting BL and EL chunks when bandwidth is severely insufficient. This leads to varying variance disparities between BL chunks and EL chunks in different bandwidth compression cases, which would accordingly affect the results of power allocation and chunk scheduling. Hence, we conduct simulations under different values of β, as illustrated in Fig. 8.5.

From Fig. 8.5 we can see that Supcast achieves graceful performance degradation with varying channel SNR, while performance of Supcast at $\beta = 0.25$ and performance of SoftCast appear saturated at high channel SNR. The reason can be explained as follows. At $\beta = 0.5$, all chunks can be transmitted and decoded by near users in Supcast. However, half chunks would be dropped in SoftCast when $\beta = 0.5$ and in Supcast when $\beta = 0.25$; especially only quarter chunks can be transmitted in SoftCast at $\beta = 0.25$. Distortion of discarding information cannot be recovered at receivers. Thus, performance of these schemes is bounded at better channel conditions.

Another interesting observation is that when channel SNR is low, Supcast can obtain higher performance gains at $\beta = 0.25$ than $\beta = 0.5$, compared with SoftCast. The reason is that at $\beta = 0.5$, poor channel condition can only support transmission of BL chunks and few superposed EL chunks. In this case, the advantage of NOMA cannot be fully utilized, thus Supcast and SoftCast achieve similar performance. However, at $\beta = 0.25$, power is intensively allocated among transmitted chunks by

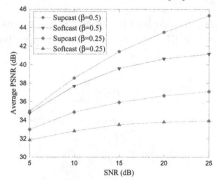

Fig. 8.5 PSNR performance at different settings of bandwidth compression ratio β, with GOP $= 4$, 64 chunks/frame.

sacrificing the transmission opportunity of some least important chunks. Therefore, more EL chunks can be superposed and decoded by near users, even when channel condition is poor. This brings about remarkable gains for Supcast.

8.5.3 Impacts of Chunk Size

Since power allocation and scheduling are both carried out over chunks, the impact of chunk size on performance of Supcast has also been investigated. As described before, DCT coefficients of each frame are divided into $N_c \times N_c$ chunks. In simulations, N_c is set as 4, 8 and 16, which produces a total number of chunks per frame as 16, 64 and 256, respectively. The results are reported in Fig. 8.6. As shown in Fig. 8.6, we can see that performance improves gradually with the increasing number of divided chunks. The reason is that with more chunks, more power scaling gains and superposition gains can be achieved due to the fine-grained power allocation and chunk scheduling. Besides, *marginal effect* can be found in Fig. 8.6, which means the performance gap between the division of 256 chunks and 64 chunks is far less than the gap between the division of 64 chunks and 16 chunks.

The above observations can provide guidelines for chunk division in Supcast, which implies that the division of 64 chunks per frame can strike a good balance between performance and complexity. Too fine division would cause heavy computational burden for chunk scheduling, according to the analysis in Sec. 8.4.2. Moreover, the huge overhead for transmitting metadata, including power scaling vectors and chunk scheduling vectors, is undesired when the number of chunks is too large. In this case, improved performance is not worth the marginal effect. It is worth noting that the choice of appropriate chunk division should be adaptively adjusted according to the GOP size and the resolution of video sequences.

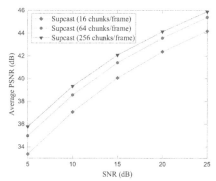

Fig. 8.6 Impact of various chunk division on the PSNR performance of Supcast, with $\beta = 0.5$, GOP = 4.

8.6 Summary

In this chapter, we presented Supcast, a novel receiver-driven scheme for video multicast in NOMA systems with heterogeneous channel conditions. The design of Supcast is jointly motivated by high spectral efficiency achieved with NOMA and robust transmission of SoftCast under heterogeneous environments. By grouping DCT coefficients into BL chunks and EL chunks for superposition, Supcast enables near users to decode both BL and EL chunks while far users decode only BL chunks. Furthermore, Supcast allows each heterogeneous user to decode video with quality proportional to its channel quality. The key module of Supcast includes power allocation and chunk scheduling to minimize video transmission distortion. With the consideration of chunk characteristics and interference formulation in decoding, we proposed a two-stage power allocation strategy. Meanwhile, by reformulating the chunk scheduling problem as a one-to-one two-sided matching problem, we propose a near-optimal and low-complexity chunk scheduling algorithm. Simulation results have shown remarkable performance improvements of Supcast over reference schemes.

Chapter 9
Joint Subcarrier Matching and Power Allocation

9.1 Introduction

Due to the diversity of mobile terminals, such as phones, tablets, laptops and so on, it is very common that receivers in video broadcast have different screen sizes. Unfortunately, transmitting a single representation of a video sequence to the range of display resolutions available in the broadcast scenario is impractical. For example, it is inequitable to design a device with low display resolution with the capacity for decoding and downsampling high resolution videos. Such a requirement could increase the cost and power consumption of the device exceeding the constraints that determine its display resolution. Meanwhile, sending the high resolution details that are ultimately not shown on the display for such a device is a waste of its receiving channel bandwidth. Therefore, how to make robust video transmission adaptive to the resolution heterogeneity with one single video representation, is a very important issue in the robust video broadcast system.

To tackle the resolution heterogeneity, original video sequence should be spatially decomposed first to accommodate diverse users with different resolutions. Two existing conventional methods can achieve spatial decomposition for video applications, i.e., the image pyramid-based method adopted in Scalable Video Coding (SVC) [5][96] and the wavelet-based method [97][98]. However, both of them are previously designed for digital source coding, and cannot be well integrated with the robust video transmission system. The image pyramid-based method is a very intuitive way of spatial decomposition, but it uses an over-complete decomposition [96], i.e., the number of image samples in the entire pyramid structure is larger than the number of samples in an original high-resolution image. This will significantly reduce the bandwidth efficiency, because the bandwidth consumption in the robust video transmission system is directly determined by the number of data samples. In contrast, the wavelet-based method belongs to critically sampled decomposition, i.e., the number of image samples is equal to that of the samples in the original high-resolution image. However, it is a computationally sophisticated method, which has inherent drawbacks such as the shift-variant nature

DOI: 10.1201/9781003118688-9

[98][99]. Thus, the wavelet-based method cannot be directly integrated with robust video transmission.

On the other hand, the original robust video transmission is designed with channel oblivious for video broadcast. In the orthogonal frequency division multiplexing (OFDM) based communication system, a wideband channel is decomposed into multiple mutually orthogonal *subcarriers*, and the channel gains on these subcarriers are usually different, sometimes by as much as 20dB [100]. Thus, the error behavior differs across subcarriers, and these subcarriers should be allocated properly as significant wireless resources. Meanwhile, video contents are usually non-uniformly distributed. According to [101] [102], matching video contents to subcarriers according to their respective sorted order of energy level, and then performing joint source-channel power allocation can effectively improve the overall error performance.

Based on the aforementioned analysis, in this chapter, we propose a robust video broadcast framework named Spatial Scalability enabled Robust Video Broadcast (SSRVB), which can accommodate diverse users with heterogeneous resolutions, as well as maintaining the scalability of robust video transmission with respect to channel conditions. In SSRVB, a novel spatial decomposition method is first designed for robust video transmission, where the input videos are decomposed into scalable layers to provide differentiated resolution demands. A base layer guarantees the base quality of the video content, while the refinement information encoded in the higher layers allows us to progressively improve video quality. Since the total number of projection values is always equal to the number of original values after each projection process, SSRVB performs critically sampled decomposition and is thus bandwidth efficient.

Exploiting the fact that the whole process of SSRVB is linear, we derive the expression of the decoding distortion of each user, as well as the average distortion of multiple users in the broadcast scenarios. Based on the analysis, we formulate the transmission distortion minimization problem with the consideration of two types resource allocation, i.e., subcarrier matching and power allocation. This formulated problem is a mixed integer non-linear programming (MINLP) problem, which is an intractable NP-hard problem. To solve this problem, we first derive a closed-form optimal power allocation solution for any given subcarrier matching. With the optimal power allocation, we then propose a near-optimal and low-complexity subcarrier matching scheme based on auction theory. Finally, an iterative algorithm is used to solve this joint subcarrier matching and power allocation problem. Extensive simulations have been carried out to validate our work. The results show that with joint subcarrier matching and power allocation, SSRVB can effectively exploit gains from robust video transmission and significantly outperforms the reference schemes under heterogeneous scenarios.

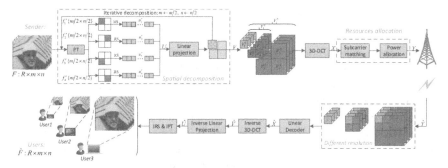

Fig. 9.1 Framework of the proposed SSRVB system.

9.2 System Model

In this section, the framework of SSRVB is introduced, as illustrated in Fig. 9.1. We consider the downlink scenario, where video data is transmitted from base station to heterogeneous users. To support resolution heterogeneity, a novel linear projection based spatial decomposition method is firstly proposed. Next, 3-Dimensional Discrete Cosine Transformation (3D-DCT) is performed to remove redundancy in source data. Then joint subcarrier matching and power allocation is applied to minimize the distortion of multiple users under the broadcast scenario. The proposed spatial decomposition and subcarrier matching between coefficient chunks and subcarriers is illustrated in Fig. 9.2.

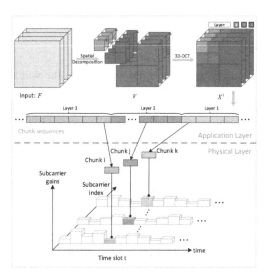

Fig. 9.2 Illustration of the proposed spatial decomposition and the subcarrier matching.

9.2.1 Overview of SSRVB

At the sender side, according to the resolution requirements of different users, a group of pictures (GOP) will be preprocessed and decomposed into multiple layers by the proposed spatial decomposition method. Since the design of the projection matrix has considered robust transmission gains, thus it can increase energy diversity across different layers in the decomposition process, according to [103]. Next 3D-DCT is applied to each cube formed by the same projection components of every frame in the GOP, which can remove the redundancy in the decomposed layers and further improve the performance of robust video transmission gains. Then the resulting coefficients are divided into equal-sized chunks. After that, subcarrier matching is performed according to the importance of different chunks and subcarriers, respectively. Subsequently, optimal power allocation is performed based on the results of subcarrier matching, which allocates power among these coefficient chunks. Next, these chunks are linearly scaled by the derived power scaling factors, and finally these scaled coefficients are delivered to all users in a broadcast way with dense constellation modulation.

At the receiver side, a certain number of layers will be received according to the resolution requirement from the user. Then a linear decoding component is used to decode the received data, after which the inverse 3D-DCT is applied to restore the corresponding multiple layers data. Finally, the inverse linear projection transformation is performed to reconstruct the video with required resolution.

9.2.2 Spatial Decomposition

9.2.2.1 Data Preprocessing

Without loss of generality, in this chapter, we assume the width and height of the adjacent resolution is with 1:2 scaling relationship, while the length of original video frames is a power of 2. For ease of description, the data preprocessing operations, including partition operation (PT) and reshape operation (RS) are defined.

The purpose of PT operation is to divide the original frames $F^r\{m \times n\}$ into four subblocks. Every four adjacent pixels is taken out of F^r, then is put into four subblocks $f_i^r \{m/2 \times n/2, 1 \leq r \leq R, 1 \leq i \leq 4\}$ respectively in the order of left to right, top to bottom, where R is the number of frames in each GOP, r represents the frame index and i denotes the subblock index, respectively. For the sake of brevity, we omit the superscript r in the following analysis. In the RS operation, results obtained by PT in each subblock f_i are vectorized into a $1 \times (mn/4)$ row vector according to the row order. Data after preprocessing operations is expressed as: $U = RS(PT(F)) = [u_1, u_2, u_3, u_4]^T$, where $\{u_i, 1 \leq i \leq 4\}$ represent the corresponding subblocks. We also use IPT and IRS to represent the inverse operations of PT and RS, respectively.

9.2.2.2 Linear Projection

After data preprocessing, the corresponding result $U = [u_1, u_2, u_3, u_4]^T$ is obtained. Then the linear projection process can be expressed as $V = T \cdot U = [v_1, v_2, v_3, v_4]^T$, where T denotes the projection matrix. After linear projection, the first projection component v_1 is regarded as the base layer, and the other three projection components v_2, v_3, v_4 constitute the enhancement layer. This projection process can be applied to the base layer v_1 in an iterative way for several times. In this case, every frame of the GOP is decomposed into multiple layers to support more resolutions. The iterative decomposition process can be expressed as $[v_1^l, v_2^l, v_3^l, v_4^l] = T \cdot RS(PT(V_1^{(l+1)})) = T \cdot [u_1^{(l+1)}, u_2^{(l+1)}, u_3^{(l+1)}, u_4^{(l+1)}]^T$, which is shown in Fig. 9.1. Since the total number of projection values is always equal to the number of original values after each projection process, the proposed decomposition method is critically sampled and thus bandwidth efficient.

9.2.2.3 Projection Matrix

According to the aforementioned analysis, the first row of T is downsampling parameters, while the remaining three rows are designed to get the enhancement layer, which can provide refinement information. Particularly, the projection matrix T is expressed as follows

$$T = \begin{bmatrix} 0.25 & 0.25 & 0.25 & 0.25 \\ 1 & -1 & 0 & 0 \\ 0 & 1 & -1 & 0 \\ 0 & 0 & 1 & -1 \end{bmatrix}.$$

After the orthogonality is normalized, the projection matrix T can be expressed as

$$T = \begin{bmatrix} 0.5000 & 0.5000 & 0.5000 & 0.5000 \\ 0.7071 & -0.7071 & 0 & 0 \\ 0.4082 & 0.4082 & -0.8165 & 0 \\ 0.2887 & 0.2887 & 0.2887 & -0.8660 \end{bmatrix}.$$

For the linear projection process $V = T \cdot U$, we have the corresponding relationship

$$v_1 = 2 \times \left(\frac{u_1 + u_2 + u_3 + u_4}{4} \right),$$

$$v_2 = 0.7071 \times (u_1 - u_2),$$

$$v_3 = 0.8165 \times \left(\frac{u_1 + u_2}{2} - u_3 \right),$$

$$v_4 = 0.8660 \times \left(\frac{u_1 + u_2 + u_3}{3} - u_4 \right).$$

It can be seen that v_1 is the average value of the four adjacent coefficients in the original frame, which also represents the downsampling data, while v_2, v_3, v_4 are intra prediction residuals. After spatial decomposition, the corresponding energy diversity of the projection values is increased, which means that more gains can be achieved during robust transmission. Thus, we can say that the proposed spatial decomposition method is specifically designed for robust video transmission.

9.2.3 Robust Video Transmission

As shown in Fig. 9.1, after spatial decomposition, 3D-DCT is applied to each cube formed by the same projection components of V, then the enhancement layer data can be expressed as

$$X^l = \{[V_2^l, V_3^l, V_4^l]^T, 2 \le l \le L\},$$

where L is the total number of layers of user's requirements, and the base layer is expressed as $X^1 = V_1^1$.

Subsequently, the layered data X^l is first divided into equal-sized chunks. Let x_i^l be the coefficients of the i-th chunk in the l-th layer, and the mean energy $\lambda_i^l = E[(x_i^l)^2]$ is estimated by averaging the energy of coefficients in that chunk. By utilizing the mean energy λ_i^l, power allocation can be implemented to get the linear power scaling factor g_i^l for each chunk. After that, the transmitted signal for coefficient x_i^l can be expressed as

$$s_i^l = g_i^l \cdot x_i^l.$$

The power allocated to the i-th chunk in the l-th layer can be obtained as $\mu_i^l = E[(s_i^l)^2] = (g_i^l)^2 \cdot \lambda_i^l$. The transmitted signal is modulated by a pair of scaled coefficients from the same chunk

$$y_i^l = [s_i^l + i \cdot (s_i^l)']/\sqrt{2}.$$

Then, all coefficients of the chunk are allocated to the j-th subcarrier and experience the same fading during transmission. The receiver receives the signal

$$\hat{y}_i^l = h_j \cdot y_i^l + n_i^l,$$

where h_j is the channel fading coefficient of the j-th subcarrier and n_i^l is a zero-mean, i.i.d. Gaussian noise variable with variance $E[n_i^l] = \sigma^2$.

Next, through low complexity linear MSE detection, the coefficients can be recovered from the real part and imaginary part of $\hat{y}_i^l$,

$$\hat{x}_i^l = Re\left(\frac{\hat{y}_i^l}{h_j g_i^l}\right) = x_i^l + Re\left(\frac{n_i^l}{h_j g_i^l}\right).$$

Correspondingly, the transmission distortion of the chunk can be expressed as

$$e_i^l = E[(x_i^l - \hat{x}_i^l)^2] = \frac{\sigma^2}{\|h_j\|^2 (g_i^l)^2}. \tag{9.1}$$

9.2.4 Spatial Scalability Analysis

Suppose that a total of L different resolutions are required, which means each frame in the GOP will be decomposed into L layers. After preprocessing operations, the corresponding result is

$$U^l = RS(PT(U_1^{(l+1)})) = [U_1^l, U_2^l, U_3^l, U_4^l]^T,$$

where the superscript l denotes the l-th layer data, and $1 \leq l \leq L-1$. Then after linear projection, we have

$$[V_1^l, V_2^l, V_3^l, V_4^l]^T = T \cdot RS(PT(V_1^{(l+1)}))$$
$$= T \cdot [U_1^l, U_2^l, U_3^l, U_4^l]^T, 1 \leq l \leq L-1,$$

where $V_1^l\{1 \leq l \leq L\}$ is the required different resolutions. Meanwhile the l-th layer data can be expressed as

$$X^l = [V_2^l, V_3^l, V_4^l]^T, 2 \leq l \leq L.$$

Particularly, for the first layer, we have $X^1 = V_1^1$.

Followed by 3D-DCT applied to each tube formed by the same projection components of every frame in the GOP, the transformed data can be obtained as

$$Y_i^l = 3D\text{-}DCT\{X_i^l\}; l = 2,3,...L; i = 2,3,4.$$

Similarly, the first layer can be expressed as $Y_1^1 = 3D\text{-}DCT\{X_1^1\}$.

According to the resolution requirements from multiple users, certain layers of the data will be received and decoded after robust video transmission. Suppose a user s is with the Ls-th resolution requirement, which means a total of Ls layers data should be received for decoding. Specifically, the decoding process can be presented as follows. Firstly, the received signal is decoded by utilizing linear MSE detection, and we get $\{\hat{Y}^l | 1 \leq l \leq L_s\}$. Next, inverse 3D-DCT is applied to $\hat{Y}_l$ and we have $\{\hat{X}^l | 1 \leq l \leq L_s\}$. After that, iterative decoding is followed to achieve higher resolution video, which is expressed as

$$\hat{V}_1^1 = \hat{X}_1^1,$$
$$\hat{V}_1^l = T^{-1} \cdot \begin{pmatrix} \hat{V}_1^{(l-1)} \\ \hat{X}^l \end{pmatrix}, 2 \leq l \leq L. \tag{9.2}$$

As we have mentioned, orthonormalization process is needed for the projection matrix design. However, this process will change the first row of the projection matrix. Therefore, during the video decoding, the decoded projection values $\hat{V}_1^{L_s}$ should be multiplied by a power of ρ to recover the original values $\hat{F}^{L_s}$, where ρ is the modulus of the first row of projection matrix T, and we have $\rho = 0.5$ in this chapter. Finally, the recovered resolution values can be expressed as

$$\hat{F}^{L_s} = IPT(IRS(\rho^{L-L_s} \cdot \hat{V}_1^{L_s})). \tag{9.3}$$

9.3 Joint Subcarrier Matching and Power Allocation

In this section, we will first formulate the transmission distortion minimization problem by considering joint subcarrier matching and power allocation, and then discuss how to optimize it. Specifically, our objective is to minimize the end-to-end transmission distortion, i.e., the distortion between the original video F and the reconstructed video $\hat{F}$. As 3D-DCT and linear projection based spatial decomposition are both orthogonal linear operations, the MSE between F and $\hat{F}$ is the same as the MSE between X and $\hat{X}$. To solve this distortion minimization problem, we decompose it into two subproblems, i.e., subcarrier matching subproblem and power allocation subproblem. We first optimally solve the power allocation subproblem with given subcarrier matching results. Then, we reformulate and solve the subcarrier matching subproblem by utilizing auction theory.

9.3.1 Problem Formulation

In this chapter, we consider a broadcast scenario, where total K users request L different resolutions. Therefore, before transmission, the input video frames are first spatial decomposed into L layers. As an OFDM system is considered, we assume that M mutually orthogonal subcarriers are available for transmission and each subcarrier experiences a slow fading so that the channel gain remains constant within each transmission interval [104].

As described in (9.1), when subcarrier is assigned, the expected chunk distortion can be obtained. Given that larger λ_i^l contributes more to the distortion, λ_i^l can reflect the importance of the i-th chunk in the l-th layer. The end-to-end distortion of a GOP for user k can be obtained as

$$MSE_k = \sum_{l=1}^{L_k}\sum_{i=1}^{N_l}\sum_{j=1}^{M} b_{ij}^l e_{ij}^l = \rho^{2(L-L_k)}\sum_{l=1}^{L_k}\sum_{i=1}^{N_l}\sum_{j=1}^{M} \frac{b_{ij}^l \sigma^2}{\|h_j\|^2 (g_i^l)^2}, \tag{9.4}$$

where b_{ij}^l is a binary value denoting whether the j-th subcarrier is allocated to the i-th chunk in the l-th layer. Here, $b_{ij}^l = 1$ means that the j-th subcarrier is allocated to i-th chunk in the l-th layer, and $b_{ij}^l = 0$ represents the other case. For multiple users, the total end-to-end distortion can be expressed as

$$MSE = \sum_{k=1}^{K} \sum_{l=1}^{L_k} \sum_{i=1}^{N_l} \sum_{j=1}^{M} b_{ij}^l e_{ij}^l = \sum_{k=1}^{K} \rho^{2(L-L_k)} \sum_{l=1}^{L_k} \sum_{i=1}^{N_l} \sum_{j=1}^{M} \frac{b_{ij}^l \sigma^2}{\|h_j\|^2 (g_i^l)^2}. \quad (9.5)$$

Let P be the total power, then the joint subcarrier matching and power allocation distortion optimization problem is formulated as

$$\min_{\{b_{ij}^l, g_i^l\}} \sum_{k=1}^{K} \rho^{2(L-L_k)} \sum_{l=1}^{L_k} \sum_{i=1}^{N_l} \sum_{j=1}^{M} \frac{b_{ij}^l \sigma^2}{\|h_j\|^2 (g_i^l)^2}, \quad (9.6a)$$

$$s.t. \ \sum_{l=1}^{L} \sum_{j=1}^{N_l} (g_i^l)^2 \lambda_i^l \le P, \quad (9.6b)$$

$$(g_i^l)^2 \lambda_i^l \ge 0, \quad (9.6c)$$

$$\sum_{l=1}^{L} \sum_{j=1}^{M} b_{ij}^l \le 1, \quad (9.6d)$$

$$\sum_{l=1}^{L} \sum_{i=1}^{N_l} b_{ij}^l \le 1, \quad (9.6e)$$

$$b_{ij}^l \in \{0, 1\}, \quad (9.6f)$$

where (9.6b) specifies the total power constraint, (9.6c) states that the power allocated to each chunk should be greater than or equal to 0. (9.6d) and (9.6e) indicates that one subcarrier can be assigned to at most one chunk in a time slot, and the reason will be explained in the following subsection.

Problem (9.6) is a mixed binary programming problem, which is NP-hard and is hard to find the global optimal solution due to the computational complexity [105]. To tackle this subcarrier-power coupled problem with low complexity yet near-optimal solution, we divide it into two subproblems. One is the power distortion subproblem which can be optimally solved; the other is the subcarrier matching subproblem which can be reformulated as an auction problem and thus efficiently solved by auction theory.

9.3.2 Power Allocation

When the subcarrier matching result $\{b_{ij}^l\}$ is determined, problem (9.6) can be rewritten as

$$\min_{\{g_i^l\}} \sum_{k=1}^{K} \rho^{2(L-L_k)} \sum_{l=1}^{L_k} \sum_{i=1}^{N_l} \frac{\sigma^2}{\|c_i\|^2 (g_i^l)^2}, \tag{9.7a}$$

$$s.t. \ \sum_{l=1}^{L} \sum_{j=1}^{N_l} (g_i^l)^2 \lambda_i^l \le P, \tag{9.7b}$$

$$(g_i^l)^2 \lambda_i^l \ge 0, \tag{9.7c}$$

where $\{c_i\}$ is the rearrangement of $\{h_j\}$ depending on the subcarrier matching results.

To tackle this subproblem, all users are first divided into L groups according to their resolution requirements. Let $G_1, G_2, \ldots, G_L$ represent the number of users in each group, and the number of layers required by each group is 1, 2, ..., L, respectively. Then problem (9.7) can be converted as

$$\min_{\{g_i^l\}} \sum_{l=1}^{L} \sum_{i=1}^{N_l} \frac{C_i^l}{(g_i^l)^2}, \tag{9.8a}$$

$$s.t. \ \sum_{l=1}^{L} \sum_{j=1}^{N_l} (g_i^l)^2 \lambda_i^l \le P, \tag{9.8b}$$

$$(g_i^l)^2 \lambda_i^l \ge 0, \tag{9.8c}$$

with the corresponding simplification

$$A_i^l = \{\rho^{2(L-L_k)} \sigma^2 \ | k \in G_g, g = l, \ldots, L\}, \tag{9.9a}$$

$$B_i^l = \{1/\|c_i\|^2 \ | k \in G_g, g = l, \ldots, L\}, \tag{9.9b}$$

$$C_i^l = \sum A_i^l \odot B_i^l, \tag{9.9c}$$

where $\odot$ denotes the Hadamard (i.e., element-wise) product for vectors. We should note that the priority of different layers has been explicitly considered in (9.8), which is determined by their contributions to the overall end-to-end distortion of the reconstructed videos. Therefore, problem (9.8) is more tractable than problem (9.7).

Theorem 9.1. The optimization problem on power allocation defined in (9.8) is convex.

Proof. As the objective function of (9.8) is monotonically decreasing in terms of g_i^l, the equality in the constraint should be hold. Thus, the power distortion optimization problem becomes

$$\min_{\{g_i^l\}} \sum_{l=1}^{L} \sum_{i=1}^{N_l} \frac{C_i^l}{(g_i^l)^2},$$

$$s.t. \ \sum_{l=1}^{L} \sum_{j=1}^{N_l} (g_i^l)^2 \lambda_i^l = P, \tag{9.10}$$

$$(g_i^l)^2 \lambda_i^l \geq 0.$$

Then the second-order derivative of (9.10) with respective to g_i^l can be derived as

$$\frac{\partial^2 (D_i^l)}{\partial^2 (g_i^l)} = \frac{6C_i^l}{(g_i^l)^4} > 0. \tag{9.11}$$

Therefore, the objective function (9.10) is a strict convex function with respect to g_i^l. As the constraints are linear, thus the optimization problem in (9.10) is a convex optimization problem.

Theorem 9.2. With optimal subcarrier matching, the number of subcarriers assigned to each chunk cannot exceed one at each time slot.

Proof. Suppose that under optimal subcarrier matching, two subcarriers j_1 and j_2 are assigned to i-th chunk for transmission. The corresponding optimal power scaling factors on the two subcarriers are g_{i_1} and g_{i_2}, respectively. Meanwhile, we assume that the channel gains on these two subcarriers satisfy $\|h_{j_1}\|^2 > \|h_{j_2}\|^2$. Now we consider another matching scheme, only subcarrier j_1 is assigned for the i-th chunk and the corresponding power scaling factor is $g_i = \sqrt{g_{i_1}^2 + g_{i_2}^2}$, which means the power usage is equal for these two matching schemes. Obviously, both of these two matching schemes satisfy the constraint in (9.10), and we have

$$\frac{\sigma^2}{\sum_{a=1}^{2} \|h_{j_a}\|^2 g_{i_a}^2} > \frac{\sigma^2}{\|h_{j_1}\|^2 \sum_{a=1}^{2} g_{i_a}^2}. \tag{9.12}$$

Thus, the second matching scheme can achieve better distortion performance, which contradicts the assumption. Therefore, under the optimal subcarrier matching, the number of subcarriers assigned to each chunk should not exceed one at each time slot.

With the Lagrange multiplier method, the optimization problem of (9.10) can be solved. The corresponding Lagrange function is

$$L = \sum_{l=1}^{L} \sum_{i=1}^{N_l} \frac{C_i^l}{(g_i^l)^2} + \gamma \left(\sum_{l=1}^{L} \sum_{i=1}^{N_l} (g_i^l)^2 \cdot \lambda_i^l - P \right). \tag{9.13}$$

By differentiating g_i^l and γ separately and setting to zero, yielding

$$\partial\gamma: \sum_{l=1}^{L}\sum_{i=1}^{N_l}\left(g_i^l\right)^2\lambda_i^l = P, \tag{9.14a}$$

$$\partial g_i^l: -2\sum_{l=1}^{L}\sum_{i=1}^{N_l}\frac{C_i^l}{\left(g_i^l\right)^3} + 2\gamma\left(\sum_{l=1}^{L}\sum_{i=1}^{N_l}g_i^l\cdot\lambda_i^l\right), \tag{9.14b}$$

$$\sqrt{\gamma} = \frac{\sum_{r=1}^{L}\sum_{s=1}^{N_r}\sqrt{C_s^r\cdot\lambda_s^r}}{P}. \tag{9.14c}$$

Then the optimal power scaling factor can be derived

$$g_i^l = \sqrt[4]{\frac{C_i^l}{\lambda_i^l\cdot\gamma}} = \sqrt{\frac{P\cdot\sqrt{C_i^l}}{\sqrt{\lambda_i^l}\sum_{r=1}^{L}\sum_{s=1}^{N_r}\sqrt{C_s^r\cdot\lambda_s^r}}}. \tag{9.15}$$

Finally, the optimal allocated power to the corresponding chunk is

$$\mu_i^l = \left(g_i^l\right)^2\cdot\lambda_i^l = \frac{P\cdot\sqrt{C_i^l\cdot\lambda_i^l}}{\sum_{r=1}^{L}\sum_{s=1}^{N_r}\sqrt{C_s^r\cdot\lambda_s^r}}. \tag{9.16}$$

9.3.3 Subcarrier Matching

With calculated optimal power allocation, we then consider the subcarrier matching subproblem. To find optimal subcarrier matching in problem (9.6), a direct approach is to calculate all the possible permutations of available matching between subcarriers and chunks, which is prohibitively complex when the numbers of users, layers, and subcarriers are large [106], [107], [108]. Therefore, an auction algorithm based subcarrier matching scheme is proposed to solve this problem, which has low complexity and memory requirement.

In auction algorithm, a competitive bidding process is mimicked, where unassigned persons raise their prices and try to become the highest bidder for their preferred objects. After getting bids from all persons, objects are assigned to the highest bidder. Specifically, the auction problem becomes a symmetric assignment problem when the number of objects and persons are equal, which can be solved very efficiently [109]. Assuming that there are M persons and M objects, there is a benefit a_{ij} associated with assigning the j-th object to the i-th person, and the i-th person should pay the price p_j. Then the profit of object j for person i is $a_{ij} - p_j$, and each person i would logically want to be assigned to an object j_i with maximal profit

$$a_{ij_i} - p_{j_i} \geq \max_{j=1,\cdots,M}\{a_{ij} - p_j\} - \varepsilon, \tag{9.17}$$

where ε is a given positive scalar, and j_i represents that person i finds the object j_i which can provide maximal value

$$j_i \in \arg \max_{j=1,\cdots,M} \{a_{ij} - p_j\}. \tag{9.18}$$

For the subcarrier matching subproblem, we suppose an assignment $\mathscr{A}$ representing a set of chunk-subcarrier pairs (i, j). Since we have assumed one-to-one matching in this chapter, then for each chunk i there is at most one pair $(i, j) \in \mathscr{A}$, and for every subcarrier j there is also at most one pair $(i, j) \in \mathscr{A}$. The goal of auction algorithm is to find an assignment with maximum total profit $\sum_{j=0}^{M} a_{ij}$. To achieve this goal, it proceeds iteratively and terminates when a feasible assignment is obtained.

Our goal is to minimize the end-to-end distortion, while the objective of auction algorithm is to maximize the total profit. Therefore, when power allocation is determined, we define the utility value of chunk i on subcarrier j as $U_{ij}^l = 1/e_{ij}^l$, and the total utility given as

$$U = \sum U_{ij}^l. \tag{9.19}$$

Then the object function of problem (9.6) can be reformulated as

$$\max_{\{b_{ij}^l\}} \sum_{l=1}^{L} \sum_{i=1}^{N_l} \sum_{j=1}^{M} b_{ij}^l \cdot U_{ij}^l, \tag{9.20a}$$

$$s.t. \sum_{l=1}^{L} \sum_{j=1}^{M} b_{ij}^l \leq 1, \tag{9.20b}$$

$$\sum_{l=1}^{L} \sum_{i=1}^{N_l} b_{ij}^l \leq 1, \tag{9.20c}$$

$$b_{ij}^l \in \{0, 1\}. \tag{9.20d}$$

This is a standard auction problem, and can be efficiently solved by the proposed *Algorithm 8*.

9.3.3.1 Convergence and Optimality Analysis

We first give the convergence analysis of *Algorithm 8*.

Definition 1 *Equilibrium*. According to (9.17), if subcarrier j is assigned to chunk i with maximal profit, we will say that the chunk i is *happy*. When all chunks are *happy*, we will say that an assignment is at *equilibrium*.

Proposition 9.1. *Once each subcarrier receives at least one bid, the auction algorithm must terminate*. To explain this, note that once a subcarrier receives a bid for the first time, the chunk assigned with the subcarrier at every subsequent round is *happy*, the reason is that a chunk is *happy* just after acquiring a subcarrier through

---

Algorithm 8 Auction algorithm for subcarrier matching

Input: Select $\varepsilon > 0$; set all M chunks as *unhappy*; set $p_j = 0, j = 1,...,N$; $\mathscr{A} = \varnothing$.
Output: Subcarrier assignment vector b_{ij}^l.
1: **repeat**
2:     Choose an *unhappy* chunk k, calculate its maximum profit $v_{kj_k} = \max_j\{a_{kj} - p_j\}$, and the second maximum profit $w_{k\bar{j}_k} = \max_{j, j \neq j_k}\{a_{kj} - p_j\}$.
3:     Assign subcarrier j_k to chunk k. If this subcarrier has been assigned to another chunk $\bar{k}$ before, remove that assignment to chunk $\bar{k}$. Further, if chunk k had been assigned with a subcarrier $\bar{j}_k$ prior to being assigned subcarrier j_k, assign subcarrier $\bar{j}_k$ to chunk $\bar{k}$.
4:     Update the price of subcarrier j_k as $b_{kj_k} = p_{j_k} + v_{kj_k} - w_{k\bar{j}_k} + \varepsilon$.
5:     Set chunk k as *happy*. Decide if chunk $\bar{k}$ is *happy* or *unhappy* with its current assignment by checking Eq. (15).
6: **until** All chunks are *happy*.

---

a bid, and continues to be *happy* as long as it holds the subcarrier. The chunks that are not *happy* must be assigned with subcarriers that have never received a bid. Thus, once each subcarrier receives at least one bid, all the chunks are *happy*, then according to *Definition 1,* the auction algorithm terminates.

Theorem 9.3. The auction algorithm always terminates in a finite number of rounds.

Proof. If a subcarrier receives a bid in m rounds, its price must exceed its initial price by at least $m\varepsilon$. Thus, when m is sufficiently large, the subcarrier will become "expensive" enough to be judged "inferior" to some subcarriers that have not received a bid so far. It follows that only for a limited number of rounds can a subcarrier receive a bid while some other subcarriers still have not yet received any bid. Therefore, there are two possibilities, *a)* the auction terminates in a finite number of rounds, with all chunks *happy* before every subcarrier receives a bid, or *b)* the auction continues until after a finite number of rounds, all subcarriers receiving at least one bid and all chunks *happy*. According to *Definition 1* and *Proposition 9.1*, the auction algorithm terminates.

Theorem 9.4. Given power allocation, if ε is small enough, the result of auction algorithm is ε-optimal.

Proof. Note that an assignment and a set of prices that are at equilibrium where all profits a_{ij} are the same as before, except for the n benefits of the assigned pairs which are modified by an amount no more than ε. Suppose now that the profits a_{ij} are all integer, which is the typical practical case (if a_{ij} are rational numbers, they can be scaled up to integer by multiplication with a suitable common number). Then, the total profit of any assignment, so if $n\varepsilon < 1$, a complete assignment that is within $n\varepsilon$ of being optimal must be optimal. It follows that, if

$$\varepsilon < \frac{1}{n}, \tag{9.21}$$

and the profits a_{ij} are all integer, the assignment obtained upon termination of the auction algorithm is optimal.

9.3.3.2 Complexity Analysis

Then we give the complexity analysis of *Algorithm 8*. For comparison, we analyze the complexity of two other matching schemes.

- Auction Algorithm Matching: The complexity of auction algorithm depends on the value of ε and on the maximum absolute utility value

$$C = \max_{i,j}|a_{ij}|.$$

  The number of bidding rounds up to termination tends to be proportional to C/ε. Meanwhile, there is also a dependence on the initial utilities; if these utilities are "near optimal", the number of rounds to terminate will be relatively small. According to [110], with ε-scalar the average complexity of auction algorithm is $O(N^2 \cdot \log(N))$, and in the worst case its complexity is $O(N^3)$.
- Optimal Exhaustive Matching: It computes the optimal results by searching all the $N!$ possible permutations of available subcarrier assignments. Thus, its complexity is $O(N!)$.
- Random Matching: Subcarriers and chunks are randomly matched with each other, without using their channel gains and importance. Therefore, its complexity is $O(N)$.

9.3.4 Iterative Solution

When the solutions of subcarrier matching and power allocation are determined, problem (9.6) can be solved in a iterative manner. As shown in [111], the setting of initial prices has a great impact on the performance of auction algorithm. If the initial prices are *near optimal*, then the number of rounds needed to solve the auction problem will be relatively small. Therefore, we first consider to set *near optimal* initial prices to reduce the computation cost. As shown in ECast [102], matching subcarriers and chunks according to their respective importance and gains can achieve the optimal transmission performance, without consideration of resolution heterogeneity. Nevertheless, there are some differences in SSRVB. Due to the operation of spatial decomposition, the energy concentration effect of SSRVB is affected, and some more important chunks will exist in higher layers. On the other hand, these higher layers will be received and decoded fewer times than these lower layers, and contribute less to the end-to-end distortion in the broadcast system. Therefore, directly matching subcarriers and chunks according to their respective importance and gains is not optimal.

The details of how to set initialization parameters as well as the iterative algorithm are given as follows. First, subcarriers are sorted according to their channel gains in descending order. Then these subcarriers are divided into L layers, with $n_1, n_2, \cdots, n_L$ representing the number of subcarriers in each layer, respectively.

Without loss of generality, we assume the number of chunks in each layer equals that of subcarriers, and we have $M = \sum_l n_l$. Next, for the matching operation within each layer, the subcarriers are matched with chunks by the descending order of channel gains and chunk importance, similar to [102]. Once subcarrier matching is initially determined, optimal power allocation $\{(g_i^l)_m, m = 1\}$ can be calculated by utilizing (9.16), where m is the iterative rounds. Then with subcarrier matching and power allocation results, the total utility $\{U_m, m = 1\}$ can be calculated by using (9.19). Meanwhile, based on the power allocation results $(g_i^l)_m$, we can get a new round subcarrier matching result $(b_{ij}^l)_{m+1}$ using *Algorithm 8*. Then the power allocation results $(g_i^l)_{m+1}$ of each block and the total utility U_{m+1} can be calculated according to (9.16). These procedures will proceed iteratively and terminate when they meet the condition $|U_{m+1} - U_m| \leq \triangle$, where $\triangle > 0$ is a scalar we choose to terminate the algorithm. The procedures are elaborated in *Algorithm 9*.

The convergence of *Algorithm 9* is analyzed as follows. In particular, *Algorithm 9* is performed through an alternative optimization manner, where the power allocation $(g_i^l)_m$ and subcarrier matching $(b_{ij}^l)_m$ are optimized sequentially while keeping the other one fixed. Since both power allocation and subcarrier matching are designed to minimize the transmission distortion, the total utility can be correspondingly improved by performing the optimization sequentially.

After the optimal power allocation is performed, it must hold that

$$U(\{g_i^l\}_m, \{b_{ij}^l\}_m) \leq U(\{g_i^l\}_{m+1}, \{b_{ij}^l\}_m). \qquad (9.22)$$

Then after Step 7 of *Algorithm 9*, the ε-optimal solution of problem (9.20) is obtained for given $\{g_i^l\}_{m+1}$, we have

$$U(\{g_i^l\}_{m+1}, \{b_{ij}^l\}_m) \leq U(\{g_i^l\}_{m+1}, \{b_{ij}^l\}_{m+1}). \qquad (9.23)$$

By combining (9.22) and (9.23), we can get

$$U(\{g_i^l\}_m, \{b_{ij}^l\}_m) \leq U(\{g_i^l\}_{m+1}, \{b_{ij}^l\}_{m+1}), \qquad (9.24)$$

which means that the total utility value is non-decreasing after each iteration of *Algorithm 9*. Since the total utility is upper bounded by a finite value, the proposed *Algorithm 9* is expected to converge.

9.3.5 Channel State Information Feedback

In the considered broadcast scenario, each user is required to feedback channel state information (CSI) on these subcarriers to the base station. Then the base station can perform the proposed joint subcarrier matching and power allocation scheme to carry out resource allocation. However, for a general broadcast scenario, the overhead of CSI feedback grows linearly with the number of users, which shall

---

Algorithm 9 Iterative algorithm for main problem

Input: Power P, layer L, subcarrier gain a_{jk}, user layer k_l, chunk number N, subcarrier number N, set $\Delta > 0$, $U_0 = 0$, $m = 1$.

Output: Power scaling vector g_i^l, subcarrier assignment b_{ij}^l

1: Arrange the N subcarriers and N chunks in a decreasing order, respectively.
2: Divide the N subcarriers into L layers, i.e., $n_1, n_2, ..., n_L$, $N = \sum_l n_l$, n_l represents the number of chunks in the l-th layer.
3: In each layer, the chunks and subcarriers are matched in a decreasing order.
4: Calculate the power allocation results g_i^l via Eq. (9.16).
5: Calculate U_i^l and the total utility U_1 via Eq. (9.19).
6: **while** $|U_m - U_{m-1}| > \Delta$ **do**
7:     Using **Algorithm 8** with $(g_i^l)_{m-1}$, recalculate subcarrier assignment results $(b_{ij}^l)_m$.
8:     Recalculate the power allocation results $(g_i^l)_m$ via Eq. (9.16).
9:     Recalculate U_i^l and the total utility U_m via Eq. (9.19), $m = m + 1$.
10: **end while**

---

degrade the system performance. Therefore, inspired by [102], we adopt an analog CSI feedback scheme to reduce the overhead.

As previously noted, all users have been grouped into L groups (i.e., $G_1, \cdots, G_L$) according to their resolution requirements. Then in SSRVB, these users will feedback CSI in sequential L time slots. Specifically, during the l-th feedback time slot, all users in $\{G_u | l \leq u \leq L\}$ transmit a group of tone signals simultaneously. Each tone signal is carried by one subcarrier with its amplitude representing the channel condition of the subcarrier. For user k, the transmitted tone signal on subcarrier j is expressed as $S_{jk}^l = \frac{\rho^{2(L-L_k)}}{\|h_j\|^4}$. Then the base station receives the superposed tone signals on the same subcarrier from users in $\{G_u | l \leq u \leq L\}$, which is represented as $S_j^l = \sum_k S_{jk}^l \|h_j\|^2 + .\sigma^2 = \sum_k \frac{\rho^{2(L-L_k)}}{\|h_j\|^2} + \sigma^2$, where $k \in \{G_u | l \leq u \leq L\}$. S_j^l is actually the C_i^l in (9.9c). After L feedback time slot, the base station will store an $N \times L$ CSI table, which can be directly applied in the joint subcarrier matching and power allocation. This feedback scheme is not sensitive to noise according to [102], and the feedback overhead is only linear to the number of resolution layers L. Therefore, the feedback overhead can be significantly reduced, and the supported number of users can be relatively large in SSRVB.

9.4 Performance Evaluation

In this section, we report and discuss the simulation results. In simulations, the luminance components are extracted to generate monochrome video content for evaluating, while the chrominance components can be evaluated in the same way. All simulations are carried out based on the following six standard video test sequences, including *foreman*, *silent*, *news*, *crew*, *akiyo* and *hall*, which can be downloaded from Xiph [78]. All these video test sequences are in standard CIF format with frame rate 30 fps and frame size 288×352. Therefore, the source bandwidth is 1.52 MHz (in complex symbols).

For fair comparison, the GOP size is set as 8 for all the schemes in our simulation. An OFDM-based PHY layer with 128 subcarriers is adopted. We use Rayleigh fading channel model with unit mean power for the evaluation, i.e., $h_m \sim \mathscr{CN}(0, 1)$. Meanwhile, we adopt AWGN model to generate random noise σ^2. For all schemes, after 3D-DCT the coefficients of each GOP will be divided into equal size chunks with chunk size 72×88. Then these chunks are transmitted over the fading channel. All simulations are implemented and performed in MATLAB® R2016a.

In this chapter, we use the objective video quality assessment, peak signal-to-noise ratio (PSNR) in dB, to evaluate the perceived video quality, which is defined as

$$PSNR = 10 \log_{10} \frac{2^M - 1}{MSE}, \tag{9.25}$$

where MSE is the mean squared error over all pixels in the video sequence, and M is the number of bits used to encode luminance pixel for original video, typically 8 bits.

9.4.1 Reference Schemes

We compare with the following reference schemes to demonstrate the superiority of SSRVB.

1. **SSRVB w/o M**: To demonstrate the effect of joint subcarrier matching and power allocation, SSRVB without subcarrier matching is evaluated in our simulations. The only difference is that the subcarriers are randomly matched with chunks, while the power allocation strategy is the same.
2. **ECast+**: Since ECast [102] has considered joint subcarrier matching and power allocation, we shall introduce resolution heterogeneity support in ECast, and term it as "ECast+". In "ECast+", after 3D-DCT the decorrelated data is first divided into equal-sized chunks. These chunks and subcarriers are sorted in descending order according to their importance and channel gains, respectively, and then one-to-one match is performed. To support resolution heterogeneity, ECast+ will transmit the full resolution video first. Then according to the user's resolution requirement, the same number of chunks as SSRVB in descending order are received. The chunks that are not received are set as zero. Finally, a specific resolution video is achieved by downsampling the reconstructed video according to the user's resolution requirement.
3. **MCast+**: Similarly, MCast [112] can be extended as MCast+ by introducing the resolution heterogeneity, while the same channel assignment and power allocation are performed as in [112]. The multi-resolution support of MCast+ is essentially similar to that in ECast+. As MCast is designed for unicast, it is adopted as a reference scheme under the single user scenarios. For fair

comparison, only one time slot is used for the transmission of each GOP in MCast+.

4. **DWT-based**: The popular 9/7 biorthogonal wavelets are adopted in the DWT-based scheme to support spatial heterogeneity. After spatial decomposition, temporal DCT is performed to remove temporal correlation. Similarly, the joint subcarrier matching and power allocation strategy is adopted in the DWT-based scheme.

5. **SVC-HM**: The SVC-HM framework is based on H.264/SVC with convolutional codes and hierarchical modulation [113]. Specially, we generate the H.264/SVC stream using the JSVM implementation [47], which allows us to control the number of spatial layers.

9.4.2 Results of Spatial Scalability and Joint Resource Allocation

We first evaluate the spatial scalability and the effect of joint subcarrier matching and power allocation, while individual video quality comparison is carried out on one stationary user. For each experiment, the test video *foreman* is evaluated for all schemes at the same SNR, while a group of such experiments are conducted under different SNR. As aforementioned, by iteratively applying the proposed spatial decomposition, SSRVB is able to provide any number of different resolutions, assuming that the user's screen size has the same resolution as the source video. For comparison, we consider decomposing the source video into three layers, and the user requests the low-resolution (LR, $L = 1$), the middle-resolution (MR, $L = 2$) and the high-resolution (HR, $L = 3$) videos, respectively. In these three cases, the number of layers requested by the user matches the available bandwidth. The requested LR and MR videos will be upsampled to the same resolution as the HR video for display. The experiment results are shown in Fig. 9.3.

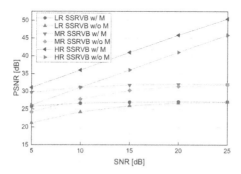

Fig. 9.3 Performance comparison under different channel SNR, while the requested resolutions are $L = 1$ (LR), $L = 2$ (MR) and $L = 3$ (HR), respectively.

From Fig. 9.3, we can see that SSRVB maintains the inherent channel scalability of robust video transmission. Compared with SSRVB w/o M, SSRVB w/ M can achieve more performance gains, no matter which resolution is requested. The reason is that SSRVB w/o M assigns subcarriers to chunks randomly, which ignores subcarrier diversity gains. For the LR and MR cases, compared with SSRVB w/o M, SSRVB w/ M can achieve more than 5dB gains at low SNR region, and this performance improvement becomes less with the SNR increases. This is because with sufficient power, as the channel quality improves, the gain of subcarrier diversity decreases. Meanwhile, the reconstructed video quality gradually becomes saturated for both LR and MR cases, since the source video is decomposed into three layers, and only part of the data is received and reconstructed by the user. Due to the loss of the remaining data information, there are upper bounds on the reconstructed video quality for the LR and MR cases, respectively. For this reason, as the channel quality increases, the reconstructed video quality of LR and MR cases improves slowly, and eventually becomes saturated.

To evaluate the optimality of SSRVB, an exhaustive search is performed to find the optimal matching results. As the computational complexity of optimal exhaustive search is $O(N!)$, we conduct small-scale simulations by setting $L = 2$, $GOP = 2$ and dividing each frame into 4 chunks. Thus 8 chunks need to be matched with subcarriers and a total of $40,320$ possibilities need to be evaluated. Fig. 9.4 shows the performance comparison between the SSRVB with subcarrier matching and the optimal exhaustive search scheme. As shown in Fig. 9.4, a near optimal performance can be achieved by the joint subcarrier matching and power allocation scheme applied in SSRVB.

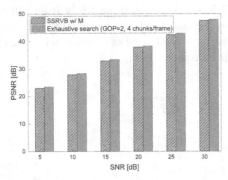

Fig. 9.4 Average PSNR comparison between the proposed SSRVB with subcarrier matching and the optimal exhaustive search scheme, where $L = 2$, GOP = 2 and 4 chunks per frame.

The convergence behavior of *Algorithm* 9 is shown in Fig. 9.5. We can see that the total utility increases gradually and the proposed algorithm converges quickly, which is inconsistent with our analysis. Actually, the total utility after first iteration depends on the initial subcarrier matching results, and the subsequent iteration is a fine-tuning of the initialization results.

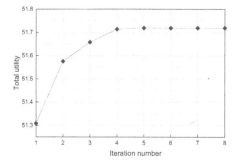

Fig. 9.5 Convergence behavior of *Algorithm 9.*

9.4.3 Results under Single User Scenarios

Although SSRVB is mainly designed for video broadcast with multiple users, it still shows a performance advantage under single user scenarios. For the scenario of single users, the video sequences are decomposed into three layers and the user requests to access the first layer and the second layer, respectively. In these two individual cases, the number of requested layers is determined by the user's screen size. Fig. 9.6 shows the comparison results of single user as the channel SNR changes. Similar simulation results can be achieved when both first and second layer videos are received. From the simulation results, we can see that SSRVB always outperforms the reference schemes under different channel SNR.

From Fig. 9.6 we can see that, comparing with ECast+ and MCast+, more than 2dB gains can be achieved by SSRVB. Specifically, the performance gain is about 2dB in low SNR ranges and is about 7~11dB in high SNR ranges. Performance gains of SSRVB come from the proposed linear projection based spatial decomposition together with the joint subcarrier matching and power allocation. With critically sampled spatial decomposition, SSRVB can inherently support resolution heterogeneity and thus can effectively exploit gains from robust transmission. Meanwhile, the proposed resource allocation scheme has considered the impact of resolution heterogeneity, which is capable of further improving the system performance. To obtain the desired resolution, ECast+ and MCast+ needs to downsample the recovered video according to the resolution requirements of users. Therefore, when channel condition gets better, the recovered video quality of ECast+ and MCast+ shall not increase accordingly, showing the saturation effect. Furthermore, SSRVB also achieves better performance compared with DWT-based scheme and the gains are more than 3dB. This is because using DWT instead of DCT to provide spatial scalability will degrade the decorrelation performance [35]. In addition, the SVC-HM scheme based on H.264/AVC presents a typical "stair effect", and SSRVB achieves more than 7dB gains over SVC-HM.

Fig. 9.7 shows the visual performance comparison. For SVC-HM, only specific number of layers can be recovered as the existence of "cliff effect", losing lots

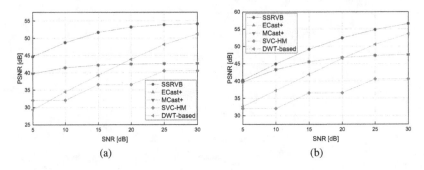

Fig. 9.6 Performance comparison under different channel SNR. (a) The user requests for the first layer video; (b) the user requests for the second layer video.

of frame details. Compared with the DWT-based scheme and the ECast+ scheme, SSRVB can achieve better reconstruction performance with fewer noise artifacts.

Fig. 9.7 Visual quality comparison of recovered frame of *foreman* and *news*, while SNR = 5dB. (a) Original; (b) DWT-based; (c) ECast+; (d) SVC-HM; (e) SSRVB.

9.4.4 Results under Multiple Users Scenarios

To evaluate the performance under broadcast scenarios with multiple users, we assume the users with different resolutions are served by a base station. The distance between the k-th user and the base station is r_k, which is randomly given. The signal power experienced by these three users is different due to large-scale fading. Suppose the transmitting power target is 5dBm; then the received power for the k-th user is approximately $5 - 10\log(r_k^\alpha)$dBm. Besides, we set the noise and interference power to -90dBm. According to users' requests, the source video is decomposed into three layers, and the 1-th, 2-th, 3-th users request the first, second and third resolution, respectively. The channel conditions of User1, User2, User3 are 8dB, 27dB and 18dB, respectively.

The simulation results are shown in Fig. 9.8, and we can see that SSRVB achieves the best average performance. Compared with the DWT-based scheme, SSRVB performs better for all users and there is about average 8dB gains, which confirms that the spatial decomposition we designed is more suitable for robust video transmission. Meanwhile, SSRVB outperforms SVC-HM about 8dB PSNR gains since SVC-HM suffers from the cliff effect, especially in broadcast scenarios. In addition, in comparison with ECast+, SSRVB performs better for User1 and User2, and a little inferior for User3. The reason is that the inter-layer redundancy cannot be totally removed by the proposed spatial decomposition method, causing a slight performance degradation on full resolution video. In other words, this degradation is the cost of supporting spatial scalability in robust video transmission. As the original version of ECast does not support spatial scalability and subcarrier matching, SSRVB can achieve better average performance than ECast+ for multiple users.

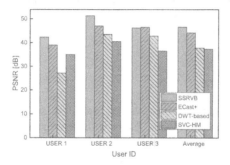

Fig. 9.8 Performance comparison of different users, where the channel SNRs of User1, User2, User3 are 8dB, 27dB and 18dB, respectively.

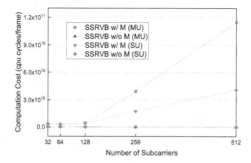

Fig. 9.9 Computation cost comparison versus different subcarrier numbers, where the channel SNR is 15dB.

9.4.5 Computation Cost Comparison

We also investigate the impact of the number of subcarriers on the computation cost performance. The simulations are conducted on the computer with an Intel Core i7-7700 CPU at the rate of 3.60 GHz, 6-GB RAM, and the video sequence *foreman* is tested. The proposed joint scheme and random scheme are compared in single user (SU) and multiple users (MU) scenarios, respectively. Each simulation is repeated 100 times and we report the average performance. The computation cost metric we adopted is the CUP cycles per frame.

The simulation results are depicted in Fig. 9.9. It can be seen that the computation cost increases as the number of subcarriers increases. When the number of subcarriers is set as 128, the average computation cost is roughly 0.126s with the proposed joint subcarrier matching and power allocation scheme. Besides, the computation cost under SU scenarios is less than that under MU scenarios, since coupling on different layers in the case of MU would involve additional calculation cost. In addition, by using a more specified hardware platform (such as DSP), the computation cost of the proposed joint subcarrier matching and power allocation scheme can be further decreased.

9.5 Summary

In this chapter, a novel robust video broadcast scheme named SSRVB is proposed to accommodate diverse users with heterogeneous resolutions as well as heterogeneous channel conditions. To fully exploit the performance gain of robust video transmission, a linear projection based spatial decomposition method is first designed in SSRVB. Then a transmission distortion minimization problem is formulated and a joint subcarrier matching and power allocation scheme is proposed to solve it efficiently. Simulation results demonstrate the superiority of SSRVB compared with reference schemes in terms of PSNR. Meanwhile, the simulation results show that the joint subcarrier matching and power allocation can achieve near-optimal performance with low computation cost. Thus, the proposed SSRVB scheme is very suitable for practical wireless video broadcast in mobile networks.

The video quality metric we adopt in this chapter is PSNR, which is an objective metric and cannot reflect the quality of human subjective perception. In the future, by taking advantage of the characteristics of the human visual system (HVS) [114], we plan to develop perception-driven resource allocation scheme to further improve the perceived visual quality of diverse users in mobile networks. Particularly, by extracting these informative features (i.e., structure information [79], gradient magnitude and phase congruency) that are more important to perceptual visual quality, and allocating more resources (i.e., more power and higher gains subcarriers) to these features we can minimize the perceptual errors. On the other hand, we believe that user resolution shall have an impact on user experience

[115]. How to accurately quantify this impact is an interesting issue for SSRVB, and we will investigate it in our future work.

Part IV
MIMO Support

MIMO technologies have been increasingly incorporated as an important building block for next-generation wireless networks. By exploiting spatial dimension across multiple antennas at the sender and the receiver, MIMO could potentially improve a wireless system's capacity, range and reliability. In this part, we will address how to support MIMO in the uncoded multimedia transmission.

In Chapter 10, we present a video transmission scheme called ParCast+ [26] designed for MIMO-OFDM channels. ParCast+ first separates the source and the channel into independent components, matches the more important source components with higher-gain channel components, allocates power weights with joint consideration to the source and the channel, and uses amplitude modulation for transmission. Such a scheme achieves fine-grained unequal error protection across source components. We implemented ParCast+ in MATLAB and on Sora. Extensive evaluation has shown that our scheme outperforms competitive schemes by notable margins, sometimes up to 6.4 dB in PSNR for challenging scenarios.

In Chapter 11, we consider image delivery in MIMO broadcasting networks with diverse channel quality and varying numbers of antennas across receivers [116]. In such systems, performance is normally constrained by the weakest users with either a low channel SNR or only a single receiver antenna. To address both dimensions of heterogeneity, we present a new uncoded image delivery scheme that adapts seamlessly along both dimensions simultaneously. The sender scales the discrete Wavelet transform (DWT) coefficients according to a power allocation strategy, and generates linear combinations of the coefficients using compressive sensing (CS), before transmitting them with amplitude modulation. On the receiving side, the received physical layer symbols are passed directly to the source decoder without conventional MIMO decoding, and the DWT coefficients are recovered using a CS decoder. Experimental results show that the presented scheme outperforms both the analog reference SoftCast and the conventional digital scheme known as HM-STBC. The average gain is 2.92 dB over SoftCast for single-antenna users and 1.53 dB over HM-STBC for two-antenna users.

In Chapter 12, we design a video multicast system that can naturally scale the video quality in the air according to the antenna settings [117]. The key innovations are the multiple similar description (MSD) coding for source processing and the multiplexed space-time block coding (M-STBC) for channel transmission. A prominent feature of the MSD coding is that any linear combination of the generated descriptions provides acceptable quality and more combinations lead to higher quality. By spatially multiplexing the MSD streams, the proposed M-STBC allows single-antenna users to benefit from transmit diversity and multi-antenna users to simultaneously achieve multiplexing gain. We build a scalable video multicast scheme named AirScale and evaluate it on Sora. In the $\{1, 2, 3, 4\} \times 4$ system, AirScale provides baseline quality for 1-antenna receiver and much higher quality for multi-antenna receivers. The gain over SoftCast is up to 3.5 dB, 3.9 dB and 4.1 dB for 2, 3 and 4-antenna receivers, respectively.

Chapter 10
Channel Allocation

10.1 Introduction

MIMO-OFDM (Multiple-Input Multiple-Output Orthogonal Frequency Division Multiplexing) technologies have become the default building blocks for next-generation wireless networks. As wireless capability continues to grow, so does the application demand. According to the Cisco Visual Networking Index [1], video-on-demand traffic is expected to double by 2022. Supporting in-home high-definition video streaming is precisely one of the motivations for 802.11ac.

While wireless links are loss prone, the original video need not be received in its entirety to ensure good visual quality. A synergy between the two sides can therefore be more effective than separately optimizing the source and the channel coding. While conventional systems perform *lossy compression over lossless digital communication*, SoftCast performs *lossless compression over lossy analog communication*. *FlexCast* [118] retains much of the MPEG encoding process, but replaces the entropy coding stage with a rateless code. The source components that contribute more to the overall distortion are represented with more channel bits. Note that allocating different amounts of power or bits to different source components is a form of unequal error protection (UEP). Both SoftCast and FlexCast use a single code to simultaneously compress and protect the source. Their performance shows that it is unnecessary to optimally compress the source, provided the amount of residual source redundancy matches the required error protection over the channel.

However, these approaches were designed with single-antenna links in mind or channel oblivious for broadcast. OFDM decomposes a wideband channel into a set of mutually orthogonal *subcarriers*, and the channel gains across these subcarriers are usually different [100], sometimes by as much as 20 dB. With MIMO, each subcarrier is further divided into a set of *spatial subchannels*, again with different channel gains. Furthermore, a channel dependent *precoding* operation is often necessary to make the spatial subchannels on the subcarrier mutually orthogonal, so that the signals do not interfere with one another along different subchannels. As a result, even for unicast, there are several issues with running SoftCast or FlexCast directly over a MIMO-OFDM link. In particular, error behavior differs across subchannels. If a one-size-fits-all code rate is used for a few or all subchannels, it generally needs to be conservative, and hence suboptimal, to accommodate the worst subchannels. In this sense, unicast over a MIMO-OFDM link resembles a broadcast channel. The need for precoding makes it difficult to ensure that a single channel oblivious error protection scheme can perform well across MIMO-OFDM links.

Given that both the source DCT component energy and subchannel gains are not uniformly distributed, if we encode the video source such that the more important, high-energy DCT components will be transmitted in high-gain subchannels, and the less important parts in lower-gain subchannels, we may better utilize the overall channel. Note, however, that the DCT and the precoding steps are essential at the source and channel, respectively, to avoid interference between source components and subchannels. This suggests that we should match DCT components to subchannels based on the respective sorted order of the energy level and then perform joint source-channel power allocation to optimize per DCT component and subchannel error performance. This is unequal error protection operating at a finer granularity than conventional layered video coding.

With these factors in mind, we present ParCast+, which tailors the video unicast quality to the MIMO-OFDM channel. ParCast+ is a revision of our earlier design, ParCast [101]. Both systems offer the same key features: (1) obtaining independent source components and subchannels, (2) matching important source components to high-gain subchannels, (3) scaling the source data with power weights computed with joint source-channel considerations, and (4) transmitting transform coefficients using amplitude modulation. Compared to ParCast, ParCast+ features improved video source decorrelation and more flexible source-channel mapping. Specifically, ParCast+ adopts a motion aligned 3D transform to decorrelate the source, which is generally considered more efficient at compacting the source energy than the 3D-DCT in ParCast. Furthermore, source components in ParCast+ are divided independently of the number of available subchannels and dynamically allocated to the channel on a per-packet basis, unlike in ParCast.

We implement the video codec in C++ and the channel dependent modules of ParCast+ both as a MATLAB simulation and on Sora [38]. We ran experiments on Sora to validate the MATLAB simulation, and then ran channel trace driven simulations to compare ParCast+ against alternatives. The results show that ParCast+ outperforms the best conventional digital scheme, sometimes by 6.4 dB, for videos with fast motion and a large energy spread over mobile links. This is a challenging case for conventional schemes, but favors ParCast+.

10.2 Background and Motivation

10.2.1 Source Characteristics

Video sources exhibit spatial correlation within a frame and temporal correlation across frames. For individual frames, DCT has been widely adopted for the compression of still images and video frames to reduce the inherent spatial redundancy between adjacent pixels. If we divide a frame into 8×8 blocks and perform a block DCT transform for each block, we can obtain the DCT coefficients in 64 different frequency bands. We compute the average energy for each frequency band and plot the energy distribution in Fig. 10.1; we can see very non-uniform distributions. The energy often spreads across 5 or 6 orders of magnitude, and the high-energy end drops very quickly. This non-uniform energy distribution is exacerbated when the inter-frame correlation is taken into account simultaneously through a temporal transform. For example, the video signal energy is always concentrated in temporal lowpass subbands in 3D subband video coding [41].

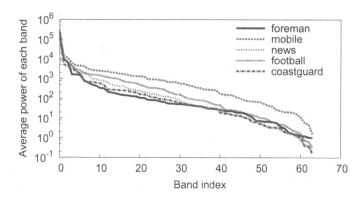

Fig. 10.1 2D 8×8 block DCT coefficient energy.

The non-uniform distribution implies statistical features and hence remaining redundancy in the coefficients. If left as is, such residual source redundancy is considered harmful, because there would be more information to transmit, with less power per unit of information. Therefore, traditional video compression schemes follow a transform with entropy coding to further compress these coefficients. Usually the coefficients in low-frequency bands have larger variations (or entropy) than those in high-frequency bands, so more bits are allocated to the low-frequency coefficients.

In current wireless systems, the allocated transmission power for each bit of the generated bit stream is the same. Therefore, the low-frequency coefficients, which are represented by more bits in source coding, are given more power for their transmission.

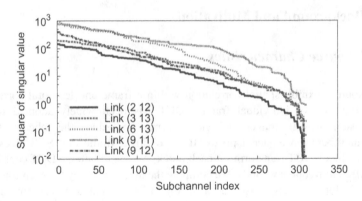

Fig. 10.2 3×3 MIMO-OFDM subchannel gains.

10.2.2 Channel Characteristics

A MIMO-OFDM link can be viewed as a set of narrowband MIMO channels. When the CSI is available at the transmitter, we are able to perform singular value decomposition (SVD)-based precoding [119] for each subcarrier, turning a MIMO-OFDM link into a set of independent single-antenna narrowband subchannels. Fig. 10.2 shows sorted subchannel gains for example 3×3 MIMO-OFDM links, with 3 antennas on either end of the link. Each link is labeled (<source ID> <destination ID>). We also see a large spread between the strongest and weakest subchannels, though with a faster drop-off at the low gain end. Having more antennas increases the spread but flattens the high end slightly.

The diverse subchannels naturally merit different quantities of information. This is the overarching goal of channel coding, so that the energy per bit sent on any subchannel appears the same. Consequently, the rate increase across a MIMO-OFDM channel is no longer monotonic with the overall channel SNR. This is unlike for single-antenna channels, which are scalar.

10.2.3 Source-channel Similarities

We have observed similarities between the operations of source and channel coding, and hence a joint source-channel scheme that exploits the synergy between the two is likely to work well.

First, SVD-based precoding for a MIMO channel can be viewed as compacting energy to diagonalize the channel matrix, whereas a decorrelation transform like DCT at the source is also expected to diagonalize the correlation matrix between the source pixels. Without precoding at the channel, the received spatial signals would interfere with one another and hurt decoding performance, as some signal strength is used to cancel out the inter-signal interference before decoding. With correlation between the source components, power or bit allocation to them would be suboptimal. Therefore, it is important to avoid correlation at both the source and the channel.

Second, Fig. 10.1 and Fig. 10.2 show a similar spread between the highest- and lowest-energy components, although the drop-off rate behavior differs. Therefore, it seems natural to match both sides, so that the high-energy DCT components are transmitted on the high-gain subchannels to avoid them acting against each other. Furthermore, the large number of subchannels allows fine-grained error protection levels.

Third, power weights can be allocated to transmitted source components to minimize the overall distortion. However, power allocation between different subchannels can also affect the achieved channel rates, which would eventually translate to the reconstructed source distortion based on a suitable rate-distortion function. Therefore, a joint source-channel power allocation strategy can optimize the overall recovery performance.

Motivated by the above observations, we have designed ParCast+ for video unicast. We use a joint source-channel coding approach to leverage the similarity.

10.3 System Design

10.3.1 Overview

The ParCast+ design follows two principles. First, the video source and the channel should be decorrelated to independent components, respectively. Second, each source component is encoded via a series of linear transforms, sent on a distinct subchannel, and decoded independently of other source components. This process ensures graceful quality degradation on each subchannel. Fig. 10.3 depicts the encoding and transmission process at the video source.

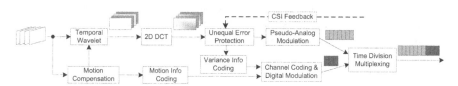

Fig. 10.3 The block diagram of the video encoding and transmission process in ParCast+.

The source encoder divides the video sequence into groups of pictures (GOPs). For each GOP, it decorrelates the source via a motion aligned 3D transform to represent each frame with the transform coefficients and a small amount of motion information. The coefficients are grouped into equal-sized chunks and a variance is computed to indicate the energy or importance of each chunk. The chunks of a GOP are grouped into source layers and then allocated to the subchannels, such that high-energy source layers are sent on high-gain subchannels in successive packets, which is a permutation transform. Power whitening is performed per source layer to even out power distribution.

The power allocation stage formulates an optimization problem to minimize the total source distortion after traversing the channel and scales the magnitude of the coefficients in each chunk by weight. The power weights are computed by taking into account both the variance of the coefficients and the corresponding subchannel gain.

Pairs of coded coefficient values are combined into complex symbols for transmission. Those for different spatial subchannels on each subcarrier are then precoded, so that they will be transmitted on orthogonal spatial channels and arrive at the receiver without interference from other spatial signals. The precoded values are then transmitted without further channel coding over the MIMO-OFDM channel using the same amplitude modulation as in SoftCast [19]. This mimics real analog modulation with a Quadrature Amplitude Modulation (QAM) of a very dense constellation.

The encoding and transmission of video data is a linear process, which can be written as:

$$\mathbf{Y} = \mathbf{H}\,\mathbf{Q}\,\mathbf{G}\,\mathbf{R}\,\mathbf{X}_p, \qquad\qquad (10.1)$$

where $\mathbf{H}$ is the overall channel matrix, $\mathbf{Q}$ is the precoding matrix, $\mathbf{G}$ is a diagonal matrix with the power weights on the diagonal, $\mathbf{R}$ implements the mapping between DCT coefficient streams to subchannels, and $\mathbf{X}_p$ contains complex symbols in one packet. The details of matrices $\mathbf{H}$, $\mathbf{Q}$ and $\mathbf{R}$ will be given in Section 10.3.3. The construction of matrix $\mathbf{X}_p$ and $\mathbf{G}$ will be explained in Section 10.3.4.2.

The video sender also transmits motion information and the source chunk energy variance in each GOP to the video receiver before sending the coefficients. The receiver feeds back channel state information (CSI) to the sender. All such metadata are compressed, sent, and decoded using conventional digital methods.

For the coefficients, the decoder does not perform regular MIMO processing to separate the signals across antennas. Instead, it collects the received signals on all the spatial and frequency domain subchannels to form an aggregate matrix, before invoking a Linear Least Square Estimator (LLSE) decoder to recover the coefficients. Then it reconstructs the frames by taking the inverse of the initial transform process.

10.3.2 Source Decorrelation

In our system, we adopt the barbell lifting based MCTF [120] to exploit the temporal correlation. Fig. 10.4 illustrates the 5/3 biorthogonal lifting structure of a recursively implemented 2-level temporal decomposition. At the first level, lowpass

L frames and highpass H frames are generated by the lifting based prediction and update step. At the second level, the lowpass frames are fed to the next MCTF level and further decomposed into LL frames and LH frames. After MCTF, the generated frames are normalized [121] and spatially decorrelated with a 2D-DCT.

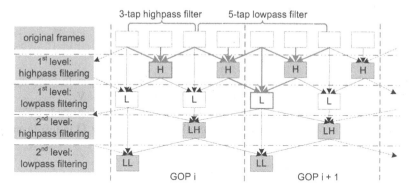

Fig. 10.4 Lifting structure of 2-level 5/3 temporal filter.

The entire source decorrelation process creates two types of metadata and a sequence of coefficients. The metadata include the motion information (mode selection and motion vectors) produced in MCTF and the variance information of the DCT coefficients. They should be transmitted with a conventional digital approach to ensure error-free reception.

The selection of the GOP size should consider the temporal characteristics of the source video [122] and the application scenario. For videos with slow or translational motion, there is temporal correlation over a long series of frames. In this case, a large GOP size is preferred because a further level of temporal filtering can exploit the inter-frame correlation between two consecutive lowpass frames. Conversely, further temporal filtering will generate high-energy highpass frames for a video with fast and complex motion like *football*, which is bad for transmission. As the codec of ParCast+ processes the video by GOPs, the GOP size also determines the complexity and the delay of the codec. To trade off the coding efficiency, complexity, and delay, we adopt a temporal filter with three levels and a GOP size of 8 frames.

10.3.3 Channel Decorrelation

Let us consider a MIMO-OFDM link with N_t transmit antennas, N_r receive antennas, and N_c subcarriers. For the sake of simplicity and without loss of generality, we assume $N_t = N_r$.

10.3.3.1 SVD-based Precoding

By design, the signals on different OFDM subcarriers are independent from one another. Let $\mathbf{H}_k$ be the complex channel matrix of the kth subcarrier. The dimension of $\mathbf{H}_k$ is $N_t \times N_t$. If it is available at the transmitter, SVD-based precoding [119] can effectively decorrelate the spatial subchannels and make the received signals mutually orthogonal. The SVD for channel matrix $\mathbf{H}_k$ can be represented as:

$$\mathbf{H}_k = \mathbf{U}_k \mathbf{S}_k \mathbf{V}_k^*, \tag{10.2}$$

where $\mathbf{U}_k$ and $\mathbf{V}_k$ are unitary matrices, $\mathbf{S}_k$ is a diagonal matrix with non-negative real values on the diagonal, and $\mathbf{V}_k^*$ is the conjugate transpose of $\mathbf{V}_k$.

SVD-based precoding simply pre-multiplies the transmitted symbols by matrix $\mathbf{V}_k$. Since there are N_c subcarriers, the overall precoding matrix $\mathbf{Q}$ in (10.1) can be formed as follows:

$$\mathbf{Q} = \begin{pmatrix} \mathbf{V}_1 & & & \\ & \mathbf{V}_2 & & \\ & & \ddots & \\ & & & \mathbf{V}_{N_c} \end{pmatrix}. \tag{10.3}$$

The dimension of this matrix is $N_c N_t \times N_c N_t$. The overall channel matrix $\mathbf{H}$ in (10.1) has the same dimension and it is similarly constructed by stacking the channel matrix of each subcarrier on the diagonal.

Meanwhile, the singular values from $\mathbf{S}_1, \mathbf{S}_2 \ldots \mathbf{S}_{N_c}$ are taken out sequentially and we construct $\mathbf{R}$ as follows. If the ith singular value is the jth largest, then the entry on the ith row and j^{th} column is set to 1, or $\mathbf{R}_{ij} = 1$. In total, there are $N_c N_t$ entries set to 1 and the other entries are all zeros.

10.3.3.2 Equivalence of Complex and Real Channels

Each complex subchannel can be further decomposed into two real subchannels with equal gain. The equivalence of complex and real channels will be used in the video decoder.

Let h be the channel gain of a particular complex subchannel, and x and y be the transmitted and received complex symbols, respectively. Ignore the channel noise for now and we can write the received symbol as $y = hx + n$ in complex values, or

$$\begin{pmatrix} Re(y) \\ Im(y) \end{pmatrix} = \begin{pmatrix} Re(h) & -Im(h) \\ Im(h) & Re(h) \end{pmatrix} \begin{pmatrix} Re(x) \\ Im(x) \end{pmatrix} \tag{10.4}$$

in real numbers, where $Re(\cdot)$ and $Im(\cdot)$ indicate the real and imaginary parts of a complex symbol. We can find that the two subchannels for $Re(x)$ and $Im(x)$ have the same channel gain $\sqrt{Re(h)^2 + Im(h)^2}$.

10.3.4 Unequal Error Protection for the Coefficients

ParCast+ provides UEP for the DCT coefficients following three steps: multi-layer source generation, source-subchannel mapping, and joint source-channel power allocation across subchannels. The overall goal of the source-channel mapping is to transmit the more important source components on the high-gain subchannels. We will discuss this in the context of the other two steps.

10.3.4.1 Multi-layer Source Generation

The DCT coefficients of each GOP in ParCast+ are first processed to generate multiple independent layers, the total number of which matches that of the number of subchannels in the MIMO-OFDM link.

Initial chunk division. The coefficients in a GOP are first divided into equal-sized rectangular-shaped chunks, used the same way as SoftCast (Fig. 3 in [19]). The variance, indicating the energy or importance, is computed for each chunk. The coefficients in the same chunk should be coded and transmitted in the same way.

Bandwidth and channel allocation. We can view the available bandwidth and channel resources as a two-dimensional matrix, where each row corresponds to complex symbols on a distinct subchannel sent over time and each column corresponds to an OFDM symbol. The dimension of the matrix is $N_c N_t \times B$, where $N_c N_t$ is the number of subchannels and B is the number of available time slots during the transmission of a GOP. Since every two real-valued DCT coefficients form one complex symbol, we prepare a real-valued data matrix $\mathbf{X}$ with dimension $N_c N_t \times 2B$ for transmission.

The channel allocation step forms matrix $\mathbf{X}_0$, which has the same dimension as $\mathbf{X}$. The reweighting and whitening step, which will be described in the following subsection, will construct $\mathbf{X}$ from $\mathbf{X}_0$. To allocate the channel, we first sort the data chunks in descending order according to their variances. Then we simply take coefficients from successive chunks and fill them into rows of matrix $\mathbf{X}_0$. If there is insufficient bandwidth, the extra elements (the least important coefficients) will be discarded. Conversely, if there is redundant bandwidth, any unfilled position is padded with 0. We refer to the data assigned to each subchannel as a *source layer*, denoted by $\mathbf{x}_0$.

Reweighting and whitening. Reweighting and whitening are performed within each source layer, or over the vector $\mathbf{x}_0$. Typically, each source layer contains coefficients from different initial chunks with different energy. If these energy values differ significantly, it is helpful to reweight the energy levels across the chunks within a layer to help decrease the overall recovery distortion. This is especially the case for the first layer, where the initial chunk variances decrease sharply. As shown in [19], this can be achieved by applying a scaling factor of $\lambda_i^{-1/4}$ for a chunk with variance λ_i. Note that the scaling factors across source layers are independent and separately calculated. If we view each coefficient within the ith chunk as a random variable with variance λ_i, the new per-layer variance λ_k' for the kth layer is the average of the variances of all data within the layer.

The average power per column of the bandwidth matrix after reweighting can vary significantly across columns. Therefore, we mix data within each source layer with a random orthogonal matrix to achieve the same effect as a Hadamard transform[1], such that the average power per OFDM symbol is the same. This also ensures the same average power across transmit antennas and eases the requirement on the dynamic range of the power amplifier at the transmitter.

The power reweighting and whitening process can be written as:

$$\mathbf{x}_r^T = \mathbf{M}\,\mathbf{W}\,\mathbf{x}_0^T, \tag{10.5}$$

where $\mathbf{M}_{2B \times 2B}$ implements per-layer whitening, $\mathbf{W}$ is a diagonal matrix with $2B$ power weights on the diagonal, $\mathbf{x}_0$ is a $1 \times 2B$ row vector representing a source layer, and the subscript T indicates a transpose. The resulting $\mathbf{x}_r$ is also a $1 \times 2B$ row vector, representing a processed source layer. Stacking all the $\mathbf{x}_r$'s, we can form the data matrix $\mathbf{X}$, and data in the same row have the same new variance, λ'.

10.3.4.2 Joint Source-channel Power Allocation

With the precoding operation at the encoder and equalization at the receiver, the MIMO-OFDM channel is separated into a set of orthogonal subchannels. After channel mapping, rows in the data matrix $\mathbf{X}$ will be sent over different subchannels. Taking both source energy and subchannel gain into account, we re-distribute the power among the rows in order to achieve the optimal performance.

The optimization problem in ParCast+ is to minimize the expected mean squared error (MSE) under the transmit power constraint with budget P. Let $\mathbf{x}_c$ be a column of data taken from the matrix $\mathbf{X}$ after channel mapping (i.e., after pre-multiply matrix $\mathbf{R}$). Assuming inverse decoding of $\mathbf{x}_c$, we can formulate the problem as:

$$\min \quad MSE = \sum_i \frac{\sigma^2}{s_i^2 g_i^2}, \tag{10.6}$$

$$\text{subject to:} \quad trace\,E[(\mathbf{G}\mathbf{x}_c)(\mathbf{G}\mathbf{x}_c)^T]$$
$$= \sum_i g_i^2 \lambda_i' \leq P,$$

where σ^2 is the average noise power, s_i is the singular value on subchannel i, and $\mathbf{G}_{N_c N_t \times N_c N_t}$ is the diagonal power weight matrix to be designed, with g_i as its ith diagonal entry. Although we perform precoding at the transmitter, the precoding matrix does not change the total transmission energy, and therefore is omitted in (10.6) for clarity. By using Lagrange multipliers, the solution is:

---

[1] Hadamard matrices can only have certain dimensions while our data can be of arbitrary dimension.

$$g_i = \sqrt{\frac{P}{\sqrt{\lambda_i' s_i^2} \sum_j \sqrt{\lambda_j'/s_j^2}}},\qquad(10.7)$$

and the derived MSE is

$$\frac{\sigma^2}{P}\left(\sum_i \sqrt{\lambda_i'/s_i^2}\right)^2.\qquad(10.8)$$

The MSE (Eq. 10.8) is determined by the mapping of λ' to s, i.e., the matrix $\mathbf{R}$ in Eq. (10.1). By the Rearrangement Inequality [123], the best $\mathbf{R}$ lets the λ_i' follow the same sorted order as s_i. This shows why the source layer with the largest variance should be assigned to the highest-gain subchannel.

Strictly speaking, this is an approximation solution for the case when the optimal LLSE decoder is used, because inverse decoding can magnify the channel noise. When the channel condition is good, however, the two decoders have comparable performance and the optimization of the MSE of inverse decoding is much simpler to solve.

If we re-formulate the optimization using LLSE instead, the derived g_i depends on the channel noise σ^2 [13]. If λ_i'/s_i^2 is too low, the corresponding g_i would be zero in the new optimization result. This means the subchannel and the corresponding source layer should be discarded and their power returned to the overall power budget. This is analogous to the water-filling power allocation strategy in MIMO systems to achieve channel capacity.

The power scaling factors can be calculated per packet to adjust to varying subchannel gain orders due to channel variation. Therefore, we write the encoding and transmission process for each data packet in (10.1). Let T be the number of OFDM symbols in one data packet. Taking $2T$ columns from matrix $\mathbf{X}$, we form a complex data matrix $\mathbf{X}_p$ with dimension $N_c N_t \times T$ that can be transmitted in one packet. In particular, every two adjacent entries in the same source layer form one complex symbol.

10.3.5 Managing Metadata

Source information from the video encoder. In order to undo the power scaling, source-channel mapping, and the MCTF stage, the video decoder needs the motion and chunk energy variance information from the video encoder. This information is compressed using standard variable length coding and sent in a regular digitally modulated packet. Since the information is critical for the recovery quality, we need to ensure error-free transmission of these packets. Currently, we use as many spatial streams as the channel quality permits and always use BPSK and $\frac{1}{2}$ rate convolutional coding for each spatial stream. The bandwidth cost of these packets is always less than 10%.

CSI from the video decoder. The video sender needs to know the channel details to perform the source-subchannel mapping, power distribution, and precoding. Since the WiFi standard 802.11ac and LTE both expect to use channel dependent precoding, it is reasonable to assume the availability of CSI.

Currently, the receiver measures the channel using the regular channel estimation technique, e.g., that for 802.11n data packets. It then feeds the CSI back to the sender in a regular, digitally modulated packet. A CSI update every 100 ms is normally considered acceptable overhead. If there is also traffic from the receiver to the sender, we can leverage channel reciprocity by letting the sender estimate the channel. Hence the CSI update overhead can be easily managed.

Note that the CSI updates in ParCast+ are *cumulative*. Since most packets are precoded, the video receiver will measure a precoded channel, $\mathbf{H}_{measured} = \mathbf{H}_{actual}\,\mathbf{V}_{previous}$. $\mathbf{H}_{measured}$ has the same singular values as the actual channel $\mathbf{H}_{actual}$, so we can assign source layers to subchannels and calculate the power weights directly. However, typically $\mathbf{V}_{actual} \neq \mathbf{V}_{measured}$, so $\mathbf{V}_{measured}$ alone cannot be used as the precoding matrix. We have two options: (1) the sender computes the actual channel as $\mathbf{H}_{actual} = \mathbf{H}_{measured}\,\mathbf{V}^*_{previous}$, and gets $\mathbf{V}_{actual}$ as the new precoding matrix; or (2) the sender gets $\mathbf{V}_{measured}$ from $\mathbf{H}_{measured}$, and uses $\mathbf{V}_{previous}\,\mathbf{V}_{measured}$ as the precoding matrix. Although $\mathbf{V}_{actual} \neq \mathbf{V}_{previous}\,\mathbf{V}_{measured}$ in general, the two sides differ by a multiplication by a unitary block diagonal matrix and achieve the same precoding effect. We have verified both options and are currently using the first one.

10.3.6 The Video Decoder

The decoder receives and decodes the digitally modulated packets following the standard decoding procedures to obtain the variance of coefficient chunks and the motion information.

With each packet containing T OFDM symbols, the ParCast+ decoder forms T length-$2N_cN_t$ real-valued vectors with the received signals on all the spatial and frequency domain subchannels. Let $\mathbf{y}$ denote one such vector and let $\mathbf{x}$ denote the corresponding transmitted vector. The dimension of $\mathbf{x}$ is also $2N_cN_t$, which equals the number of decomposed real channels. Given the linear encoding process, we use the LLSE decoder to recover the coefficients in $\mathbf{x}$, which is the optimal decoder [13]. That is:

$$\hat{\mathbf{x}} = \Lambda \mathbf{C}^T (\mathbf{C}\Lambda\mathbf{C}^T + \Sigma)^{-1}\mathbf{y}, \tag{10.9}$$

where $\mathbf{C}$ is the overall encoder written in real numbers and Σ and Λ are both diagonal matrices. The dimensions of the three matrices are all $2N_cN_t \times 2N_cN_t$. The ith diagonal element of Σ is the channel noise experienced by the packet carrying the ith row of the received $\mathbf{y}$. The $(2i-1)^{th}$ and $2i^{th}$ diagonal element of Λ is λ_i'/s_i^2, where λ_i' is the variance of the ith row of $\mathbf{X}_p$ (complex with dimension $N_cN_t \times 1$) and s_i is the gain on the corresponding subchannel.

After decoding the coefficients, ParCast+ follows the inverse processes for multi-layer source generation, 2D-DCT, and MCTF to reconstruct the frames.

10.4 Implementation

10.4.1 ParCast+ Implementation

We divide the whole system into the application layer video codec and physical layer operations.

At the video sender side, the video encoder performs the MC-based 3D transform, generates source layers from these coefficients, and passes them, as well as the metadata (chunk variances and motion information from MCTF), to the PHY module. The PHY module performs subchannel allocation, power distribution, and precoding, before grouping enough OFDM symbols into individual packets for transmission. In addition, the PHY module on the video sender sends the source metadata digitally and processes the CSI feedback from the video receiver to calculate the SVD of each subcarrier channel matrix.

Note that although we currently implement the entire source encoder at the transmitter, this is not strictly necessary. The motion-aligned 3D transform is independent of the channel and could easily take place on a remote video server connected with a wireless transmitter over the wire. If the server is notified of the available bandwidth, chunk division, bandwidth allocation, per-layer power reweighting and whitening can also be performed remotely, leaving only the PHY operations to be performed at the wireless transmitter.

At the video receiver, the PHY module performs channel estimation, compensation for carrier frequency offsets (CFO), and OFDM pilot phase tracking without compensating for the channel, before passing the received complex samples to the video decoder. It also decodes the digital packets with the source metadata and feeds back the estimated channel matrices to the video sender. The video decoder then finds the LLSE solution of video coefficients and performs the inverse process of source layer generation, DCT and MCTF to reconstruct the video frames.

We use Sora [38] as our experimental platform. Since the current Sora platform can support real-time 20 MHz wideband packet transmission and reception, but not single-device MIMO, we need to emulate MIMO with multiple single-antenna boxes. Due to the pseudo-analog modulation of the transform coefficients, we need to send raw signal samples to the sending nodes separately and copy the received signals from the receiving nodes to one box, both via Ethernet. The latency from moving the samples across the network makes it currently unfeasible to run the whole system in real time. However, since CSI updates can be sent using a single antenna, we can still run the channel dependent components in real time to assess the latency of PHY processing.

Therefore, we currently implement the PHY modules using Sora SDK 1.5 to run in real time. The actual video codec is implemented in MATLAB and interfaces with the PHY module via the generated video data as real values and the received complex samples. The video data packets follow an 802.11n-like packet structure, so that we can leverage the techniques for CFO compensation, channel estimation, and precoding in 802.11n. In contrast to 802.11n, however, the pilot subcarriers for each antenna are used alternately across different OFDM symbols, similar to the approach in [124], so that we can update all the estimated channel coefficients for one transmit antenna per symbol. Noise is estimated from the error vector magnitude of the signal field in the packet preamble, and passed to the video decoder to be plugged into the LLSE decoder.

We also implement a channel simulation that can act in place of the Sora-based PHY modules but replay measured channel traces. This allows us to study a larger variety of channel instances and compare different schemes more easily and fairly.

10.4.2 Schemes for Comparison

ParCast+ was inspired by SoftCast and follows a similar linear codec process. Although SoftCast only exploits source property in its design, it appears to be near optimal for unicast over a single antenna. Therefore, we compare ParCast+ with SoftCast to assess the importance of exploiting the source-channel synergy in MIMO-OFDM systems. Additionally, we compare ParCast+ with a version of omniscient H.264/MPEG-4 [125] over 802.11n-like channel rates (Omni-MPEG), which represents the best possible performance for a conventional scheme with separate source and channel coding.

SoftCast. SoftCast starts with a 3D-DCT and divides the coefficients into chunks. It then reweights the power across the chunks-based on the chunk energy distribution. Next, a Hadamard matrix-based whitening is applied across chunks within a frame, before these coded coefficients are packaged and transmitted over an uncoded MIMO-OFDM channel using pseudo-analog modulation. The decoder performs LLSE decoding to recover the DCT coefficients. The chunk variance information is transmitted the same way as in ParCast+ for a fair comparison.

There are two high-level differences between SoftCast and ParCast+. First, SoftCast adopts 3D-DCT transform to decorrelate the source, while ParCast+ uses MC-based 3D transform. Second, SoftCast does not de-correlate the channel and does not perform precoding, whereas ParCast+ implements channel precoding and specifically optimizes for each subchannel individually. In particular, SoftCast performs Hadamard-based whitening for the DCT coefficients and the mixed coefficients are sequentially mapped to the I and Q components of the complex symbols over each subcarrier. In contrast, ParCast+ de-correlates the channel and incorporates channel details in power allocation.

Omni-MPEG. H.264/MPEG-4 specifies that a sequence of raw frames is encoded into three types of frames. An *I-frame* is an independently compressed still image and it is divided into blocks in encoding. A *P-frame* encodes changes in the image from the previous frame, whereas a *B-frame* includes changes from both the previous and the future frames. Blocks in P- and B-frames are compared to their references to identify the closest matches. The corresponding motion vector and the differences between the matching blocks are stored. The blocks for all kinds of frames then go through DCT transform, quantization, and entropy coding for further compression.

Typically, the source encoder needs to know the expected channel throughput in order to select an appropriate quantization level, and the physical layer transmitter should determine the most suitable bit rate accordingly. We alter the standard MPEG-4 encoding and transmission process to optimally choose the source and channel rates based on the given CSI.

We implement H.264/MPEG-4 based on the reference implementation JM16.1 [126]. The source first generates encoded data under different Quantization Parameter (QP) values. We derive a table of PSNRs under various QPs, the corresponding data stream size and the channel throughput required.

The data is transmitted using 802.11n-like modulation and coding, and we select the channel rate based on the effective SNR of the given channel [100]. Depending on the number of antennas on both sides, a sender can choose between sending 1 to 4 concurrent spatial streams (i.e., packet fragments) at a time. To ensure a good rate, we precode the transmitted streams and allow a different modulation and coding combination for each transmitted spatial stream. This allows a higher overall rate than those provided by unequal modulation across streams in 802.11n [127]. If the worst spatial stream is too weak to support even BPSK, we allocate the power to a stronger spatial stream instead, using a high rate where possible. If any stream is decoded incorrectly, the entire packet is dropped at the receiver and retransmitted.

To compare Omni-MPEG with ParCast+ under the same bandwidth constraint, we select an encoded data size that requires the transmission time closest to ParCast+, look up the proper QP, and use the corresponding PSNR as the performance of Omni-MPEG.

10.5 Evaluation

10.5.1 Experimental Setup

We evaluate the video delivery quality using the standard PSNR metric. Again, we average the PSNR across frames to produce a single value for each video sequence.

Test videos. We select a few representative video sequences [128], including *foreman*, *mobile*, *news*, *bus*, *football*, *soccer*, *tennis*, and *coastguard*. They are in *.cif*, with a frame size of 352×288 pixels. Fig. 10.1 shows the energy distribution of the first frame of some of these. These videos have different motion characteristics, background textures, and energy distributions. For example, *news* has a smooth background and little motion. It is therefore easily compressed with a conventional video codec. *mobile* has many small moving objects and there is continuous movement in the whole scene due to camera movement. *football* and *coastguard* both include large texture areas and complex motion. Consequently, both are challenging cases for conventional compression systems.

We set the GOP size to 8 frames for source processing. We adopt block sizes of 8×8, 8×16, 16×8, and 16×16 pixels as a motion unit in MC process. The search range is 32×32 pixels, and the motion vector precision is $\frac{1}{4}$ pixel. Smaller motion unit sizes like 4×4 are not included, because we have found that such a small size increases the transmission cost for motion information with negligible improvement in the video recovery performance.

When coding coefficients, we divide each video frame into 64 chunks. For a 3×3 link, we could send up to 2 values per complex symbol, 3 symbols per subcarrier, and 52 data subcarriers, or 312 values total in a single 802.11n OFDM symbol. We currently send 300 values in each OFDM symbol and skip the worst 12 subchannels, so that an entire video frame takes about 337 OFDM symbols. For a fair comparison with other schemes, we define the packet size T in terms of the number of OFDM symbols and we set $T = 33$.

Sora setup. We use four single-antenna Sora boxes to emulate a 2×2 MIMO link in an indoor environment, and move the antennas to different locations to get different channel instances. The carrier frequencies of all four radios are configured to be within a few hundred Hz of one another. This is the precision we can achieve given the configuration tool, and we have verified that pilot tracking can correct residual CFO between each transmit-receive pair sufficiently well. We calibrate the CPU clocks of all the boxes offline and use a SourceSync [124]-like approach to achieve synchronized transmissions from the two transmit antennas.

While the current experimental evaluation is not real-time due to Sora's lack of MIMO capabilities, we believe that we can carry out real-time experiments in the near future with the fast development of software radio platforms.

Channel traces. We use two sets of channel traces of 3×3 802.11n MIMO-OFDM links from previous work [100] for trace-driven simulations, one including around 120 stationary links and the other a mobile trace. These were collected on commodity Intel `iwl5300` NICs in an indoor environment. Fig. 10.2 shows the squared singular value distributions for example links. The average SNR for the stationary link (9 11) is 27.87dB, and the average SNR for the stationary link (9 12) is 22.42dB. For the mobile link, the average SNR is about 25.46dB.

For each stationary trace, there is one packet approximately every 6 ms. Our experiments show that the results differ mainly in whether there is a CSI feedback delay and are not sensitive to the delay period. Therefore, we simply present the results for one-packet delay, or around 6 ms. For the mobile trace, we select a CSI sample approximately every 10 ms to ensure channel variation.

10.5.2 ParCast+ Microbenchmarks

We run a few benchmarks to assess the individual contribution of the operations of ParCast+, including MC in source decorrelation, channel precoding, UEP, and pseudo-analog modulation. We choose two representative 3×3 channel traces for stationary links (9 11) and (9 12), which feature a very small and large spread of squared singular values, respectively. We will also assess the effects of inaccurate CSI.

In general, the amount of CSI inaccuracy due to delayed CSI and its effects on the channel-dependent components depends on the channel characteristics. For the most common scenario with stationary links, CSI inaccuracy is mainly caused by estimation noise and precision errors. For the mobile trace, inaccurate CSI is due to changing channels.

The precoding and UEP operations depend on the SVD of the channel matrix. With inaccurate CSI, precoding is unable to entirely decorrelate spatial streams and the effective subchannel gains cannot be estimated correctly. This makes the source-channel matching and the joint power allocation suboptimal. Detailed discussion about the impact of CSI accuracy on these operations will be combined with the system benchmarks in this subsection. For other experiments, delayed CSI is used, unless otherwise stated.

Motion compensation. Softcast and our previous scheme ParCast both use 3D-DCT, while ParCast+ adopts MCTF+2D-DCT (referred to as M+2D subsequently). Table 10.1 shows that ParCast+ with M+2D often outperforms ParCast+ with 3D-DCT, by 1.49 dB in PSNR on average and up to 3.20 dB for sequence *mobile*. However, the 3D-DCT version of ParCast+ performs better for *football*.

Table 10.1 Comparison between ParCast+ with M+2D and 3D-DCT

Video	Bandwidth Ratio		PSNR (9 11)		PSNR (9 12)	
	M+2D	3D-DCT	M+2D	3D-DCT	M+2D	3D-DCT
foreman	5.79%	2.44%	52.38	50.91	45.97	44.33
mobile	5.33%	3.38%	48.63	45.72	41.68	38.19
news	2.80%	1.82%	53.93	52.52	49.40	47.63
bus	9.17%	3.19%	49.22	46.95	42.58	39.85
football	14.75%	2.40%	49.97	50.81	43.66	44.60
soccer	8.29%	2.28%	52.40	51.62	46.05	45.49
tennis	6.57%	2.86%	50.24	49.07	43.97	42.08
coastguard	4.94%	2.50%	52.26	50.63	45.89	44.01

From a pure source coding perspective, M+2D is normally considered more effective for exploiting inter-frame correlation and usually can better compact the source energy, i.e., the energy in the frame is more concentrated in the lowest frequency bands. However, the MC process also produces motion vectors, which need to be transmitted to the video decoder, too. As shown in Table 10.1, the proportion of bandwidth needed to transmit all metadata from the video source increases from 2.61% to 7.21% on average due to the transmission of the motion information. For the overall video delivery quality, therefore, whether MC is worthwhile depends on the trade-off between energy compaction quality and the bandwidth consumption of the motion information.

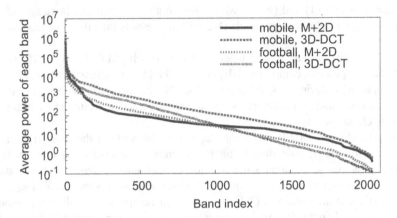

Fig. 10.5 The chunk energy distribution of coefficients in the first 4 GOPs for video *mobile* and *football*.

For sequences with little motion, M+2D produces little motion information and coefficients of a similar energy distribution to those after 3D-DCT. Therefore, the overall recovery PSNR is comparable using either source decorrelation approach. For videos with high but translational motion, such as *mobile* and *bus*, MC across frames could significantly improve the energy compaction of the coefficients (Fig. 10.5). Using M+2D then is more likely to produce a higher PSNR. *football* has fast and complex motion, and the energy compaction property of its coefficients could not be improved much with MC. Worse, the motion information is difficult to compress and its transmission would consume a great deal of bandwidth. As a result, 3D-DCT works better for this sequence.

Ideally, we would design a system to support both M+2D and 3D-DCT, and adapt between the two source decorrelation methods dynamically based on the motion characteristics of the video at hand. However, given M+2D performs better for most natural videos, we do not incorporate the source-based adaptation in ParCast+ to simplify the design.

Channel precoding. We compare between ParCast+ with and without channel precoding. Even without precoding, we can still calculate the gains of the correlated spatial subchannels [100] and permute the source layers to match them. Fig. 10.6(a) and Fig. 10.6(b) show that we cannot use the channel effectively without precoding whether we get accurate CSI. Although we only show the results for source *mobile* and *football*, the performances for the other six sequences are similar.

Without precoding, the signals on different spatial subchannels of the same subcarrier will interfere with each other and on average the performance drops by

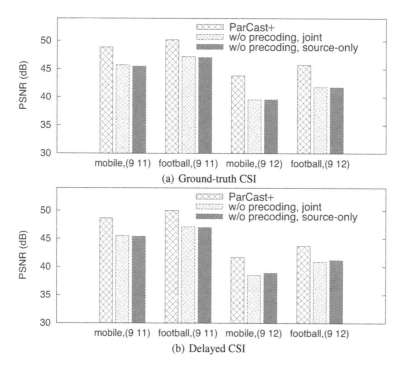

Fig. 10.6 Effects of channel precoding over MIMO.

about 3.58 dB. It should be noted that the matching is performed differently with and without precoding, so the figures show the combined effects of the various system components. Furthermore, when there is no precoding, it makes little difference whether we consider the channel for power allocation. Further simulation results show that performing precoding is still much better than not precoding at all for the mobile trace, whether with accurate or delayed CSI.

Unequal error protection. In this section, we examine the importance of source-channel matching, joint source-channel power allocation, and reweighting as part of source layer generation.

Fig. 10.7(a) and Fig. 10.7(b) show the performance comparison between ParCast+ with and without matching, given the ground-truth CSI and delayed CSI, respectively. Without matching indicates that the source layers are simply allocated to the subchannels in a random order. The comparison shows that as much as 7.18 dB in PSNR can be attributed to matching when joint power allocation is performed. Even for source-only power allocation, matching is still clearly beneficial. For stationary links, even with channel estimation noise, it is likely that the subchannel order will only be slightly wrong, so matching is little affected. When the channel details might be completely wrong due to mobility, matching

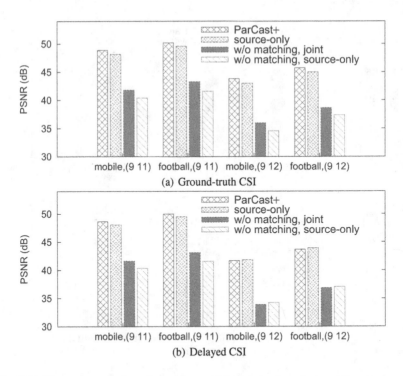

Fig. 10.7 Effects of source-channel matching and joint source-channel power allocation.

is statistically the same as not matching in the worst case. Otherwise there is always a benefit, so matching should always be done for both stationary and mobile links.

In Fig. 10.7(a) and Fig. 10.7(b), we also compare the performance between ParCast+ with joint power allocation and with source-only power allocation. Recall that a source layer and subchannel pair is discarded if its λ_i'/s_i^2 is too low (Section 10.3.4.2), hence joint power allocation can skip the worst subchannels at low SNR. With ground-truth CSI, joint power allocation outperforms the source-only approach by 0.60 to 0.82 dB. The more diverse the subchannels, the more valuable joint power allocation appears for different links. When there is a CSI delay, the larger the singular value spread, the larger the effect of inaccurate CSI. For example, joint power allocation is still helpful with CSI delay for link (9 11) but incurs a slight PSNR loss for link (9 12). Further experiments show that for the mobile trace, source-only power allocation is better than the joint approach, while the joint approach is helpful if the link is mostly stationary.

Finally, we compare between ParCast+ with and without the per-row source layer reweighting. The reweighting gain in our simulation ranges from 0.10 dB to 0.32 dB for different videos. The gain is insignificant because only two or three initial chunks are involved in each layer under our system setting. The reweighting step would be more useful for a larger GOP size, such that each layer may contain data from several initial chunks.

Summary. As we saw in previous discussions, motion compensation is helpful for better source decorrelation and is unaffected by CSI accuracy. Channel precoding and source-channel matching are very important components of ParCast+, whose contribution is much larger than joint power allocation in UEP. When considering the effects of CSI inaccuracy in practice, we always use precoding and perform source-channel matching. The joint power allocation is only utilized for stationary links, and the source-only power allocation is used for more dynamic channels.

10.5.3 Comparison against Alternative Schemes

We next compare ParCast+, SoftCast and OMNI-MPEG for different videos and channel conditions. The comparison between ParCast+ and ParCast is made over two typical stationary links. The setting of ParCast+ is chosen according to the type of channels and matches the summary in the previous subsection.

Stationary links. We first study the performance of all three schemes over all stationary 3×3 links, with delayed CSI feedback. This represents the most common scenario. Channel precoding is assumed for both ParCast+ and OMNI-MPEG but not SoftCast, since our previous work [101] showed that directly adding channel precoding to SoftCast had a negligible effect.

Fig. 10.8 shows ParCast+ often achieves a much higher PSNR than SoftCast for all sequences over all links. Note that we set the maximum PSNR value to 55 dB. Moreover, the performance of ParCast+ improves more quickly with the channel quality than SoftCast. This is mainly because ParCast+ optimizes the performance on individual subchannels, whereas SoftCast treats the channel as a whole. Furthermore, SoftCast includes a Hadamard transform to even out the energy between different packets, which actually mixes together the source layers with unequal importance. This correlation at the source eventually manifests as a correlation at the channel [101]. Effectively, Hadamard acts as *random* precoding, which is statistically equivalent to not precoding at all [129]. This also precludes source-channel matching. As we evaluated previously, precoding and source-channel matching are important for ParCast+, and the system performance degrades significantly without them.

ParCast+ often outperforms OMNI-MPEG except for *news*, *foreman*, and *tennis* over some low SNR links. When averaging over all links, OMNI-MPEG slightly outperforms ParCast+ only for the fairly compressible video *news* among these test sequences. For each of the other sequences, ParCast+ achieves more than 5 dB PSNR improvement on average and the gain is as high as 8.7 dB for video *coastguard*.

For several stationary traces with low SNR, OMNI-MPEG performs better for the sequences *news*, *foreman*, and *tennis* by adopting high compression ratios combined with strong channel coding, since these three sequences have relatively high compressibility at low bitrates. In contrast, ParCast+ uses pseudo-analog transmission and cannot efficiently overcome the channel noise by discarding subchannels.

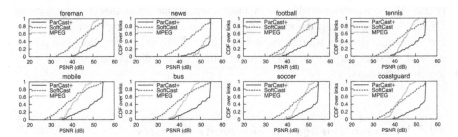

Fig. 10.8 PSNR for ParCast+, SoftCast and H.264 for all stationary traces.

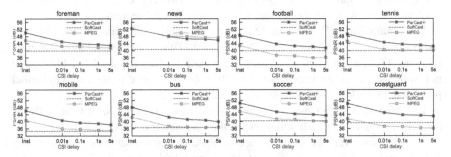

Fig. 10.9 PSNR for ParCast+ vs MPEG and SoftCast given different CSI delay.

For the traces with higher SNR, the high source compression capability of OMNI-MPEG becomes less valuable. In contrast, the pseudo-analog modulation approach in ParCast+ is very helpful in MIMO-OFDM situations to fully utilize the diverse channel gains without much overhead. Otherwise, the transmitter would also need to signal to the receiver how to demodulate each subchannel, and even a FARA [130]-like scheme may not work well. With delayed CSI, precoding would not be able to entirely decorrelate the spatial streams and could cause modulation selection to be too optimistic for Omni-MPEG.

Mobility case. We next compare the three schemes using the mobile trace. For OMNI-MPEG with SVD-based precoding, delayed CSI could cause modulation selection to be too optimistic and eventually inaccurate modulation selection would cause decoding errors. Hence, no precoding is adopted for MPEG.

We consider CSI delay periods of 0 (No delay), 1 packet (10 ms), 10 packets (100 ms), 100 packets (around 1 s), and 500 packets (around 5 s). To reduce the randomness of the error between the available CSI and the ground truth for large

CSI delay periods, we run the simulations over four different parts of the mobile trace and report the average performances.

Fig. 10.9 summarizes the results. The error margin is about ±0.5 dB for MPEG and ±0.9 dB for ParCast+ for any delay period. As expected, SoftCast has a flat performance curve since it does not utilize the CSI information. While the performance of both schemes degrades with increasing CSI delay, the degradation stabilizes around 1s delay. The reason is that once the delay becomes sufficiently large, the error between the available and the ground-truth CSI becomes random, and the average PSNR value over the whole transmission becomes independent of the exact CSI delay. This is why we have not considered delay periods longer than 5 seconds, and the performance degradation with delayed CSI is not strictly monotonic when the delay period becomes large.

We find that compared with OMNI-MPEG, the performance of ParCast+ degrades more with CSI delay due to inaccurate precoding, especially for the sequences *foreman* and *tennis*. On the other hand, OMNI-MPEG without precoding cannot benefit much from the accurate CSI information in the case of no delay. Among these sequences, only *news* favors OMNI-MPEG, and the largest gain is less than 1.4 dB.

10.6 Summary

ParCast+ is motivated by non-uniform energy distribution at both the source and the channel. It divides the source into layers with unequal energy and sends them on independent subchannels, with the more important layers on higher-gain subchannels, joint source-channel power allocation, and pseudo-analog modulation to optimally leverage source redundancy for error protection at the channel. We have shown that such a design can significantly outperform conventional digital schemes by turning challenging MIMO-OFDM links into opportunities.

Chapter 11
Compressive Sampling Code

11.1 Introduction

A broadcast system suffers from heterogeneous channel conditions across receivers. To ensure reception by all, the performance of a conventional system is always constrained by the worst channel. This would be exacerbated in MIMO-based systems, where devices may be equipped with different numbers of antennas. We refer to this as receive antenna heterogeneity. Fig. 11.1 shows an example. The base station can send two concurrent streams that are either distinct, to achieve a higher rate, or duplicate, for better reliability. The former is only possible if the receiver also has two antennas. If we design a system based on B1's higher rate capability, the single-antenna users (1-ant RXs) A1 and A2 may get no information. Conversely, some of B1's channel capacity would be wasted. Ideally, we need one strategy so that both types of users can derive information of a quality commensurate with the antenna setting and the channel SNR.

Some previous work has considered channel SNR heterogeneity or antenna heterogeneity, but not both. Hierarchical modulation (HM) [65, 11] and Softcast [131, 19] consider SNR heterogeneity for single-antenna systems. The latter achieves smooth rate increase with the channel SNR through a linear codec design, where the transmitted signal strength is proportional to the source magnitude. However, its decoder expects a near full-rank matrix, or the performance would degrade significantly. Therefore, it cannot be readily extended to address antenna heterogeneity. Diversity embedded space time codes [132] do address antenna heterogeneity. The scheme separates the source into layers of different priorities, and superimposes different layers in each transmission. Each receiver derives an amount of information matching its antenna number. Various superimposed MIMO codes have also been designed for cooperative channels [133], 2×1 MIMO [134] and 2×2 MIMO systems [135]. In these schemes, the strong users are expected to decode both layers of data with the help of relay nodes or good channel conditions, with weak users only able to derive the base layer. As with HM, however, only a few discrete levels of recovery quality can be achieved, and

DOI: 10.1201/9781003118688-11

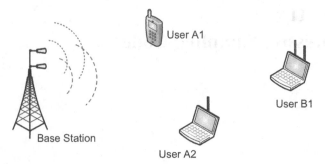

Fig. 11.1 A MIMO broadcast system with receiver antenna heterogeneity.

the bandwidth of the weak receivers is reduced by the transmission of low-priority data. To the best of our knowledge, no existing system addresses both dimensions of heterogeneity simultaneously.

In this chapter, we present a compressive broadcast framework which layers compressive sensing (CS) over MIMO transmissions to simultaneously address the two types of heterogeneity. This framework is applicable to compressible multimedia content where CS helps solve an under-determined linear system. The sender transmits linear combinations, or measurements, of raw signals instead of the quantized and digitized bits. The received measurement number depends on the number of receive antennas, whereas the measurement quality reflects the channel SNR. Consequently the recovery quality or the perceived rate scales with the antenna number and the channel SNR.

We show through analysis and simulations that the MIMO channel does not invalidate CS recovery. The rate in our framework approaches a linear increase with the per-antenna channel SNR for a fixed number of antennas, and the rate gap between receivers with different numbers of antennas approaches a constant for fixed SNRs regardless of the number of transmitted symbols. More importantly, extensive simulations indicate that our framework is capable of simultaneously achieving higher rates for multi-ant RXs and better reliability for 1-ant RXs.

11.2 Compressive Image Broadcasting

We propose an uncoded image delivery scheme over MIMO links with receiver antenna heterogeneity as shown in Fig. 11.1. The base station is equipped with two antennas, i.e., $n_t = 2$, and single-antenna and two-antenna receivers coexist, i.e., $n_r = 1$ or $n_r = 2$. For simplicity, we will refer to such a setup as a $2 \times \{1, 2\}$ MIMO system throughout this chapter. We assume the number of available time slots is $T = N/4$ to transmit an image of size $N = W \times H$ in this scheme.

Fig. 11.2 depicts a block diagram of our proposed compressive image broadcasting scheme. There are four steps on the encoder side: DWT transform,

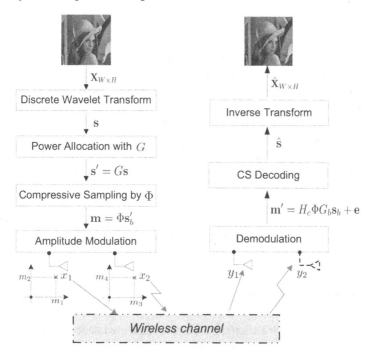

Fig. 11.2 Block diagram of the compressive image broadcasting scheme.

power allocation, compressive sampling to generate measurements, and amplitude modulation and transmission of the measurements. The main decoding steps are CS decoding and inverse transform.

The power allocation strategy and the CS module combine to address CSNR heterogeneity and receiver antenna heterogeneity simultaneously. Our power allocation strategy adjusts the source data so that the subsequent CS module is more effective, specifically tuning the performance trade-off between receivers with varying antenna numbers.

CS theory makes it feasible to decode under-determined systems at single-antenna users, as shown when we previously proved that the MIMO channel would not invalidate CS recovery [136]. On the other hand, multi-antenna receivers are able to benefit from additional antennas via higher rates, because the CS recovery quality scales with the number of received measurements. Furthermore, the lower the noise level in each measurement, the higher the CS decoding performance. With the antenna setting determining the number of received measurements, and the CSNR governing the quality of each measurement, the overall recovery quality will then be simultaneously in line with the antenna number and the CSNR.

11.3 Sender Design

The encoder first transforms the image to the frequency domain to remove the spatial correlation of the raw image using DWT, as in the JPEG2000 standard [7]. We use orthogonal Daubechies wavelets [137] as the DWT basis, with a filter length of 8 and decomposition level $L = 5$. Next, the encoder redistributes power across the DWT coefficients of different frequency bands. The scaled coefficients are then divided into a number of base vectors for the compressive sampling stage, from which measurements are generated by using a Hadamard sensing matrix. Finally, the measurements are directly transmitted as real (I) or imaginary (Q) components of complex wireless signals instead of being quantized and digitized. A distinct complex symbol is sent from each transmit antenna via spatial multiplexing. The per-chunk variance information is also broadcasting to all receivers as metadata, but through a reliable digital modulation and coding scheme.

11.3.1 Power Allocation

Since we transmit the DWT coefficient via amplitude modulation, the energy carried in a coefficient can serve as protection at the channel to guard against noise. Therefore, transmit power allocation directly affects the reconstructed image's quality. In particular, we need to adjust the relative power differences between the coefficients of different frequency bands. This is essential for two reasons. First, the energy of DWT coefficients is concentrated in low-frequency bands. If the coefficients are transmitted verbatim without any power redistribution, low-frequency coefficients would consume most of the transmit power, so much so that high-frequency coefficients would be left with very little power budget. Second, receivers with different capabilities would favor different power allocation strategies. Since we target a heterogeneous broadcast system with diverse antenna settings, we need to balance the reconstruction performance of all types of users with a single scheme. This is a distinctive feature of our scheme.

It has been proven that, for a SISO (single-input single-output) AWGN channel and a linear decoder, linear scaling proportional to $\lambda^{-1/4}$ achieves optimal performance under the mean square error (MSE) criterion [13], [19]. Here, λ denotes the variance of the random variable representing the transform coefficients. Although this works well for SoftCast, it is suboptimal for our scheme for two reasons. First, the optimality of a power allocation scheme depends on the decoding algorithm. Unlike SoftCast, our scheme adopts CS decoding instead of LLSE. Second, since single-antenna and two-antenna users coexist in our target broadcasting scheme, the power allocation strategy should balance the achievable multiplexing capability of two-antenna users and the diversity benefit for single-antenna users.

Let us first provide some intuition to this problem. The purpose of power allocation is to adjust the compressibility of the DWT coefficients **s**. The parameter

p dominates the degree to which the signal $\mathbf{s}$ is compressible. Therefore, we limit our discussion to scaling operations in which the power scaling factors are exponential functions of the coefficients, or mathematically:

$$g_i = C_1 \cdot s_i^{2\alpha}, \tag{11.1}$$

where g_i is the scaling factor for coefficient s_i, and C_1 is a constant to ensure that the allocated power satisfies the total transmit power constraint. The constant 2 in the exponent is included so that α can be compared directly to its counterpart in SoftCast.

Since we have assumed that the compressibility parameter of the wavelet coefficients $\mathbf{s}$ is p, the scaled coefficient s_i' after power adjustment is:

$$|s_i'| = g_i \cdot |s_i| = C_1 \cdot |s_i|^{1+2\alpha} \lesssim C_1 \cdot C_0^{1+2\alpha} \cdot i^{-\frac{1}{p/(1+2\alpha)}}. \tag{11.2}$$

The compressibility parameter now becomes $p/(1 + 2\alpha)$. Since a smaller p indicates higher compressibility, a positive α improves compressibility and a negative α does the opposite. From a channel protection perspective, on the other hand, a larger α tends to provide more protection to low-frequency bands. Conversely, the smaller the α value, the better protected the high-frequency bands.

From Eq. (11.2), we can see that setting $\alpha = -1/2$ means flattening out all coefficients, and setting $\alpha = 0$ means transmitting the coefficients as they are. In SoftCast, α is selected to be $-1/4$, which sets larger power scaling factors for high-frequency coefficients to avoid overprotecting the low-frequency bands. In our scheme, however, two types of receivers have different preferences. In particular, two-antenna users receive as many CS measurements as the number of unknown coefficients. They prefer a power scaling factor that properly amplifies high-frequency coefficients as in SoftCast, while single-antenna users only receive half of the CS measurements and would prefer a larger α which suppresses the high-frequency coefficients, because those coefficients cannot be decoded anyway. Therefore, the best α that optimizes the entire multicast performance would depend on the proportion of the two types of receivers. In our design, we simply assume an equal number of single-antenna and two-antenna receivers, and choose α based on extensive simulations. We finally select $\alpha = -1/8$ which strikes a good balance for system performance. More detailed simulation results will be presented in the next section.

A practical problem arises as the power scaling parameters need to be reliably transmitted to the receivers. If we select unique scaling factors for each of the coefficients and transmit them all, it immediately makes our scheme a trivial design at a huge overhead, because all s_i can be directly computed from the scaling factors. Fortunately, it has been shown [19] that adjacent coefficients in the same frequency band can be viewed as samples of the same zero-mean Gaussian distributed random variable. Therefore, we can group the coefficients into chunks and perform power scaling on a per-chunk basis. All coefficients in the same chunk share the same scaling factor g_i, in the computing of which the s_i^2 in (11.1) will be replaced by the

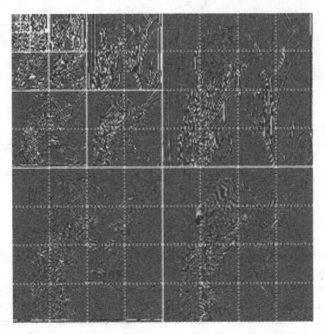

Fig. 11.3 Pyramidal structure of 5-level wavelet decomposition and chunk division for *Lena*.

variance of chunk i, denoted by λ_i. Then, the variance information used to calculate scaling factors is broadcasting to all receivers through a reliable modulation and coding scheme.

Obviously, smaller chunks allow for finer-grained adjustment, but they will incur higher overhead when transmitting metadata. We find that using 70 chunks achieves a good trade-off between overhead and performance gain. The variance metadata are quantized into integers and then encoded by Exponential-Golomb codes. After this step, they are transmitted using 1/2 rate channel coding, QPSK and STBC. The chunk division details are shown in Fig. 11.3. The 10 upper left wavelet bands correspond to 10 chunks, while each of the remaining 6 bands is split into several chunks of equal size. The chunks in the upper left corner are smaller than the others because there are fewer coefficients in the lowest-frequency band, and coefficients from different frequency bands should not be mixed into the same chunk.

In summary, in the power allocation module, the DWT coefficients are divided into 70 chunks, and the transmit power is allocated among these chunks according to their variance. The matrix representation of the power allocation process is:

$$\mathbf{s}' = \mathbf{Gs}, \qquad (11.3)$$

where G is a diagonal power weight matrix with diagonal elements g_i defined in Eq. (11.1), while $\mathbf{s}$ and $\mathbf{s}'$ are the image coefficient vectors before and after power scaling.

11.3.2 Compressive Sampling and Transmission

After power allocation, the CS sampling module generates measurements through linear projections. However, the number of DWT coefficients to represent an image is usually in the hundreds of thousands. Performing CS sampling and decoding on such a large vector is impractical. Since coefficients in the same chunk have the same statistical characteristics, we may form short vectors with the same compressibility characteristic by taking one element from each chunk.

However, due to the wavelet transform, not all chunks are the same size. We tackle this problem with an approximation. In particular, we merge the 7 upper left bands into one sampling chunk, while still computing and transmitting the variance for each band separately, and retain the other 63 chunks. As such, we form 64 new chunks of equal size. Since CS decoding favors a larger source dimension for better recovery performance [138], we generate compressible source vectors of length 256 by taking 4 coefficients from each chunk at a time. $n = 256$ is chosen to strike a balance between good recovery performance and decoding complexity.

Let s_b' be one such source vector of length n and s_b be the corresponding vector before power allocation. Therefore $s_b' = G_b s_b$ where G_b is the corresponding submatrix of G. Then we can obtain the linear projections m_i of s_b' by:

$$\mathbf{m} = (m_1, m_2, \ldots, m_n)^T = \Phi s_b', \tag{11.4}$$

where Φ is an $n \times n$ sensing matrix.

To ensure information capture capability and CS decoding performance, Φ should satisfy some requirements, such as the restricted isometry property (RIP) and mutual coherence [139], [140]. The most commonly used sensing matrix ensembles, such as random Gaussian matrices and Hadamard matrices, have normalized or approximately normalized columns. This means that the transmit power distribution among different coefficients will not be changed in the sampling process. We use a Hadamard sampling matrix in the proposed scheme. It has been shown [141], [142] that a Hadamard sampling matrix has the same desirable properties and comparable recovery performance as the optimal random Gaussian matrix ensemble, but allows us to generate measurements at a lower complexity. It is known that using the Hadamard sampling matrix may impose some constraints on the size of the source vector. We circumvent this problem by dividing the image coefficients into length-256 vectors according to the method described above.

Since the measurements generated after the power allocation and linear sampling steps are compact and resilient representations of the original coefficients, further channel coding, such as that defined in the conventional 802.11 PHY layer, is not necessary. Instead, pairs of these linear projections are directly mapped to the I and Q components of the complex signal to be transmitted. This is the same pseudo-analog modulation as proposed in SoftCast. Each transmit antenna at the base station sends out a distinct complex symbol.

Mathematically, the sender transmits x_1^t and x_2^t on the two antennas in the tth time slot, where

$$x_1^t = m_{4t-3} + j\, m_{4t-2},$$
$$x_2^t = m_{4t-1} + j\, m_{4t}. \tag{11.5}$$

For each source vector with length n, the sender generates n measurements and takes $T_0 = n/4$ time slots to transmit them.

11.4 Receiver Design

At the receiver, the real and imaginary parts of the complex symbol on each antenna are separated and collected into the overall measurement vector. Regular MIMO decoding is skipped, and the original coefficients per vector are recovered via a weighted l_1-minimization CS decoder with the help of the variance metadata. The raw image is then reconstructed from the coefficients through an inverse DWT.

11.4.1 CS Decoder

For each receiver, the received signal quality is determined by the matrix channel defined by the n_t transmit antennas and n_r receiver antennas. Within the broadcasting scheme, the source transmission strategy is independent of the exact channel details between the sender and any receiver, and we assume such knowledge is not available to the sender. However, the receivers can normally obtain such knowledge through the frame preamble. Let H^t be the $n_r \times n_t$ channel matrix in the tth time slot, and each matrix element $h_{i,j}^t$ denotes the path gain from transmit antenna j to receiver antenna i.

For a single-antenna receiver, or a 2×1 case, the path gain from the two transmit antennas to the receiver antenna are $h_{1,1}^t$ and $h_{1,2}^t$ respectively in the tth time slot. Then the received signal y^t in the tth time slot is:

$$y^t = h_{1,1}^t x_1^t + h_{1,2}^t x_2^t + e^t, \tag{11.6}$$

where e^t is the Gaussian noise. From y^t, the receiver obtains two new measurements:

$$\begin{pmatrix} m_{2t-1}' \\ m_{2t}' \end{pmatrix} = H_{2\times 1}^t \begin{pmatrix} m_{4t-3} \\ m_{4t-2} \\ m_{4t-1} \\ m_{4t} \end{pmatrix} + \begin{pmatrix} \Re(e^t) \\ \Im(e^t) \end{pmatrix}. \tag{11.7}$$

Matrix $H_{2\times 1}^t$ can be written as:

$$H_{2\times 1}^t = \begin{pmatrix} \Re(h_{1,1}^t) & -\Im(h_{1,1}^t) & \Re(h_{1,2}^t) & -\Im(h_{1,2}^t) \\ \Im(h_{1,1}^t) & \Re(h_{1,1}^t) & \Im(h_{1,2}^t) & \Re(h_{1,2}^t) \end{pmatrix}. \tag{11.8}$$

where $\Re(\cdot)$ and $\Im(\cdot)$ are the real and imaginary parts of a complex number.

For two-antenna receivers, or 2×2 cases, each receiver derives four new measurements per time slot, 2 on each antenna:

$$\begin{pmatrix} m'_{4t-3} \\ m'_{4t-2} \\ m'_{4t-1} \\ m'_{4t} \end{pmatrix} = H^t_{2\times 2} \begin{pmatrix} m_{4t-3} \\ m_{4t-2} \\ m_{4t-1} \\ m_{4t} \end{pmatrix} + \begin{pmatrix} \Re(e^t_1) \\ \Im(e^t_1) \\ \Re(e^t_2) \\ \Im(e^t_2) \end{pmatrix}, \tag{11.9}$$

where the matrix $H^t_{2\times 2}$ can be written as:

$$H^t_{2\times 2} = \begin{pmatrix} \Re(h^t_{1,1}) & -\Im(h^t_{1,1}) & \Re(h^t_{1,2}) & -\Im(h^t_{1,2}) \\ \Im(h^t_{1,1}) & \Re(h^t_{1,1}) & \Im(h^t_{1,2}) & \Re(h^t_{1,2}) \\ \Re(h^t_{2,1}) & -\Im(h^t_{2,1}) & \Re(h^t_{2,2}) & -\Im(h^t_{2,2}) \\ \Im(h^t_{2,1}) & \Re(h^t_{2,1}) & \Im(h^t_{2,2}) & \Re(h^t_{2,2}) \end{pmatrix}. \tag{11.10}$$

After T_0 time slots, the single-antenna receiver gets $2T_0$ new measurements. Stacking these new measurements to form a vector $\mathbf{m}_1$:

$$\mathbf{m}_1 = \begin{pmatrix} H^1_{2\times 1} & 0 & \cdots & 0 \\ 0 & H^2_{2\times 1} & \cdots & 0 \\ \vdots & \vdots & \ddots & \vdots \\ 0 & 0 & \cdots & H^{T_0}_{2\times 1} \end{pmatrix} \begin{pmatrix} m_1 \\ m_2 \\ \vdots \\ m_{4T_0-1} \\ m_{4T_0} \end{pmatrix} + \mathbf{e}$$

$$= H_c \Phi \mathbf{s}'_b + \mathbf{e}$$

$$= H_c \Phi G_b \mathbf{s}_b + \mathbf{e}. \tag{11.11}$$

The two-antenna receiver gets $4T_0$ new measurements, and the measurement vector $\mathbf{m}_2$ can be represented similarly.

For both types of users, the conventional MIMO decoding at the channel is skipped, and the receiver collects the raw signal samples for the measurements across all of its antennas over T_0 time slots. Decoding over many slots permits CS operations over a much larger matrix than a typical MIMO channel matrix, whose dimension is far too small to satisfy CS requirements.

Since the variance information can be sent to the decoder as metadata, we adopt the weighted l_1-minimization decoder [143], instead of the standard l_1-minimization for better recovery performance. Define $w_i = 1/\sqrt{\lambda_i}$, where λ_i is the known variance of the ith source element at the decoder. Then the minimization problem for decoding the source vector $\mathbf{s}_b$ is:

$$\hat{\mathbf{s}}_b = \min_{\mathbf{s}_b \in \mathbb{R}^n} \|W\mathbf{s}_b\|_{l_1} \quad s.t. \|\mathbf{m}_1 - H_c \Phi G_b \mathbf{s}_b\| < \varepsilon, \tag{11.12}$$

where W is the diagonal matrix with w_i on the diagonal and ε represents the noise power at the receiver.

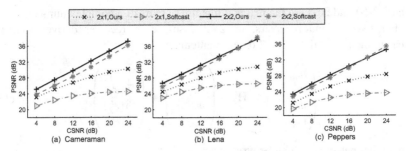

Fig. 11.4 Our scheme vs. SoftCast using images *Cameraman*, *Lena*, and *Peppers* under different CSNRs.

The weighted l_1-minimization decoding problem for two-antenna users can be presented similarly. As we stated before, $T_0 = n/4$ time slots are needed to transmit each source vector. Therefore, the problem to be solved for single-antenna users is under-determined, and the CS decoding algorithm based on Eq. (11.12) is quite efficient. Although the linear system for two-antenna users has full rank, we find that the performance of the weighted l_1-minimization based CS decoder matches that of the optimal linear decoder LLSE.

11.5 Simulation Evaluation

In this section, we compare our proposed scheme with representatives of two classes of broadcast schemes. One reference scheme is SoftCast, which adopts a similar analog framework and was originally designed for SISO broadcast. We extend it to MIMO settings and adopt a spatial multiplexing-based MIMO transmission to transmit the Hadamard whitened linear projections. The other class encompasses conventional digital schemes that adopt layered source-channel schemes.

In line with our previous description, we mainly focus on the $2 \times \{1, 2\}$ MIMO setting and will discuss cases with more antennas later. Block Rayleigh fading channel with perfect receiver CSI is assumed if not otherwise stated. For clarity and without loss of generality, we assume that the two receiver antennas of two-antenna users have the same average per receiver antenna SNR. The recovery performance is evaluated using the standard objective measure PSNR.

11.5.1 Comparison with SoftCast

SoftCast implements power allocation with $\alpha = -1/4$ and adopts LLSE decoding for all receivers. Fig. 11.4 shows the comparison between our scheme and SoftCast when transmitting the three test images. Not surprisingly, our scheme achieves significant gains of up to 4.96 dB over SoftCast for single-antenna users. Meanwhile, our scheme does not incur any performance degradation for two-antenna users. For test image *Cameraman*, our scheme even achieves a 1 dB gain in 2×2 cases because DWT compacts energy much better than frame-based DCT for this image. This comparison clearly demonstrates the importance of power allocation and weighted CS decoding in a MIMO broadcast system with antenna heterogeneity.

11.5.2 Comparison with Conventional Digital Schemes

We compare our scheme with two layered source-channel schemes. They adopt the same layered source coding but different MIMO transmission strategies.

In these two schemes, the state-of-the-art image codec JPEG2000 [6] is used to generate a layered source. A (204,188) short Reed-Solomon code is employed as suggested by the DVB-H standard. The encoded bit stream is then divided into the base layer and the enhancement layer. The encoded packets of both layers are subjected to convolutional coding and interleaving before modulation. The convolutional coding rate for the base and the enhancement layers is set to $1/2$ and $2/3$, respectively, in our simulation. Correspondingly, the receiver performs de-interleaving, de-convolution, and RS decoding to obtain the JPEG2000 stream.

Regarding MIMO transmission, our first reference scheme, referred to as HM-STBC, relies on STBC to fully exploit transmit diversity from multiple antennas on the base station [144, 145]. In this scheme, the channel coded bit stream is modulated into HM symbols. We implemented two typical HM variants, namely QPSK-in-16QAM (i.e., hierarchical 4/16QAM, QPSK for both layers) and QPSK-in-64QAM (i.e., hierarchical 4/64QAM, QPSK and 16QAM for the two layers, respectively) [11]. The parameter that governs the ratio of protection of the base over the enhancement layer is set to 2. The HM symbols are sent using the Alamouti scheme.

Our second reference scheme, referred to as SP-MIMO, employs superposition MIMO coding [135, 133]. In this scheme, the base layer data are coded with the Alamouti scheme for higher reliability, and spatial multiplexing is used to code the enhancement layer to leverage the higher capacity of strong receivers. The transmitter combines them into HM symbols with a parameter ρ [133], which is the ratio of the amplitude of the second layer to that of the first layer. The value of ρ determines the extent of protection of the two layers in signal superposition, and based on experiments we set $\rho = 0.3$ to balance protecting both layers. As an example, if x_1 and x_2 are two successive symbols for the base layer data, and x_i, for $i = 3, 4, 5, 6$ represents successive enhancement layer data symbols, then SP-MIMO transmits $(x_1 + x_3)$ and $(x_2 + x_4)$ on the two antennas in the first time slot, and $(-x_2^* + x_5)$ and $(x_1^* + x_6)$ in the second slot, where '+' means superposition. Weak receivers with low CSNRs or a single antenna are expected to decode x_1 and x_2, while two-antenna receivers with good channel conditions can also decode

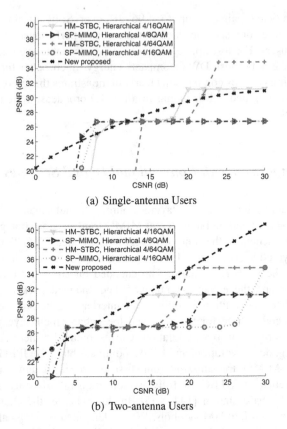

(a) Single-antenna Users

(b) Two-antenna Users

Fig. 11.5 Our scheme vs. two conventional reference schemes, HM-STBC and SP-MIMO, using the image *Cameraman*.

x_3 to x_6. To ensure that SP-MIMO sends the enhancement layer at the same rate as in HM-STBC, we use both BPSK and QPSK to match the two HM settings in HM-STBC.

Fig. 11.5 (image Cameraman) and Fig. 11.6 (image Lena) show the performance of our scheme as well as the two reference digital schemes. For the same enhancement layer data rate, we can make three major observations between the two reference digital schemes. First, for both single-antenna and two-antenna users, the CSNR required to decode the base layer in SP-MIMO is always lower than for HM-STBC. Second, single-antenna users cannot decode the enhancement layer at all in SP-MIMO, but they can in HM-STBC when the channel condition permits it. Third, in order to decode the enhancement layer, two-antenna users in SP-MIMO need much higher CSNRs than in HM-STBC.

When comparing our scheme with HM-STBC and SP-MIMO, an immediate observation is that the two digital schemes only obtain stair-shaped incremental increases in quality while our scheme has a very smooth quality scaling behavior.

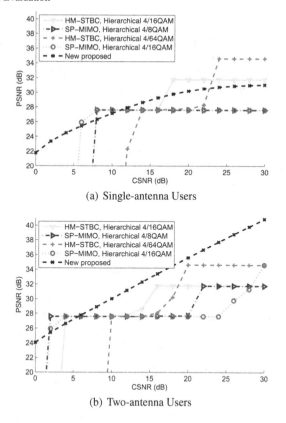

(a) Single-antenna Users

(b) Two-antenna Users

Fig. 11.6 Our scheme vs. two conventional reference schemes, HM-STBC and SP-MIMO, using the image *Lena*.

Furthermore, in our scheme, two-antenna users always derive higher PSNRs over the single-antenna users when the per-antenna CSNR is the same. In HM-STBC and SP-MIMO, however, the additional antenna is under-utilized in most cases, because the scheme performance stops improving when the CSNR exceeds a threshold (known as the *level-off effect* of digital schemes).

Between our scheme and SP-MIMO, we find that both single-antenna and two-antenna users in our scheme can derive higher PSNRs at most CSNRs. The exceptions are when the CSNR is just high enough to allow the decoding of the base layer data, for example at 6 dB for single-antenna users and 4 dB for two-antenna users.

Between our proposed scheme and HM-STBC, our scheme always performs better for two-antenna users at CSNRs of 8 dB or higher. At a CSNR of 26 dB, the PSNR from our scheme is more than 3 dB higher than that for the QPSK-in-16QAM variant of HM-STBC, and about 7 dB higher than the QPSK-in-64QAM variant of HM-STBC. For single-antenna receivers, our scheme is superior over HM-STBC at low CSNRs. However, when the channel is good enough to allow single-antenna users to correctly receive enhancement layer bits, our scheme incurs some performance loss. This is the cost our scheme has to pay in order to trade off the performance between single-antenna and two-antenna users. However, although HM-STBC with hierarchical 4/64QAM can achieve high PSNR at high CSNR, the single-antenna users can barely get anything at a CSNR below 15 dB. In contrast, our scheme has a significantly larger operational range.

Fig. 11.7 and Fig. 11.8 show the visual quality of Cameraman and Lena, respectively. Our scheme consistently produces better visual quality than SoftCast, especially for single-antenna users. Compared to HM-STBC, although our scheme delivers images that appear less smooth in some places, the image details are better preserved.

Table 11.1 Comparison between our scheme, SoftCast, and J2K

	Single-antenna users			Two-antenna users		
	Ours	SoftCast	J2K	Ours	SoftCast	J2K
Cameraman	27.73	23.76	27.14	31.58	30.13	29.56
Lena	28.76	25.77	28.55	32.77	32.18	30.08
Peppers	26.16	22.80	25.94	29.73	29.30	28.49
Boat	29.42	28.02	28.39	33.32	34.13	31.26
Couple	30.26	26.25	30.86	33.32	32.22	33.23
Girl	30.45	27.17	31.35	33.62	33.39	33.16
House	32.41	29.86	33.24	35.91	36.32	34.45
Tree	26.48	24.72	25.76	30.23	31.07	28.01
Average	**28.96**	**26.04**	**28.90**	**32.56**	**32.34**	**31.03**

11.5.3 Overall Performance in a Broadcasting Session

We compare the overall performance of our scheme with two reference schemes, namely SoftCast and HM-STBC, in a broadcasting session. We assume 100 single-antenna users and 100 two-antenna users in the session, with average per-antenna SNR 15 dB, and variance 4 dB. Table 11.1 lists the average received PSNR for eight test images. In the table, J2K denotes the digital scheme which encodes images with JPEG2000 standard and transmits them using HM-STBC scheme. We do not show the results for SP-MIMO, because previous experiments have shown that it significantly underperforms our scheme.

From the last row of the table, we can see that our scheme achieves the highest PSNR among the three schemes for both types of receivers. On average, our scheme obtains 2.92 dB gain over SoftCast for single-antenna users, and 1.53 dB gain over HM-STBC for two-antenna users. As more advanced techniques on CS reconstruction for images are proposed, the compressive image broadcast scheme is

(a) Ours, 2x1, 26. 8dB   (b) SoftCast, 2x1, 23. 4dB   (c) J2K, 2x1, 26. 7dB

(d) Ours, 2x2, 29. 8dB   (e) SoftCast, 2x2, 28. 3dB   (f) J2K, 2x2, 26. 7dB

Fig. 11.7 Visual quality comparison of decoded *Cameraman* at CSNR=12 dB. The images in the top and bottom rows show the perceived quality by the single-antenna (labeled 2×1) and two-antenna users (labeled 2×2).

(a) Ours, 2x1, 28. 6dB   (b) SoftCast, 2x1, 25. 8dB   (c) J2K, 2x1, 27. 6dB

(d) Ours, 2x2, 32. 3dB   (e) SoftCast, 2x2, 31. 6dB   (f) J2K, 2x2, 27. 6dB

Fig. 11.8 Visual quality comparison of decoded *Lena* at CSNR=14 dB.

expected to achieve even better performance. For example, it is reported in a recent body of work [146] that the reconstruction PSNR for Lena (256×256) could be as high as 29.16 dB and 33.58 dB when the number of available CS measurements is only 15% and 30% of the original pixel numbers. This suggests great potential for the proposed scheme.

11.6 Summary

In this chapter we have presented a compressive image broadcast scheme to simultaneously address heterogeneity across receiving antenna numbers and diverse channel SNRs. By integrating compressive sensing into the MIMO transmission of multimedia data, our framework ensures decoding for single-antenna users while two-antenna users can achieve multiplexing gain.

Our scheme is likely more beneficial for schemes with more antennas. A digital approach would be even more constrained in such a scenario, since we would need to divide the source into more layers. Hybrid multiplexing and STBC schemes would also be limited by the inherent difficulty of designing efficient STBC codes for large channel dimensions. The LLSE decoder in SoftCast would suffer further if the number of received measurements becomes even smaller, e.g., for a 3×1 or 4×1 scenario. In comparison, the main components in our scheme naturally cope with higher channel dimensions, merely using slightly different parameter choices for two possible reasons. First, the most suitable power scaling factor may be different. Second, it is likely that the scheme should send more measurements than are needed by the user with the most antennas. This would trade off more multiplexing gain for diversity gain and help the single-antenna users.

Finally, although this work focuses on image transmission, we can treat images as intra-coded video frames without considering temporal correlation among successive frames. Our scheme can be extended to video broadcasting by using a 3D wavelet transform, which requires consideration of the trade-off between system performance and the decoding complexity.

Chapter 12
Multiple Similar Description Code

12.1 Introduction

A key challenge facing wireless multicast is user heterogeneity. Currently, *antenna heterogeneity* brought by the prevalence of MIMO technology has not received much attention. As shown in Fig. 12.1, devices in the same multicast session may be equipped with varying numbers of receiver antennas. In such a system, the number of spatial streams (or multiplexing gain) is limited by the least number of receiver antennas. In this research, we aim to design a video multicast system in which each receiver can obtain a video quality that gracefully scales with the number of its antennas.

Our idea to solve this problem is inspired by multiple description (MD) coding [27]. In the simplest implementation, two $B/2$-Hz descriptions of a signal are generated from the odd and the even samples of a B-Hz description. In a $\{1,2\} \times 2$ system, if the sender transmits the adjacent odd and even samples, the symbol received by 1-antenna user is a weighted average of the two samples and the weights are the corresponding channel parameters. A sequence of the received symbols can be looked on as another $B/2$-bits/s description of the original signal created in the air. Meanwhile, the 2-antenna user is able to decode both odd and even samples and reconstruct a B-bits/s signal with full quality.

However, the implementation of this idea is facing three main challenges. First, the channel parameters are not under control. In the worst case, signals from different antennas may cancel out each other. To solve this problem, we propose multiplexed space-time block coding (M-STBC), which ensures that all transmitted signals will be weighed by a positive factor in the received signal. Second, we discover that the key to the success of M-STBC is to construct similar streams to be concurrently transmitted on multiple antennas. We propose multiple similar description coding (MSDC) which produces highly similar streams through sub-sampling and pixel-shift prediction. Note that the conventional MD coding only ensures that any description alone is decodable, but the proposed MSDC ensures that any linear combinations of the descriptions are decodable and more combinations

DOI: 10.1201/9781003118688-12

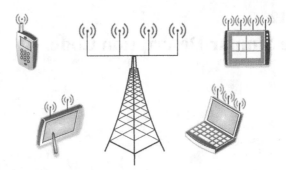

Fig. 12.1 Scenario: a MIMO video multicast system with both SNR and antenna heterogeneity.

lead to higher quality. However, the third challenge arises as similar streams contain too much redundancy which, if not removed, will greatly affect the power efficiency of the transmission. We tackle this problem by a two-phase transform. We create and transmit similar discrete cosine transform (DCT) coefficients but perform power allocation over Hadamard coefficients. With this design, we manage to transmit multiple similar streams with the same power efficiency as transmitting a single stream.

Based on seamless integration of these key technologies, we design and implement a scalable video multicast system named *AirScale* and evaluate it on Sora MIMO kit [38]. Results show that AirScale overcomes the cliff effect and stair-shaped rates of conventional digital schemes and outperforms the state-of-the-art video multicast scheme SoftCast [19]. In a $\{1,2\} \times 2$ system, AirScale achieves performance gain for both 1-antenna and 2-antenna receivers up to 0.9dB and 1.5dB in video PSNR. In a $\{1,2,3,4\} \times 4$ system, AirScale achieves significant gains over SoftCast up to 3.5 dB, 3.9 dB and 4.1 dB for 2, 3 and 4-antenna receivers with less than 2.8 dB loss for 1-antenna receiver.

12.2 Intuition

We first provide intuitions and illustrate the basic ideas in a simplified system model. Let us consider a $\{1,2\} \times 2$ system, where the sender has two transmitter (Tx) antennas and receivers may have one or two receiver (Rx) antennas. When the sender transmits two spatial streams, the 2-antenna receiver can decode both streams through standard MIMO detection. However, in conventional wisdom, the 1-antenna receiver will fail to decode any information.

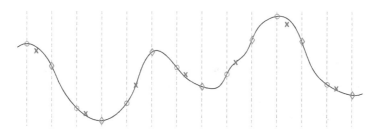

Fig. 12.2 The transmitted samples (circles (odd) and diamonds(even)) and the received samples by 1-antenna user (crosses).

12.2.1 Basic Idea

We seek a solution that allows a 1-antenna receiver to decode useful information from the interfered spatial streams. For simplicity of illustration, we assume in this example that all the transmitted symbols and channel coefficients are real numbers. Let a and b be the transmitted symbols in a particular time slot. Let us ignore the noise, the received signal at 1-antenna receiver is:

$$c = \alpha \cdot a + \beta \cdot b, \tag{12.1}$$

where α and β are the corresponding channel state information (CSI), which are assumed to be known at the receiver and normalized to $\alpha + \beta = 1$. With only one equation, it is almost impossible to decode two unknowns, but interestingly, c is an interpolation of the two transmitted symbols.

Let us consider transmitting a signal as shown in Fig. 12.2. The signal is sampled at B Hz, which is likely to be greater than the Nyquist rate. We create two $B/2$-Hz descriptions by separating odd samples, which are represented by circles, and even samples, which are represented by diamonds in the figure. The two descriptions are transmitted verbatim as two spatial streams in MIMO. The crosses in Fig. 12.2 mark the possible positions of the symbols received by a 1-antenna receiver when channel coefficients are $\alpha = 1/3$ and $\beta = 2/3$. Interestingly, these interpolations can be looked on as another description of the original signal, though the sample values may not be equal to the values in the original description. In a nutshell, the 1-antenna receiver obtains a sub-sampled signal through "interpolation in the air" and the sub-sampling ratio equals the ratio of the Tx antenna number to the Rx antenna number.

The main problem in this idea is that unfavorable CSI may cause the two transmitted symbols to cancel out each other. When $sign(\alpha) = sign(\beta)$, no matter which coefficient is larger in absolute value, c is an interpolation of a and b. However, when $sign(\alpha) \neq sign(\beta)$, the received signal becomes an extrapolation of a and b. Depending on the values of α and β, the extrapolation may still be close to or seriously deviate from the original signal. This is definitely an undesired result.

12.2.2 Innovations

We propose in this research multiplexed space-time block coding (M-STBC) to put uncontrolled CSI under our control. Let x_1 and x_2 be two complex symbols formed by the samples in one description and x_1' and x_2' be symbols formed by corresponding samples in the other description. If $x_1 \approx x_1'$ and $x_2 \approx x_2'$, we can construct the M-STBC code as:

$$\mathcal{MC}_2 = \begin{pmatrix} x_1 & -x_2'^* \\ x_2 & x_1'^* \end{pmatrix}, \tag{12.2}$$

where * denotes a complex conjugate. Each column represents a time slot and each row represents an antenna. A 2-antenna receiver can decode x_1, x_2 in the first time slot and decode x_1', x_2' in the second time slot, through standard MIMO detection.

A 1-antenna receiver receives two signals in two time slots, denoted by $y^{(1)}$ and $y^{(2)}$. We have

$$\left(y^{(1)} y^{(2)} \right) = (h_1 \ h_2) \cdot \mathcal{MC}_2, \tag{12.3}$$

where h_1 and h_2 are channel coefficients which are assumed to be unchanged in the two time slots. The 1-antenna receiver only tries to decode two values. Therefore, it assumes that $x_1 = x_1'$ and $x_2 = x_2'$. Then $\mathcal{MC}_2$ becomes the Alamouti's code [147], and the transmitted signals can be decoded by:

$$\widehat{x}_1 = \frac{h_1^* y^{(1)} + h_2 y^{(2)*}}{\|h_1\|^2 + \|h_2\|^2}, \widehat{x}_2 = \frac{h_2^* y^{(1)} - h_1 y^{(2)*}}{\|h_1\|^2 + \|h_2\|^2}.$$

Simple deduction will give:

$$\widehat{x}_1 = \frac{\|h_1\|^2 x_1 + \|h_2\|^2 x_1'}{\sum_{i=1,2} \|h_i\|^2} + \frac{h_1^* h_2}{\sum_{i=1,2} \|h_i\|^2} (x_2 - x_2'),$$

$$\widehat{x}_2 = \frac{\|h_2\|^2 x_2 + \|h_1\|^2 x_2'}{\sum_{i=1,2} \|h_i\|^2} + \frac{h_1 h_2^*}{\sum_{i=1,2} \|h_i\|^2} (x_1 - x_1').$$

The first terms on the right sides of both equations are the linear interpolations of two signals, regardless of the values of the channel coefficients. The second terms can be considered as artificial errors, which would be small if $|x_1 - x_1'|$ and $|x_2 - x_2'|$ are small. Now it is clear that the key to the success of M-STBC is to have very similar descriptions of the original signal. This is the reason our source processing technique is named multiple similar description (MSD) coding.

For natural video signals, the pixel values at adjacent spatial or temporal positions are likely to be similar. One step further, if we represent the two descriptions in transform domain, such as DCT domain (as shown in Fig. 12.3), the transform-domain coefficients will be similar too, given that the sampling offsets of the two streams are properly aligned. Note that both the encoded MSD streams and the transmitted signals should be uncoded, because digitization will destroy

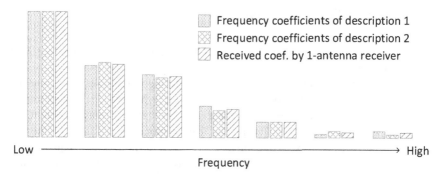

Fig. 12.3 Transform-domain representation of the two descriptions and a possible interpolation.

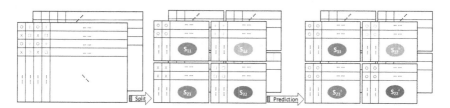

Fig. 12.4 Generating MSD sequences through spatial sub-sampling and pixel-shift prediction.

the similarity between symbols. We could adopt the pseudo-analog transmission as SoftCast[19]. The transmitted signals still go through the digital communication hardware, but the modulation constellation is much denser than that used in standard digital communications.

12.3 AirScale System Design

In this section, we detail the design of AirScale for the two most representative cases where the sender has two or four Tx antennas. The number of Rx antennas varies from one to two or four.

The three key steps in AirScale sender processing are generating MSD streams, transform and power allocation, and M-STBC code construction. While the basic ideas behind the first and the third steps have been illustrated in Section 12.2, the second step also contains key technical contribution, which we call two-phase transform, that greatly improves the power efficiency. We have a uniform and neat design for AirScale receivers. All receivers with any number of antennas adopt the same reconstruction algorithm. These key steps and contributions will be detailed consecutively in the following subsections.

12.3.1 Generating MSD Sequences

Given a video sequence S with resolution of $W \times H$, a sender generates four MSD sequences from S through two steps, as shown in Fig. 12.4.

First, we perform spatial sub-sampling and split the original sequence into four low-resolution ($\frac{W}{2} \times \frac{H}{2}$) sequences, denoted by S_{11}, S_{12}, S_{21} and S_{22}. As an example, S_{11} contains odd samples in both horizontal and vertical directions, as denoted by circles in Fig. 12.4. Note that the pixels at corresponding positions of the four sequences are adjacent pixels in a small 2×2 block in the original sequence, and therefore are likely to have similar values. Actually, sub-sampling can be performed in either spatial or temporal domain, or a combination of the two.

Next, we perform pixel-shift prediction to align the sampling offsets of the four sequences, such that their transform-domain representation will be more similar. In our design, we keep sequence S_{11} unchanged and generate three predicted copies of S_{11} from the other three sequences. To this end, three prediction functions, denoted by $P_{\leftarrow}(\cdot), P_{\uparrow}(\cdot)$ and $P_{\nwarrow}(\cdot)$, are designed. The predicted sequences are:

$$S'_{12} = P_{\leftarrow}(S_{12}), S'_{21} = P_{\uparrow}(S_{21}) \text{ and } S'_{22} = P_{\nwarrow}(S_{22}).$$

Note that the three predicted sequences contain the values of the same sampling positions as sequence S_{11} (marked with circles in the first picture of Fig. 12.4).

The prediction functions $P_{\leftarrow}(\cdot)$ and $P_{\uparrow}(\cdot)$ are performed on row and column basis, respectively. The function $P_{\nwarrow}(\cdot)$ can be realized by $P_{\leftarrow}(P_{\uparrow}(\cdot))$. The key operation in all three prediction tasks is a forward half-pixel prediction for a one-dimensional signal. According to the property of Fourier transform that sample shift is equivalent to phase rotation in transform domain. We implement the pixel shift in three steps: FFT (fast Fourier transform), phase rotation and IFFT (inverse FFT). These operations are invertible so that there exists a backward half-pixel prediction function such that

$$S_{12} = P_{\rightarrow}(S'_{12}) = P_{\rightarrow}(P_{\leftarrow}(S_{12})). \tag{12.4}$$

Therefore, a receiver who obtains all four transmitted sequences S_{11}, S'_{12}, S'_{21} and S'_{22} is able to reconstruct S_{12}, S_{21} and S_{22}, and consequently reconstruct the original sequence.

12.3.2 Transform and Power Allocation

We consider a communication system with total power constraint. In order to optimize the system performance under the mean squared error (MSE) criterion, the video signal should first be de-correlated and then power scaled [19]. In SoftCast, signal is de-correlated through 3D-DCT transform. However, simply applying 3D-DCT for each MSD sequence does not sufficiently de-correlate the entire video signal. This is because there are still strong correlations among the generated streams (comprising the DCT coefficients). This puts us in a dilemma. On one hand, we shall maintain the similarity among MSD streams so that M-STBC can behave as we expected. On the other, if the inter-stream correlations are not removed, the subsequent power scaling will be less efficient.

We get out of this dilemma through an innovative way to decouple power allocation and transmission. Specifically, we perform 3D-DCT for each MSD sequence. Then, we take out the DCT components from the same frequency band of the four sequences and perform a length-4 Hadamard transform. It de-correlates the four similar streams and makes the subsequent power allocation very efficient. Then we perform an inverse Hadamard transform and form M-STBC codewords based on (altered) DCT coefficients. Note that the inverse Hadamard transform is orthonormal, so it does not change the total transmission power.

Mathematically, consider a GOP with F frames. Let $c_{11}[i]$, $c_{12}[i]$, $c_{21}[i]$ and $c_{22}[i]$ ($i = 1...\frac{W}{2} \cdot \frac{H}{2} \cdot F$) denote the 3D-DCT coefficients of sequence S_{11}, S'_{12}, S'_{21} and S'_{22} respectively. We perform Hadamard transform for the four DCT coefficients drawn from the same position of the four streams:

$$\begin{pmatrix} \mathbf{d}_1[i] \\ \mathbf{d}_2[i] \\ \mathbf{d}_3[i] \\ \mathbf{d}_4[i] \end{pmatrix} = \mathbf{T}_{H4} \begin{pmatrix} \mathbf{c}_{11}[i] \\ \mathbf{c}_{12}[i] \\ \mathbf{c}_{21}[i] \\ \mathbf{c}_{22}[i] \end{pmatrix}, \tag{12.5}$$

where $\mathbf{T}_{H4}$ is the 4×4 Hadamard transform matrix.

The Hadamard coefficients are divided into $K \cdot F$ rectangular chunks (K chunks per frame) and the coefficients in each chunk are modeled as random variables of the same distribution. The variance of the four Hadamard coefficients in the kth chunk is denoted by λ_1^k, λ_2^k, λ_3^k and λ_4^k ($1 \leq k \leq K \cdot F$). The power scaling factor for each chunk, which minimizes the reconstruction MSE, is inversely proportional to the fourth root of its variance [19]. Thus, g_j^k ($j = 1...4$) can be computed by:

$$g_j^k = \left(\lambda_j^k \right)^{-\frac{1}{4}} \sqrt{\frac{P}{\sum_{k=1}^{KF} \sum_{j=1}^{4} \sqrt{\lambda_j^k}}}, \tag{12.6}$$

where P is the total power budget for this GOP.

Then, inverse Hadamard transform is performed. Assume that index i corresponds to a position in the kth chunk of the GOP. We have the altered DCT coefficients as follows:

$$\begin{pmatrix} \tilde{\mathbf{c}}_{11}[i] \\ \tilde{\mathbf{c}}_{12}[i] \\ \tilde{\mathbf{c}}_{21}[i] \\ \tilde{\mathbf{c}}_{22}[i] \end{pmatrix} = \mathbf{T}_{H4}^{-1} \begin{pmatrix} g_1^k \mathbf{d}_1[i] \\ g_2^k \mathbf{d}_2[i] \\ g_3^k \mathbf{d}_3[i] \\ g_4^k \mathbf{d}_4[i] \end{pmatrix}, \tag{12.7}$$

where $\mathbf{T}_{H4}^{-1}$ is the inverse Hadamard transform matrix which is the same as $\mathbf{T}_{H4}$.

Note that not all Hadamard coefficients should be transmitted. The reasons are two-fold. First, for natural signals such as video, the high-frequency (DCT and Hadamard) coefficients are likely to be very small. If these coefficients are not transmitted, the receivers can simply assume them to be zeros without much information loss, but the saved bandwidth and power can be used by more important coefficients. Second, for receivers with fewer antennas than the number of spatial streams, the small Hadamard coefficients are treated as noises during reconstruction. Therefore, discarding some small coefficients would benefit weak receivers. How to discard the coefficients is a design choice, which will change the performance trade-off between receivers with different numbers of antennas. We will provide a feasible implementation in Section 12.4.

12.3.3 M-STBC Code Construction

M-STBC codes are constructed based on STBC codes and the key is to put similar symbols to corresponding space-time positions such that they can be decoded as the same symbol when there are not sufficient Rx antennas.

We first consider a $\{1,2,3,4\} \times 4$ system. The length-4 M-STBC code is constructed based on the quasi-orthogonal STBC proposed by Jafarkhani [148]. Let $\mathbf{x}_{11}[\cdot]$, $\mathbf{x}_{12}[\cdot]$, $\mathbf{x}_{21}[\cdot]$ and $\mathbf{x}_{22}[\cdot]$ be the symbol vectors formed by the altered (real-valued) DCT coefficients of the four MSD streams. For example,

$$\mathbf{x}_{11}[i] = \tilde{\mathbf{c}}_{11}[2i-1] + \sqrt{-1} \cdot \tilde{\mathbf{c}}_{11}[2i]. \tag{12.8}$$

Though it is not necessary to always combine adjacent coefficients, the real and imaginary parts of the complex symbols with the same index in the four vectors should be aligned in the four MSD streams, so that they can be assumed to be similar.

The length-4 M-STBC codeword is constructed as:

$$
\begin{array}{c}
\text{time-slots} \\
\xrightarrow{\hspace{6cm}} \\
\text{Tx antennas} \downarrow
\begin{pmatrix}
\mathbf{x}_{11}[1] & -\mathbf{x}_{12}[2]^* & -\mathbf{x}_{21}[3]^* & \mathbf{x}_{22}[4] \\
\mathbf{x}_{11}[2] & \mathbf{x}_{12}[1]^* & -\mathbf{x}_{21}[4]^* & -\mathbf{x}_{22}[3] \\
\mathbf{x}_{11}[3] & -\mathbf{x}_{12}[4]^* & \mathbf{x}_{21}[1]^* & -\mathbf{x}_{22}[2] \\
\mathbf{x}_{11}[4] & \mathbf{x}_{12}[3]^* & \mathbf{x}_{21}[2]^* & \mathbf{x}_{22}[1]
\end{pmatrix}
\end{array}
$$

We next consider a $\{1,2\} \times 2$ system. To construct length-2 M-STBC code, only pair-wise similar symbols are needed. Therefore, we group the four similar coefficients into two pairs, based on the SAD (sum of absolute differences) criterion. This process is called directional pairing and the intuition behind it is that the spatial correlation at different positions of a video frame could have different directions. If the horizontal correlation is stronger, symbols $\mathbf{x}_{11}$ and $\mathbf{x}_{12}$ should be more similar,

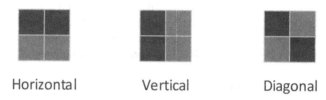

Horizontal   Vertical   Diagonal

Fig. 12.5 Three directional pairing choices.

and if the vertical correlation is stronger, symbols x_{11} and x_{21} should be more similar. We provide three directional pairing choices as shown in Fig. 12.5.

After directional pairing, every two symbols from the four MSD streams will be sent through two codewords. As an example, when horizontal pairing is adopted in a particular block, the codewords are:

$$\begin{pmatrix} x_{11}[1] & -x_{12}[2]^* \\ x_{11}[2] & x_{12}[1]^* \end{pmatrix}, \begin{pmatrix} x_{21}[1] & -x_{22}[2]^* \\ x_{21}[2] & x_{22}[1]^* \end{pmatrix}.$$

Actually, directional pairing is useful in the 4 Tx antenna case too. It can be performed before the Hadamard transform. If the pairing selection is vertical, the vector on the right-hand side in (12.5) will be changed to $(c_{11}[i], c_{21}[i], c_{12}[i], c_{22}[i])^T$. This will make the energy of Hadamard coefficients more compact in the statistical sense.

12.3.4 Reconstruction Algorithm

All receivers in AirScale will decode signals with a unified process, regardless of the number of receiver antennas N_r. The unknowns to be detected are Hadamard coefficients instead of DCT coefficients because only the variances of Hadamard coefficients (λ_i^k's) are known. Therefore, the received symbols can be conceptually written as:

$$Y = H \cdot T_H^{-1} \cdot G \cdot d + N, \tag{12.9}$$

where H is the channel matrix, T_H^{-1} is the inverse Hadamard matrix, G is the scaling factors and N is the channel noise. The underlined part can be looked on as a combined encoder C.

We adopt the standard MMSE (minimum mean-squared error) decoder to reconstruct d. In order to precisely represent the MMSE decoder in matrix form, the real parts and imaginary parts need to be separated. The decoder can be written as:

$$\hat{d} = \Lambda \cdot C^T \cdot \left(C \Lambda C^T + \sigma^2 \cdot I \right)^{-1} \cdot \begin{pmatrix} \mathscr{R}(y) \\ \mathscr{I}(y) \end{pmatrix},$$

where $\mathscr{R}(\cdot)$ and $\mathscr{I}(\cdot)$ denote the real and imaginary parts of a complex vector and $\hat{\mathbf{d}}$ is the estimated Hadamard coefficients, with the first half corresponding to the real parts of the transmitted symbols and the second half corresponding to the imaginary parts. Λ is a diagonal matrix containing the variance information and σ^2 is the noise power.

Although receivers with fewer than four antennas are not able to decode all the Hadamard coefficients, solving the M-STBC code in an under-determined system instead of a full-rank system (i.e., decodes the same number of Hadamard coefficients per group as the number of Rx antennas) can achieve a better performance. This is because we can fully utilize the variance information of each AC (alternating current) coefficient instead of treating them as a whole. The reconstruction algorithm is also justified in the next section.

From the decoded Hadamard coefficients, we can compute the 3D-DCT coefficients through inverse Hadamard transform and reconstruct the four MSD sequences S_{11}, S'_{12}, S'_{21} and S'_{22} through inverse 3D-DCT. Then, backward prediction is performed to obtain S_{12}, S_{21} and S_{22}. Finally, the original sequence is reconstructed by putting pixels from the four sub-sampled sequences back to the corresponding positions.

12.4 Evaluation

12.4.1 Implementation

The kernel of AirScale system includes two key modules, application layer video codec and physical layer (PHY) amplitude modulation.

The video codec is implemented in MATLAB Compiler Runtime (MCR) and provides an interface to the PHY module. The PHY module is built on Sora MIMO Kit [38]. The PHY leverages the Sora SDK 2.0 software implementation of OFDM, data scrambling, convolution coding, interleaving, digital modulation, preamble for channel estimation and frequency offset correction, cross-correlation based time synchronization and pilot phase correction. The 16-bit data representation in the Sora MIMO Kit is fully utilized to transmit the uncoded data. In addition, the cyclic shift delay (CSD) is implemented to prevent unintentional beamforming.

We evaluate the system performance through comparing with three alternatives, namely SoftCast [19], SVC with Hierarchical Modulation [10] (SVC-HM) and SVC with Time-Division multiplexing (SVC-TD). SoftCast is also implemented in MCR for codec and shares the same PHY with AirScale. The video stream of SVC-HM and SVC-TD is generated by the H.264 reference software JSVM [47] and is configured with Medium-Grain SNR (MGS) scalability. The PHY of these two digital schemes is based on the standard 802.11 PHY in the SDK.

The MIMO channel gain is estimated through the training symbols before the PLCP header. The channel noise power is estimated based on the four known pilots that cover four sub-bands of the 48 data sub-carriers. To detect packet loss, an OFDM symbol that contains packet ID is inserted between the PLCP header and data symbols.

In order to fairly compare the four schemes under the same channel condition, we trace the raw sampling data from the radio board and replay them for different schemes.

12.4.2 Environment and Settings

Testbed: The experiments are run on a nine-node Sora MIMO Kit testbed with one sender and eight receivers as shown in Fig. 12.6. Each node includes one MIMO RCB, 4-way RAB and four RF daughter-boards which operate on 2.4 GHz. The MIMO RCB connects to the PC with one external PCIe extension cables.

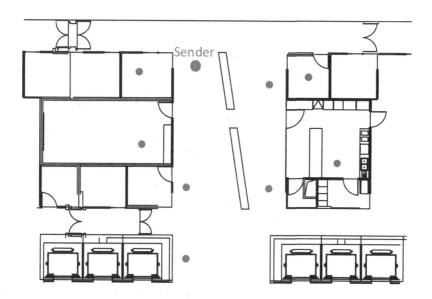

Fig. 12.6 Testbed for trace-driven evaluation.

Test Video: We use a diverse set of 1280×720 (720p) standard test video sequences, indexed from 1 to 10: *IntoTree, Jets, City, SpinCalendar, ShuttleStart, Sheriff, Stockholm, Shields, Mobcal,* and *Parkrun*. The frame rate is 30 fps (frames per second) and the sample format is YUV420. For all evaluation schemes, the GOP size is set to 16. Video quality is assessed by the subjective metric PSNR.

Wireless Setting: At each node, all 4 radios are synchronized with the same clock and operate on 2.437 GHz. Eight combinations of receiver Low Noise

Amplify (LNA) and Power Gain are tuned to obtain various channel SNR conditions. Auto Gain Control is enabled to avoid power saturation. One PLCP frame contains up to 152 OFDM symbols and lasts 632 μs together with preamble and header. With 48 sub-carriers, the total number of complex symbols in one PLCP frame is 7296. Therefore, it takes 32 PLCP frames (20.2 ms, i.e., 49 fps) to transmit one 720p video frame for two Tx antennas and 16 PLCP frames (10.1 ms, i.e., 98 fps) for four Tx antennas. To combat frequency-selective fading, we interleave coefficients within each frame. The metadata bits of all four schemes are encoded with rate-1/2 channel coding, modulated with BPSK and transmitted with STBC working in full diversity MIMO mode.

AirScale Setting: All the encoding operations are based on GOPs. The coefficients are divided into 8×8 chunks per frame. The variance and the power scaling factor are computed for each chunk. Part of the Hadamard coefficients are set to zero according to the following procedure. First, we compute the PSNR of the video that is reconstructed from 1/4 largest Hadamard coefficients (1/2 in 2 Tx antenna case). This baseline video quality, denoted by Q_0dB in PSNR, provides a performance upper bound for all types of receivers if we do not want to introduce any inter-stream interference to 1-antenna receivers. Then, we decide ΔQ which is the desired increase of performance upper bound for multi-antenna receivers, and keep the n largest coefficients that correspond to PSNR $Q_0 + \Delta Q$. Note that if all four Hadamard coefficients are discarded, the saved time slots can be allocated to other important coefficients and increase their diversity gain.

SoftCast Setting: Although it gracefully handles SNR heterogeneity, SoftCast has to transmit in full diversity MIMO mode when there is antenna heterogeneity. We have evaluated SoftCast in multiplexing mode, the 1-antenna receiver in a $\{1,2\} \times 2$ system only obtains around 26dB PSNR when the channel SNR varies from 5dB to 30dB. The visual quality is extremely poor. Therefore, this option is not considered in the evaluation. We follow almost all the parameter settings in the standard SoftCast implementation, except that the sender needs to drop a certain portion of the 3D-DCT coefficients to ensure the same bandwidth cost. In a 2-Tx-antenna system, half of the coefficients are transmitted with the Alamouti's code. In a 4-Tx-antenna system, one quarter of the coefficients are transmitted with the quasi-orthogonal STBC code.

SVC-HM and SVC-TD Setting: SVC-HM is used in the digital video broadcasting (DVB) standard [86] to address SNR heterogeneity. It always operates in diversity mode and uses Alamouti's code or quasi-orthogonal STBC code for 2 and 4-Tx-antenna systems. Video is encoded into three source layers, corresponding to the three layers of HM, which is (QPSK,1/2) + (QPSK,1/2) + (QPSK,1/2). Reed-Solomon (RS) code (188, 204) is used as the outer code.

SVC-TD handles antenna heterogeneity through time-division multiplexing. In particular, video is encoded into two or four source layers and the available transmission time is divided into two or four equal slots. Different slots are used to transmit different source layers and except for the base layer which is transmitted in diversity mode, all enhancement layers are transmitted in multiplexing mode. In the four Tx antenna system, the first, second and third enhancement layers are transmitted with two, three and four antennas, respectively. Again, (QPSK,1/2) is used for each source layer and RS-code (188, 204) is applied as the outer code.

12.4.3 System Comparisons

In order to carry out comprehensive evaluations of the four comparison schemes, we divide the SNR range into 1dB bins and pick four channel traces in each bin. Each channel trace is applied to transmit each test video sequence and the received PSNR is averaged across the ten sequences and the four traces in the same bin.

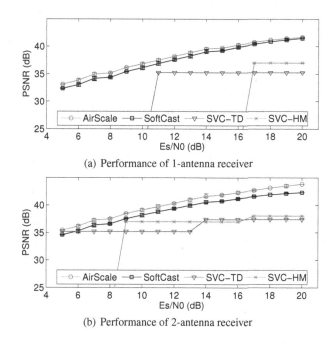

(a) Performance of 1-antenna receiver

(b) Performance of 2-antenna receiver

Fig. 12.7 Received video PSNR in a $\{1,2\} \times 2$ MIMO video multicast system.

Fig. 12.7 shows the results in a $\{1,2\} \times 2$ MIMO system. Both digital schemes show obvious cliff effects and stair-shaped rates. The minimum SNR required by SVC-HM to receive the base layer information is higher than that of SVC-TD. This is due to the inter-layer interference in each wireless symbol. When the SNR is sufficiently high, SVC-HM performs better, but the performance of both schemes will saturate below 40dB. Though the coding, modulation and time division strategies in these two digital schemes are not optimized and other strategies may result in different trade-offs, the advantage of uncoded transmission over digital methods is clear.

It can be seen that AirScale and SoftCast both achieve graceful performance degradation with SNR, but AirScale achieves better performance for both types of receivers. The PSNR gain is up to 0.8 dB and 1.5 dB for 1- and 2-antenna receivers. This gain comes from the directional pairing operation which further increases the similarity of the symbols in M-STBC codeword. If we do not adopt directional pairing, the 1-antenna receiver would have performance similar to that of SoftCast. For the AirScale results presented in this figure, ΔQ is set to 1dB. We have also tested the cases when ΔQ is 2dB or 3dB. When ΔQ is larger, the performance gain of a 2-antenna receiver is larger, but that of a 1-antenna receiver is smaller.

Fig. 12.8 shows the results in a $\{1, 2, 3, 4\} \times 4$ MIMO system. The advantage of uncoded schemes over digital schemes is still obvious. Different from the two Tx antenna case, the performance of AirScale and SoftCast diverges for different receivers. AirScale significantly outperforms SoftCast for 2-, 3- and 4-antenna receivers, but incurs some PSNR loss for 1-antenna receivers. When the channel SNR is 23dB, AirScale achieves 3.5 dB, 3.9 dB and 4.1 dB gain over SoftCast for 2-, 3- and 4-antenna receivers with 2.8 dB loss for 1-antenna receiver. We would like to point out that, AirScale still achieves an acceptable video PSNR between 30dB to 35dB for 1-antenna receiver when the channel SNR varies from 7dB to 23dB. Moreover, we find that the subjective quality of the reconstructed video does not degrade much when compared to SoftCast results. This is consistent with our initial analysis that the combined description obtained by the 1-antenna receiver is a meaningful description of the video but would differ in values from the original descriptions.

For the results presented in the figure, ΔQ is set to 4dB. We set a larger ΔQ than in the 2-Tx antenna case because the baseline PSNR is computed from only 1/4 of the coefficients and therefore is much lower. We also evaluated other ΔQ choices. A larger ΔQ will set a lower performance upper bound for a 1-antenna receiver but bring larger gains at multi-antenna receivers. Overall, the small quality degradation at 1-antenna receiver is always well paid off by significantly increased video quality at multi-antenna receivers.

12.4.4 Robustness to Radio Failures

Although the CSD is implemented to prevent the unintentional beamforming, it creates pseudo multipath in the received signal and may cause performance degradation of cross-correlation based timing synchronization. Since different receiving radios experience different multipaths, detection failure may occur on some radios. In order to evaluate the robustness to radio failure, we run the experiment during working hours when the wireless environment is noisy and there are people walking around.

The lowest and middle sub-figure in Fig. 12.9 shows the instantaneous working radio numbers and channel SNRs, both of which vary dramatically. From the top sub-figure, we can find that AirScale is very robust to radio failures and achieves a

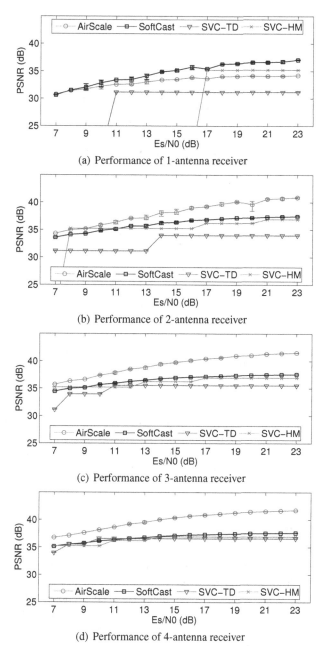

(a) Performance of 1-antenna receiver

(b) Performance of 2-antenna receiver

(c) Performance of 3-antenna receiver

(d) Performance of 4-antenna receiver

Fig. 12.8 Received video PSNR in a $\{1,2,3,4\} \times 4$ MIMO video multicast system.

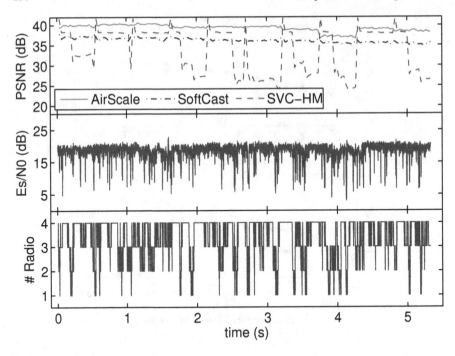

Fig. 12.9 Comparing the performance of AirScale and SoftCast for video sequence "intotree" when there are frequent radio failures.

consistent gain around 3dB over SoftCast, while the digital method SVC-HM only recovers a choppy video. We intentionally present the result of this trace where there is an obvious performance drop of AirScale when the radio failure is too frequent. In most other traces, AirScale shows very small quality variations.

12.5 Summary

We have described in this chapter an uncoded video multicast system named AirScale, which allows the received video quality to gracefully scale with the channel SNR and the number of Rx antennas. The proposed MSD coding and M-STBC fully tap the potential of uncoded transmission to address the various types of user heterogeneity in a MIMO multicast system. The proposed AirScale is readily extended to other antenna settings. When the number of Tx antennas increases to 8 or even larger, we could also generate more MSD streams through the described method. As we have shown earlier, sub-sampling in temporal domain also generates very similar sequences. Therefore, we can combine spatial and temporal multi-layer sub-sampling in various ways to generate MSD sequences.

Part V
Hybrid Digital and Analog Transmission

An analog (uncoded) system has the advantage of graceful degradation when the channel condition varies dramatically. However, in a point-to-point setting with stable channel conditions, an analog system is generally inferior to a digital system in terms of the distortion-power performance. An HDA framework can potentially benefit from both the high distortion-power performance of digital systems and the graceful performance degradation of analog systems. We shall answer two key questions for this framework: One is how to separate a video signal into digital and analog parts, and the other is how to allocate limited energy and bandwidth resources between and within digital and analog transmissions.

In Chapter 13, we introduce a practical HDA framework [149] which models video frames as a parallel Gaussian source. The source is separated into digital and analog parts through scalar quantization. Given the worst-case CSNR, we are able to derive a closed-form expression of the overall distortion. However, minimizing it is a mixed-integer non-linear programming problem which is generally NP-hard. By making reasonable and justified simplifications, we approach the optimal solution through a practical scheme. Evaluations show that the proposed practical scheme outperforms SoftCast by a large margin. The gain in received video PSNR is up to 5.0dB for various types of videos.

In Chapter 14, we present a structure-preserving HDA video delivery system, named SharpCast [79], to improve both the objective and subjective visual quality. SharpCast decomposes a video into the *content* part and the *structure* part. The latter is important to the human perception and therefore is protected with a robust digital transmission scheme. Then, the energy-intensive part in the content information is extracted and transmitted in digital for energy efficiency while the residual is transmitted in analog to achieve the desired smooth adaptation. We formulate the resource (power and bandwidth) allocation problem in SharpCast and solve the problem with a greedy strategy.

In Chapter 15, we propose a hybrid digital-analog superimposed modulation (HDA-SIM) scheme [150] for soft video delivery. The motivation of the work is that uncoded video delivery also suffers from the leveling-off effect when the allocated channel bandwidth is severely insufficient. In HDA-SIM, we treat the bandwidth of competing digital traffic as hidden resources for the video delivery system. The key problem in this scheme is how to allocate the bandwidth and power resources among various modulation symbols so that we can improve the performance of video delivery without sacrificing the throughput of existing digital traffic. In addition to the theoretical analysis, we implement the proposed scheme for SoftCast and SharpCast. Both simulations and testbed evaluations show that the HDA-SIM version can achieve significant gains in the received video quality over their original designs.

In Chapter 16, we propose an Adaptive Hybrid Digital-Analog Video Transmission scheme (A-HDAVT) [151] for robust video streaming in mobile networks with realistic fading channels. Each GOP in A-HDAVT is first transformed into one Low-pass frame and several High-pass frames with MCTF. The critical Low-pass frame is reliably transmitted as base layer in a digital mode, while High-pass frames are transmitted as enhancement layers in an analog mode to achieve desired graceful degradation performance. In analog transmission, we introduce a channel Prediction based Adaptive Power Distortion Optimization (P-APDO) scheme to combat channel fading in mobile networks. The basic idea behind P-APDO is to perform power allocation based on the video content as well as the predicted channel status. Furthermore, we also investigate the multi-user scenarios in which the content diversity and channel diversity among users are appropriately exploited. Extensive simulations show that A-HDAVT can achieve significant performance gains over competing schemes.

Chapter 13
A Practical HDA Design

13.1 Introduction

In general, a video source after decorrelation transformation can be described by a parallel Gaussian source, with each source component representing the transform coefficients in some adjacent frequency bands. Previous work on analog video transmission has shown that the source components representing low-frequency coefficients have much larger variances than those representing high-frequency coefficients, and the difference can reach a few orders of magnitude [131, 152]. In such cases, previous theoretical research on HDA transmission [21] has proved that analog transmission is definitively suboptimal to digital transmission. The loss in performance of the analog approach with respect to the digital approach for sufficiently large transmission powers is

$$\frac{D_{analog}}{D_{digital}} = \left(\frac{(\sigma_1 + \sigma_2 + \cdots + \sigma_M)/M}{(\sigma_1 \sigma_2 \cdots \sigma_M)^{1/M}} \right)^2, \tag{13.1}$$

where M is the number of source components, σ_i^2 ($i = 1...M$) is the variance of the ith source component and D_{analog} and $D_{digital}$ are the MSE distortions of the analog and the digital approach, respectively [20]. We can tell from Eq. (13.1) that the analog system is as good as the digital system only when the variances of all M source components are equal. The more diverse the source components are, the larger the performance gap is.

Given the clear pros and cons of the digital and analog approaches, researchers have investigated the HDA framework to strike a balance between distortion-power performance and adaptation capability. Theoretical works include the HDA coding for the transmission of a single Gaussian source [30, 29, 31, 15] and, a parallel Gaussian source [20, 21]. However, the problem of finding an optimal power allocation policy among digital coding and analog coding to optimize overall distortion is still open [33]. For practical applications of video transmission, several HDA schemes have been proposed [35, 121, 34]. These schemes explore video

DOI: 10.1201/9781003118688-13

characteristics and require complicated digital video signal processing techniques. Furthermore, the resource allocations between digital coding and analog coding are mostly based on heuristics.

In this chapter, we explore the HDA framework for wireless video transmission with an objective to reduce the performance gap with the digital transmission while still keeping the graceful degradation property. We shall answer two key questions for this framework. One is how to separate the video signal into digital and analog parts; the other one is how to allocate the limited energy and bandwidth resources between and within digital and analog transmissions. We find that, without employing complicated video processing techniques such as motion estimation/compensation or entropy coding, the scalar quantization of the transform coefficients is a practical and efficient way to separate the digital and analog parts. Specifically, we perform quantization on the sources with large variances, encode the quantization coefficients, and transmit them using a conventional digital method. The residuals, together with the instances which are not quantized, are transmitted in analog.

We formulate the resource allocation problem, and derive the closed-form expression of the distortion at any given energy and bandwidth budget and the channel SNR. Based on this derived distortion expression, we make two reasonable simplifications and propose a practical algorithm to minimize the distortion at any target channel SNR. This is achieved by determining the quantization steps for each Gaussian source. Thanks to the graceful degradation property of analog transmission, when the actual channel SNR deviates from the target value, there is no abrupt change in distortion performance. Extensive simulations and trace-driven emulations show that the proposed solution achieves significant gain over the state-of-the-art analog scheme under the time varying channel.

13.2 The Proposed HDA Framework

We propose an HDA framework based on scalar quantization for the transmission of a parallel Gaussian source with diverse variances over an energy and bandwidth constrained channel. The motivation behind our proposal is that analog transmission, amplitude modulation in particular, is not energy efficient for sources with large variances. In contrast, digital encoding and transmission of such sources do not cost as much energy, but at the cost of consuming more bandwidths. Therefore, we shall leverage their respective advantages to optimize overall performance. Investigation on how to optimally allocate energy and bandwidth between digital coding and analog coding is nontrivial.

As mentioned earlier, for the sake of low complexity, we do not use complex video signal processing techniques. Instead, a decorrelation transform (i.e., 3D-DCT) is adopted and the transform coefficients are divided into chunks. Previous research has shown that the coefficients in each chunk can be treated as instances drawn from a Gaussian distribution. As such, the video signal is modeled as a

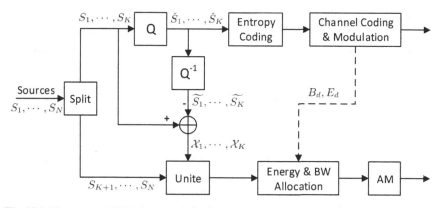

Fig. 13.1 The proposed HDA framework for the transmission of a parallel Gaussian source.

parallel Gaussian source [20]. Let S_i, $i = 1, 2, \cdots, N$ denote N i.i.d. Gaussian sources (variables) with zero mean and variance λ_i, i.e., $S_i \sim \mathcal{N}(0, \lambda_i)$. We also use $\sigma_i = \sqrt{\lambda_i}$ to denote the standard deviation of S_i. Without loss of generality, we assume that these N sources have already been sorted in descending order according to their variances, i.e., $\lambda_1 \geq \lambda_2 \geq \cdots \geq \lambda_N$. We consider the transmission of a block of data, which contains L instances of each source. Therefore, there are NL real-valued coefficients in total to be transmitted.

Fig. 13.1 provides an overview of the proposed HDA framework. For the N sources, we perform scalar quantization (Q) over the instances from the first K sources $S_1, S_2, \cdots, S_K$. The quantized sources, denoted by $\check{S}_1, \check{S}_2, \cdots, \check{S}_K$, are coded in digital while the residuals, denoted by $\mathcal{X}_1, \mathcal{X}_2, \cdots, \mathcal{X}_K$, and the rest of the sources $S_{K+1}, S_{K+2}, \cdots, S_N$ are coded in analog. The digital and analog coding are performed under both energy and bandwidth constraints. For clarity, we convert the bandwidth constraint into the number of wireless symbols that can be transmitted for each data block (i.e., a Group of Pictures), and denote it by B. Since each wireless symbol can carry two real-valued coefficients in its I and Q plane in the amplitude modulation (AM), $B = NL/2$ when the channel bandwidth equals the data source bandwidth. This is also referred to as the *full bandwidth case* in the rest of this chapter. Let $2P_s$ be the (two-dimensional) average per-symbol energy, which is usually determined by the transmission system, then the energy constraint (total available energy) is $E = 2P_s \times B$.

Let Q_i denote the quantization step for source S_i. Effectively we have $Q_i = \infty$ for $S_{K+1}, S_{K+2}, \cdots, S_N$. The number of K will be determined based on source characteristics. The quantized data will be entropy coded and digitally transmitted. In order not to compromise the channel adaptation capability of the analog transmission, we adopt a robust modulation scheme and a low rate channel code (strong protection) for the digital transmission, and both the modulation and channel coding schemes remain unchanged even if the actual channel condition is much better than expected. With the fixed digital transmission parameters, once the quantization steps for each source are determined, the energy and bandwidth consumed by the digital parts, denoted by E_d and B_d, can be computed.

The quantization residuals (with reduced variances) of the first K sources and the remaining $N - K$ non-quantized sources will be transmitted in the analog manner. Since the variances of the residuals are much smaller than those of the original coefficients, they require much less energy to be transmitted. The remaining bandwidth and energy resources, denoted by B_a and E_a, are allocated among these sources for analog transmission. The power-scaled data are transmitted with AM.

Note that not all non-quantized sources will be transmitted. Some of them, which have very small variances, may be dropped at the sender to save precious bandwidth resources. The receiver can simply estimate these instances with their mean values (i.e., zero). Although this may increase the distortion of the small-variance sources, the saved bandwidth allows the sender to transmit more digital bits, which translates to smaller quantization steps and smaller distortions for the large-variance sources.

13.3 Optimization in Resource Allocation

13.3.1 Problem Formulation

Our optimization task is to determine the number K of the sources to be quantized and the quantization steps Q_i for sources S_i, where $i = 1, 2, \cdots, K$, so that the overall distortion (D) can be minimized. The optimized solution should trade off the energy (E) and bandwidth (B) allocated between digital transmission and analog transmission. The resource allocation problem in HDA can be formulated as:

$$\underset{Q_i, i=1,\cdots,N}{\arg\min} \ D$$
$$s.t. \ B_d + B_a \leq B$$
$$E_d + E_a \leq E. \tag{13.2}$$

In order to get the optimal performance, equality should be achieved in both constraints. In other words, once E_d and B_d is known, we shall allocate all remaining energy $E_a = E - E_d$ and bandwidth $B_a = B - B_d$ to the analog part.

In this work, we are interested in the cases where B is no greater than $NL/2$. When $B = NL/2$, there are just enough channel uses to transmit all the data in analog, and some instances (from small-variance sources) have to be dropped if the sender generates any digital data. When $B < NL/2$, $(NL - 2B)$ coefficients belonging to the sources with the smallest variances are dropped even before we start the optimization process. In addition, we define P_d and $2P_a$ as the average energy of a (two-dimensional) digital symbol and (two-dimensional) analog symbol, respectively.

13.3.2 Problem Analysis

13.3.2.1 Quantization

For the ith memoryless Gaussian source S_i, $S_i \sim \mathcal{N}(0, \sigma_i^2)$, we perform mid-tread uniform quantization with step Q_i. Then, the source after the quantization (quantized source) $\check{S}_i$ can be calculated as

$$\check{S}_i = sign(S_i) \times \lfloor \frac{S_i}{Q_i} + \frac{1}{2} \rfloor, \tag{13.3}$$

where $sign(\cdot)$ is the sign function and $\lfloor \cdot \rfloor$ indicates the rounding down to the nearest integer operation. The quantization coefficients from $\check{S}_i$ approximately follow a Gaussian distribution: $\check{S}_i \sim \mathcal{N}(0, \lambda_i/Q_i^2)$. Correspondingly, the inverse quantization is:

$$\widetilde{S}_i = \check{S}_i \times Q_i, \tag{13.4}$$

and the residual source $\mathscr{X}_i$ can be obtained by

$$\mathscr{X}_i = S_i - \widetilde{S}_i. \tag{13.5}$$

When the quantization step is small (relative to the standard deviation of the source), the quantization error (residual) can be modeled as a source with zero mean and variance λ_i' [153] where the variance is

$$\lambda_i' = Q_i^2/12. \tag{13.6}$$

13.3.2.2 Digital Encoding and Transmission

The average bit consumption b_i for the coefficient from the quantized source $\check{S}_i$ can be approximated by its entropy when the quantization step Q_i is small relative to σ_i [154]:

$$b_i = H(\check{S}_i) = \frac{1}{2}log_2(2\pi e \lambda_i) - log_2(Q_i), \tag{13.7}$$

where e is the base of the natural logarithm.

Let r (bits/symbol) denote the digital transmission rate, which is the product of modulation rate and channel coding rate. For example, $r = 1$ for (QPSK,1/2) where the source bits are first encoded by a rate-1/2 channel code and then modulated by quadrature phase-shift keying (QPSK). Similarly, $r = 0.5$ for (BPSK,1/2). Since L instances are transmitted for a source, the bandwidth consumption (channel uses) c_i for coding source $\check{S}_i$ is

$$c_i = Lb_i/r. \tag{13.8}$$

When K sources are quantized, the bandwidth consumption of the digital transmission can be computed by:

$$B_d = \sum_{i=1}^{K} c_i = L \sum_{i=1}^{K} b_i/r. \qquad (13.9)$$

Recall that we are considering the full bandwidth case. If the digital part of source S_i occupies c_i channel uses, t_i $(t_i = 2c_i/L = 2b_i/r)$ analog sources (with the smallest variances) should be dropped without transmission. Thus, in order to transmit the digital parts of the first K sources, the total number of sources to be dropped without transmission is $T = \sum_{i=1}^{K} t_i = \sum_{i=1}^{K} 2b_i/r = 2B_d/L$. Therefore, $B_d = LT/2$.

We have denoted the per-symbol energy for digital transmission as P_d. Simply put, we can set it as $P_d = 2P_s \times \beta$ with $\beta = 1$. Given the tolerable worst channel SNR, we can choose the transmission rate r to ensure error-free transmission by simply looking up a table [155]. To assure the error-free decoding of the digital bits at varying channel, we conservatively choose a fixed transmission rate even though the time-varying channel could experience better channel states. For (QPSK,1/2) with $r = 1$, the tolerable channel SNR is 7dB when $\beta = 1$. To be tolerant of the channel SNR of 4dB (=7dB-3dB), the per-symbol energy for digital transmission could be doubled as $P_d = 4P_s$ by setting β as 2.

In our implementation, we adopt (QPSK,1/2). Although QPSK is less robust than BPSK, it can achieve exactly the same bit error rate (BER) as BPSK, if the per-symbol energy is doubled, while saving half of the bandwidth that BPSK would need. For the HDA transmission in the bandwidth-constrained channel, leaving more bandwidth for analog transmission will bring performance gain in most cases.

13.3.2.3 Analog Coding and Transmission

The K residual sources and the $N - K$ non-quantized sources are transmitted in analog. To make full use of the limited bandwidth resource, we let $B_a = B - B_d$. We only consider amplitude modulation in this work, and every complex-valued wireless symbol carries two real-valued instances so that $2B_a$ instances can be transmitted. As in [19], we shall transmit the instances of the sources with the largest variances in order to minimize distortion. Then M $(M = 2B_a/L)$ sources with the largest variances are transmitted in analog. Without loss of generality, we denote these sources by $\mathscr{X}_i$ and their variances and standard deviations by λ_i' and σ_i', respectively, where $i = 1, 2, \cdots, M$. For the non-quantized sources (i.e., $Q_i = \infty$), we have $\mathscr{X}_i = S_i$ and $\lambda_i' = \lambda_i$.

In order to minimize distortion at the receiver, instances of source $\mathscr{X}_i$ should be scaled by a factor g_i, which is inversely proportional to the square root of its standard deviation [131]. When SNR is sufficiently high, the expression of g_i is:

$$g_i = \sqrt{\frac{E_a/L}{\sigma_i' \sum_{j=1}^{M} \sigma_j'}}. \qquad (13.10)$$

When SNR is low, not all sources should be transmitted, or $g_i = 0$ for some sources. Details will be given in the next subsection.

Mathematical expectation of the energy consumption for transmitting a signal from source $\mathscr{X}_i$ is:

$$P_{ai} = \mathbb{E}((g_i\mathscr{X}_i)^2) = g_i^2\lambda_i' = \frac{E_a\sigma_i'}{L\sum_{j=1}^{M}\sigma_j'}. \tag{13.11}$$

We observe that the average energy consumption for transmitting a signal from source $\mathscr{X}_i$ is proportional to the standard deviation of the source, i.e., $P_{ai} \propto \sigma_i'$.

13.3.2.4 Distortion in Analog Transmission

For each instance x_{ij} from source $\mathscr{X}_i$, the power-scaled signal $y_{ij} = g_ix_{ij}$ is transmitted. In a block fading channel, the received signal is $\hat{y}_{ij} = hy_{ij} + z$, where h is the channel parameter which can be estimated at the receiver, and z denotes the noise of the additive white noise channel. The original signal can be decoded as

$$\hat{x}_{ij} = \frac{\hat{y}_{ij}}{hg_i} = x_{ij} + \frac{z}{hg_i} = x_{ij} + \frac{z'}{g_i}, \tag{13.12}$$

The equivalent noise, as a random variable, can be rewritten as $z' = z/h$ with variance N_0, i.e., $\mathbb{E}(z'^2) = N_0$. We represent the decoded signal as $\hat{\mathscr{X}}_i$. Following the derivation of expected distortion under the additive white noise channel for SoftCast [131], we obtain the expected distortion (in terms of MSE) of a signal from source $\mathscr{X}_i$ as

$$d_{ai} = \mathbb{E}((\hat{\mathscr{X}}_i - \mathscr{X}_i)^2) = \frac{\mathbb{E}(z'^2)}{g_i^2} = \frac{N_0\sigma_i'}{E_a/L}\sum_{j=1}^{M}\sigma_j' = \frac{N_0\sigma_i'}{P_aM}\sum_{j=1}^{M}\sigma_j'. \tag{13.13}$$

Note that $E_a = 2P_aB = P_aML$. Here, we notice $SNR = 2P_a/2N_0$ is just the channel SNR. The SNR value is usually expressed using the logarithmic decibel scale as $SNR_{dB} = 10log_{10}(SNR)$. We observe that the expected distortion for a signal from source $\mathscr{X}_i$ is proportional to the standard deviation of the source, i.e., $d_{ai} \propto \sigma_i'$. In addition, the expected distortion is a function of the channel SNR. We notice that for very small P_a/N_0, the expected distortion as in (13.13) could be large. To avoid an unreasonable case, if $d_{ai} > \lambda_i'$, such source will not be transmitted since the distortion without transmission is λ_i'. The final number of sources M' to be transmitted can be determined by

$$M' = f(N_0, E_a/L, M, \Sigma) = \arg\max_{V \leq M} V,$$

$$s.t. \quad \forall i, i \leq V : \sigma_i'\frac{N_0}{E_a/L}\sum_{j=1}^{V}\sigma_j' \leq \lambda_i', \tag{13.14}$$

where $\Sigma = \{\sigma'_i | i = 1, 2, \cdots, M\}$. The solution can be easily found by the half-interval search. An approximate solution is to find the first source $\mathscr{X}_i$ which satisfies $\sigma'_i < \frac{N_0}{E_a/L} \sum_{j=1}^{M} \sigma'_j$ and then $M' = i - 1$. $m = M - M'$ sources are not to be transmitted.

Note that if a source S_i is dropped without transmission, the expected MSE is

$$d_{ti} = \mathbb{E}((S_i - 0)^2) = \lambda_i. \tag{13.15}$$

The summation of the expected MSE over M sources is

$$D_{analog}(\mathscr{X}) = \sum_{i=1}^{M} d_{ai} = \frac{N_0}{E_a/L} \left(\sum_{i=1}^{M'} \sigma'_i \right)^2 + \sum_{i=M'+1}^{M} \lambda'_i. \tag{13.16}$$

13.3.2.5 Overall Distortion Optimization

To achieve the optimized overall distortion, we are to find the quantization steps Q_i and the number of sources to be quantized (K). From the above analysis, given the sources, we know that the number of digital bits, total energy (E_d) and bandwidth (B_d) for the digital bits, and the number of dropped sources (T) are all functions of K and the quantization step $Q_i, i = 1, \cdots, K$. Thus, the proposed quantization serves the role of energy and bandwidth allocation between digital coding and analog coding.

In the full bandwidth case, i.e., $B = NL/2$, the bandwidth for analog coding is $B_a = B - B_d = L(N - T)/2$ and $M = 2B_a/L = N - T$ sources are transmitted in analog ($M \leq N$). The energy allocated to analog coding (E_a) is

$$E_a = E - E_d = P_s NL - P_d B_d = P_s NL - 2\beta P_s B_d. \tag{13.17}$$

Correspondingly, the average per-symbol energy P_a for transmitting an analog signal is $P_a = E_a/(M'L)$. Note that given M sources, N_0, E_a, the number of sources M' which are transmitted can be determined as discussed in the previous subsection ($M' \leq M$), i.e., $M' = M - m = N - T - m$.

In the optimization, the overall distortion consists of two parts: the distortion from analog transmission and the distortion caused by the dropping of sources. It is the overall distortion since we have assured zero distortion over the digital coding part. Based on the derived optimal distortion of the analog coding in (13.16), we can get the analog transmission distortion over the set of residual sources and the non-quantized sources, which is the expected distortion statistically. The summation of the expected distortion for N sources is

$$D_{hyb}(K) = \frac{N_0}{E_a/L} \underbrace{(\sum_{i=1}^{K} \sigma_i' + \sum_{i=K+1}^{M'} \sigma_i)^2 + \sum_{i=M'+1}^{M} \lambda_i + \underbrace{\sum_{i=M+1}^{N} \lambda_i}_{\text{dropping distortion}}}_{\text{analog transmission distortion}}$$

$$= \frac{N_0}{P_s N - P_d B_d/L} (\sum_{i=1}^{K} \sigma_i' + \sum_{i=K+1}^{M'} \sigma_i)^2 + \sum_{i=M'+1}^{N} \lambda_i$$

$$= \frac{N_0}{P_s(N - \frac{2\beta B_d}{L})} (\sum_{i=1}^{K} \frac{Q_i}{\sqrt{12}} + \sum_{i=K+1}^{M'} \sigma_i)^2 + \sum_{i=M'+1}^{N} \lambda_i. \tag{13.18}$$

In (13.18), we assume $Q_i \leq 2\sigma_i$ for $i = 1, 2, \cdots, K$ to assure the accuracy of the model. Note that when the quantization step Q_i is far larger than the source standard deviation σ_i, the quantized coefficients are prone to be zeros and it is equivalent to the case that no quantization is performed for source S_i. Note that in the time-varying channel, N_0 is the equivalent variance of the additive white noises during the transmission of these N sources. The channel SNR within such time duration is $SNR_{tar} = 10 log_{10}(P_s/N_0)$, which we also refer to as target SNR in our optimization. Generally, channel SNR is unknown at the sender ahead of the transmission. We will discuss the influence when the target SNR does not match the actual channel SNR in Section 13.5.

Finally, the optimization over the distortion is written as

$$\underset{K; Q_i, i=1, \cdots, K}{\arg\min} \quad D_{hyb}(K). \tag{13.19}$$

13.4 A Practical Design

We find from the distortion expression given in (13.18) that, for a given set of Gaussian sources, finding the optimal quantization-based HDA scheme under energy and bandwidth constraints is a mixed integer nonlinear programming (MINLP) problem, which is in general NP-hard [75]. In this section, we propose a practical algorithm to efficiently find a sub-optimal solution.

The algorithm is based on two simplifications. First, we prioritize sources with different variances for quantization. In the following, we present a theorem which suggests that quantizing sources with larger variances brings larger gains.

Theorem 1. *For sources with diverse variances, given the same digital bit budget, the distortion reduction for quantizing a source with larger variance is larger than quantizing a source with smaller variance.*

The proof of Theorem 1 can be found in [149]. We provide some hints in the following. In analog coding, for a set of Gaussian sources with diverse variances, the sources with large variances will be assigned with smaller scaling factors (g_i) in the optimal power allocation. As a result, the recovered values of these large-variance sources will have larger distortions as indicated in (13.10), (13.11) and (13.13).

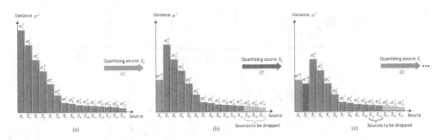

Fig. 13.2 Illustration of the proposed algorithm. Horizontal axis indicates the source identity while the vertical axis shows the variance of the corresponding source. (a) and (b) indicate the 1st round quantization over source S_1. After the quantization, the variance for the residual source as marked by blue is $\sigma_1'^2$. $T \doteq t_1 = 3$ sources with the smallest variances as marked in yellow are to be dropped. (b) and (c) indicate the 2nd round quantization over source S_2. Another 2 ($t_2 = 2$) sources with the smallest variances as marked by red are to be dropped.

Applying quantization to such sources will significantly reduce the variance of residuals so that they can be assigned with much larger scaling factors. This will greatly increase the perceived SNR of the analog parts and results in much smaller distortion in the recovered values. This explains why we select the first K sources with largest variances for quantization rather than over the sources with small variances.

The second simplification in our practical design is to discretize the quantization steps. In round i operation, we pick the source S_i and evaluate the quantization choices $Q_i = \omega\sigma_i, \omega \in \Omega = \{1/1024, 1/512, 1/256, 1/128, 1/64, 1/32, 1/16, 1/8, 1/4, 1/2, 1, 2, 4.133$ [1] $\}$. For each choice, we evaluate the overall distortion using (13.18). We then compare the distortion with that achieved in the last round and see whether there is any distortion reduction. If the largest distortion reduction ΔD among all the quantization choices is larger than zero, we quantize this source using the corresponding optimal quantization step. Then, we proceed to the next source S_{i+1} (next round of $i + 1$). If, in any step, there is no distortion reduction, the quantization process stops and the selected quantization steps are output. The complete practical algorithm is presented in Algorithm 10.

Fig. 13.2 illustrates our algorithm with an example. The horizontal axis indicates the source identity, with the sources already being sorted based on the variances, while the vertical axis shows the variance of the corresponding source. A total of 15 Gaussian sources will be transmitted under the bandwidth ratio of one (i.e., there is just sufficient bandwidth for pure analog transmission). In the 1st round operation as shown in (a) and (b), we determine Q_1^* for source S_1. The variance for the residuals of this source is reduced to $\sigma_1'^2$. Due to the digital coding of the quantized coefficients, $t_1 = 3$ sources with the smallest variances as marked in yellow need to be dropped. With the energy and bandwidth consumed by the digital coding

---

[1] 4.133 is obtained by setting b_i to 0 in (13.7). It is equivalent to the case that no quantization is performed, i.e., $\omega = \infty$.

Algorithm 10 Quantization-based resource allocation

Input: $S = \{S_i\}, \Sigma = \{\sigma_i | i = 1, 2, \cdots, N\}; \Sigma_i = \sigma_i; P_s, N_0; B = NL/2; \beta$
Output: $K^*; Q_i^*, i = 1, 2, \cdots, K^*$
1: $B_d = 0; D_{opt} = \infty$ ▷ Initialization
2: **for** $i = 1$ to N **do**
3:      $B_d' = B_d; \Sigma' = \Sigma$
4:      **for** each ω in Ω **do**
5:          $Q_i = \omega\sigma_i$ ▷ set the quantization step
6:          Based on (13.7) (or actual entropy coding result) and (13.8), calculate b_i and c_i
7:          $B_d = B_d' + c_i$ ▷ bandwidth for digital coding
8:          $\sigma_i' = Q_i/\sqrt{12}$
9:          $\Sigma_i' = \sigma_i'$
10:         $T = 2B_d/L$
11:         $E_a = P_s(NL - 2\beta B_d)$
12:         $M = N - T$
13:         Based on (13.14), calculate M'
14:         Based on the first row of (13.18), calculate $D_{hyb}(i)$
15:         Record $\mathscr{D}_{hyb}(i, Q_i) = D_{hyb}(i), \mathscr{C}(Q_i) = c_i, \mathscr{A}(Q_i) = \sigma_i'$
16:      **end for**
17:      $Q_i^* = \arg\min_{Q_i} \mathscr{D}_{hyb}(i, Q_i)$
18:      $\Delta D = D_{opt} - D_{hyb}^*(i)$
19:      **if** $\Delta D <= 0$ **then**
20:          $K^* = i - 1$; break
21:      **else**
22:          $D_{opt} = \mathscr{D}_{hyb}(i, Q_i^*)$
23:          $B_d \leftarrow B_d' + \mathscr{C}(Q_i^*)$
24:          $\Sigma_i' = \mathscr{A}(Q_i^*); \Sigma = \Sigma';$
25:      **end if**
26: **end for**

---

excluded, analog coding is conducted on the residual sources and non-quantized sources (with dropped sources excluded). Similarly, (b) and (c) show the 2nd round operation which makes quantization over source S_2.

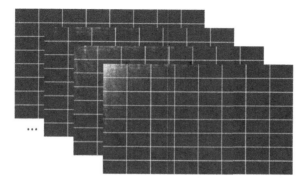

Fig. 13.3 Partition of 3D-DCT coefficients into chunks.

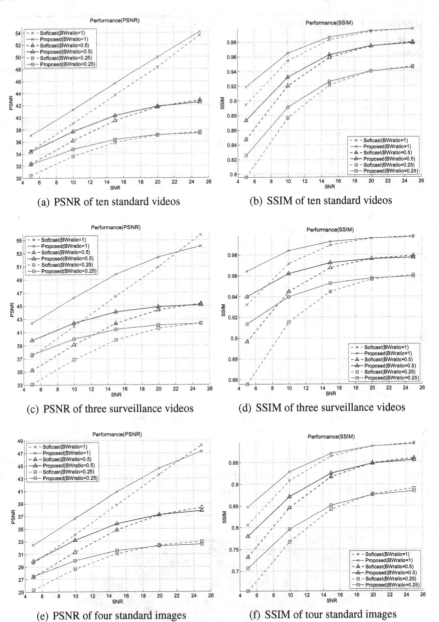

(a) PSNR of ten standard videos

(b) SSIM of ten standard videos

(c) PSNR of three surveillance videos

(d) SSIM of three surveillance videos

(e) PSNR of four standard images

(f) SSIM of tour standard images

Fig. 13.4 Average PSNR and SSIM performance of three data sets (target SNR 10dB).

13.5 Implementation and Evaluation

In this section, we evaluate the performance of the proposed HDA scheme through a wireless video transmission system.

13.5.1 Implementation

The video transmission system is implemented based on SoftCast [19]. First, a three dimensional discrete cosine transform (3D-DCT) is applied to a Group of Pictures (GOP) (e.g., 16 frames) to de-correlate the pixel values. If image transmission is considered, 2D-DCT will be used instead of 3D-DCT. Second, the transform coefficients in each transformed temporal plane are uniformly partitioned into blocks, referred to as chunks, as illustrated in Fig. 13.3. The chunks in the upper-left corner correspond to low spatial frequencies while those in the bottom-right corner correspond to high frequencies. Based on the observation that neighboring coefficients exhibit similar statistics, coefficients in the same chunk are treated as instances from the same zero-mean Gaussian source. Third, the chunks are sorted according to their computed variances, and those with the largest variances can be transmitted under a given bandwidth budget. The power scaling factors are computed for each chunk and the scaled coefficients are transmitted using amplitude modulation. We strictly follow the implementation details of SoftCast as described in [19], including the GOP size of 16 frames and 64 chunks per frame.

In the implementation of the proposed HDA scheme, we make quantization decisions for the sorted chunks and allocate energy and bandwidth resources according to the proposed practical algorithm. Since we know the exact signal realizations of each source, i.e., transform coefficients in a given chunk, we use Huffman coding [156] to encode the quantized coefficients and obtain the exact number of bits during the optimization process. Based on the observation which will be shown later, that the quantization steps for different sources tend to be similar, we will use the optimized quantization step of the first chunk as the quantization steps for other chunks to reduce the computation cost.

Careful readers may have noticed that the channel SNR is an input parameter of the distortion optimization procedure as described in (13.18). However, we do not assume the exact knowledge of channel SNR at the sender. Therefore, we will set a fixed target SNR, denoted by SNR_{tar} during the optimization and compute P_s/N_0 accordingly. In the next subsection, we will show that the performance is not very sensitive to this value.

We use QPSK modulation and rate-1/2 convolutional code to transmit the digital bits. The average per-symbol energy for carrying digital bits is selected such that error-free transmission can be guaranteed when the channel SNR is above 4dB, i.e., $\beta = 2$. The physical-layer (PHY) implementation is assumed to be OFDM (orthogonal frequency division multiplexing), so that the PAPR (peak to average power ratio) will not be a severe issue for analog transmission.

13.5.2 Settings

Source signals: We test on three sets of visual signals. (i) The first set contains ten standard 720p (1280 × 720) test videos with a frame rate of 30 fps (frame per second). They are *In_to_tree*, *Jets*, *City*, *Spincalendar*, *ShuttleStart*, *Sheriff*, *Stockholm_ter*, *Shields_ter*, *Mobcal_ter* and *Parkrun*. These videos were captured from natural scenes using the moving cameras, so they contain rich details and present global motions. (ii) The second set of videos is captured by fixed cameras, often seen in surveillance scenarios. We use three videos *Ballet*, *Breakdancers* [157] and *BookArrival* [158] with resolution 1024×768^2. (iii) The third set of visual signals contains four standard 512×512 gray-scale test images, including *Lena*, *Boat*, *Barbara*, and *Peppers*.

Note that we only evaluate the transmission of the luminance (Y) component in the YUV video. In a practical video transmission system, the chrominance (U and V) components can be processed in the same way.

Channel configurations: We consider the memoryless noise channel with a wide range of channel SNRs. In the simulations, channel SNRs of 5dB, 10dB, 15dB, 20dB, and 25dB are tested. We also consider the effect of bandwidth ratio (*BW ratio*), which is defined as the ratio of channel bandwidth to data source bandwidth. Three cases are tested, corresponding to $BW\,ratio = 1, 0.5$ and 0.25. They are also referred to as full, half and quarter bandwidth cases. When $BW\,ratio < 1$, we first discard $(1 - BW\,ratio) \times N$ chunks with the smallest variances before we execute the resource allocation algorithm.

Evaluation metrics: Both the objective quality measure PSNR and the structural similarity measure SSIM [159] are used for evaluation. We also show some reconstructed frames for perception experience comparison (some displayed images are cropped images).

13.5.3 Results

13.5.3.1 System Comparisons

We first perform a system-level comparison between the proposed HDA scheme and the state-of-the-art pure analog scheme SoftCast. The comparison is carried out under both simulated channel conditions and real wireless environment using trace-based emulation.

Simulated AWGN channel: We evaluate the performance under simulated AWGN channel by considering a practical scenario where the encoder does not know the channel SNRs. In the optimization process of our proposed HDA scheme, the encoder uses a fixed target channel SNR of 10dB. Therefore, the results obtained in this set of simulations are also valid for block fading channels. Fig. 13.4 shows

---

[2] The three videos are from multi-view videos. We use videos from the first view as our test videos.

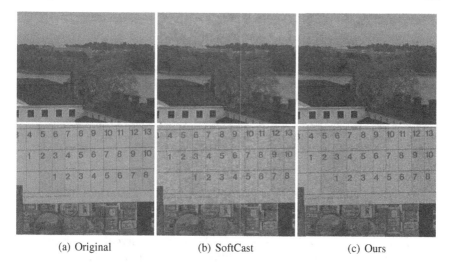

(a) Original   (b) SoftCast   (c) Ours

Fig. 13.5 The standard video set: *In-to-tree* and *Spincalendar* (cropped region size 320 × 250), channel SNR 5dB.

(a) Original   (b) SoftCast   (c) Ours

Fig. 13.6 The surveillance video set: *Ballet* (frame size 1024 × 768), channel SNR 5dB.

the PSNR and SSIM comparisons for the three sets of test videos/images. In each subfigure, the performance curves under different bandwidth ratios are included. Results show that the proposed HDA scheme outperforms SoftCast, in terms of both PSNR and SSIM, in most SNR regions for all bandwidth settings. On average, the proposed scheme can achieve up to 2.5dB, 5.0dB, 2.9dB gains in terms of PSNR on the three data sets, respectively. We notice that at a higher SNR of 25dB, there is some performance loss in PSNR of the proposed scheme. This is because the results presented in this figure are based on the optimization at a 10dB channel SNR. When the actual channel condition deviates from the targeted one by 15dB, the results are not optimal any more. However, if the channel SNR is expected to vary in a higher SNR value range, the encoder could set the target SNR to a higher value too. Later, we will show the performance curve of different target SNR settings. For now, in practical wireless environments, we find that setting target SNR to 10dB achieves a good performance trade-off between low-SNR regime and high-SNR regime.

(a) Original   (b) SoftCast   (c) Ours

Fig. 13.7 The standard image set: *Peppers* (image size 512×512), channel SNR 10dB.

Among the three types of test signals, the gain for surveillance videos is the largest. That is because the variances of different sources from the surveillance video differ by a larger number of magnitudes. The visual quality comparisons are given in Fig. 13.5, Fig. 13.6 and Fig. 13.7. Due to space limitations, only representative HDA/quantization/images/videos of each category are shown.

Performance on mobile trace: To evaluate the performance under varying channels, we test the performance under a real wireless environment with the mobile trace captured using Sora [38] (equipped with a WARP radio board) over 802.11a/g-based WLAN. The test sequences we use are *Sheriff* and *In_to_tree* (12 GOPs, 192 frames). The comparative results are shown in Fig. 13.8. It is clear that our proposed scheme can achieve consistent significant gain in comparison with SoftCast. Note that the target SNR is set as 10dB here.

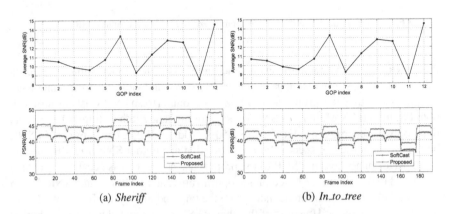

(a) *Sheriff*   (b) *In_to_tree*

Fig. 13.8 Performance comparisons on *Sheriff* and *In_to_tree* under fast varying channel. For each video, the top subfigure shows the average channel SNR for each GOP and the bottom subfigure shows the received quality for each frame. GOP size is 16. Target SNR is set as 10dB.

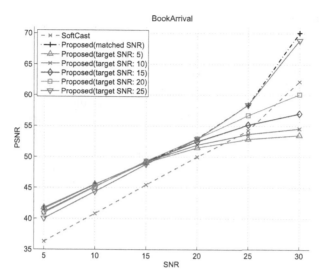

Fig. 13.9 Performance comparison on *BookArrival* under different target SNR settings. GOP size is 16.

13.5.3.2 Micro-benchmarks — Impact of Target SNR (SNR_{tar})

In the system level comparison, we have fixed the SNR_{tar} to 10dB. Now, we set SNR_{tar} to 5dB, 10dB, 15dB, 20dB, and 25dB, respectively, to evaluate its influence on the overall performance. Fig. 13.9 shows the performance curves of different target SNRs for test video *BookArrival* when the bandwidth ratio is one. All the SNR_{tar} settings have pretty good adaptation capabilities. When SNR_{tar} is set too low, the performance tends to saturate at high SNRs; when SNR_{tar} is set too high, it incurs some performance loss at low SNR regime. In a practical system, the encoder could set SNR_{tar} based on a rough estimation of the channel to achieve the desired trade-off.

We have also evaluated different SNR_{tar}'s over the ten standard test videos, and under the bandwidth ratios of 1, 0.5 and 0.25. Due to space limitations, we do not plot the performance curves. They basically show the same trend as that in Fig. 13.9, but the differences between different curves are smaller. When the actual channel SNR is 5dB but the encoder parameters are optimized for SNR_{tar}=20dB, the received video PSNR is about 0.6dB lower than the optimal result. Similarly, when the actual channel SNR is 20dB but the encoder parameters are optimized for SNR_{tar}=5dB, the received video PSNR is around 0.4dB lower than the optimal result. A mid-level target SNR, e.g., 10dB, can maintain high performance over a wide range of channel SNRs, providing less than 0.3dB difference from the performance at matched SNRs. These results justify our proposed HDA scheme for the video transmissions in time-varying channels.

13.6 Summary

In this work, we propose an HDA scheme for the transmission of wireless video, which is modeled as a parallel Gaussian source with diverse variances. We have found that selective scalar quantization is a simple but efficient way to separate the content for digital and analog transmissions. Specifically, the sources with large variances should be quantized while the sources with small variances should be left unchanged. Within the proposed scalar quantization-based HDA framework, we have solved the optimal resource allocation problem and have derived a practical scheme to achieve sub-optimal performance. Experimental results show that the proposed scheme can outperform the state-of-the-art analog scheme by up to 5.0dB and 2.9dB in terms of received signal PSNR for video and image transmissions, respectively.

Chapter 14
Structure-Preserving Hybrid Digital-Analog Transmission

14.1 Introduction

The crux of the HDA transmission problem is what type of information is more efficiently represented and transmitted in digital form than in analog. The previous chapter presents a solution where the decisions are made based on the objective video quality, or the mean squared error (MSE) criterion. The human visual perception is largely ignored. The only work we could find along the line of pseudo-analog (or HDA) transmission that takes subjective visual quality into consideration is G-Cast [160], but it only considers image transmission. G-Cast[160] splits an image into a base layer which contains the DC and some low-frequency components and an enhancement layer which contains the gradient information. The former is digitally encoded and transmitted while the latter is transformed and transmitted in pseudo-analog way. Results show that, by transmitting image gradients instead of pixel intensities, the reconstructed visual quality can be significantly improved. However, G-Cast is not readily extended to video transmission because it is harder to compact the energy of gradient values than intensity values for motion pictures. In other words, the gradient information in a video cannot be easily decorrelated, which will greatly affect the transmission efficiency.

It is well known that human visual system (HVS) creates the *Mach bands illusion* because HVS performs spatial high-boost filtering on the luminance channel and sharpens the edges of what we perceive [161]. This is why the structural information widely existing in natural images is considered very important and why the structural similarity (SSIM) index [159] was designed to improve on traditional objective image measurement metrics like PSNR or MSE. However, structural information such as texture and edges mainly resides in intermediate and high-frequency bands. Unfortunately for pseudo-analog transmission, when the bandwidth is not sufficient, only the low-frequency bands will be kept in order to minimize MSE. This is common when the transmitted videos are high-definition (HD) ones. Fig. 14.1 shows a fraction of a reconstructed 720p (1280 × 720) video

DOI: 10.1201/9781003118688-14

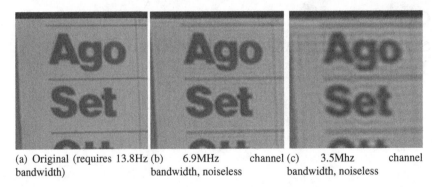

(a) Original (requires 13.8Hz (b)   6.9MHz   channel (c)   3.5Mhz   channel
bandwidth)   bandwidth, noiseless   bandwidth, noiseless

Fig. 14.1 A reconstructed block in a 720p video *spincalendar* from analog transmission. Even under a noiseless channel, the visual quality degradation due to dropping intermediate and high-frequency coefficients is huge.

spincalendar when the channel bandwidth is 6.9MHz and 3.5MHz, respectively. The visual quality is quite poor even when the channel is noiseless.

In this chapter, we present a structure-preserving HDA wireless video delivery scheme, named SharpCast, which simultaneously achieves continuous quality adaptation to varying wireless channels and high-quality visual experience of the reconstructed video. The basic approach of SharpCast is to decompose video into *content* part (smooth image) and *structure* part. Human visual system is sensitive to the structure part, so it is digitized, channels coded and reliably transmitted. Then, the content part will be transmitted under the constraint of remaining bandwidth and power. We notice that although transmitting the highest-energy DCT coefficients in analog saves bandwidth, the energy consumption is huge. Conversely, if they are transmitted in digital, the benefits of energy saving outweighs the drawbacks of consuming additional bandwidth. Therefore, in the proposed SharpCast scheme, both the structural information and the highest-energy DCT coefficients are transmitted in digital and the rest of the information is transmitted in analog.

In the design of SharpCast, the key technical challenge is the bandwidth and power allocation among the structure part, highest-energy coefficients and the remaining coefficients with an objective to optimize the received video quality. We tackle this problem by splitting it into two sub-problems. First, we determine the bandwidth share of the structure part assuming that the remaining content part will be transmitted in analog. Second, given the remaining share of the bandwidth and power, we determine the number of coefficients in the content part that will be transmitted in digital as well as the quantization parameter (QP) to digitize them. Both digital parts will be protected with strong channel codes and robust modulation schemes to ensure their correct reception even under very poor channel conditions. The analog part has the ability to adapt to varying channel conditions.

Our implementation of SharpCast is evaluated over standard 720p test video sequences and the performance is compared to the state-of-the-art HEVC-based digital method, the pioneering pseudo-analog method SoftCast [19] and a recent HDA scheme called WSVC [35]. Both the traditional PSNR measure and the SSIM measure are considered. The results show that when channel SNR ranges from $5dB$ to $20dB$, SharpCast achieves a comparable or slightly better performance than an omniscient HEVC-based digital scheme in which the exact channel state information (CSI) of the next time instance is assumed to be known. Compared to SoftCast and WSVC, SharpCast outperforms in almost the entire SNR range and the gain is significant in poor channel conditions. When the SNR is 5dB, the PSNR gain over WSVC is between 2.1dB and 2.9dB and that over SoftCast is between 4.4dB and 6.0dB under different channel bandwidth settings. The SSIM gains are also significant. More importantly, the visual quality of the reconstructed pictures from SharpCast is notably better.

14.2 SharpCast System Design

14.2.1 Overview

SharpCast is a structure-preserving HDA video delivery scheme aiming to achieve both graceful quality degradation and high visual fidelity even under bandwidth constrained scenarios. At the core of the SharpCast system is the separation of the digital and analog parts. SharpCast encodes and transmits two types of information in digital form. One is the structural information which human perception is very sensitive to. The other is the most energy-intensive chunks in the content information in order to achieve high energy efficiency. The encoded bit streams for both types of information are protected by strong channel codes and transmitted with a robust digital modulation scheme to ensure error-free delivery even under very unfavorable channel conditions. The rest of the video will be transmitted in pseudo-analog fashion to achieve the desired channel adaptation properties.

The block diagram of the SharpCast sender is depicted in Fig. 14.2. In the rest of this section, we will detail the SharpCast sender design, including video decomposition and the processing and transmission of the decomposed digital and analog parts. We will leave the discussion of the resource allocator, which is responsible for bandwidth and power allocation, to the next section. Although the resource allocator is not explicitly shown in Fig. 14.2, it determines the key parameters in various modules, including the quantization parameter Q for structure compression, the number N_0 of energy-intensive chunks to be digitized, and the quantization step q to be used. It also determines the average symbol energy for digital and analog transmissions, denoted by P_d and P_a in the figure, respectively.

Fig. 14.3 shows the block diagram of the SharpCast receiver. The symbols from digital transmissions, denoted by Y_d, are fed into the demodulator and channel decoder sequentially. The decoded bit streams S_{d1} and S_{d2} are used to reconstruct the structure part and the quantized chunks, respectively. By using a robust digital

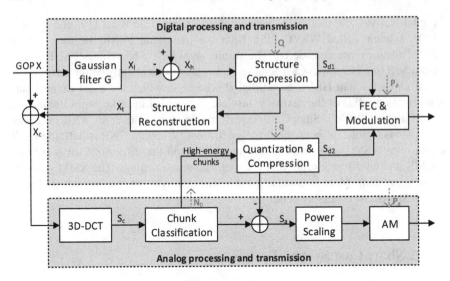

Fig. 14.2 Block diagram of the SharpCast sender. All the parameters marked with red font and dotted arrow lines are determined by the resource allocation algorithms.

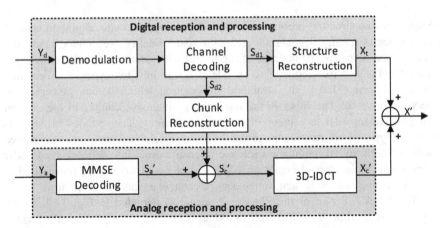

Fig. 14.3 Block diagram of the SharpCast receiver.

modulation and coding scheme, we can ensure that the digital parts are received error-free, so the structure reconstruction X_t is exactly what is transmitted by the sender. The quantized parts of the energy-intensive chunks are also faithfully reconstructed. Meanwhile, the received pseudo-analog symbols, denoted by Y_a, are processed with an MMSE decoder and S_a' is estimated. Summing up the quantized chunks and S_a', we will obtain the estimation of the 3D-DCT coefficients, denoted by S_c'. Then the estimation of the content information, denoted by X_c', is obtained by applying a 3D-IDCT. The final reconstruction of the original video, denoted by X', is obtained by summing up X_t and X_c'.

(a) X_l: low-frequency part after Gaussian filtering

(b) X_h: intermediate and high-frequency part after Gaussian filtering

(c) X_c: content part (with structure residual) for transmission

(d) X_t: structure part for digital transmission, QP=34

Fig. 14.4 Demonstrating the decomposition of the first frame in sequence *spincalendar* for HDA transmission: $X = X_l + X_h = X_c + X_t$.

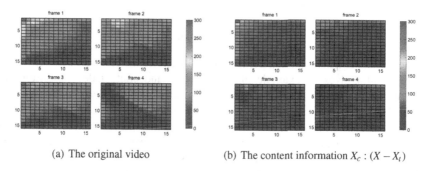

(a) The original video

(b) The content information $X_c : (X - X_t)$

Fig. 14.5 Comparing the energy distributions of the original video and the analog part, video *spincalendar*, GOP size is 4, Q=30.

14.2.2 Video Decomposition

In SharpCast, all processing and transmissions are based on group of pictures (GOP). The video source X is first decomposed into *content* part X_c and *structure* part X_t and then some energy-intensive chunks are further extracted from the content part for digital transmission. The residuals in the content part will be transmitted in analog.

The decomposition into content and structure parts is accomplished through two phases: the initialization phase and the refinement phase, on a per frame basis. In the initialization phase, we apply a two-dimensional low-pass Gaussian filter G to each frame to obtain the low-frequency part X_l and the intermediate and high-frequency part X_h. Mathematically,

$$X_l = X \bigotimes G;$$
$$X_h = X - X_l.$$

(14.1)

The discrete convolutional kernel [161] G can be written as:

$$G_{i,j}(d, \sigma_G) = \beta e^{-\frac{(i-\lceil d/2 \rceil)^2 + (j-\lceil d/2 \rceil)^2}{2\sigma_G^2}},$$

(14.2)

where d is an odd number denoting the width and height of the Gaussian window, σ_G is the standard deviation, and β is a normalization factor. Although different parameter selections will create different decomposition results, we found through experiments that setting $d = 13, \sigma_G = 4$ is a good choice in general.

In the refinement phase, the intermediate and high-frequency part X_h is encoded into bit stream S_{d1} with a digital video encoder. Note that the quantization step in digital coding will create difference between the original and the reconstructed signals. The *structural information* X_t is actually referred to the quantized intermediate and high-frequency part, or the reconstruction from S_{d1}:

$$X_t = X_h(Q);$$
$$X_c = X - X_t,$$

(14.3)

where Q is the quantization parameter and X_c denotes the *content information*.

Fig. 14.4 gives an example of the structure and content decomposition. The picture is cropped from the first frame of video sequence *spincalendar*. We could find that the structure part (Fig. 14.4(d)) contains important information which, when correctly recovered, will greatly enhance the perceived video quality. In SharpCast, setting aside some network resources for structural information not only improves the perceived visual quality, but also allows the residual information to have a better energy packing. Fig. 14.5 shows the comparison of energy distributions (variances of DCT coefficients) before and after the structure part is extracted from the video signal. We can find that the content part has much more concentrated energy than the original video, suggesting that the sender could discard a large portion of chunks without much performance loss when the bandwidth is not sufficient. This is a very favorable feature for analog transmission. For illustration purposes, we use a GOP size of 4 in this figure, but in our final implementation the GOP size is set to 16.

After the structure and content decomposition, the structural information is treated as a whole and processed as in a conventional digital communication framework. The content information X_c, on the other hand, needs to be further decomposed. As we have seen in Fig. 14.5, several chunks in the low-frequency band have very high energy. If they are transmitted in analog using amplitude modulation, the energy cost will be extremely high. Digitizing these chunks and transmitting the encoded bits through the digital method can significantly reduce the energy consumption. Although the digitized bit stream occupies more bandwidth, the cost of discarding small-energy chunks is well paid by the huge energy savings. In particular, we pick N_0 chunks with the highest energy and quantize them with step size q. The encoded bit stream is denoted as S_{d2}. Similarly, the digital encoding of the N_0 chunks will create residuals. The residual information together with all the other chunks constitute the analog part.

14.2.3 Digital Processing and Transmission

Both the structural information and the energy-intensive content chunks are processed and transmitted in digital. We adopt the state-of-the-art high-efficiency video coding (HEVC) for structural information compression. Once the quantization parameter Q is determined for structural information, HEVC encoder will generate a bit stream denoted by S_{d1}. The quantized content chunks contains DCT coefficients instead of pixel values. Therefore, we simply adopt arithmetic coding [162] for the compression and the encoded bit stream is denoted by S_{d2}. In the process of generating S_{d1} and S_{d2}, the key parameters are the quantization step Q for structure and q for content chunks. We leave the discussion of QP selection to the next section.

Here, we would like to note a practical implementation issue in structure compression. The intermediate and high-frequency information X_h is computed by $X_h = X - X_l$, so its dynamic range, denoted by $[X_{h,min}, X_{h,max}]$ could be as large as [-255,255]. Although HEVC codec supports bit depth larger than 8, its coding efficiency will degrade. Therefore, in order to achieve a high compression efficiency, we linearly scale the structure representation to [0, 255] before feeding it to the HEVC encoder. At the receiver, the output from the HEVC decoder is descaled according to $X_{h,min}$ and $X_{h,max}$. These two values are treated as metadata and will be transmitted faithfully. The scaling/descaling operations are considered as a part of the structure codec.

Strong protection should be provided to the digital bit stream, so we adopt a rate-1/2 convolutional code for forward error correction (FEC). Although there exist FEC codes with even lower rates, we choose to be compliant with the IEEE 802.11a standard [163] so that our system can be easily implemented and has higher potential to be actually deployed.

Among the four modulation schemes specified in 802.11a, BPSK is certainly the most robust one. However, we decided to use QPSK instead of BPSK in SharpCast. The reason is that QPSK could achieve exactly the same bit error rate (BER) as BPSK, if the per-symbol energy is doubled, while saving half of the bandwidth BPSK would need. For a hybrid video transmission in bandwidth-limited channel, leaving more bandwidth to pseudo-analog transmission will bring substantial gain. Although using higher-order modulation schemes such as 16-QAM and 64-QAM could save more bandwidth, these two modulation schemes are not energy-efficient.

Simulations also confirm that using QPSK with doubled per-symbol energy is the best choice under most channel conditions.

14.2.4 Analog Processing and Transmission

The content information X_c is transformed into the frequency domain by 3D-DCT. The DCT coefficients, denoted by S_c, are divided into M equal-size rectangular-shaped chunks. Coefficients in each chunk are treated as instances of the same Gaussian distribution and their variances, denoted by λ_i ($i = 1...M$), are computed. Then, chunks are sorted in descending order according to their variances. Without loss of generality, we assume that $\lambda_1 \geq \lambda_2 \geq \lambda_M$. Trading off bandwidth and energy, the sender quantizes N_0 highest-energy chunks (the selection of N_0 is also detailed in the next section). The quantization residual of the N_0 chunks and all the other chunks form the analog part, denoted by S_a.

Given the bandwidth budget, a sender will only transmit K chunks with the largest variances or energies. All the selected coefficients will be transmitted using amplitude modulation. It has been derived in SoftCast [19] that, in order to minimize the MSE at the receiver, coefficients in the ith chunks should be scaled by g_i, which can be computed by

$$g_i = \lambda_i'^{-\frac{1}{4}} \cdot \sqrt{\frac{P_a/N_a}{\frac{1}{K}\sum_{j=1}^{K}\sqrt{\lambda_j'}}}, \tag{14.4}$$

where P_a and N_a are the total transmission power and the number of transmitted coefficients, respectively. λ_i' is the variance of the ith chunk in S_a or $S_{a,i}$.

Although the variances of the first N_0 chunks can be computed after quantization, there is a much easier way to estimate them. Actually, after performing quantization with step q, the residuals can be modeled as uniformly distributed random variables in the range of $[0, q)$. Therefore, the variances used in (14.4) can be written as:

$$\lambda_i' = \begin{cases} q^2/3, & 1 \leq i \leq N_0 \\ \lambda_i, & N_0 + 1 \leq i \leq K \end{cases} \tag{14.5}$$

14.3 Resource Allocation

14.3.1 Problem Formulation

SharpCast is a HDA wireless video delivery scheme under power and bandwidth constraints. Both types of resources need to be properly allocated between digital and analog transmissions for the optimal video reception quality. Let B and P be the total bandwidth and power for transmitting a GOP of video, and let (B_d, P_d)

and (B_a, P_a) be the resources allocated to digital and pseudo-analog transmissions, respectively. Denote D_d and D_a as the distortions incurred to the digital and the analog parts. The objective of resource allocation is to minimize D_a while ensuring that $D_d = 0$. The problem can be formulated as:

$$
\begin{aligned}
\min\nolimits_{P_d, B_d, P_a, B_a} \ & D_a, \\
s.t. \ & D_d = 0 \\
& B_d + B_a \le B \\
& P_d + P_a \le P \\
& B_d, B_a \ge 0 \\
& P_d, P_a \ge 0.
\end{aligned}
\tag{14.6}
$$

For digital transmission, the most important parameter is the number of bits to be transmitted, denoted by N_d, although B_d is also determined by the coding and modulation scheme and P_d is further affected by the average symbol power p_d. Recall that the structural information is compressed into binary bits by HEVC and the N_0 quantized chunks are arithmetically encoded, so N_d is a function of the quantization parameter Q of the HEVC encoder as well as N_0 and q. The resources consumed by digital transmission can be explicitly written as:

$$
\begin{aligned}
B_d(Q, N_0, q) &= \alpha^{-1} \times N_d(Q, N_0, q); \\
P_d &= p_d \times B_d,
\end{aligned}
\tag{14.7}
$$

where α is the product of the coding and modulation rates. When rate-1/2 channel coding and QPSK modulation are used, α equals 1. α and p_d should be selected to ensure error-free transmission of the digital stream, which could be very sensitive to bit errors. When the digital transmission is successful, the distortion of the digital part is zero, i.e., $D_d = 0$.

Obviously, in order to make full use of network resources, equality should be achieved in both bandwidth and power constraints in (14.6). Therefore, under the condition that $B_d \le B$ and $P_d \le P$, the resources consumed by pseudo-analog transmission are:

$$
\begin{aligned}
B_a &= B - B_d, \ N_a = 2B_a; \\
P_a &= P - P_d,
\end{aligned}
\tag{14.8}
$$

where N_a is the number of coefficients in S_a that can be transmitted. It is twice B_a because every wireless symbol can carry two coefficients on its I and Q planes. Therefore, we shall sort the DCT coefficient chunks according to their variances and only the top K chunks (containing N_a coefficients) will be transmitted. Without loss of generality, we here assume that B_a is divisible by chunk size.

By definition, the distortion of the pseudo-analog transmission is:

$$
D_a = E\left\{ (S_a - S_a')^T (S_a - S_a') \right\}.
\tag{14.9}
$$

It can be derived into the following form in an additive white Gaussian noise (AWGN) channel with noise power σ^2:

$$D_a = \frac{1}{M} \left(\sum_{i=1}^{K} \frac{\sigma^2/2}{g_i^2} + \sum_{i=K+1}^{M} \lambda_i' \right), \tag{14.10}$$

where g_i is the power scaling factor for the ith chunk, λ_i is the variance of the ith chunk of S_a and M is the total number of chunks. The first term on the right-hand side corresponds to the transmitted chunks while the second term corresponds to the discarded chunks. The coefficients in the discarded chunks will be padded with zero at the receiver as it is the best estimate for a zero-mean Gaussian variable in order to minimize MSE.

14.3.2 The Proposed Solution

The joint optimization of bandwidth and power as defined in (14.6) is a mixed nonlinear programming problem. Increasing Q will reduce N_d but increase the structure residual energy thus increasing λ_i, and decreasing Q will have the opposite effect. Meanwhile, q, N_0 and λ_i will also make a difference on N_d and λ_i'. To tame the complexity, we propose a greedy strategy to solve the problem.

We first make a simplification by fixing the coding and modulation for digital transmission. In particular, rate-1/2 channel coding and QPSK modulation are always used. Thus, parameter α in (14.7) is fixed to 1. The constraint $D_d = 0$ will be guaranteed by adjusting the average symbol power p_d of digital transmission. Actually, for any given coding and modulation scheme, there exists a signal-to-noise ratio threshold beyond which the transmission will be error-free with high probability. Let γ denote the SNR threshold for (QPSK, 1/2) and let σ^2 be the noise power, then p_d is selected such that

$$\frac{p_d}{\sigma^2} \geq \gamma. \tag{14.11}$$

To make the best use of the power resource, $p_d = \gamma\sigma^2$.

Then, we divide the original problem into two subproblems:

Sub-Problem 1: Assuming all the content information is transmitted in analog, i.e., no chunks are quantized, how should bandwidth and power be allocated between the structure and the content parts? In other words, what is the optimal Q for structure compression?

Sub-Problem 2: Given the bandwidth and power share for the content part, how should we optimally choose N_0 and q, so that the MSE can be minimized?

14.3.3 Solving Sub-problem 1

In sub-problem 1, the total number of digital bits $N_d^{(1)}$ is simply a function of Q, denoted as $N_d^{(1)}(Q)$. Similar to the derivation of Equation (14.4) and (14.10), we could re-formulate sub-problem 1 as follows:

$$\min_{Q} \quad \frac{\sigma^2 B_a^{(1)}}{K^{(1)} P_a^{(1)}} \left(\sum_{i=1}^{K^{(1)}} \sqrt{\lambda_i} \right)^2 + \sum_{i=K^{(1)}+1}^{M} \lambda_i$$

$$s.t. \quad B_d^{(1)}(Q) \leq B \tag{14.12}$$

$$\gamma \sigma^2 B_d^{(1)} \leq P_d^{(1)} \leq P.$$

$$P_a^{(1)}, B_a^{(1)} \geq 0$$

where $B_a^{(1)}/P_a^{(1)}$ and $B_d^{(1)}/P_d^{(1)}$ is bandwidth / power for content information and digital structural information bit stream, respectively. $K^{(1)}$ denotes the number of chunks that $B_a^{(1)}$ bandwidth can afford. Equation (14.8) and Equation (14.7) still hold if the notations are replaced correspondingly. Again, to make the best use of the power resource, $\gamma \sigma^2 B_d^{(1)} = P_d^{(1)}$ should be achieved when σ^2 is known. Note that in a multicast session, in order to guarantee that the receiver who experiences the worst channel condition can decode and reconstruct the digital part, σ^2 should be set to the noise power of the worst receiver.

Recall that $X_c = X_l + X_{\Delta t}$, where $X_{\Delta t}$ is the residual of the structure part and is a function of the quantization parameter Q. Let S_c, S_l and $S_{\Delta t}$ denote the DCT coefficients of X_c, X_l and $X_{\Delta t}$ respectively. We further use $S_{c,i}$, $S_{l,i}$ and $S_{\Delta t,i}$ to denote the coefficients in the ith chunk of the corresponding signal. Then we have:

$$\lambda_i = var\{S_{c,i}\}$$
$$= var\{S_{l,i} + S_{\Delta t,i}\} \tag{14.13}$$
$$= \lambda_{l,i} + \lambda_{\Delta T,i} + cov\{S_{l,i}, S_{\Delta t,i}\}.$$

Next, we approximate λ_i based on several observations. To help readers understand these observations, we show the values of $\lambda_{c,i}$, $\lambda_{l,i}$ and $\lambda_{\Delta T,i}$ for video sequence *spincalendar* in Figure 14.6. The QP use in HEVC encoding is 30.

1. For natural pictures, the content part and the residual of the structure part can be considered independent, i.e., $cov\{S_{l,i}, S_{\Delta T,i}\} \approx 0$. Therefore, it is reasonable to approximate λ_i by the sum of $\lambda_{l,i}$ and $\lambda_{\Delta T,i}$;
2. The energy of the low-pass information is very compact. $\lambda_{l,i}$ could be a few magnitude larger than $\lambda_{\Delta T,i}$ when i is small($\leq M_1$), but it decays very fast. Therefore, it is reasonable to ignore $\lambda_{\Delta T,i}$ when $i \leq M_1$;
3. The residual of the structure part exhibits little spatial correlation. Therefore, performing 2D-DCT in spatial domain results in nearly uniform distribution of the coefficients. However, since temporal correlation may exist, performing

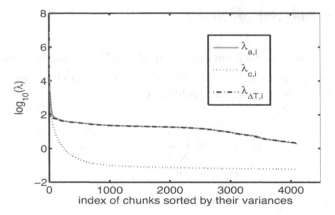

Fig. 14.6 The illustration of variances of each chunk of "Spincalendar720p" when QP = 30

DCT along the temporal dimension will compact the energy. A quick drop of energy will be observed in the 3D-DCT coefficients when i is larger than a certain threshold (M_2). Therefore, it is appropriate that we model $\lambda_{\Delta T,i}$ as a constant when $M_1 < i \leq M_2$ and make an approximation that $\lambda_{\Delta T,i}$ shows log-linearity when $i > M_2$.

In order to estimate $\lambda_{\Delta T,i}$, let us introduce $err(Q)$, which denotes the average energy of $X_{\Delta t}$ when the quantization parameter is Q in HEVC encoding. Due to the randomness of structure residual, we can model $S_{\Delta t,i}$ as i.i.d. Gaussian distribution. Equation (14.14) holds because the DCT transform is orthogonal.

$$\sum_{i=1}^{M} \lambda_{\Delta T,i} = M * err(Q). \tag{14.14}$$

Therefore, we model $\lambda_{c,i}$ as a piece-wise function as follows:

$$\lambda_i \approx \begin{cases} \lambda_{l,i} + \lambda_{\Delta T,i} \approx \lambda_{l,i} & 1 \leq i \leq M_1 \\ \lambda_{l,i} + err(Q) & M_1 < i \leq M_2 \\ \lambda_{l,i} + \{err(Q)\}^{\frac{M-i}{M-M_2}} & M_2 < i \leq M \end{cases} \tag{14.15}$$

$err(Q)$ can be calculated from $mse(Q)$ by a simple scaling:

$$err(Q) = \left(\frac{X_{h,max} - X_{h,min}}{255}\right)^2 mse(Q), \tag{14.16}$$

where $X_{h,max}$ and $X_{h,min}$ are the maximum and minimum values in the high-pass X_h, and $mse(Q)$ is the MSE of the reconstructed scaled structural information by HEVC when QP equals Q.

To find the optimal Q in (14.12), we also need to model the mapping from Q to $N_d^{(1)}(Q)$. $N_d^{(1)}(Q)$ can be calculated from $b(Q)$ which is the compression rate (bit per pixel) when $QP = Q$. To obtain $b(Q)$ and $mse(Q)$, our approach is to compress the scaled structure part of the first GOP using three QPs (small, medium and large), and fit the $b(Q)$ and $mse(Q)$ curves. Many related studies have been done on R-D modeling; we follow [164] and use the Cauchy-based distortion estimation formula $mse(\Delta) = b * \Delta^\beta$, where Δ is the quantization step. In HEVC, the relationship between Δ and QP is $\Delta = 2^{(QP-4)/6}$. For simplicity, we equivalently use (14.17) as the D-QP model:

$$mse(Q) = a_0 + a_1 \exp\{a_2 Q\} \tag{14.17}$$

As for the R-QP mapping, in TM5 [165], a simple model, i.e., $R = X/\Delta$ is used to estimate the rate given quantization step. Therefore, to fit the $b(Q)$, we also equivalently use an exponential function as specified in (14.18).

$$b(Q) = a_0' + a_1' \exp\{a_2' Q\} \tag{14.18}$$

In addition, the $var\{S_{\Delta t,i}\}$ calculated at the medium $QP = q_m$ setting will be used to determine M_2, while M_1 is set to a constant 50. In particular, we choose M_2 by minimizing the total absolute error of $var\{S_{\Delta t,i}\}, i = M_1 + 1, ..., M$:

$$
M_2 = \min_k \sum_{i=M_1+1}^{k} |var\{S_{\Delta t,i}(q_m)\} - err(q_m)|
$$
$$
+ \sum_{i=k+1}^{M} |var\{S_{\Delta t,i}(q_m)\} - \{err(q_m)\}^{\frac{M-i}{M-k}}| \tag{14.19}
$$

Based on the fitted curves, SharpCast encoder can find the optimal Q^* according to Equation (14.12) and encode the first GOP, the actual $(Q^*, b(Q^*))$ and $(Q^*, mse(Q^*))$ value-pairs of the first GOP are used to refine the fitted curves before encoding the second GOP, and so on. Once Q^* is obtained, the bandwidth and power for digital structure bit stream and content information transmission is determined accordingly, i.e., $B_a^{(1)}$ (or $K^{(1)}$) and $P_a^{(1)}$ are available for content information transmission.

14.3.4 Solving Sub-problem 2

The objective of sub-problem 2 is to find the optimal N_0 and q to quantize the energy-intensive chunks to further reduce the distortion of content information. N_0 and q are also treated as metadata and they can be faithfully received at the receiver side. Now that Q^* is decided, the SharpCast sender can compress the structural information and obtain the actual λ_i instead of approximating it as is done in solving sub-problem 1. We formulate the sub-problem 2 in the following.

The 3D-DCT coefficients of the content information can be described by a mixed Gaussian model, $S_c \sim N(0, \lambda_i)$. The first N_0 chunks are quantized by step q. We can still model the N_0 chunks as a Gaussian distribution with zero mean and variance equal to $\lambda = \sum_{i=1}^{N_0} \lambda_i / N_0$. The mean quantization distortion of these chunks is $D = q^2/3$. According to the rate-distortion theory of Gaussian source [154], the rate of entropy coding these quantized coefficients is:

$$R(N_0, q) = \frac{1}{2} log_2(\frac{\lambda}{D}) = \frac{1}{2} log_2(\frac{3 \sum_{i=1}^{N_0} \lambda_i}{q^2 N_0})$$ (14.20)

Let $B_d^{(2)}$ and $P_d^{(2)}$ denote the bandwidth and power for bit stream S_{d2} transmission, and $N_d^{(2)}$ denote the number of bits in S_{d2}, which can be calculated by $N_d^{(2)} = R(N_0, q) * N_0 * N_c$, where N_c is the number of coefficients per chunk. Then the following relationships can be easily derived when S_{d2} is transmitted using QPSK 1/2 modulation and coding scheme:

$$\begin{aligned} K &= K^{(1)} - 2R(N_0, q) * N_0 \\ P_a &= P_a^{(1)} - P_d^{(2)} \\ P_d^{(2)} &= p_d N_d^{(2)} \\ B_a &= B_a^{(1)} - N_d^{(2)} \end{aligned}$$ (14.21)

Given that total bandwidth $B_a^{(1)}$ and power $P_a^{(1)}$ are allocated for content information transmission, sub-problem 2 can be formulated as follows:

$$\min_{N_0, q} \frac{\sigma^2 B_a}{K P_a} \left(\sum_{i=1}^{K} \sqrt{\lambda_i'} \right)^2 + \sum_{i=K+1}^{M} \lambda_i'$$

$$\begin{aligned} s.t. \quad & N_d^{(2)} + B_a \leq B_a^{(1)} \\ & P_a + P_d^{(2)} \leq P_a^{(1)}. \\ & P_a, B_a \geq 0 \end{aligned}$$ (14.22)

where λ_i' is defined in (14.5) and K denotes the maximum number of chunks that can be transmitted when bandwidth for analog transmission is constrained by B_a. Again, in video multicast, to ensure the faithful reception of digital signals of the weakest receiver, σ in the above optimization problem should be the largest noise power. Closed form solutions of N_0 and q are impossible, so we solve this problem with the help of the following two properties:

1. Owing to the good energy packing of S_a, the first several λ_is are magnitudes bigger than the rest. Quantizing large energy chunks can lead to higher energy

efficiency. If q is fixed, when N_0 increases by 1 starting from 0, the distortion D_a will initially decrease and then increase;

2. When N_0 is fixed, when q decreases starting from a large value, the distortion D_a will initially decrease and then increase, because large q leads to large λ_i' while too small q will result in large $R(N_0, q)$ thus more chunks will have to be discarded.

Therefore, we firstly initiate a large q and increase N_0 until the distortion D_a doesn't decrease, then we decrease q to a half and find the optimal N_0 again. This process stops when decreasing q does not provide any gain.

14.4 Evaluation and Results

14.4.1 Methodology

We evaluate the performance of the proposed SharpCast through extensive simulations. First, benchmark evaluation will be presented to illustrate the gains achieved by video decomposition and digitizing energy-intensive chunks, respectively. Then, we will present results on video multicast and compare SharpCast with several state-of-the-art reference schemes of different categories.

Video source: The resolution of the test video sequences is 1280×720. Nine typical test sequences (*stockholm, parkrun, city, spincalendar, sheriff, shuttlestart, in-to-tree, shields and jets*) are used.

Wireless channel: We consider AWGN channel and the target SNR range is $5\text{-}20dB$. To evaluate the performance under bandwidth constraints, we conduct experiments with bandwidth ratio setting of 0.25, 0.5 and 1, respectively. Here, bandwidth ratio *BwRatio* is defined as:

$$BwRatio = \frac{B}{N_c * M / 2} \tag{14.23}$$

where B is the available bandwidth (i.e., number of wireless symbols) and $N_c * M / 2$ is the bandwidth in need.

Evaluation metrics: Both the objective quality measure PSNR and the structural similarity measure SSIM [159] are used for evaluation. We also show some reconstructed frames for perception experience comparison. (The images displayed are cropped.)

Reference schemes: We implement three reference schemes, namely omniscient digital, SoftCast [19] and WSVC[35], and compare their performance with SharpCast. The omniscient digital scheme uses HEVC for source coding and standard modulation and coding schemes as defined in IEEE 802.11. The term *omniscient* means that we assume the sender knows the exact channel condition and therefore is able to select the best modulation and coding for the highest throughput.

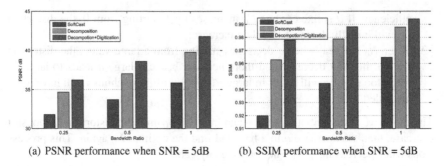

(a) PSNR performance when SNR = 5dB   (b) SSIM performance when SNR = 5dB

Fig. 14.7 The performance for benchmark comparison.

Practically, the performance of omniscient digital scheme is not achievable. We simply use it as an upper bound for possible digital implementations.

For fair comparison, all the analog or HDA schemes divide each frame into 256 chunks with equal size of 80×45. The GOP size is set to 16 for SoftCast, WSVC and SharpCast. Omniscient digital scheme and the digital transmission part in both SharpCast and WSVC all take hard Viterbi decoder for channel decoding. We follow the original implementation of WSVC which uses 1/8 convolutional codes and BPSK modulation except that we replace H264 codec with HEVC codec for better performance and fair comparison.

14.4.2 Benchmark Evaluation

The main insight of SharpCast is two-fold. First, extracting structural information from a video not only helps preserve the perceptually important structural information but leads to better energy packing of the remaining content information. Second, digitizing energy-intensive chunks of content information, which basically trades bandwidth for energy, is beneficial. We evaluated the gain of each individual component when channel SNR is 5dB and the results are shown in Fig. 14.7.

From the figures, it can be easily observed that both the decomposition and digitization bring significant performance gain, in both PSNR and SSIM, for all the tested bandwidth ratio. Decomposing video and transmitting structural information with heavy protection can greatly improve the structural similarity. In addition, extracting structural information leads to better energy packing of content information, thus bringing PSNR gain. We can see that digitization of high-energy chunks is also beneficial; there is an additional $2dB$ gain in PSNR and, of course, SSIM index is also improved.

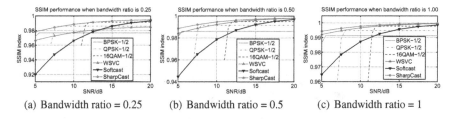

Fig. 14.8 The average SSIM performance comparison among different schemes.

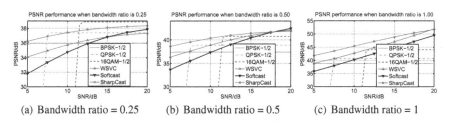

Fig. 14.9 The average PSNR performance comparison among different schemes.

14.4.3 Performance Comparison

In this section, we evaluate the performance of SharpCast in various channel conditions and compare it with reference schemes. The digital parts of SharpCast are transmitted such that any receiver with a channel SNR above 5dB can correctly decode. Therefore, the results presented in this subsection are achievable in multicast sessions. Fig. 14.8 and Fig. 14.9 present the SSIM and PSNR performance achieved by all four schemes when bandwidth ratio is 0.25, 0.5 and 1, respectively.

Results show that SharpCast outperforms Softcast up to $6.0dB$, $4.9dB$ and $4.4dB$, and outperforms WSVC up to $2.9dB$, $2.3dB$ and $2.1dB$ in PSNR, when bandwidth ratio is 1, 0.5 and 0.25, respectively. In terms of SSIM, SharpCast achieves improvements up to 0.03, 0.044 and 0.058 over Softcast, and up to 0.002, 0.004 and 0.012 over WSVC, when bandwidth ratio equals 1, 0.5 and 0.25, respectively. We can also observe that the digital scheme, which adopts separate source compression and channel coding, suffers from an obvious "cliff effect". Even compared with the performance envelope of the omniscient HEVC-based digital scheme, SharpCast still excels. When the bandwidth ratio is 0.5 and 1, SharpCast outperforms the digital scheme in both PSNR and SSIM. When the bandwidth ratio is 0.25, SharpCast also achieves a higher SSIM index.

Among the three reference schemes, WSVC performs the closest to SharpCast. It achieves smooth rate adaptation and the performance gap with respect to SharpCast is small when the bandwidth ratio is 0.5 and 1. However, when the bandwidth ratio is 0.25, the performance gap becomes significantly larger. This is because WSVC loses too much structural information in low-variance chunks. In contrast, the chunks dropped by SharpCast only contain less important high-frequency information.

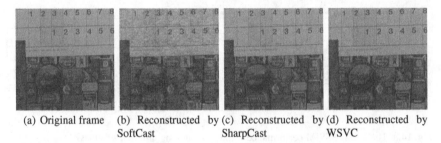

(a) Original frame (b) Reconstructed by (c) Reconstructed by (d) Reconstructed by
                        SoftCast   SharpCast   WSVC

Fig. 14.10 The first reconstructed frame of *spincalendar* using different schemes when bandwidth ratio is 0.25 and channel SNR equals 5dB.

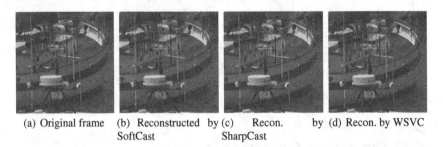

(a) Original frame (b) Reconstructed by (c)   Recon.   by (d) Recon. by WSVC
                        SoftCast   SharpCast

Fig. 14.11 The first reconstructed frame of *sheriff* using different schemes when bandwidth ratio is 0.25 and channel SNR equals 5dB.

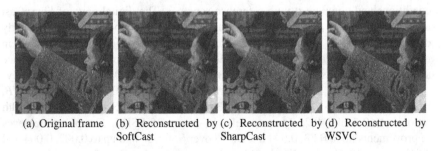

(a) Original frame (b) Reconstructed by (c) Reconstructed by (d) Reconstructed by
                        SoftCast   SharpCast   WSVC

Fig. 14.12 The first reconstructed frame of *shields* using different schemes when bandwidth ratio is 0.25 and channel SNR equals 5dB.

The gain in visual quality is also significant. Fig. 14.10, Fig. 14.11 and Fig. 14.12 compare part of the first frame in sequences *spincalendar*, *sheriff* and *shields* when the bandwidth ratio is 0.25 and channel SNR is *5dB*. It is quite surprising that the perceived quality of SharpCast videos is so close to the original even under such challenging channel conditions. It is also obvious that SharpCast allows the receivers to recover much sharper videos than SoftCast and WSVC.

14.5 Summary

In this chapter, we present a structure-preserving HDA video delivery scheme, named SharpCast, for wireless networks. The crux of an HDA transmission problem is what type of information is more efficiently represented and transmitted in digital form than in analog. We believe that human perception should be taken into consideration in making this decision. Based on the fact that human visual system is sensitive to structural information, SharpCast improves the received visual quality by decomposing a video into content and structure parts and setting aside sufficient network resources for structure transmission. The decomposition also leads to a compact energy packing of the content part so that analog transmission of the content part in bandwidth-limited scenarios does not degrade the received video quality as much as that of the original video. SharpCast is readily applicable to video multicast as well as unicast in varying wireless channels.

Chapter 15
Superimposed Modulation for Soft Video Delivery with Hidden Resources

15.1 Introduction

The work in this chapter is motivated by the following question: by using analog transmission, does a soft video delivery system completely avoid the leveling-off effect? The leveling-off effect refers to the fact that the system performance remains constant even when the CSNR is increased above and beyond the threshold [29]. For digital transmission, the channel coding and modulation schemes are determined based on channel estimation. If the actual channel is better than estimated, no additional gain can be obtained. Analog transmission avoids such an effect because the sender does not try to estimate the channel and the noise level in the received symbol faithfully reflects the instantaneous channel condition. As the CSNR increases, the received symbol quality continues to grow.

However, the system-wise, leveling-off effect is also observed in soft video delivery systems, when the allocated channel bandwidth is severely insufficient. Fig. 15.1 shows the performance of the pioneering soft video delivery system called SoftCast, in the received video PSNR versus CSNR. The test video sequence is the monochrome *Shields_720p* with resolution 1280×720 and frame rate 30fps. The source bandwidth is 27.6MHz and the matching channel bandwidth is 13.8MHz (every complex wireless symbol carries two real-valued coefficients on I- and Q-planes, respectively). During low CSNR range, the channel noise will play an important role in the distortion of video and the performance gap with different bandwidth is relatively small. When the CSNR decreases to -30dB. This gap will become negligible. However, during high CSNR range, it is clear that the received video quality suffers from a severe leveling-off effect. The root cause of this effect is that even when the CSNR is very high, a complex wireless symbol cannot carry more than two analog symbols, or the symbol is not decodeable[1]. Therefore, when the channel bandwidth is insufficient, a certain portion of the source data is discarded before transmission, creating a non-negligible error floor.

---

[1] There do exist some bandwidth compaction techniques such as the spiral coding, but they will sacrifice the adaptation capability.

DOI: 10.1201/9781003118688-15   273

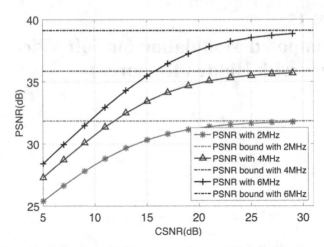

Fig. 15.1 Illustrating the leveling-off effect in the soft video delivery system due to bandwidth deficiency. The test sequence is Shields_720p.

It seems that this problem cannot be solved unless the soft video delivery system is allocated with more bandwidth. However, the bandwidth resource is usually limited. According to Cisco VNI [1], video streaming accounts for 31% of the IP consumer traffic. The other traffic, including web, email and data (18%) and gaming (47%), still needs to be transmitted with conventional digital method. It is very common in our daily lives that a user watches a video while syncing with his/her cloud storage as a background task. Thus a video delivery application needs to compete for the bandwidth with other applications or even other users (in a multi-user network), whose traffic is mostly digital. This situation creates troubles but also brings opportunities. The opportunity arises from the fact that the analog traffic can share bandwidth with the digital traffic through superimposed modulation [166]. Therefore, the bandwidth allocated to the competing digital traffic can be treated as hidden resources for the analog video traffic. However, the challenge is how to take advantage of these hidden resources without compromising the BER requirement for digital traffic.

In this work, we design and analyze the HDA scheme with Superimposed modulation, named as HDA-SIM, for soft video delivery when the hidden bandwidth resource is available. We shall answer the following questions. First, how to design the HDA-SIM scheme to make it *imperceptible* to digital traffic? The short answer is to let the video application trade power for bandwidth. Specifically, when we decode the digital symbols from superimposed symbols, their BER is determined by the signal to interference and noise ratio (SINR), where the interference comes from the superimposed analog symbols. If the video application gives some power to the digital symbols, the interference brought to the digital symbols can be balanced out. Then the second question arises: if the video application has to give out some transmission power, is the trade *worthwhile*?

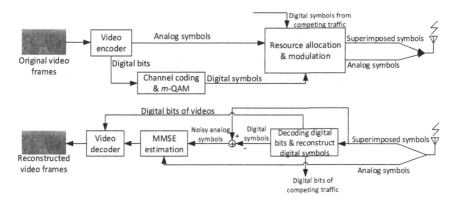

Fig. 15.2 The general soft video delivery framework with HDA-SIM.

In order to answer the second question, we formulate the resource allocation problem for the proposed HDA-SIM scheme. At any given CSNR and under the constraint that the BER requirement of the competing digital traffic is not compromised, the optimal bandwidth and power allocation can be found that maximizes the received video PSNR. The optimized solution helps us derive the necessary and sufficient condition for the proposed HDA-SIM scheme to achieve better video delivery performance (i.e., when the trade is worthwhile). To verify our analysis and evaluate the efficiency of the proposed HDA-SIM, we implement the HDA-SIM version for two state-of-the-art soft video delivery systems, known as SoftCast and SharpCast. Both simulations and trace-driven testbed evaluations show that significant gains can be achieved.

15.2 Soft Video Delivery with HDA-SIM

15.2.1 An Overview of the Soft Video Delivery Framework

The soft video delivery framework with HDA-SIM is shown in Fig. 15.2. Note that we are not proposing any specific video delivery scheme; instead, any existing HDA-based or analog-based soft video delivery system can be reformed by this framework. At the sender, we keep the video encoder intact. If the original video delivery scheme is an HDA scheme, the video encoder outputs both digital and analog symbols; if the original scheme is pure analog based, the video encoder only outputs analog symbols.

Normally for an HDA scheme, the digital bits will be protected by channel coding and then transmitted by a standard m-order quadrature amplitude modulation (m-QAM). As for analog symbols, they are often divided into equal-sized chunks, and symbols in the same chunk are treated as instances drawn from the same

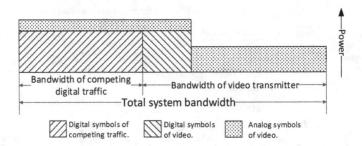

Fig. 15.3 Illustrating the design of HDA-SIM.

Gaussian distribution. For convenience in the following discussion, we assume that a complex (analog) symbol is always generated from a pair of symbols in the same chunk. We use $X_i, i = 1, 2, ..., N_s$ to denote a complex symbol of the ith chunk and N_s is the number of chunks. In general, X_i can be modeled as a complex Gaussian variable with $\mathbb{E}(X_i) = 0$. We assume that the real and the imaginary parts of X_i are mutually independent, and that all X_is are mutually independent.

In addition to analog traffic and digital traffic (if any) generated by the soft video delivery system, our proposed framework further considers competing digital traffic. All three types of traffic are fed into the resource allocation and modulation (RA-M) module, which is the kernel of the proposed framework. The output of the RA-M module is two types of modulation symbols, the superimposed HDA symbols and the pure analog symbols.

At the receiver, the three types of traffic are reconstructed successively. First, the digital symbols (of both the competing traffic and the video delivery system) are decoded from the superimposed symbols by taking the superimposed analog symbols as noise. Then, the decoded digital symbols are deducted from the superimposed symbols to obtain the superimposed analog symbols. These analog symbols, together with the received pure analog symbols, are fed into a (optional) minimum mean squared error (MMSE) decoder. Finally, the video decoder takes the digital (if any) and analog symbols to reconstruct the video. Again, we do not change the MMSE estimation and the video decoder modules in the original soft video delivery scheme.

The implementation of such a system needs reconfiguration of the base stations. With the development of software defined radio (SDR) technologies [167], such reconfiguration can be easily implemented in the future.

15.2.2 Introduction of HDA-SIM

The basic idea of HDA-SIM for soft video delivery is illustrated in Fig. 15.3. Due to the existence of competing digital traffic, only part of the system bandwidth is allocated to video application. If the video encoder is an HDA encoder, the digital symbols of the video source will further occupy some bandwidth. In this work, we model the system bandwidth as a number of parallel channels. The channels for transmitting digital symbols (from both video source and competing traffic) are called *occupied channels* and the rest are called *vacant channels*. Normally, the number of vacant channels is much smaller than the number of analog symbols. Therefore, the analog symbols of the video are divided into two parts. Some of them are transmitted in the vacant channels using AM and the others are superimposed on digital symbols to multiplex the occupied channels.

Given the limited channel and power resources in wireless communications, the resource allocation problem arises. The channel allocation problem is essentially a set partitioning problem. It determines whether the analog symbols in the ith chunk, i.e., $X_i, i = 1, 2, ..., N_s$, will be modulated in vacant channels or superimposed on the digital symbols in occupied channels. Once the channel allocation is determined, the power allocation problem is addressed to determine the transmission power of all X_i's as well as the transmission power of digital symbols. As mentioned earlier, power allocation needs to be designed carefully to ensure that the superimposed analog symbols do not compromise the BER requirement of the digital transmission. We will formulate and solve the above two problems in Section 15.3.

Note that, after power allocation, the analog symbols allocated to the occupied channels will be transformed through an orthonormal matrix. The transformed symbols, instead of the original analog symbols, will be superimposed on the digital symbols. This transformation greatly simplifies the resource allocation problem in HDA-SIM, as the transformed symbols can be looked on as instances drawn from the same Gaussian distribution.

At the receiver, the digital bits and digital symbols are reconstructed first. If the channel condition is not too bad, the digital symbols can be reconstructed correctly with very high probability. Then by subtracting the digital symbols from the received symbols, we get the noisy symbols of X_i, denoted $\widetilde{X}_i$. Let $\widehat{X}_i$ denote the estimation of X_i. Then $\widehat{X}_i$ is obtained through an MMSE decoder, i.e.,

$$\widehat{X}_i = \frac{P_i^{(X)}}{P_i^{(X)} + \sigma_c^2} \widetilde{X}_i, \tag{15.1}$$

where $P_i^{(X)}$ is the power allocated to X_i and σ_c^2 is the channel noise power. Then it is easy to derive the mean squared error (MSE) between all $\widehat{X}_i$ and X_i as

$$D = \frac{1}{N_s} \sum_{i=1}^{N_s} \mathbb{E}\left(\|\widehat{X}_i - X_i\|^2\right) = \frac{1}{N_s} \sum_{i=1}^{N_s} \frac{\mathbb{E}(\|X_i\|^2)}{1 + P_i^{(X)}/\sigma_c^2}, \tag{15.2}$$

where $\mathbb{E}(\cdot)$ means expectation. Equation (15.2) is the optimization objective in the resource allocation of HDA-SIM, which will be discussed in detail in the next section.

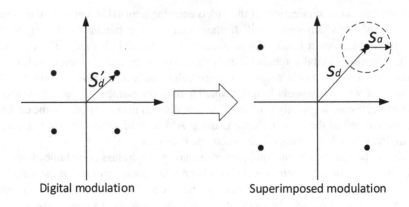

Digital modulation   Superimposed modulation

Fig. 15.4 The idea of SIM with QPSK as an example. The digital symbol needs to be scaled up to resist the interference brought by the superimposed analog symbol.

15.2.3 Analysis of HDA-SIM

In this part, we will analyze the behavior of HDA-SIM in an intuitive way and show its potential to improve the performance of soft video delivery.

15.2.3.1 Influence of HDA-SIM to Digital Traffic

Let s_a and s_d be a complex analog symbol and a complex digital symbol, respectively. They are to be superimposed into s_{sim} for transmission. As shown in Fig. 15.4, the superimposed symbol (SIM symbol) s_{sim} is generated by

$$s_{sim} = s_a + s_d. \qquad (15.3)$$

In order to resist the interference brought by the superimposed analog symbol, the digital symbol needs to be scaled up, as shown in Fig. 15.4. A formal mathematical explanation will be given later (see (15.10)). At the receiver, the received SIM symbol can be written into:

$$y_{sim} = s_{sim} + n = s_a + s_d + n, \qquad (15.4)$$

where n is the complex channel noise which follows $\mathscr{CN}(0, \sigma_c^2)$.

The decoder first decodes the digital bits from y_{sim} by taking both s_a and n as noise. We use P_a and P_d to denote the average power of s_a and s_d respectively. The total noise power in decoding the digital bits is $P_a + \sigma_c^2$ and the SNR of digital symbols, denoted as SNR_d, is

$$SNR_d = \frac{P_d}{P_a + \sigma_c^2}. \qquad (15.5)$$

Given the BER requirement of digital decoding, the SNR of digital symbols needs to be larger than a threshold, which is determined by channel coding and modulation rate. We use γ to denote this threshold. Therefore, the following inequality (15.6) needs to be satisfied to guarantee that the digital bits can be decoded with required BER.

$$SNR_d = \frac{P_d}{P_a + \sigma_c^2} \geq \gamma. \tag{15.6}$$

In order to analyze the influence of HDA-SIM to digital transmission, we use s_d' to denote the original digital symbol without superimposed modulation and P_d' to denote its average power. Obviously, the SNR of digital symbols in this case, denoted as SNR_d', is P_d'/σ_c^2. If the BER requirement is satisfied in original digital traffic without superimposed modulation, we have

$$SNR_d' = \frac{P_d'}{\sigma_c^2} \geq \gamma. \tag{15.7}$$

Since the superimposed modulation cannot compromise the BER requirement of digital traffic, the inequality (15.6) must be guaranteed to be valid if (15.7) holds. This is the most important constraint in HDA-SIM. We define $\sigma_m^2 = P_d'/\gamma$. It is not difficult to deduce that this constraint can be simplified as

$$\frac{P_d}{P_a + \sigma_m^2} \geq \gamma. \tag{15.8}$$

However, if (15.7) does not hold, meaning that the BER requirement is not satisfied in original digital traffic, the inequality (15.6) does not need to be satisfied because HDA-SIM has no responsibility to enhance the robustness of digital transmission.

Although the power allocation problem is not addressed yet, it is not hard to see that the equality holds in (15.8) under the optimal power allocation. Otherwise, some power of digital symbols can be allocated to analog symbols without violating (15.8) to further decrease the distortion of analog transmission. With optimal power allocation in HDA-SIM (i.e., the equality holds in (15.8)), if the BER requirement is satisfied in original digital traffic, i.e., the inequality (7) holds, we have

$$\frac{P_d'}{\sigma_c^2} = \frac{\gamma \sigma_m^2}{\sigma_c^2} = \frac{P_d}{P_a + \sigma_m^2} \cdot \frac{\sigma_m^2}{\sigma_c^2} > \frac{P_d}{P_a + \sigma_c^2}. \tag{15.9}$$

where the last inequality follows from $\sigma_m^2 > \sigma_c^2$ if (7) holds. Not surprisingly, we see from (15.9) that HDA-SIM will decrease the SNR of digital symbols, resulting in the increase of BER. However, it does not sacrifice the BER requirement. For example, if the BER requirement is 10^{-5}. Without HDA-SIM, the BER could be as low as 10^{-7} in a good channel condition, but with HDA-SIM, the BER becomes 10^{-6}, which still meets the requirement.

For the HDA video transmission systems, it is not necessary to involve the BER of digital traffic in measuring the received video quality. This is because a digital communication system usually does not pass the PHY bit error to the application layer. When bit errors are detected in a packet, the entire packet is discarded and a retransmission is requested. If the BER of digital transmission is kept low, the retransmission mechanism can ensure error-free transmission of the digital part with little bandwidth overhead. Therefore, in the following discussion of the received video quality, we only consider the distortion caused by analog traffic.

15.2.3.2 Influence of HDA-SIM to Analog Traffic

According to (15.2), the distortion of analog traffic presented depends on the transmission power of X_i. Specifically, $P_i^{(X)} = 0$ if X_i is not transmitted. When the bandwidth for analog traffic is not sufficient, some $P_i^{(X)}$'s are forced to zero no matter how much the total available power is. This is exactly the reason why the leveling-off effect in pseudo-analog or HDA video transmission systems will appear.

With HDA-SIM, more analog symbols have opportunity to be transmitted. However, according to (15.8), it is easy to show that if some analog symbols are superimposed on the digital symbols, we have

$$P_d \geq \gamma(P_a + \sigma_m^2) > \gamma\sigma_m^2 = P_d', \tag{15.10}$$

meaning that the transmission power of digital symbols needs to be raised to satisfy the BER requirement. With fixed system available power, the average transmission power allocated to analog traffic, i.e., $\sum_{i=1}^{N_s} P_i^{(X)}$, has to be decreased. Therefore, the essence of HDA-SIM is to get additional bandwidth at the cost of power. Now, the core question is whether this exchange is worthwhile. This question will be answered in Theorem 15.2 after solving the resource allocation problem in HDA-SIM.

The above analysis about analog traffic is based on the premise that the digital decoding is successful and digital symbols are reconstructed correctly. If the digital decoding fails, not only are the digital symbols affected, but also the superimposed analog symbols have to be discarded. As a result, the soft video delivery performance will be significantly reduced. However, as we have discussed in Section 15.2.3.1, if the BER of digital traffic is kept low, this undesirable situation is unlikely to happen.

15.3 Resource Allocation in HDA-SIM

15.3.1 Problem Formulation and Definitions

There are two types of resources that we consider in this research, bandwidth and power. Accordingly, the resource allocation problem in HDA-SIM can be divided into channel allocation and power allocation problems. For clarity of presentation, we first formulate the problem mathematically and give key definitions that will be used in the rest of the section.

15.3.1.1 Source and Channel Model

As introduced in Section 15.2.1, HDA-SIM needs to address multiple uncorrelated Gaussian sources X_i. In the literature, this kind of source model is called a parallel Gaussian source. We name each source component X_i as a sub-source in this work. For convenience, in the following discussion we rearrange all sub-sources in the descending order of their variances. We denote the new arrangement of sub-sources as $\left(X_{(1)}, X_{(2)}, ..., X_{(N_s)}\right)$ and we also define $\mathbb{E}(\|X_{(i)}\|^2) = \lambda_i$. Thus, we have $\lambda_1 \geq \lambda_2 \geq ... \geq \lambda_{N_s}$.

The channel can be modeled as follows. A total of N_c uncorrelated complex sub-channels with the same noise power σ_c^2 is available. Let N_d be the number of sub-channels occupied by the digital symbols. Specifically, N_d is represented as

$$N_d = N_d^{(o)} + N_d^{(s)}. \tag{15.11}$$

where $N_d^{(o)}$ is the number of channels occupied by the digital symbols of competing digital traffic while $N_d^{(s)}$ denotes the number of channels occupied by the digital part of the video transmitter. For pure (pseudo-)analog systems, $N_d^{(s)} = 0$. Then the remaining $N_c - N_d$ sub-channels are available to the analog transmission of $X_{(i)}$.

Without loss of generality, we focus on a special case where the source bandwidth equals the total channel bandwidth, i.e., $N_s = N_c$ when solving the resource allocation problem in HDA-SIM. In practice, if the source bandwidth is larger, the sub-sources with the smallest variances have to be discarded before transmission. If conversely, the total channel bandwidth is larger, we could introduce some auxiliary sub-sources with a variance of zero.

15.3.1.2 Definitions of Channel and Power Allocation

We use π to denote a channel allocation. We also define two sets A_π and B_π, where A_π is the set of sub-sources to be transmitted in vacant channels and B_π is the set of sub-sources to be transmitted through HDA superimposed modulation in the occupied channel. Further, we only consider cases in which each instance from each sub-source is transmitted at most once in an occupied or vacant sub-channel. Mathematically, a channel allocation π can be characterized by A_π and B_π which satisfy the following conditions:

- $|A_\pi| = N_c - N_d$; $|B_\pi| = N_d$;
- $A_\pi \cup B_\pi = \{X_{(i)} | i = 1...N_s(N_c)\}$;
- $A_\pi \cap B_\pi = \emptyset$.

We use $\mathbf{P}$ to denote a power allocation. $\mathbf{P}$ decides the average power P_d of digital symbols, as well as the transmission power P_i for each sub-source $X_{(i)}$. If $P_i > 0$, $X_{(i)}$ is actually transmitted; otherwise, $X_{(i)}$ is discarded without transmission. $\mathbf{P}$ is called a feasible power allocation for π if and only if the total power constraint is not violated and the inequality (15.8) is satisfied, where

$$P_a = \frac{1}{N_d} \sum_{\{i|X_{(i)} \in B_\pi\}} P_i. \qquad (15.12)$$

If $\mathbf{P}$ is a feasible power allocation for π, let $D(\pi, \mathbf{P})$ denote the MSE when π and $\mathbf{P}$ are adopted. We use $\mathbf{P}^*(\pi)$ to denote the optimal power allocation which minimizes the MSE for channel allocation π and $P_i^*(\pi)$ to denote the power allocated to $X_{(i)}$ in $\mathbf{P}^*(\pi)$. π is an optimal channel allocation if and only if it satisfies

$$D(\pi, \mathbf{P}^*(\pi)) \le D(\pi', \mathbf{P}^*(\pi')), \forall \pi'. \qquad (15.13)$$

Note that the optimal channel allocation which satisfies (15.13) may not be unique. However, all the optimal channel allocations should result in the same minimum MSE.

15.3.2 Channel Allocation

We first give a specific channel allocation π^* in Definition 15.1 and then prove its optimality based on Lemma 15.1.

Definition 15.1. Channel allocation π^* is defined as : $A_{\pi^*} = \{X_{(i)}|1 \le i \le N_c - N_d\}$ and $B_{\pi^*} = \{X_{(i)}|N_c - N_d < i \le N_s\}$.

The intuition behind π^* is quite straightforward. Vacant channels are allocated to the most significant sub-sources and the other sub-sources are superimposed to digital symbols to opportunistically utilize the channel.

Lemma 15.1. *For a channel allocation π, if there exists a pair of sub-sources $(X_{(i)}, X_{(j)}), i < j$ such that $X_{(i)} \in B_\pi$ and $X_{(j)} \in A_\pi$, then swapping their allocated channels, i.e., let $X_{(i)} \in A_\pi$ and $X_{(j)} \in B_\pi$, does not increase the MSE under the optimal power allocation.*

Based on this lemma, we give the following theorem.

Theorem 15.1. *The channel allocation π^* as defined in Definition 15.1 is an optimal channel allocation scheme.*

The proof of the Theorem can be found in [150].

15.3.3 Power Allocation

Now that we have proven π^* is the optimal channel allocation scheme, we next consider the optimal power allocation for π^*. For clarity, we change the notations for sub-sources as follows:

$$
\left(X_{(1)},X_{(2)},...,X_{(N_c-N_d)}\right) \Rightarrow \left(X_{\alpha,1},...,X_{\alpha,N_\alpha}\right),
$$
$$
\left(X_{(N_c-N_d+1)},X_{(N_c-N_d+2)},...,X_{(N_s)}\right) \Rightarrow \left(X_{\beta,1},...,X_{\beta,N_\beta}\right), \tag{15.14}
$$

where $N_\alpha = N_c - N_d$ and $N_\beta = N_d$. We also denote the variance of $X_{\alpha,i}$ and $X_{\beta,i}$ as $\lambda_{\alpha,i}$ and $\lambda_{\beta,i}$ respectively. The allocated power is denoted by $P_{\alpha,i}$ or $P_{\beta,i}$. According to the channel allocation scheme π^*, $X_{\alpha,i}$ is modulated in a vacant channel and $X_{\beta,i}$ is modulated in an occupied channel.

Hence, the constraint in (15.8) can be re-written into:

$$
\frac{P_d}{\frac{\sum_{i=1}^{N_\beta}P_{\beta,i}}{N_d} + \sigma_m^2} \geq \gamma. \tag{15.15}
$$

As mentioned before, the equality in (15.15) holds for an optimal power allocation scheme. Thus we formulate the power allocation problem as follows.

P1 (Optimal power allocation problem):

$$
\min_{P_{\alpha,i},P_{\beta,i},P_d} \sum_{i=1}^{N_\alpha} \frac{\lambda_{\alpha,i}}{1+\frac{P_{\alpha,i}}{\sigma_t^2}} + \sum_{i=1}^{N_\beta} \frac{\lambda_{\beta,i}}{1+\frac{P_{\beta,i}}{\sigma_t^2}}, \tag{15.16}
$$

$$
\text{s.t.} \quad P_{\alpha,i} \geq 0, P_{\beta,i} \geq 0, P_d \geq 0,
$$

$$
\sum_i^{N_\alpha} P_{\alpha,i} + \sum_i^{N_\beta} P_{\beta,i} + N_d P_d = E_t, \tag{15.17}
$$

$$
\sum_{i=1}^{N_\beta} P_{\beta,i} - N_d\left(\frac{P_d}{\gamma} - \sigma_m^2\right) = 0, \tag{15.18}
$$

where E_t is the total power budget. In a traditional transmission system without HDA-SIM, it is reasonable to assume that the system allocates the same average power for soft video delivery and competing digital traffic. Thus E_t can be represented as

$$
E_t = P_d' N_c = \gamma \sigma_m^2 N_c. \tag{15.19}
$$

Constraint (15.18) follows (15.15) by taking the equality.

Note that it is not easy to minimize MSE for all possible channel conditions, so our strategy is to set a target CSNR and to minimize the expected MSE for this CSNR. When the actual channel condition deviates from the target, the analog part can always achieve graceful adaptation. Notation σ_t^2 in (15.16) is the noise power under the target channel condition.

The optimal power allocation problem as defined in **P1** is a convex optimization problem. We solve it by exploiting Lagrangian function and KKT conditions [105]. Finally, the optimal power allocation can be obtained through a water-filling algorithm, i.e., finding a constant C to satisfy

$$(1+\gamma)\sum_{i=1}^{N_\beta} P_{\beta,i}^* + \sum_{i=1}^{N_\alpha} P_{\alpha,i}^* = E_t\left(1 - \frac{N_d}{N_c}\right). \tag{15.20}$$

where

$$P_{\alpha,i}^* = \begin{cases} C\sigma_t\sqrt{(1+\gamma)\lambda_{\alpha,i}} - \sigma_t^2, & C\sqrt{1+\gamma} > \frac{\sigma_t}{\sqrt{\lambda_{\alpha,i}}}, \\ 0, & \text{Otherwise.} \end{cases} \tag{15.21}$$

$$P_{\beta,i}^* = \begin{cases} C\sigma_t\sqrt{\lambda_{\beta,i}} - \sigma_t^2, & C > \frac{\sigma_t}{\sqrt{\lambda_{\beta,i}}}, \\ 0, & \text{Otherwise.} \end{cases} \tag{15.22}$$

With the optimal power allocation $\mathbf{P}^*(\pi^*)$, we are able to know which sub-sources should be transmitted and which should be discarded. If all sub-sources in B_{π^*} are allocated with zero power, it means that HDA-SIM is not necessary. A natural question is under what conditions HDA-SIM improves the performance. The following theorem answers this question.

Theorem 15.2. *Define* $\gamma_t = \frac{E_t}{N_c\sigma_t^2}$ *and* $\sqrt{\lambda_\alpha} = \frac{\sum_{i=1}^{N_\alpha}\sqrt{\lambda_{\alpha,i}}}{N_\alpha}$. *HDA-SIM achieves performance gain if and only if*

$$\frac{1+\gamma_t}{\sqrt{1+\gamma}} > \frac{\sqrt{\lambda_\alpha}}{\sqrt{\lambda_{\beta,1}}}. \tag{15.23}$$

According to Theorem 15.2 and (15.23), we give some insights about the benefits of HDA-SIM. First, the ratio $\sqrt{\lambda_\alpha}/\sqrt{\lambda_{\beta,1}}$ implies the distribution of the variances of the parallel Gaussian source. If the variances of different sub-sources $((\lambda_1,\lambda_2,...,\lambda_{N_s}))$ do not differ too much, utilizing hidden bandwidth resources tends to achieve performance gain. Second, γ_t is the target CSNR under which the MSE is minimized in the power allocation problem. Equation (15.23) indicates that the transmission of a parallel Gaussian source benefits more from HDA-SIM in a high-quality channel than in a low-quality channel. Third, γ is the lowest CSNR that the digital system is designed to support. Generally, the selection of coding rate and modulation of the digital traffic in wireless communication is quite conservative because the wireless channel is changing all the time. Hence, γ tends to be relatively small and HDA-SIM is very likely to achieve gain in this case.

15.4 Implementations

In order to verify the performance of the proposed HDA-SIM, we implement it for two soft video delivery systems, namely SoftCast [19] and SharpCast [79], and compare the performance with their original design.

15.4.1 SoftCast-SIM

The implementation of SoftCast-SIM is quite straightforward. We set the video encoder/decoder module in Fig. 15.2 to the SoftCast encoder/decoder. As SoftCast is a pure analog scheme, no digital symbol is generated from the video encoder.

15.4.2 SharpCast-SIM

The SharpCast-SIM system is implemented by setting the video encoder/decoder in Fig. 15.2 to SharpCast encoder/decoder [79]. In order to perform a fair comparison between SharpCast and SharpCast-SIM, we make a few slight changes to SharpCast encoder/decoder as follows.

First, in the original design of SharpCast[79], the digital bits are always transmitted with $\frac{1}{2}$-rate channel coding and QPSK modulation. We relax this constraint in our implementation and allow SharpCast to use other channel coding and modulation schemes. Normally, the digital traffic from SharpCast will use the same transmission scheme as the competing digital traffic. Second, the original SharpCast encoder doubles the average power of digital symbols to ensure reliable transmission of QPSK symbols when the CSNR is above 5dB. However, if a rough estimation of the CSNR is available, as assumed in our evaluation, it is not necessary to stick to the 5dB threshold. Therefore, in our implementation, we select an appropriate channel coding and modulation scheme according to the CSNR and do not double the symbol power for digital traffic. Note that this adjustment will improve the performance of SharpCast at the targeted channel condition.

In the implementation of SoftCast-SIM and SharpCast-SIM, we do not perform joint optimization of the video encoder and HDA-SIM resource allocation, although such optimization is possible and will definitely improve overall performance. In our evaluations, we try to keep the two modules uncoupled so that the performance gain brought by HDA-SIM is well-defined.

15.5 Evaluations

We carry out extensive simulations, as well as a trace-driven emulation, to validate the effectiveness of HDA-SIM.

15.5.1 Settings

Video source: A total of nine high-definition (720p with resolution 1280×720) videos are used for evaluation. They are *Shields, Stockholm, City, In_to_tree, Jets, Parkrun, Sheriff, Shuttlestart, Spincalendar.* These sequences are indexed as $1, 2, ...9$. In our simulation, we follow the configuration in SharpCast [79]. The GOP size is 16 and a total of 4096 chunks are produced for each GOP. If not otherwise specified, the first two GOPs of each sequence are used for simulations. With a frame rate of 30fps, the source bandwidth is 13.8 MHz.

Channel: We evaluate under both a simulated AWGN channel and a real OFDM channel for 802.11a/g collected by software radio named Sora [38]. The bandwidth resources in the simulated AWGN channel are also set according to the Sora trace. Specifically, the channel is divided into 64 subcarriers and 48 of them are used to transmit modulation symbols. To reduce the overhead of the PLCP header, we use 100 OFDM symbols in each PLCP frame for data transmission. Overall, the channel bandwidth is 12 MHz and the data bandwidth is about 11.4 MHz. This is the case where $N_s > N_c$, so only around 82% of the chunks will be considered for transmission in HDA-SIM.

For digital symbols, from both video transmitter and other competing digital traffic, we consider four coding and modulation settings as defined in 802.11a [168]. They are (4QAM, $\frac{1}{2}$), (4QAM, $\frac{3}{4}$), (16QAM, $\frac{1}{2}$) and (16QAM, $\frac{3}{4}$). In all evaluations, the BER requirement is set to 10^{-5}. The corresponding threshold SNR γ in the four settings is around 7dB, 10dB, 13dB and 17dB, respectively.

Evaluation metric: We adopt the standard video quality measurement PSNR as the evaluation metric. For each system setting, we repeat the simulation for ten times and the average results are reported.

15.5.2 Benchmark Evaluations of HDA-SIM

Before making the system-level comparison, we first show in this subsection some benchmark results which corroborate the HDA-SIM design.

HDA-SIM allows more transmitted chunks: First, a major motivation of this research is that soft video delivery exhibits a severe leveling-off effect when the bandwidth is not sufficient because some chunks have to be dropped before transmission. Therefore, the number of transmitted chunks is an important index of how HDA-SIM improves bandwidth proficiency. The results in this test are

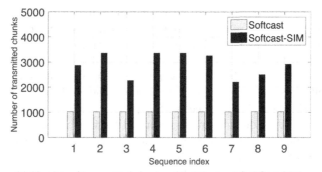

(a) Number of transmitted chunks of SoftCast and SoftCast-SIM.

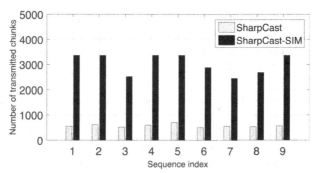

(b) Number of transmitted chunks of SharpCast and SharpCast-SIM.

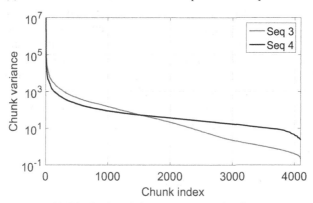

(c) Distribution of chunk variances in SoftCast.

Fig. 15.5 Comparison of the number of transmitted chunks in different systems. The bandwidth ratio allocated to video is 0.25. γ_t is set as 15dB for HDA-SIM.

obtained when the digital transmission adopts (4QAM, $\frac{1}{2}$) and the target CSNR is 15dB. Fig.15.5(a) compares the average number of transmitted chunks of SoftCast and the SoftCast-SIM for the first GOP of the nine test sequences. We set the available bandwidth ratio to 0.25, i.e., $(N_c - N_d^{(o)})/N_s = 0.25$, where $N_d^{(o)}$ denotes the channel numbers allocated to other competing digital traffic. Since there are 4096 chunks per GOP, SoftCast can only transmit a fixed number of 1024 chunks. In contrast, by adopting HDA-SIM, the video transmitter is able to transmit many more chunks, with an average of 2900 chunks. Note that the number of transmitted chunks in HDA-SIM slightly varies with the digital modulation scheme and the target CSNR. We also compare the number of transmitted chunks of SharpCast and SharpCast-SIM in Fig. 15.5(b). Because SharpCast will allocate part of the available bandwidth of video to digital symbols generated by video encoder, only 569 chunks can be transmitted in average. However, SharpCast-SIM can transmit an average of 3036 chunks, which is a huge increase.

It should be noted that the number of transmitted chunks in SoftCast-SIM varies greatly for different sequences. This is decided by the distribution of the chunk variances. When the distribution is flat over sub-sources, HDA-SIM tends to transmit more sub-sources. To illustrate this point, we show in Fig. 15.5(c) the variance distributions of sequence 3 and 4. Obviously, the distribution of sequence 4 is more flat, and it benefits more from the proposed HDA-SIM because more chunks of sequence 4 are transmitted.

HDA-SIM satisfies the BER requirement: Another important issue about HDA-SIM is how it affects digital traffic. We illustrate this by plotting the SNR of digital symbols in SoftCast (w/o HDA-SIM) and SoftCast-SIM (w/ HDA-SIM) with analog symbols and channel noise as interference versus the actual CSNR. Fig. 15.6 shows the results for the first GOP of sequence 1 when two different digital coding and modulation schemes are used. The threshold SNR γ for these two schemes is 7dB and 10dB, respectively. We find that HDA-SIM does not bring noticeable change to the SNR of digital symbols when the actual CSNR is around γ. When the actual SNR is significantly larger than γ (i.e., channel is better than digital traffic expected), the SNR of digital symbols is lower than the actual value, corresponding to the analysis in (15.9). However, since the SNR is far larger than the threshold SNR, the BER in this case is extremely small and the bit error event is hard to detect in our simulation. Therefore, superimposed modulation will only cause negligible influence to the behavior of digital systems.

15.5.3 Performance Comparison

In this section, we evaluate the performance of HDA-SIM from different perspectives. As we have mentioned in Section 15.2, the threshold SNR γ is usually lower than the actual CSNR. Otherwise, the digital transmission itself will fail. Therefore, in our experiments, we will set different values for γ, but for each γ, we will only evaluate the cases in which the actual CSNR is larger than γ.

First, Fig. 15.7 shows the comparison under different available bandwidth ratios for video transmitter, i.e., $(N_c - N_d^{(o)})/N_s$. In this test, the digital transmission adopts $(4QAM, \frac{1}{2})$. A total of four curves are plotted in each figure. They are the performance curves of SoftCast, SoftCast-SIM, SharpCast and SharpCast-SIM. It

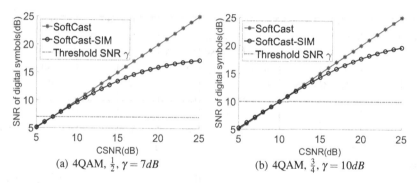

Fig. 15.6 The perceived SNR of digital traffic in SoftCast and SoftCast-SIM. The bandwidth ratio allocated to video is 0.25. 4QAM is used and γ_t is set to 15dB for HDA-SIM.

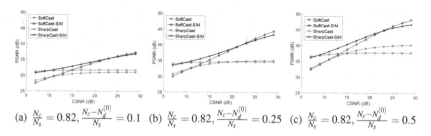

(a) $\frac{N_c}{N_s} = 0.82, \frac{N_c - N_d^{(0)}}{N_s} = 0.1$ (b) $\frac{N_c}{N_s} = 0.82, \frac{N_c - N_d^{(0)}}{N_s} = 0.25$ (c) $\frac{N_c}{N_s} = 0.82, \frac{N_c - N_d^{(0)}}{N_s} = 0.5$

Fig. 15.7 Performance comparison under different bandwidth ratio. 4QAM and $\frac{1}{2}$ coding rate are used for digital transmission.

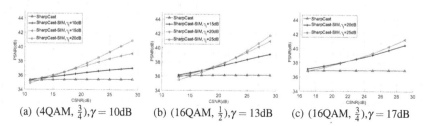

(a) (4QAM, $\frac{3}{4}$),$\gamma = 10$dB (b) (16QAM, $\frac{1}{2}$),$\gamma = 13$dB (c) (16QAM, $\frac{3}{4}$),$\gamma = 17$dB

Fig. 15.8 Performance comparison under different modulation and channel coding rate settings in occupied channels. $\frac{N_c}{N_s} = 0.82, \frac{N_c - N_d^{(0)}}{N_s} = 0.25$.

is clear that both SoftCast and SharpCast suffer from a severe leveling-off effect when the available bandwidth ratio is below 0.5. When the ratio is 0.1, SoftCast can only achieve an average of 31.08dB for transmitted videos even when the CSNR is 29dB. Although SharpCast could achieve about 3dB gain in low CSNR range, it still suffers from a similar leveling-off effect in high SNR range. However, when HDA-SIM is exploited to utilize the hidden bandwidth resource, the leveling-off effect is alleviated. For example, in Fig. 15.7(a), HDA-SIM significantly improves the received video quality of SoftCast and SharpCast by 6.25dB and 5.17dB when the CSNR is 29dB. The improvement is even more significant when the bandwidth ratio for video transmitter is 0.25 or 0.5, as shown in Fig. 15.7(b) and Fig. 15.7(c).

The performance of HDA-SIM is also largely affected by the targeted SNR γ_t and how digital traffic is transmitted. Fig. 15.8 presents the results under different coding and modulation selections. In each sub-figure of Fig. 15.8, we have included three performance curves of SharpCast+SIM with different target SNRs γ_t. The available bandwidth ratio in this group of tests is 0.25. We find that SharpCast-SIM achieves larger gain over SharpCast when the digital modulation rate is lower, or γ is lower. When the CSNR is 29dB and γ_t is 20dB, SharpCast-SIM improves the received video PSNR by 3.56, 4.79 and 5.47dB, respectively, for different coding and modulation schemes, which correspond to $\gamma = 17$dB, $\gamma = 13$dB and $\gamma = 10$dB.

As for the selection of γ_t, it is also observed from Fig. 15.8 that γ_t controls the trade-off between the system performance during high and low CSNR ranges. Generally speaking we can aggressively choose a larger γ_t in order to achieve larger gains during high CSNR range. When the real CSNR is mismatched with γ_t, there will be a small gap between the real performance and its optimum. If the real CSNR is much smaller than γ_t, the mismatch may cause a little performance loss compared to the existing schemes. However, with proper selection of γ_t, the performance loss is quite small.

15.5.4 Trace-driven Emulations

We also carry out trace-driven emulations to show the performance of HDA-SIM in a typical 802.11a/g wireless environment. The trace is obtained using a software radio system named Sora [38]. We fix the sender antenna and move the receiver antenna to simulate a mobile environment. Fig. 15.9(a) reports the CSNR and we find that it varies in a wide range and is generally larger than 7dB most cases. Therefore, we use (4QAM and 1/2) for the digital traffic and the γ is around 7dB. The available bandwidth ratio is set to 0.25 in this evaluation, which is around 3.45MHz.

We first extract the first five GOPs (80 frames) of each test sequence and produce a combined sequence consisting of 45 GOPs (720 frames). We then carry out the trace-driven emulations for this combined sequence and draw the PSNRs of each GOP achieved by SharpCast and SharpCast-SIM in Fig. 15.9(b). It should be noted that the PSNR value not only depends on the channel condition but also on the property of the transmitted sequence. Thus the trend of PSNR changes does not fully match the CSNR changes. It is clear that HDA-SIM improves the received video quality in most of the time. Compared to SharpCast, SharpCast-SIM achieves an average of 2.5dB PSNR gain for the combined test sequence. It is observed in Fig. 15.9 that, for few GOPs, SharpCast-SIM does not perform better than SharpCast. This is because we choose a relatively large target CSNR and this will cause a little performance loss when actual CSNR is much lower than the target.

We also compare the visual quality of the received videos in Fig. 15.10. The two frame clips are from the sequence Shields and Parkrun, respectively. We see that SharpCast-SIM preserves more details compared to SharpCast because more high-frequency coefficients are transmitted.

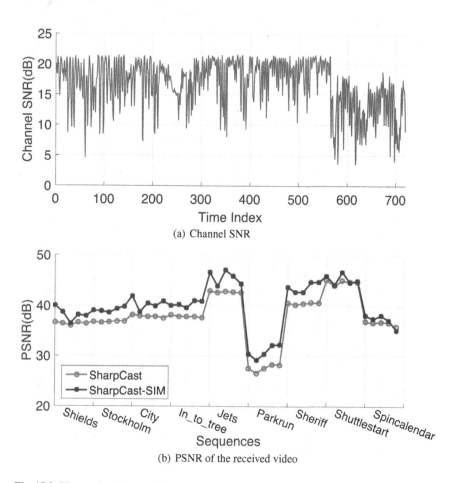

(a) Channel SNR

(b) PSNR of the received video

Fig. 15.9 The results of a trace-driven simulation. The modulation and coding rate of digital traffic are 4QAM and $\frac{1}{2}$. Bandwidth ratio of video is 0.25. Targeted SNR for HDA-SIM is 15dB.

15.6 Summary

In this work, we propose HDA-SIM to exploit hidden bandwidth resources to improve the performance of soft video delivery systems with constrained bandwidth. The superposition of analog symbols over existing digital symbols

(a) Original   (b) Original

(c) SharpCast   (d) SharpCast

(e) SharpCast-SIM   (f) SharpCast-SIM

Fig. 15.10 The visual quality comparison. The frames in the left column are from Shields and the right column frames are from Parkrun.

alleviates the leveling-off effect and brings significant performance gain especially when CSNR is high. We explicitly solve the resource allocation problem and point out the sufficient and necessary condition under which the utilization of hidden bandwidth resource by HDA-SIM is beneficial. The simulation and emulation results also validate our proposed scheme. In the future, we plan to work on the resource allocation problem of HDA-SIM in fading channels.

Chapter 16

Adaptive HDA Video Transmission in Mobile Networks

16.1 Introduction

The uncoded part in HDA transmission exploits statistical channel states to achieve robust uncoded video transmission. However, in mobile networks, statistical or feedback channel states might be very different from instantaneous channel states with which video data is being transmitted. This fact might result in significant degradation in performance. Moreover, the characteristics of video content is usually not fully exploited during wireless transmission. Consequently, new strategies need to be developed to overcome the challenges of channel fading in video transmission over mobile networks.

In this spirit, we develop A-HDAVT for real-time video streaming applications in mobile networks. A-HDAVT attempts to achieve excellent rate-distortion-capacity performance for digital transmission as well as graceful degradation performance for analog transmission in mobile networks where channel fading cannot be neglected. First, to facilitate hybrid digital-analog video transmission, Motion-Compensated Temporal Filtering (MCTF) [169][170] is adopted to compress and transform each Group of Pictures (GOP) into a Low-pass frame and several High-pass frames. Then, a joint power allocation scheme is designed to achieve simultaneously reliable digital transmission for reference frames and adaptive analog transmission for High-pass frames based on channel prediction in mobile networks. Besides content diversity, A-HDAVT exploits channel diversity to optimize power allocation during video transmission. The main contributions of this research are

1) In A-HDAVT, a power allocation strategy for hybrid digital-analog video transmission is developed. The critical Low-pass frame is allocated with sufficient power and transmitted in reliable digital transmission to ensure basic video quality even in poor channel states. The remaining power is then allocated to the High-pass frames in analog transmission to achieve graceful degradation performance. This enables robust video transmission with guaranteed minimum acceptable video

DOI: 10.1201/9781003118688-16

quality as well as maximum possible video quality in mobile networks with wireless fading channels.

2) In analog transmission, an algorithm for channel Prediction-based Adaptive Power Distortion Optimization (P-APDO) in A-HDAVT is designed to combat channel fading in mobile networks and to improve the user perceived video quality. With P-APDO, each High-pass frame is hierarchically decomposed and proper power is allocated to various data units according to their relative importance. This enables the exploitation of video content diversity at multi-resolution level.

3) In multi-user scenarios, an extended P-APDO is also developed assuming that each user is transmitting with an independent sub-channel. In this case, the extended P-APDO is able to exploit both content diversity and channel diversity among users. Both power pre-allocation and power re-allocation are executed. Power pre-allocation is performed to allocate power among video data of all users based only on their content importance. However, power re-allocation is applied to re-allocate power among video data being transmitted with additional consideration of the predicted channel states for each particular user in mobile networks.

4) Various simulations are carried out to evaluate the performance of the proposed A-HDAVT under various scenarios. The performance of A-HDAVT is also compared with that of Softcast [18][19][171], Parcast [101] and RUVT [25] under the same channel condition in both single-user and multi-user scenarios, to demonstrate the inherent advantage of A-HDAVT when the wireless channels are experiencing inevitable fading in mobile networks.

16.2 System Overview

The framework of A-HDAVT is shown in Fig. 16.1. The main components of A-HDAVT are digital encoder, analog encoder, packaging and modulation, and decoder. In A-HDAVT, MCTF is first employed at the sender side to separate a video GOP for digital encoding and analog encoding, respectively. Different from the 3D-DCT adopted in analog schemes [18][19][24][101], MCTF can provide better support for temporal scalability while removing the inter-frame redundancy efficiently.

In single-user scenarios, the transmitting power for each GOP is assumed to be constrained. In multi-user scenarios, a sending window is used to indicate the video data that should be simultaneously transmitted in sub-channels of all users, and the transmitting power for video data in the sending window is assumed to be constrained. In this research, we focus on the novel power allocation scheme in A-HDAVT, which has been carefully designed with the consideration of the importance of video content in different units of particular granularity (i.e., frames, chunks, subbands). Another novel feature of this A-HDAVT is the design of effective channel prediction based on the Long Range Prediction (LRP) algorithm [172], which is capable of combating channel fading in mobile networks and improving A-HDAVT's adaptive ability under highly dynamic network environments.

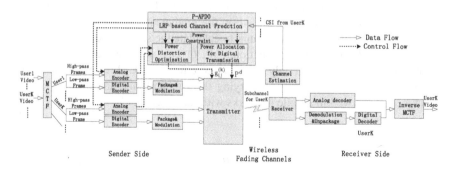

Fig. 16.1 Overview of the proposed A-HDAVT scheme.

16.2.1 Digital Encoder

In the digital encoder of A-HDAVT, H.264/AVC is introduced as the source encoder for the purpose of video compression, while convolution code is applied for the purpose of FEC for the reference frames. As channel states vary frequently in the mobile networks, reliable digital transmission is utilized for the Low-pass frame to ensure basic video quality. Low-order modulation such as Binary Phase Shift Keying (BPSK) and low rate FEC are adopted to ensure successful digital transmission. In addition, sufficient power is allocated for digital transmission to further ensure its reliability.

In [19][101], power distortion optimization is performed in units of GOPs to provide error resilience and graceful degradation performance. In mobile networks, due to the limited range of channel prediction, the transmission time for one video GOP is generally much larger than the prediction range. However, for APDO in the proposed A-HDAVT, we need to know CSI during the transmission of whole video GOP. Thus, performing APDO in units of GOPs or High-pass frames is not realistic. We propose to separate High-pass frames into chunks and allocate the transmitting power within each chunk. The chunk size is determined by the predicted range of the channel prediction algorithm. As the energy of chunks usually presents a non-uniform distribution after DWT and MCTF, the transmitting power can be allocated among these chunks according to their content importance to provide differentiated error resilience. For multi-user parallel transmission, we re-allocate power among the chunks of all users to minimize the average Mean Squared Error (MSE) distortion.

In the analog part, LRP-based channel prediction provides CSI for the proposed APDO in chunk transmission and power re-allocation in multi-user parallel transmission. In this case, the chunk size should be set within the prediction range. By considering the channel coherence time, we further divide each chunk into subbands with appropriate size. Based on the predicted CSI, APDO is performed among the subbands within each chunk to calculate the scaling factors for subband transmission. With channel prediction, APDO can achieve better adaptability compared with schemes that only utilize delayed feedback CSI for power distortion optimization [101]. Moreover, by varying the subband size and scaling factors, APDO can work well in mobile networks with fading channels.

16.2.2 Packaging and Modulation

Instead of the superposition or parallel transmission used in recent HDA schemes [173][24], a hybrid and serial transmission strategy is adopted in A-HDAVT. In this strategy, the outputs of digital encoder for each user, including metadata and coded bitstream, are first packaged together. Next, these digital packets are modulated with low-order modulation schemes such as BPSK to ensure reliable transmission. On the other hand, analog signals are transmitted directly in the forms of real valued symbols. Digital packets and analog symbols are transmitted in sequential manner. In multi-user scenarios, video data for different users are simultaneously transmitted over independent sub-channels.

16.2.3 Maintaining the Integrity of the Specifications

At the receiver side, metadata and coded bitstream of the Low-pass frame are first demodulated and unpacked, and then decoded by utilizing the digital decoder. For digital decoding, Viterbi and H.264/AVC decoder are performed to decode the Low-pass frame. Meanwhile, analog symbols are received directly and decoded by the analog decoder. For analog decoder, Linear Least Squares Estimate (LLSE) decoder with estimated channel fading factors is introduced to obtain the optimal estimation of linear analog symbols. After merging subbands and chunks, inverse DWT is applied to obtain the High-pass frames. Finally, inverse MCTF is utilized to recover the original video GOP. Particularly, CSI is also estimated at the receiver side, and delivered to the sender side to determine the levels of power allocation for adaptive video transmission.

16.3 Effect of Channel Prediction on Video Transmission in Mobile Networks

16.3.1 Long-range Prediction Algorithm

As described previously, CSI is critical for adaptive video transmission. However, feedback CSI from the receiver side might not be effective due to the time-varying channel states. In this case, the prediction of channel coefficients (e.g., tens or hundreds of symbols ahead) is indispensable. LRP [172][174][175][176] is a class of algorithms for channel prediction, which calculates the linear Minimum Mean Squared Error (MMSE) estimation of the future channel coefficients based on the past observation samples. The most distinct feature of LRP is that it has a lower sampling rate compared with other methods. Generally, the sampling rate of LRP is much lower than the data rate. However, it should be greater than twice the maximum Doppler frequency shift.

In single-user scenarios, with LRP, the predicted channel coefficient $\hat{\alpha}_j$ based on p historical samples $\alpha_{j-1}, \alpha_{j-2}, \cdots, \alpha_{j-p}$ can be written as follows [176]

$$\hat{\alpha}_j = LRP(\alpha_{j-1}, \cdots, \alpha_{j-p}) = \sum_{k=1}^{p} \beta_k \alpha_{j-k}, \tag{16.1}$$

where p denotes the order of Auto-Regression (AR) model proposed in [177], and β_k is the optimal coefficient determined by the orthogonality principle with $q(q > p)$ observed samples. Let f^{sample} denote the sampling rate of fading coefficients. Generally, f^{sample} is much lower than data rate r^{data}. However, it should be larger than $2f^{dm}$, where f^{dm} is the maximum Doppler frequency shift. As long as r^{data} and p are fixed, a lower sampling rate will result in a larger memory range (observation time span), which shall facilitate prediction further into the future. For example, given $r^{data} = 25$ $kbps$ and sampling rate $f^{sample} = 500$ Hz. As predicted channel fading coefficient $\hat{\alpha}_1$ is based on $\alpha_{-p+1}, \cdots, \alpha_0$, we will get it after $\frac{r^{data}}{f^{sample}} - 1 = 49$ symbols. In this case, the prediction range is equal to 50 symbols. Consequently, the prediction range of the LRP algorithm can be obtained as follows

$$PRL = \frac{r^{data}}{f^{sample}}, \quad f^{sample} \geq 2f^{dm}. \tag{16.2}$$

From Eq. (16.2), we can see that slower mobility will result in a larger prediction range. The reason is that slower mobility produces less channel fluctuation, and we can predict further into future channel states. In A-HDAVT, training symbols are inserted into the data packets for channel estimation at the receiver side. When the receiver side obtains the estimated channel coefficient α_j, it sends feedback containing α_j to the sender side immediately. Then the sender side uses $\alpha_j, \cdots, \alpha_{j-q+1}$ to calculate the AR model coefficient β_k and uses $\alpha_j, \cdots, \alpha_{j-p+1}$ to predict $\hat{\alpha}_{j+1}$ with Eq. (16.1).

In multi-user scenarios, video data is transmitted to multiple users over independent sub-channels. Let S denote the number of users. Similar to single-user scenarios, the predicted sub-channel coefficient for user i $(1 \leq i \leq S)$ can be obtained based on p historical samples from user i (i.e., $\alpha_{i,j-1}, \alpha_{i,j-2}, \cdots, \alpha_{i,j-p}$), which is expressed as

$$\hat{\alpha}_{i,j+1} = LRP(\alpha_{i,j-1}, \cdots, \alpha_{i,j-p}) = \sum_{k=1}^{p} \beta_k^i \alpha_{i,j-k}, \qquad (16.3)$$

where β_k^i is the optimal coefficient of the sub-channel of user i determined by the orthogonality principle with $q(q > p)$ observed samples. The prediction range for the sub-channel of user i can be expressed as

$$PRL_i = \frac{r_i^{data}}{f_i^{sample}}, \ f_i^{sample} \geq 2f_i^{dm} \ and \ 1 \leq i \leq S, \qquad (16.4)$$

where r_i^{data} and f_i^{sample} denote data rate and sampling rate for user i, respectively. f_i^{dm} is the maximum Doppler frequency shift determined by the speed of user i.

The complexity of the LRP algorithm mainly lies in calculating the AR model coefficients β_k or β_k^i $(1 \leq k \leq p, 1 \leq i \leq S)$, with time complexity $O(q^2)$. In general, an AR model with limited order $(p < 20)$ is used for channel prediction. In this case, q is usually less than 30. In this case, the time complexity of calculating β_k or β_k^i is acceptable.

16.3.2 Video Content Division Strategy

In single-user scenarios, each High-pass frame in analog transmission is divided into chunks and the chunk size is set to PRL derived from Eq. (16.2). That is, LRP can provide the whole chunk transmission process with predicted CSI. Each chunk is further divided into subbands such that the channel state can keep constant during subband transmission, while the subband size is set according to the channel coherence time. Channel coefficients $\alpha_j^{(k)}$ $(1 \leq k \leq M)$ utilized for transmitting subband k in chunk j can be calculated as $\alpha_j^{(k)} = I(\alpha_j, \hat{\alpha}_{j+1})$. M is the number of subbands in chunk j. $I(\cdot)$ denotes Raised Cosine Filter (RCF) interpolation [172] which is described as follows.

1) Uniformly insert zero-points into sequence $[\alpha_{j-1}, \alpha_j, \hat{\alpha}_{j+1}, \hat{\alpha}_{j+2}]$ to generate temporary sequence α_j^L at data rate r^{data}.

2) Use RCF to produce channel coefficients at data rate r^{data}.

$$\hat{\alpha}_j^L[n] = \alpha_j^L[n] * h[n]$$
$$\alpha_j^{(k)} = \hat{\alpha}_j^L[L+k], (k=0,1,\cdots,L-1), \qquad (16.5)$$

where $L = r_{data}/f_{sample}$ and "*" denotes the convolution operation. $h[\cdot]$ denotes time domain impulse response of Raised Cosine Filter. Based on the predicted coefficients, adaptive scaling factors are derived to allocate power for each subband transmission.

In the multi-user scenario, chunk transmission of different users should be synchronized. In this case, power pre-allocation and re-allocation can be performed among chunks of all users, as described in Sections 16.5.2 and 16.5.3. When the videos of all users have equal resolution, the chunk size for these videos are also the same, which can be set as $min(PRL_1, \cdots, PRL_S)$. When the video resolutions for different users are different, the chunk size for each user should be set carefully to guarantee the same chunk transmission duration for all users. In this case, both PRL_i ($1 \leq i \leq S$) and video resolution should be considered, and different chunk sizes might be set for different users. Similar to the single-user scenarios, for user i, each chunk may be further divided into subbands with the consideration of sub-channel coherence time. Finally, the sub-channel coefficients $\alpha_{i,j}^{(k)}$ ($1 \leq i \leq S$, $1 \leq k \leq M_i$) for the delivery of subband k in chunk j of user i can also be obtained as $\alpha_{i,j}^{(k)} = I(\alpha_{i,j}, \hat{\alpha}_{i,j+1})$.

16.3.3 Time Complexity of Proposed System

In A-HDAVT, besides the time complexity of digital encoder, including H.264/AVC, low-order modulation and convolutional, extra time complexity comes from analog encoder, i.e., MCTF/IMCTF, 2D-DWT/2D-IDWT and LRP channel prediction. For a video GOP containing G frames, the time complexity of MCTF operation is $O(G \cdot L \cdot W)$ [170], where L and W describe the frame size. With parallel computing in matrix addition, the time complexity of MCTF can be reduced to $O(G)$. For $n - points$ DWT/IDWT, its time complexity is $O(n)$ [178]. The time complexity of LRP channel prediction is $O(q^2) + O(p^2)$, where q is the number of samples to compute AR coefficients and p is the order of AR model. For $p < q$ in LRP [172], the time complexity of LRP is $O(q^2)$. Therefore, the additional time complexity of the proposed scheme is $O(G) + (G - 1) \cdot O(L \cdot W) + O(q^2)$. As L and W are usually much larger than G and q, the additional time complexity of the proposed scheme is $O(L \cdot W)$.

In addition, we obtain the runtime of A-HDAVT to demonstrate that it can support real time video transmission. The simulations are conducted on our office computer with Intel (R) Core (TM) i3-3220 CPU @ 3.30GHz, 6GB RAM. The test video sequence is "Foreman_cif" and the GOP size is 8. The average runtime of transmitting one frame is about 52ms and the average runtime of decoding one frame is about 22ms. Since only the High-pass frame is coded using digital encoder in A-HDAVT, the average runtime for one frame is much less than that of H.264/AVC encoder. In addition, by utilizing a faster hardware platform (such as DSP), the runtime of A-HDAVT can be further reduced. Therefore, it can be concluded that the time complexity of the proposed scheme is acceptable.

16.4 P-APDO in Single-user Scenarios

In single-scenarios, three power allocation procedures are performed in P-APDO in different data units of granularities (i.e., frame, chunk, and subband). Intuitively, more power should be allocated to more important video content to achieve better performance. For example, the Low-pass frame should be given higher priority than the High-pass frames when power allocation is performed. Moreover, in mobile networks with fading channels, power allocation should be adaptive to channel states. For this purpose, LRP-based channel prediction is designed to predict CSI for future video transmission. Also, with LRP, High-pass frames are divided according to the strategy described in Section 16.3.2.

We assume that the transmission power is fixed to P for each video GOP. The overall power consumed to deliver both digital data (P^d) and analog symbols (P^a) should not exceed P, namely $P^d + P^a \leq P$. In digital transmission, the modulation mode is characterized by modulation order Δ which can be set according to channel states. Better channel states will result in a higher Δ.

16.4.1 Power Allocation Strategy in Hybrid Digital-Analog Transmission

Since digital transmission has been adopted to delivery the most important data in each GOP, sufficient power should be allocated to ensure that the Bit Error Rate (BER) should not exceed a given threshold (i.e., BER_0). In this research, we assume that the coded bits of the Low-pass frame and metadata are packaged into T packets with size Q determined by the channel coherence time. Let P_t^d denote the transmitting power for $t^{th}(1 \leq t \leq T)$ packet. Then we have

$$\frac{P_t^d \cdot |\hat{\alpha}_t|^2 \cdot \log_2 \Delta}{Q \cdot \sigma^2} \geq SNR(BER_0), \qquad (16.6)$$

where $\hat{\alpha}_t$ denotes the predicted channel coefficient for delivering t^{th} digital packet and σ^2 is the Gaussian noise power. $SNR(BER_0)$ denotes the minimum SNR required to achieve the given BER_0 at the receiver side.

A threshold-based strategy is proposed to save power in the digital transmission. Since the channel states vary frequently in mobile networks, much power is required to ensure reliable digital transmission when poor channel states occur. The basic idea is to perform digital transmission only when channel state is better than a given threshold with α^{th}. Actually, α^{th} can be set to a proper value based on the results from channel prediction. According to Eq. (16.6), the threshold based strategy for power allocation between digital and analog transmission can be described as

$$
P_t^d =
\begin{cases}
Q \cdot \sigma^2 \cdot SNR(BER_0)/(|\hat{\alpha}_t|^2 \cdot \log_2 \Delta), \\
\quad \hat{\alpha}_t \geq \alpha^{th} \\
\\
0, \quad \hat{\alpha}_t < \alpha^{th},
\end{cases}
\tag{16.7}
$$

$$
P^a = P - \sum_{t=1}^{T} P_t^d.
\tag{16.8}
$$

16.4.2 Chunk-based Power Allocation

In analog transmission, each High-pass frame is divided into chunks. After MCTF and 2D-DWT, the variances of these chunks are unevenly distributed. Therefore, power allocation should be performed among these chunks. Chunk with larger variance means that it is more important for video decoding [19]. In this research, analog transmitting power is allocated among chunks based on their variances, and the power allocation strategy can be formulated as

$$
min \ \frac{1}{N} \sum_{j=1}^{N} \frac{\lambda_j}{P_j^a}
$$
$$
s.t. \ \sum_{j=1}^{N} P_j^a \leq P^a,
\tag{16.9}
$$
$$
\frac{(G-1) \cdot L \cdot W}{N} \leq PLR,
$$

where λ_j denotes the variance of chunk j. P_a and P_j^a are the allocated power to transmit High-pass frames and chunk j, respectively. N is the number of chunks constrained by PRL, and PRL can be derived from Eq. (16.2). By utilizing the technique of Lagrange multipliers, Eq. (16.2) can be solved and the power allocated to chunk j can be obtained as

$$
P_j^a = \frac{\sqrt{\lambda_j}}{\sum_{j=1}^{N} \sqrt{\lambda_j}} P^a.
\tag{16.10}
$$

According to Eq. (16.10), it can be seen that a chunk with larger variance (i.e., a more important chunk) will be allocated more power.

16.4.3 Subband-based Adaptive Power Distortion Optimization

Similar to power allocation in Softcast [18][19], APDO proposed in A-HDAVT also scales the magnitudes of transformed signals to provide error resilience over noisy channels. However, APDO is also different from Softcast-based schemes. That is, the power allocation via APDO not only considers the importance of video chunks, but also facilitates adaptation to combat channel fading. In APDO, each chunk is further divided into subbands, while the size of these subbands is set to ensure their transmission time is less than the channel coherence time. Thus, the basic unit for channel adaptation is a subband. Specifically, according to channel fading coefficients, APDO is performed among subbands within each chunk through adjusting the scaling factors of subbands.

Let $X_j^{(k)} (j = 1 \cdots N, k = 1 \cdots M)$ denote subband k in chunk j, $Y_j^{(k)} = g_j^{(k)} \cdot X_j^{(k)}$ represent the transmission signal that can combat both channel fading and Gaussian noise. $g_j^{(k)}$ is the optimal scaling factor for subband $X_j^{(k)}$, and M is the number of subbands in each chunk. Then the received signal can be expressed as

$$\hat{Y}_j^{(k)} = \alpha_j^{(k)} \cdot g_j^{(k)} \cdot X_j^{(k)} + N_j^{(k)}, \tag{16.11}$$

where $\hat{Y}_j^{(k)}$ denotes k^{th} received subband in chunk j, and $N_j^{(k)}$ is the Gaussian noise vector. Channel coefficient $\alpha_j^{(k)}$ can be obtained as described in Section 16.3.2. The MSE distortion of chunk j can be derived as

$$MSE(j) = E[(\hat{X}_j^{(k)} - X_j^{(k)})^T (\hat{X}_j^{(k)} - X_j^{(k)})] = \sum_{k=1}^{M} \frac{\sigma^2}{|\alpha_j^{(k)}|^2 \cdot |g_j^{(k)}|^2}, \tag{16.12}$$

where $\hat{X}_j^{(k)}$ is the estimate of $X_j^{(k)}$ at the receiver side and is equal to $\frac{\hat{Y}_j^{(k)}}{\alpha_j^{(k)} \cdot g_j^{(k)}}$. The objective of APDO is to find an optimal scaling factor g_j^k to minimize the MSE distortion for chunk j with given power P_j^a. Then the power distortion optimization problem can be formulated as

$$\min MSE(j)$$
$$s.t. \sum_{k=1}^{M} |g_j^{(k)}|^2 \cdot E[|X_j^{(k)}|^2] \le P_j^a. \tag{16.13}$$

By utilizing the technique of Lagrange multipliers, Eq. (16.13) can be solved and the optimal scaling factors can be obtained as

$$g_j^{(k)} = \sqrt{\frac{P_j^a}{\sqrt{\lambda_j^{(k)} |\alpha_j^{(k)}|^2} \cdot \sum_{k=1}^{M} \sqrt{\lambda_j^{(k)} / |\alpha_j^{(k)}|^2}}}, \tag{16.14}$$

where $\lambda_j^{(k)}$ denotes the variance of $X_j^{(k)}$. From Eq. (16.14), we can see that APDO will increase the transmitting power of the subbands that are with low signal power. When the channel state deteriorates, more power will be allocated to the current transmitting subband. Therefore, with estimated channel states, the transmitting power is adaptively allocated for a subband.

Accordingly, the MSE distortion of the High-pass frames in one GOP can be derived as

$$MSE_{Hf} = E[MSE(j)] = \frac{\sigma^2}{P_a} \sum_{j=1}^{N} [\frac{E[\sqrt{\lambda_j}]}{\sqrt{\lambda_j}} (\sum_{k=1}^{M} \sqrt{\lambda_j^{(k)} / |\alpha_j^{(k)}|^2})^2]. \qquad (16.15)$$

Then the MSE of the GOP can be written as follows

$$MSE_{GOP} = \frac{1}{G} MSE_{Lf} + (1 - \frac{1}{G}) MSE_{Hf}, \qquad (16.16)$$

where G is the GOP size and MSE_{Lf} is the MSE distortion of the Low-pass frames. Generally, MSE_{Lf} can be ignored when the channel SNR is above the threshold $SNR(BER_0)$ as indicated in Eq. (16.7).

16.5 P-APDO in Multi-user Scenarios

In multi-user scenarios, we consider Base Station (BS) simultaneously transmitting different videos for several mobile users. In such multi-user video transmission scenarios, the proposed P-APDO performed at the BS is able to exploit both content diversity and channel diversity among users, to further improve the user perceived video quality. With the development of programmable and re-configurable techniques in communication networks, the BS is assumed to support the content-aware processing such as the proposed P-APDO.

In multi-user scenarios, video contents for multiple users are transmitted over independent sub-channels. As shown in Fig. 16.2, sending window is adopted instead of GOP to indicate the amount of video data that are transmitted for each user. In P-APDO, power pre-allocation is initially performed to allocate power to the chunks of all users according to their content importance. Next, power re-allocation is further applied among chunks with the additional consideration based on the predicted channel states. Chunk synchronization for different users should be accomplished to facilitate such power pre-allocation and re-allocation. To meet this requirement, the chunk sizes for different users should be set according to the following principles.

1) For user i, the chunk size should be set to be less than PRL_i.

2) The number of chunks of each user within the sending window should be the same.

3) The chunk transmission time for each user should also remain the same. With such guiding principles, the chunk sizes of different users may be different in order to meet the synchronization requirements.

The transmission power budget for video data of all users in the sending window is assumed as P. Let P^d and P^a represent the power of digital transmission and analog transmission, respectively, and we have $P^d + P^a \leq P$. For user i, the modulation mode in digital transmission is determined by the modulation order Δ_i, where Δ_i is determined by the sub-channel states of user i.

16.5.1 Multi-user Power Allocation Strategy in Hybrid Digital-Analog Transmission

Similar to single-user scenarios, in multi-user scenarios, video in the sending window is transformed into one reference and several High-pass frames. Low-pass frame and metadata are transmitted in digital mode over the given sub-channel. Sufficient power should be allocated for digital transmission to ensure its reliability. However, different from the single-user scenarios, multi-user scenarios have the ability to further exploit channel diversity among users to reduce overall power consumption. For instance, assigning transmission priority to users with better channel states can be applied when performing power allocation.

Specifically, reference frames and metadata of all users are packaged into packets for transmission. Let $P_{i,t}^d$ denote the power allocated to transmit t^{th} packet of user i in the digital mode. Q_i is the packet size, and BER_i^0 is the minimum BER required by user i. Specifically, we describe the multi-user power allocation strategy for digital transmission in the following Algorithm 11.

Algorithm 11 Hybrid power allocation in multi-user scenarios

Input: $\{\hat{\alpha}_{i,t}\},\{Q_i\},\{BER_i^0\},1 \leq i \leq S, 1 \leq t \leq T$
Output: $\{P_{i,t}^d\},1 \leq i \leq S, 1 \leq t \leq T$
1: **initial procedure:**
2:   Define set $coef = \{\hat{\alpha}_{i,t}(1 \leq i \leq S, 1 \leq t \leq T)\}$
3: **end initial procedure**
4: **while** $coef \neq \phi$ **do**
5:   $\hat{\alpha}_{i,t} = max\{coef\}$
6:   **if** $\hat{\alpha}_{i,t} < \alpha_i^{th}$ **then**
7:       break(stop transmission temporarily)
8:   **end if**
9:   $P_{i,t}^d = Q_i \cdot \sigma_i^2 \cdot SNR(BER_i^0)/(|\hat{\alpha}_{i,t}|^2 \cdot \log_2 \Delta_i)$
10:   $coef = coef - max\{coef\}$
11: **end while**

In Algorithm 11, σ_i^2 and Δ_i are Gaussian noise power and the modulation order in the sub-channel of user i, respectively. α_i^{th} represents the transmitting threshold of user i. Digital transmission for user i shall stop temporarily when the sub-channel state of user i deteriorates below α_i^{th}. $\hat{\alpha}_{i,t}$ is the predicted channel coefficient when delivering t^{th} digital packet of user i, which can be obtained through $LRP(\alpha_{i,t-1}, \cdots, \alpha_{i,t-p})$. It can be seen that power will always be allocated to the user with the best channel state. After power allocation for digital transmission, the remaining power shall be utilized for analog transmission, which is elaborated as follows:

$$P^a = P - \sum_{i=1}^{S}\sum_{t=1}^{T} P_{i,t}^d. \tag{16.17}$$

16.5.2 Chunk-based Power Pre-allocation for Multi-user Parallel Transmission

In multi-user scenarios, power pre-allocation is first introduced to exploit content diversity among users. High-pass frames of different users are divided into chunks, with the consideration of prediction range of LRP and the synchronization requirement. Compared with the single-user scenarios, variances of the chunks are distributed unevenly with respect to users. This kind of content diversity of users can be utilized to further optimize power allocation.

Let $X_{i,j}$ ($1 \leq i \leq S$, $1 \leq j \leq N$) denote chunk j of user i. $P_{i,j}^a$ is the power allocated to $X_{i,j}$ and $\lambda_{i,j}$ is the variance of $X_{i,j}$. P^a is allocated among chunks of all users. The basic idea is that the power budget for a chunk should be proportional to the importance of the chunk. The optimization problem for power pre-allocation is formulated as follows

$$min \frac{1}{S \cdot N}\sum_{i=1}^{S}\sum_{j=1}^{N}\frac{\lambda_{i,j}}{P_{i,j}^a}$$

$$s.t. \sum_{i=1}^{S}\sum_{j=1}^{N} P_{i,j}^a \leq P^a. \tag{16.18}$$

Eq. (16.18) shows that more power will be allocated to chunks with larger variances. By using the method of Lagrange multipliers, we can obtain the power pre-allocated to chunk $X_{i,j}$ as follows:

$$P_{i,j}^a = \frac{\sqrt{\lambda_{i,j}}}{\sum_{i=1}^{S}\sum_{j=1}^{N}\sqrt{\lambda_{i,j}}}P^a. \tag{16.19}$$

16.5.3 Power Re-allocation among Chunks Being Transmitted

We have pre-allocated power to the chunks with the consideration of content diversity of all users. In mobile networks, the sub-channel states vary with respect to users, and this kind of sub-channel diversity can also be explored to further optimize power allocation.

Video chunks of all users in the sending window are shown in Fig. 16.2, with which we can better understand the process of power re-allocation.

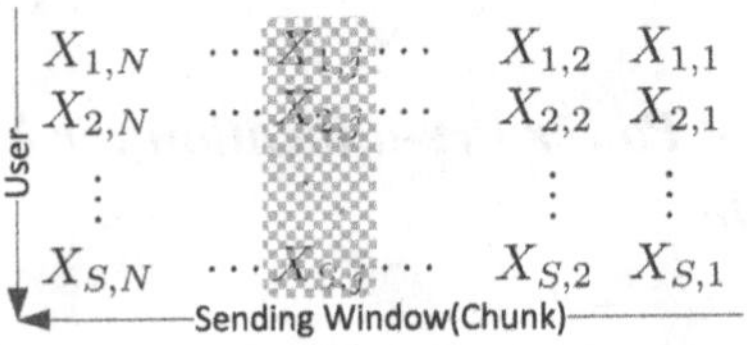

Fig. 16.2 Chunks in sending window in multi-user scenario.

In the sending window, each column contains S chunks transmitted in parallel over independent sub-channels. Let $\mathbf{X}_j = (X_{1,j}, X_{2,j}, \cdots, X_{S,j})$ represent these S chunks. With the LRP algorithm described in Section 16.3.1, we can derive $\hat{\alpha}_{i,j+1}$ ($1 \leq i \leq S$) for transmitting $\mathbf{X}_j$. Then, the power re-allocation is performed among chunks in $\mathbf{X}_j$.

Specifically, the objective of power re-allocation is to minimize the average MSE distortion of chunks in $\mathbf{X}_j$. We will first derive the MSE distortion for each chunk. Let $\hat{P}_{i,j}^a$ denote the pre-allocated power to chunk $X_{i,j}$. Considering coherence time of the sub-channel assigned to user i, $X_{i,j}$ is divided into M_i subbands (i.e., $X_{i,j}^{(k)}, 1 \leq k \leq M_i$), which is similar to that in single-user scenarios. Based on predicted $\hat{\alpha}_{i,j+1}$, sub-channel coefficient $\alpha_{i,j}^{(k)}$ for subband $X_{i,j}^{(k)}$ is obtained as described in Section 16.3.2. Then the MSE distortion of chunk $X_{i,j}$ can be expressed as

$$MSE(i,j) = \frac{\sigma^2}{\hat{P}_{i,j}^a} (\sum_{k=1}^{M_i} \sqrt{\lambda_{i,j}^{(k)} / |\alpha_{i,j}^{(k)}|^2})^2, \qquad (16.20)$$

where $\lambda_{i,j}^{(k)}$ is the variance of subband $X_{i,j}^{(k)}$. Based on Eq. (16.20), the power re-allocation optimization problem can be expressed as

$$min \sum_{i=1}^{S} \frac{\sigma^2}{\hat{P}_{i,j}^a} (\sum_{k=1}^{M_i} \sqrt{\lambda_{i,j}^{(k)} / |\alpha_{i,j}^{(k)}|^2})^2$$

$$s.t. \sum_{i=1}^{S} \hat{P}_{i,j}^a \leq \sum_{i=1}^{S} P_{i,j}^a. \qquad (16.21)$$

Similarly, with the technique of Lagrange multipliers, Eq. (16.21) can be solved and the power allocated to each chunk after power re-allocation is

$$\hat{P}_{i,j}^a = \frac{\sum_{k=1}^{M_i} \sqrt{\lambda_{i,j}^{(k)} / |\alpha_{i,j}^{(k)}|^2}}{\sum_{i=1}^{S} \sum_{k=1}^{M_i} \sqrt{\lambda_{i,j}^{(k)} / |\alpha_{i,j}^{(k)}|^2}} \cdot \frac{\sum_{i=1}^{S} \sqrt{\lambda_{i,j}}}{\sum_{i=1}^{S} \sum_{j=1}^{N} \sqrt{\lambda_{i,j}}} \cdot P^a. \tag{16.22}$$

In Eq. (16.22), it can be seen that not only the content diversity (i.e., $\lambda_{i,j}$) but also the sub-channel diversity (i.e., $\alpha_{i,j}^{(k)}$) are taken into account in the power re-allocation process. Exploiting these two types of diversities can significantly improve the reconstructed video quality for multiple users in multi-user scenarios.

16.5.4 Subband-based Adaptive Power Distortion Optimization

As mentioned before, each chunk $X_{i,j}$ is divided into M_i subbands to perform APDO. That is, the basic unit for each sub-channel adaptation is a subband. Since the subband size is set according to the sub-channel coherence time, the sub-channel state can be considered as constant during the transmission of each subband. As shown in Section 16.3.2, the sub-channel coefficient $\alpha_{i,j}^{(k)}$ for subband $X_{i,j}^{(k)}$ ($1 \leq k \leq M_i$) can be derived. Similar to APDO in single-user scenarios, power allocation for subbands of $X_{i,j}$ is based on their importance and sub-channel states. The optimal scaling factor of subband $X_{i,j}^{(k)}$ can be obtained according to Eq. (16.14), which is shown as

$$g_{i,j}^{(k)} = \sqrt{\frac{\hat{P}_{i,j}^a}{\sqrt{\lambda_{i,j}^{(k)} |\alpha_{i,j}^{(k)}|^2} \cdot \sum_{k=1}^{M_i} \sqrt{\lambda_{i,j}^{(k)} / |\alpha_{i,j}^{(k)}|^2}}}. \tag{16.23}$$

With Eq. (16.22), Eq. (16.23) can be rewritten as

$$g_{i,j}^{(k)} = \left(\frac{\frac{1}{\sqrt{\lambda_{i,j}^{(k)} |\alpha_{i,j}^{(k)}|^2}} \cdot \frac{\sum_{i=1}^{S} \sqrt{\lambda_{i,j}}}{\sum_{i=1}^{S} \sum_{j=1}^{N} \sqrt{\lambda_{i,j}}}}{\sum_{i=1}^{S} \sum_{k=1}^{M_i} \sqrt{\lambda_{i,j}^{(k)} / |\alpha_{i,j}^{(k)}|^2}} \cdot P^a \right)^{\frac{1}{2}}. \tag{16.24}$$

16.6 Performance Evaluation

Simulations are carried out to verify the performance of proposed A-HDAVT. In this research, all simulations are implemented and performed in MATLAB R2013a. PSNR is adopted as metric to measure the video transmission performance in both single-user and multi-user scenarios, as defined as follows

$$PSNR = 20 \lg \frac{2^L - 1}{\sqrt{MSE}},$$ (16.25)

where L is the number of bits to encode the pixel luminance, and generally we have $L = 8$. MSE is the mean square error between all original and decoded pixel values and lg denotes the logarithmic function.

In A-HDAVT, MCTF [169] is adopted to transform the original video GOP into a Low-pass frame and several High-pass frames, and the main steps of MCTF are described as follows.

1) Input video GOP $S_n = \{S_{n,l}, 0 \le l \le 2^n - 1\}$ that consists of 2^n frames.

2) Separate S_n into 2^{n-1} pairs $\{S_{n,2l}, S_{n,2l+1}\}$ $(l = 0, 1, \cdots, 2^{n-1} - 1)$. Then for each pair, transformation is performed to obtain High-pass frames d_{n-1} and Low-pass frames S_{n-1}, where $S_{n-1,l} = \frac{S_{n,2l+1} + S_{n,2l}}{2}$ and $d_{n-1,l} = S_{n,2l+1} - S_{n,2l}$. Both S_{n-1} and d_{n-1} consist of 2^{n-1} frames.

3) Recursively repeat the above transformation on S_{n-1}, S_{n-1}, ..., S_1, until there left only one low-pass frame S_0.

In simulations, the GOP size and the sending window size are set to 8. Six standard CIF video sequences are adopted, including 'Foreman', 'News', 'Tempete', 'Flower' (352×288, 30 fps) and 'Football', 'Tennis' (352×240, 30 fps). Specifically, the luminance components of these video sequences are extracted to produce monochrome video sequences. Meanwhile, the chunk size and subband size are set according to the simulation scenario with highest mobility. In this case, the chunk size and the subband size will not exceed the prediction range and the channel coherence time, respectively. Particularly, default chunk size is set to 99 for 'Foreman', 'News', 'Tempete', 'Flower', and 165 for 'Football', 'Tennis'. Meanwhile, default subband size is set to 33 for 'Foreman', 'News', 'Tempete', 'Flower', and 55 for 'Football', 'Tennis'. In Table 16.1, some common parameters of wireless channels and sub-channels are given for simulations, including single-user and multi-user scenarios.

In A-HDAVT, H.264/AVC reference software JM 18.6 [179] is adopted as the digital encoder. Some main parameters are given as follows, i.e., FramesToBeEncoded = 1, IntraPeriod = 1, NumberReferenceFrames = 1, NumberBFrames = 0, YUVFormat = 4:2:0 and other parameters are configured as default values in the file "encoder.cfg". To ensure reliable transmission of reference frames and metadata, the received SNR should be higher than 3 dB. Therefore, the BER is limited to 10^{-6} [180] by using $(2, 1, 41)$ convolutional codec with polynomials $\{133, 171\}$, soft Viterbi decoding algorithm and BPSK modulation for digital bitstreams. In addition, we adopt *Jakes Model* [176] to simulate the fading channel/subchannel. In *Jakes Model*, channel/sub-channel fluctuations are caused by the path gain of multipath transmission and the user mobility. During simulations, parameters of multipath are fixed as described in Table 16.1. Thus, we can control the degree of channel/sub-channel fading by adjusting the speed of each user. We use maximum Doppler frequency shift f^{dm} to indicate the speed of the user in each simulation.

Table 16.1 Parameters of wireless channels/sub-channels

Parameter and Description	Value
Power budget of each user	10^3
BER_0	10^{-6}
Average path gain	$-10\,dB$
Variance of path gain	$0.55\,dB$
Number of paths	9
Carrier frequency (f_c)	$2100\,MHz$

Three reference schemes are adopted for comparison with A-HDAVT in both single-user and multi-user scenarios, including Softcast [18][19], Parcast [101] and RUVT [25]. Particularly, Softcast is strictly as the system framework described in [18]. First, 3D-DCT is employed to remove the intra- and inter-frame redundancy of the video GOP. Then, the scaling factor of each chunk is calculated, followed by a Hadamard Transform. Finally, these transformed chunks are transmitted over a fading channel. At the receiver side, to ensure fairness, we first use an equalizer to eliminate the effect of channel fading on the transmitted signals. After that, inverse Hadamard transform, linear decoding and inverse 3D-DCT are applied to reconstruct the original video GOP.

For Parcast, the encoder and decoder part are similar to that of Softcast. However, Parcast has considered MIMO-OFDM channels and the optimal match between video chunks and MIMO-OFDM sub-channels. First, the CSI of all sub-channels is sent back to the transmitter as feedback. Then the transmitter makes singular value decomposition on the feedback channel matrix. Then, each video chunk and MIMO-OFDM sub-channel are matched according to the principles proposed in Parcast. Finally, we calculate the optimal scaling factor for each chunk according to its variance and the CSI of relative sub-channel. At the receiver side, we use inverse pre-coding, linear decoding, inverse Hadamard Transform, inverse match and inverse 3D-DCT in sequence to recover the original video frames.

For RUVT, original video GOP is firstly decorrelated with 3D-DCT. Then optimal power and bandwidth allocation are performed with the algorithm proposed in [25]. Finally, the scaled coefficients are directly modulated with AQM. At the receiver side, symbols with multiple transmission are combined with maximum ratio combining.

16.6.1 Simulation Results in Single-user Scenarios

16.6.1.1 Performance in Scenarios with Different Channel Noise

In simulations, the noise power is determined by the target channel SNR once the transmitting power is given. Thus, by varying the noise power, we can specify different channel SNR. The channel fading coefficients are generated by *Jakes model* [176] and f^{dm} is set to 70 Hz. Other parameters are set as shown in Table 16.1.

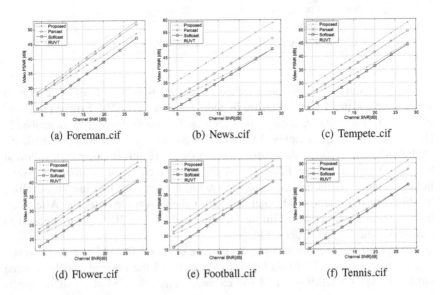

(a) Foreman_cif   (b) News_cif   (c) Tempete_cif

(d) Flower_cif   (e) Football_cif   (f) Tennis_cif

Fig. 16.3 Performance comparison in noisy scenarios.

Fig. 16.3 shows the performance comparison of six video sequences with A-HDAVT and three reference schemes in fading channels. The average channel SNR varies from 4 dB to 28 dB. It can be seen that A-HDAVT outperforms RUVT [25] about $1.6 \sim 7.5\,dB$, Parcast for about $1.8 \sim 7.9\,dB$ and Softcast for about $6.5 \sim 12.1\,dB$, respectively. In addition, it also can be seen that the performance improvement differs for different video sequences. The reason is that different video sequences are with different motion. For videos with larger motion, MCTF and 2D-wavelet transform are not efficient, since some blocks in the High-pass frames cannot find good prediction.

Visual quality comparison is provided in Fig. 16.4. The channel SNR is fixed to 6 dB. The 12th frame of video sequence 'Foreman' is chosen for comparison. We can see that the visual performance of A-HDAVT outperforms the other three reference schemes.

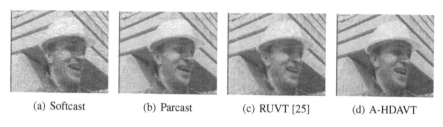

(a) Softcast   (b) Parcast   (c) RUVT [25]   (d) A-HDAVT

Fig. 16.4 Visual video quality comparison.

16.6.1.2 Performance in Scenarios with Different User Mobility

Multipath channel fluctuations in mobile network depend heavily on the Doppler frequency shift, which is proportional to the movement velocities of the users. By adjusting f^{dm}, channel coefficients in low, medium and high mobility with movement velocities at 36 km/h, 72 km/h and 144 km/h can be generated. In all simulations, the channel SNR is fixed to 10 dB, and we adopt video sequences 'tempete' for test. Simulation results are given in Fig. 16.5.

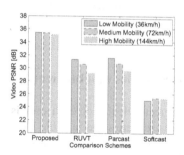

Fig. 16.5 Performance comparison in mobility scenarios.

From Fig. 16.5 we can see that A-HDAVT outperforms RUVT [25], Parcast and Softcast. Since P-APDO is adopted to adaptively combat channel fading, it can be seen that the PSNR of A-HDAVT only decreases slightly as the user velocity increases. Therefore, it can be concluded that A-HDAVT can provide better support for robust video transmission in mobile networks. For RUVT [25], only statistical CSI is adopted for resource allocation. However, statistical CSI might be very different from instantaneous CSI. This fact results in the performance degradation of RUVT. In addition, CSI feedback from the receiver side in Parcast may not catch the dynamics of channel change, which will result in non-optimal power allocation. Softcast shows the worst performance. The reason is that it is designed for AWGN channels and cannot cope with channel fading effectively.

16.6.2 Simulation Results in Multi-user Scenarios

In multi-user scenarios, through adjusting the channel SNR and velocity of user movement, we can generate multi-user scenarios. Jakes model is employed to simulate the channel state for each user and the channels are independent from each other. In multi-user scenarios, the number of users is set to 4. Four different video sequences (i.e., 'Foreman', 'News', 'Tempete' and 'Flower') are transmitted for four users, respectively.

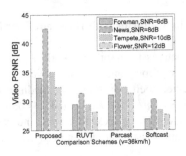

Fig. 16.6 Performance comparison in noisy scenarios with four users.

16.6.2.1 Performance in Scenarios with Different Channel Noise

In simulations, the movement velocity of each user is fixed at 36 km/h. Other sub-channel parameters for users are set as in Table 16.1. The channel SNR is set as 6 dB, 8 dB, 10 dB and 12 dB, respectively. Simulation results are given in Fig. 16.6. It can be seen that A-HDAVT performs best in all simulations. It outperforms RUVT [25] about 6.4 dB, Parcast at least 3.9 dB and SoftCast at least 7.7 dB in terms of PSNR. Particularly, the performance gain comes from power re-allocation among the users as well as the power optimization in each chunk based on both predicted channel states and the importance of video content. Meanwhile, we can see that the PSNR does not monotonically decrease as the average channel SNR increases, due to the diversity of both video content and users.

16.6.2.2 Performance in Scenarios with Different User Mobility

We also study the effects of user mobility on the performance of A-HDAVT, RUVT [25], Parcast and Softcast in terms of PSNR. During simulations, we fixed the average channel SNR to 10 dB and set the movement velocities of four users at 18 km/h, 54 km/h, 90 km/h and 108 km/h, respectively. Other sub-channel parameters for users remain same as that in Table 16.1.

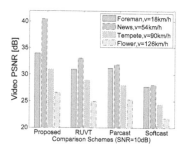

Fig. 16.7 Performance comparison in mobility scenarios with four users.

The results are shown in Fig. 16.7. We can see that A-HDAVT outperforms RUVT [25], Parcast and Softcast about 3.5 *dB*, 4.0 *dB* and 7.5 *dB*, respectively, in terms of average PSNR gains. The PSNR gains come from P-APDO in the multi-user scenarios and such gains vary with respect to video content and user movement velocity.

16.7 Summary

In this chapter, we proposed a novel scheme A-HDAVT, aiming at substantially improving the user perceived video quality in mobile networks with fading channels. A-HDAVT has two distinct features: (i) Hybrid digital-analog video transmission. Reliable digital transmission is employed to transmit the Low-pass frame to guarantee the basic video quality for users even with poor channel states while analog transmission is adopted to transmit remaining video data within a GOP to achieve graceful degradation performance. (ii) P-APDO with the LRP algorithm in analog transmission. The basic idea behind P-APDO is to optimize power allocation for video transmission based on the predicted channel states as well as the importance of video content. In multi-user scenarios, content diversity and channel diversity among users are also explored to further improve the performance of video transmission. The simulation results show that A-HDAVT achieves more significant performance gains than reference schemes in both single-user and multi-user scenarios.

In the future, we plan to extend A-HDAVT to more complicated mobile networks with relays and/or multiple hop transmissions. Moreover, we shall also study the effect of user mobility models on the performance of A-HDAVT.

16E Summary

References

1. Cisco. Cisco visual networking index: Global mobile data traffic forecast update, 2017-2022 white paper. Technical report, https://www.cisco.com/c/en/us/solutions/collateral/service-provider/visual-networking-index-vni/white-paper-c11-738429.html, February 2019.
2. Claude E Shannon. A mathematical theory of communication. *Bell System Technology Journal*, 27:379–423, 1948.
3. Sridhar Vembu, Sergio Verdu, and Yossef Steinberg. The source-channel separation theorem revisited. *IEEE Transactions on Information Theory*, 41(1):44–54, 1995.
4. Thomas Wiegand, Gary J Sullivan, Gisle Bjontegaard, and Ajay Luthra. Overview of the h. 264/avc video coding standard. *IEEE Transactions on Circuits and Systems for Video Technology*, 13(7):560–576, 2003.
5. Heiko Schwarz, Detlev Marpe, and Thomas Wiegand. Overview of the scalable video coding extension of the h.264/avc standard. *IEEE Transactions on Circuits and Systems for Video Technology*, 17(9):1103–1120, Sept, 2007.
6. Majid Rabbani and Rajan Joshi. An overview of the jpeg 2000 still image compression standard. *Signal Processing: Image Communication*, 17(1):3–48, 2002.
7. William B Pennebaker and Joan L Mitchell. *JPEG: Still image data compression standard*. Springer, 1993.
8. Yao Wang and Qin-Fan Zhu. Error control and concealment for video communication: A review. *Proceedings of the IEEE*, 86(5):974–997, 1998.
9. Jeongseok Ha, Jaehong Kim, and Steven W McLaughlin. Rate-compatible puncturing of low-density parity-check codes. *IEEE Transactions on Information Theory*, 50(11):2824–2836, Nov, 2004.
10. Kannan Ramchandran, Antonio Ortega, K. Metin Uz, and Martin Vetterli. Multiresolution broadcast for digital hdtv using joint source/channel coding. *IEEE Journal on Selected Areas in Communications*, 11(1):6–23, 1993.
11. Tomas Kratochvil. Hierarchical modulation in dvb-t/h mobile tv transmission. In *Multi-Carrier Systems & Solutions*, pages 333–341. Springer, 2009.
12. Michael Gastpar, Bixio Rimoldi, and Martin Vetterli. To code, or not to code: lossy source-channel communication revisited. *IEEE Transactions on Information Theory*, 49(5):1147–1158, May, 2003.
13. Kyonghwa Lee and D Petersen. Optimal linear coding for vector channels. *IEEE Transactions on Communications*, 24(12):1283–1290, Dec, 1976.
14. Z Reznic, Meir Feder, and Ram Zamir. Distortion bounds for broadcasting with bandwidth expansion. *IEEE Transactions on Information Theory*, 52(8):3778–3788, Aug, 2006.
15. Makesh Pravin Wilson, Krishna Narayanan, and Giuseppe Caire. Joint source channel coding with side information using hybrid digital analog codes. *IEEE Transactions on Information Theory*, 56(10):4922–4940, 2010.

16. Yuval Kochman and Ram Zamir. Analog matching of colored sources to colored channels. *IEEE Transactions on Information Theory*, 57(6):3180–3195, June, 2011.

17. T Goblick. Theoretical limitations on the transmission of data from analog sources. *IEEE Transactions on Information Theory*, 11(4):558–567, Oct, 1965.

18. Szymon Jakubczak and Dina Katabi. Softcast: one-size-fits-all wireless video. In *ACM SIGCOMM Computer Communication Review*, 2010.

19. Szymon Jakubczak and Dina Katabi. A cross-layer design for scalable mobile video. In *Proceedings of the 17th Annual International Conference on Mobile Computing and Networking*, MobiCom'11, pages 289–300, 2011.

20. Vinod M Prabhakaran, Rohit Puri, and Kannan Ramchandran. Colored Gaussian source-channel broadcast for heterogeneous (analog/digital) receivers. *IEEE Transactions on Information Theory*, 54(4):1807–1814, 2008.

21. Vinod M Prabhakaran, Rohit Puri, and Kannan Ramchandran. Hybrid digital-analog codes for source-channel broadcast of Gaussian sources over Gaussian channels. *IEEE Transactions on Information Theory*, 57(7):4573–4588, 2011.

22. Szymon Jakubczak, Hariharan Rahul, and Dina Katabi. Softcast: One video to serve all wireless receivers. In *MIT Technical Report, MIT-CSAIL-TR-2009-005*, 2009.

23. Ruiqin Xiong, Jizheng Xu, Feng Wu, and Shipeng Li. Barbell-lifting based 3-D wavelet coding scheme. *IEEE Transactions on Circuits and Systems for Video Technology*, 17(9):1256–1269, 2007.

24. Xiaopeng Fan, Feng Wu, Debin Zhao, and Oscar C Au. Distributed wireless visual communication with power distortion optimization. *IEEE Transactions on Circuits and Systems for Video Technology*, 23(6):1040–1053, June, 2013.

25. Hao Cui, Chong Luo, Chang Wen Chen, and Feng Wu. Robust uncoded video transmission over wireless fast fading channel. In *INFOCOM 2014. Thirty-Third Annual Joint Conference of the IEEE Computer and Communications Societies. Proceedings. IEEE*, pages 73–81, 2014.

26. Xiao Lin Liu, Wenjun Hu, Chong Luo, Qifan Pu, Feng Wu, and Yongguang Zhang. ParCast+: Parallel Video Unicast in MIMO-OFDM WLANs. *IEEE Transactions on Multimedia*, 16:2038–2051, 2014.

27. Yao Wang, Amy R Reibman, and Shunan Lin. Multiple description coding for video delivery. *Proceedings of the IEEE*, 93(1):57–70, Jan, 2005.

28. Igor Kozintsev and Kannan Ramchandran. A wavelet zerotree-based hybrid compressed/uncompressed framework for wireless image transmission. In *Signals, Systems & Computers, 1997. Conference Record of the Thirty-First Asilomar Conference on*, volume 2, pages 1023–1027. IEEE, 1997.

29. Mikael Skoglund, Nam Phamdo, and Fady Alajaji. Hybrid digital-analog source-channel coding for bandwidth compression/expansion. *IEEE Transactions on Information Theory*, 52(8):3757–3763, 2006.

30. Mikael Skoglund, N Phamdo, and Fady Alajaji. Design and performance of vq-based hybrid digital-analog joint source-channel codes. *IEEE Transactions on Information Theory*, 48(3):708 –720, Mar, 2002.

31. Udar Mittal and Nam Phamdo. Hybrid digital-analog (HDA) joint source-channel codes for broadcasting and robust communications. *IEEE Transactions on Information Theory*, 48(5):1082–1102, 2002.

32. Yuval Kochman and Ram Zamir. Joint Wyner-Ziv/dirty-paper coding by modulo-lattice modulation. *IEEE Transactions on Information Theory*, 55:4878–4899, Nov, 2009.

33. Hamid Behroozi, Fady Alajaji, and Tamás Linder. On the performance of hybrid digital-analog coding for broadcasting correlated Gaussian sources. *IEEE Transactions on Communications*, 59(12):3335–3342, 2011.

34. Yadong Wang, Fady Alajaji, and Tamás Linder. Design of VQ-based hybrid digital-analog joint source-channel codes for image communication. In *Proceedings of the Data Compression Conference*, pages 193–202. IEEE, 2005.

35. Lei Yu, Houqiang Li, and Weiping Li. Wireless scalable video coding using a hybrid digital-analog scheme. *IEEE Transactions on Circuits and Systems for Video Technology*, 24(2):331–345, 2014.

36. Hao Cui, Zhihai Song, Zhe Yang, Chong Luo, Ruiqin Xiong, and Feng Wu. Cactus: A hybrid digital-analog wireless video communication system. In *Proceedings of the 16th ACM International Conference on Modeling, Analysis, Simulation of Wireless and Mobile Systems*, MSWiM'13, pages 273–278, 2013.

37. Hao Cui, Ruiqin Xiong, Chong Luo, Zhihai Song, and Feng Wu. Denoising and resource allocation in uncoded video transmission. *IEEE Journal of Selected Topics in Signal Processing*, 9(1):102–112, 2014.

38. Kun Tan, He Liu, Jiansong Zhang, Yongguang Zhang, Ji Fang, and Geoffrey M Voelker. Sora: high-performance software radio using general-purpose multi-core processors. *Commun. ACM*, 54(1):99–107, Jan, 2011.

39. Xiaopeng Fan, Feng Wu, Debin Zhao, Oscar C Au, and Wen Gao. Distributed soft video broadcast (DCAST) with explicit motion. In *Data Compression Conference (DCC), 2012*, pages 199–208, 2012.

40. Feng Wu, Xiulian Peng, and Jizheng Xu. Linecast: Line-based distributed coding and transmission for broadcasting satellite images. *IEEE Transactions on Image Processing*, 23(3):1015–1027, 2014.

41. Seung-Jong Choi and John W Woods. Motion-compensated 3-D subband coding of video. *IEEE Transactions on Image Processing*, 8(2):155–167, Feb, 1999.

42. W. K. Pratt. Median filtering. Technical report, Image Processing Institute, University of Southern California, Sept, 1975.

43. Kostadin Dabov, Alessandro Foi, Vladimir Katkovnik, and Karen Egiazarian. Image denoising by sparse 3-d transform-domain collaborative filtering. *IEEE Transactions on Image Processing*, 16(8):2080–2095, Aug, 2007.

44. Ruiqin Xiong, Feng Wu, Xiaopeng Fan, Chong Luo, Siwei Ma, and Wen Gao. Power-distortion optimization for wireless image/video softcast by transform coefficients energy modeling with adaptive chunk division. In *2013 Visual Communications and Image Processing (VCIP)*, pages 1–6. IEEE, 2013.

45. Bm3d algorithm and its extensions. Technical report, http://www.cs.tut.fi/ foi/GCF-BM3D/.

46. S. H. Y. Wong, H. Yang, S. Lu, and V. Bharghavan. Robust Rate Adaptation for 802.11 Wireless Networks. pages 146–157, Los Angeles, CA, USA, 2006. ACM.

47. *JSVM reference software.* http://www.hhi.fraunhofer.de/.

48. Anne Aaron, Rui Zhang, and Bernd Girod. Wyner-Ziv coding of motion video. In *Signals, Systems and Computers, 2002. Conference Record of the Thirty-Sixth Asilomar Conference on*, volume 1, pages 240–244, 2002.

49. Bernd Girod, Anne Margot Aaron, Shantanu Rane, and David Rebollo-Monedero. Distributed video coding. *Proceedings of the IEEE*, 93(1):71–83, 2005.

50. Rohit Puri and Kannan Ramchandran. Prism: A new robust video coding architecture based on distributed compression principles. In *the Annual Allerton Conference on Communication Control and Computing*, 2002.

51. Rohit Puri, Abhik Majumdar, and Kannan Ramchandran. Prism: A video coding paradigm with motion estimation at the decoder. *IEEE Transactions on Image Processing*, 16(10):2436–2448, 2007.

52. David Slepian and Jack Wolf. Noiseless coding of correlated information sources. *IEEE Transactions on Information Theory*, 19(4):471–480, 1973.

53. Aaron Wyner and Jacob Ziv. The rate-distortion function for source coding with side information at the decoder. *IEEE Transactions on information Theory*, 22(1):1–10, 1976.

54. Qian Xu and Zixiang Xiong. Layered wyner–ziv video coding. *IEEE Transactions on Image Processing*, 15(12):3791–3803, 2006.

55. Qian Xu, Vladimir Stankovic, and Zixiang Xiong. Distributed joint source-channel coding of video using raptor codes. *IEEE Journal on Selected areas in communications*, 25(4):851–861, 2007.

56. A Secker and David Taubman. Lifting-based invertible motion adaptive transform (limat) framework for highly scalable video compression. *IEEE Transactions on Image Processing*, 12(12):1530–1542, 2003.

57. Yixuan Zhang, Ce Zhu, and Kim-Hui Yap. A joint source-channel video coding scheme based on distributed source coding. *IEEE Transactions on Multimedia*, 10(8):1648–1656, 2008.

58. Mei Guo, Zixiang Xiong, Feng Wu, Debin Zhao, Xiangyang Ji, and Wen Gao. Witsenhausen-wyner video coding. *IEEE Transactions on Circuits and Systems for Video Technology*, 21(8):1049–1060, 2011.

59. Xiaopeng Fan, Feng Wu, and Debin Zhao. D-cast: Dsc based soft mobile video broadcast. In *Proceedings of the 10th International Conference on Mobile and Ubiquitous Multimedia*, 2011.

60. A Secker and David Taubman. Highly scalable video compression with scalable motion coding. *IEEE Transactions on Image Processing*, 13(8):1029–1041, 2004.

61. Elliott D Kaplan and Christopher J Hegarty. *Understanding GPS: principles and applications*. Artech House, 2005.

62. Google. Google can track ships at sea. Technical report, http://defense.aol.com/2012/05/17/google-satellites-can-track-every-ship-at-sea-including-us-na/, 2012.

63. Geoeye website, http://www.geoeye.com/corpsite/.

64. S. Sandeep Pradhan and Kannan Ramchandran. Distributed source coding using syndromes (discus): design and construction. *IEEE Transactions on Information Theory*, 49(3):626–643, 2003.

65. Xiulian Peng, Jizheng Xu, You Zhou, and Feng Wu. Highly parallel line-based image coding for many cores. *IEEE Transactions on Image Processing*, 21(1):196–206, 2012.

66. The usc-sipi image database, http://sipi.usc.edu/database/.

67. Hao Cui, Chong Luo, Chang Wen Chen, and Feng Wu. Robust linear video transmission over rayleigh fading channel. *IEEE Transactions on Communications*, 62(8):2790–2801, 2014.

68. Dongliang He, Cuiling Lan, Chong Luo, Enhong Chen, Feng Wu, and Wenjun Zeng. Progressive pseudo-analog transmission for mobile video streaming. *IEEE Transactions on Multimedia*, 19(8):1894–1907, 2017.

69. Xiaoda Jiang, Hancheng Lu, Chang Wen Chen, and Feng Wu. Receiver-driven video multicast over noma systems in heterogeneous environments. In *IEEE INFOCOM 2019-IEEE Conference on Computer Communications*, pages 982–990. IEEE, 2019.

70. Yongqiang Gui, Hancheng Lu, Feng Wu, and Chang Wen Chen. Robust video broadcast for users with heterogeneous resolution in mobile networks. *IEEE Transactions on Mobile Computing*, 2020.

71. Wai Wong, R Steele, B Glance, and D Horn. Time diversity with adaptive error detection to combat Rayleigh fading in digital mobile radio. *IEEE Transactions on Communications*, 31(3):378–387, 1983.

72. Gwo-Tsuey Chyi, John G Proakis, and Catherine M Keller. On the symbol error probability of maximum-selection diversity reception schemes over a Rayleigh fading channel. *IEEE Transactions on Communications*, 37(1):79–83, 1989.

73. Akshay Kashyap, Tamer Basar, and R Srikant. Minimum distortion transmission of Gaussian sources over fading channels. In *Proceedings of the 42nd IEEE Conf. on Decision and Control*, volume 1, pages 80–85. IEEE, 2003.

74. Jin-Jun Xiao, Zhi-Quan Luo, and Nihar Jindal. Linear joint source-channel coding for gaussian sources through fading channels. In *IEEE Globecom 2006*, pages 1–5. IEEE, 2006.

75. Christodoulos A Floudas. *Nonlinear and mixed-integer optimization: fundamentals and applications*. Oxford University Press, 1995.

76. Jo Bo Rosen. The gradient projection method for nonlinear programming. part i. linear constraints. *Journal of the Society for Industrial and Applied Mathematics*, 8(1):181–217, 1960.

77. Ruiqin Xiong, Feng Wu, Jizheng Xu, and Wen Gao. Performance analysis of transform in uncoded wireless visual communication. In *2013 IEEE International Symposium on Circuits and Systems (ISCAS2013)*, pages 1159–1162. IEEE, 2013.

78. Xiph test media. https://media.xiph.org/.

79. Dongliang He, Chong Luo, Cuiling Lan, Feng Wu, and Wenjun Zeng. Structure-preserving hybrid digital-analog video delivery in wireless networks. *IEEE Transactions on Multimedia*, 17(9):1658–1670, Sept, 2015.

80. Linglong Dai, Bichai Wang, Zhiguo Ding, Zhaocheng Wang, Sheng Chen, and Lajos Hanzo. A survey of non-orthogonal multiple access for 5g. *IEEE Communications Surveys & Tutorials*, 20(3):2294–2323, 2018.

81. Zhiguo Ding, Xianfu Lei, George K Karagiannidis, Robert Schober, Jinhong Yuan, and Vijay K Bhargava. A survey on non-orthogonal multiple access for 5g networks: Research challenges and future trends. *IEEE Journal on Selected Areas in Communications*, 35(10):2181–2195, 2017.

82. SM Riazul Islam, Nurilla Avazov, Octavia A Dobre, and Kyung-Sup Kwak. Power-domain non-orthogonal multiple access (noma) in 5g systems: Potentials and challenges. *IEEE Communications Surveys & Tutorials*, 19(2):721–742, 2016.

83. Xiaoda Jiang, Hancheng Lu, and Chang Wen Chen. Enabling quality-driven scalable video transmission over multi-user noma system. In *IEEE INFOCOM 2018-IEEE Conference on Computer Communications*, pages 1952–1960. IEEE, 2018.

84. Jinho Choi. Minimum power multicast beamforming with superposition coding for multiresolution broadcast and application to noma systems. *IEEE Transactions on Communications*, 63(3):791–800, 2015.

85. Zhengquan Zhang, Zheng Ma, Ming Xiao, Xianfu Lei, Zhiguo Ding, and Pingzhi Fan. Fundamental tradeoffs of non-orthogonal multicast, multicast, and unicast in ultra-dense networks. *IEEE Transactions on Communications*, 66(8):3555–3570, 2018.

86. *Digital Video Broadcast, en_300744v010601p.* http://www.etsi.org/.

87. Daosen Zhai, Ruonan Zhang, Lin Cai, Bin Li, and Yi Jiang. Energy-efficient user scheduling and power allocation for noma-based wireless networks with massive iot devices. *IEEE Internet of Things Journal*, 5(3):1857–1868, 2018.

88. Yuan Wu, Li Ping Qian, Haowei Mao, Xiaowei Yang, HaiBo Zhou, and Xuemin Shen. Optimal power allocation and scheduling for non-orthogonal multiple access relay-assisted networks. *IEEE Transactions on Mobile Computing*, 17(11):2591–2606, 2018.

89. Fang Fang, Haijun Zhang, Julian Cheng, Sébastien Roy, and Victor CM Leung. Joint user scheduling and power allocation optimization for energy-efficient noma systems with imperfect csi. *IEEE Journal on Selected Areas in Communications*, 35(12):2874–2885, 2017.

90. Boya Di, Siavash Bayat, Lingyang Song, Yonghui Li, and Zhu Han. Joint user pairing, subchannel, and power allocation in full-duplex multi-user ofdma networks. *IEEE Transactions on Wireless Communications*, 15(12):8260–8272, 2016.

91. Shen Pei-Ping and Yuan Gui-Xia. Global optimization for the sum of generalized polynomial fractional functions. *Mathematical Methods of Operations Research*, 65(3):445–459, 2007.

92. Elizabeth Bodine-Baron, Christina Lee, Anthony Chong, Babak Hassibi, and Adam Wierman. Peer effects and stability in matching markets. In *International Symposium on Algorithmic Game Theory*, pages 117–129. Springer, 2011.

93. AE Roth and Oliveira Sotomayor. Two-sided matching: A study in game-theoretic modeling and analysis. 1992.

94. Siavash Bayat, Raymond HY Louie, Zhu Han, Branka Vucetic, and Yonghui Li. Distributed user association and femtocell allocation in heterogeneous wireless networks. *IEEE Transactions on Communications*, 62(8):3027–3043, 2014.

95. David Gale and Lloyd S Shapley. College admissions and the stability of marriage. *The American Mathematical Monthly*, 69(1):9–15, 1962.

96. C Andrew Segall and Gary J Sullivan. Spatial scalability within the h. 264/avc scalable video coding extension. *IEEE Transactions on Circuits and Systems for Video Technology*, 17(9):1121–1135, 2007.

97. Nicola Adami, Alberto Signoroni, and Riccardo Leonardi. State-of-the-art and trends in scalable video compression with wavelet-based approaches. *IEEE Transactions on Circuits and Systems for Video Technology*, 17(9):1238–1255, 2007.

98. Amir Averbuch, Danny Lazar, and Moshe Israeli. Image compression using wavelet transform and multiresolution decomposition. *IEEE Transactions on Image Processing*, 5(1):4–15, 1996.

99. Po-Yuen Cheng, Jin Li, and C-C Jay Kuo. Multiscale video compression using wavelet transform and motion compensation. In *Proceedings, International Conference on Image Processing*, volume 1, pages 606–609. IEEE, 1995.

100. Daniel Halperin, Wenjun Hu, Anmol Sheth, and David Wetherall. Predictable 802.11 packet delivery from wireless channel measurements. *ACM SIGCOMM Computer Communication Review*, 41(4):159–170, 2011.

101. Xiao Lin Liu, Wenjun Hu, Qifan Pu, Feng Wu, and Yongguang Zhang. Parcast: Soft video delivery in mimo-ofdm wlans. In *Proceedings of the 18th Annual International Conference on Mobile Computing and Networking*, Mobicom'12, pages 233–244, 2012.

102. Zhilong Zhang, Danpu Liu, Xiaoli Ma, and Xin Wang. Ecast: An enhanced video transmission design for wireless multicast systems over fading channels. *IEEE Systems Journal*, 11(4):2566–2577, 2015.

103. Ruiqin Xiong, Feng Wu, Jizheng Xu, Xiaopeng Fan, Chong Luo, and Wen Gao. Analysis of decorrelation transform gain for uncoded wireless image and video communication. *IEEE Transactions on Image Processing*, 25(4):1820–1833, 2016.

104. Zhilong Zhang, Danpu Liu, and Xin Wang. Joint carrier matching and power allocation for wireless video with general distortion measure. *IEEE Transactions on Mobile Computing*, 17(3):577–589, 2017.

105. Stephen Boyd and Lieven Vandenberghe. *Convex optimization*. Cambridge University Press, 2004.

106. Zan Yang and Xiaodong Wang. Scalable video broadcast over downlink mimo–ofdm systems. *IEEE Transactions on Circuits and Systems for Video Technology*, 23(2):212–223, 2012.

107. Guocong Song and Ye Li. Cross-layer optimization for ofdm wireless networks-part i: theoretical framework. *IEEE Transactions on Wireless Communications*, 4(2):614–624, 2005.

108. Ya-Feng Liu and Yu-Hong Dai. On the complexity of joint subcarrier and power allocation for multi-user ofdma systems. *IEEE Transactions on Signal Processing*, 62(3):583–596, 2013.

109. Kai Yang, Narayan Prasad, and Xiaodong Wang. An auction approach to resource allocation in uplink ofdma systems. *IEEE Transactions on Signal Processing*, 57(11):4482–4496, 2009.

110. Dimitri P Bertsekas. Auction algorithms for network flow problems: A tutorial introduction. *Computational Optimization and Applications*, 1(1):7–66, 1992.

111. Dimitri P Bertsekas. Auction algorithms. *Encyclopedia of Optimization*, 1:73–77, 2009.

112. Chaofan He, Huiying Wang, Yang Hu, Yan Chen, Xiaopeng Fan, Houqiang Li, and Bing Zeng. Mcast: High-quality linear video transmission with time and frequency diversities. *IEEE Transactions on Image Processing*, 27(7):3599–3610, 2018.

113. Cornelius Hellge, Shpend Mirta, Thomas Schierl, and Thomas Wiegand. Mobile tv with svc and hierarchical modulation for dvb-h broadcast services. In *2009 IEEE International Symposium on Broadband Multimedia Systems and Broadcasting*, pages 1–5. IEEE, 2009.

114. Jian Shen, Lei Yu, Li Li, and Houqiang Li. Foveation-based wireless soft image delivery. *IEEE Transactions on Multimedia*, 20(10):2788–2800, 2018.

115. Tiesong Zhao, Qian Liu, and Chang Wen Chen. Qoe in video transmission: A user experience-driven strategy. *IEEE Communications Surveys & Tutorials*, 19(1):285–302, 2016.

116. Xiao Lin Liu, Wenjun Hu, Chong Luo, and Feng Wu. Compressive image broadcasting in mimo systems with receiver antenna heterogeneity. *Signal Processing: Image Communication*, 29(3):361–374, Mar, 2014.

117. Hao Cui, Chong Luo, Chang Wen Chen, and Feng Wu. Scalable video multicast for mu-mimo systems with antenna heterogeneity. *IEEE Transactions on Circuits and Systems for Video Technology*, 26(5):992–1003, 2016.

118. Siripuram Aditya and Sachin Katti. Flexcast: graceful wireless video streaming. In *Proceedings of International Conference on Mobile Computing and Networking (MobiCom'11)*, pages 277–288, 2011.

119. Hemanth Sampath and Arogyaswami J Paulraj. Joint transmit and receive optimization for high data rate wireless communication using multiple antennas. In *Signals, Systems, and Computers, 1999. Conference Record of the Thirty-Third Asilomar Conference on*, volume 1, pages 215–219, 1999.

120. Ruiqin Xiong, Feng Wu, Jizheng Xu, Shipeng Li, and Ya-Qin Zhang. Barbell lifting wavelet transform for highly scalable video coding. pages 237–242, 2004.

121. Xiaopeng Fan, Ruiqin Xiong, Feng Wu, and Debin Zhao. Wavecast: Wavelet based wireless video broadcast using lossy transmission. In *VCIP*, pages 1–6. IEEE, 2012.

122. G. H. Park, M. W. Park, S. Jeong, K. Kim, and J. Hong. Improve svc coding efficiency by adaptive gop structure (svc ce2). *ISO/IEC JTC1/SC29/WG11 and ITU-T SG16 Q*, 6, 2005.

123. Godfrey Harold Hardy, John Edensor Littlewood, and George Pólya. Inequalities, (2nd ed.), Cambridge Mathematical Library, 1989.

124. Hariharan Rahul, Haitham Hassanieh, and Dina Katabi. Sourcesync: a distributed wireless architecture for exploiting sender diversity. *ACM SIGCOMM Computer Communication Review*, 41(4):171–182, 2011.

125. Iain E Richardson. *H. 264 and MPEG-4 video compression*, volume 20. Wiley Online Library, 2003.

126. H.264/AVC JM Reference Software. http://iphome.hhi.de/suehring/tml/.

127. IEEE Std. 802.11n-2009: Enhancements for Higher Throughput.

128. http://videocoders.com/yuv.html.

129. David Tse and Pramod Viswanath. *Fundamentals of Wireless Communication*. Cambridge University Press, 2005.

130. Hariharan Rahul, Farinaz Edalat, Dina Katabi, and Charles G Sodini. Frequency-aware rate adaptation and MAC protocols. In *ACM MobiCom*, pages 193–204, 2009.

131. Szymon Jakubczak and Dina Katabi. Softcast: One-size-fits-all wireless video. In *Proceedings of the ACM SIGCOMM 2010 conference*, pages 449–450, 2010.

132. Chihhung Kuo and C C J Kuo. An embedded space-time coding (stc) scheme for broadcasting. *IEEE Transactions on Broadcasting*, 53(1):48–58, March, 2007.

133. Chihhung Kuo, Chienming Wang, and Jiungliang Lin. Cooperative wireless broadcast for scalable video coding. *IEEE Transactions on Circuits and Systems for Video Technology*, 21(6):816–824, 2011.

134. Cagdas Bilen, Elza Erkip, and Yao Wang. Layered video multicast using diversity embedded space time codes. In *Sarnoff Symposium*, pages 1–5. IEEE, 2009.

135. Seok-Ho Chang, Minjoong Rim, Pamela C Cosman, and Laurence B Milstein. Superposition mimo coding for the broadcast of layered sources. *IEEE Transactions on Communications*, 59(12):3240–3248, 2011.

136. Xiao Lin Liu, Chong Luo, Wenjun Hu, and Feng Wu. Compressive broadcast in mimo systems with receive antenna heterogeneity. In *IEEE INFOCOM'12*, pages 3011–3015, March, 2012.

137. Ingrid Daubechies. Orthonormal bases of compactly supported wavelets. *Communications on Pure and Applied Mathematics*, 41(7):909–996, 1988.

138. Yi Yang, Oscar C Au, Lu Fang, Xing Wen, and Weiran Tang. Perceptual compressive sensing for image signals. In *2009 IEEE International Conference on Multimedia and Expo*, pages 89–92. IEEE, 2009.

139. Emmanuel J Candes and Terence Tao. Decoding by linear programming. *IEEE transactions on information theory*, 51(12):4203–4215, 2005.

140. Emmanuel J Candès and Michael B Wakin. An introduction to compressive sampling. *Signal Processing Magazine, IEEE*, 25(2):21–30, 2008.

141. Lu Gan, Thong T Do, and Trac D Tran. Fast compressive imaging using scrambled block Hadamard ensemble. *2008 16th European Signal Processing Conference*, pages 1–5, 2008.

142. Saeid Haghighatshoar, Emmanuel Abbe, and Emre Telatar. Adaptive sensing using deterministic partial Hadamard matrices. In *IEEE International Symposium on Information Theory Proceedings (ISIT)*, pages 1842–1846, 2012.

143. Emmanuel J Candes, Michael B Wakin, and Stephen P Boyd. Enhancing sparsity by reweighted L1 minimization. *Journal of Fourier Analysis and Applications*, 14(5):877–905, 2008.

144. Ping Luo. Hierarchical modulation for the downlink of mimo multi-user channels. In *Proc. of 1st International Conference on CCSP with Special Track on Biomedical Engineering*, pages 77–80. IEEE, 2005.

145. Amrico MC Correia, Joo CM Silva, Nuno MB Souto, Lusa AC Silva, Alexandra B Boal, and Armando B Soares. Multi-resolution broadcast/multicast systems for mbms. *IEEE Transactions on Broadcasting*, 53(1):224–234, March, 2007.

146. Jian Zhang, Debin Zhao, Chen Zhao, Ruiqin Xiong, Siwei Ma, and Wen Gao. Image compressive sensing recovery via collaborative sparsity. *IEEE Journal on Emerging and Selected Topics in Circuits and Systems*, 2(3):380–391, 2012.

147. Siavash Alamouti. A simple transmit diversity technique for wireless communications. *IEEE Journal on Selected Areas in Communications*, 16(8):1451–1458, Oct, 1998.

148. Hamid Jafarkhani. A quasi-orthogonal space-time block code. *IEEE Transactions on Communications*, 49(1):1–4, Jan. 2001.

149. Cuiling Lan, Chong Luo, Wenjun Zeng, and Feng Wu. A practical hybrid digital-analog scheme for wireless video transmission. *IEEE Transactions on Circuits and Systems for Video Technology*, 28(7):1634–1647, 2017.

150. Fei Liang, Chong Luo, Ruiqin Xiong, Wenjun Zeng, and Feng Wu. Superimposed modulation for soft video delivery with hidden resources. *IEEE Transactions on Circuits and Systems for Video Technology*, 28(9):2345–2358, 2017.

151. Xiao Zhao, Hancheng Lu, Chang Wen Chen, and Jun Wu. Adaptive hybrid digital–analog video transmission in wireless fading channel. *IEEE Transactions on Circuits and Systems for Video Technology*, 26(6):1117–1130, 2015.

152. Xi Liu, Osvaldo Simeone, and Elza Erkip. Energy-efficient sensing and communication of parallel Gaussian sources. *IEEE Communication Letter*, 60(12):3826–3835, 2012.

153. James E Mazo. Quantizing noise and data transmission. *Bell System Technical Journal*, 47(8):1737–1753, 1968.

154. Thomas M Cover and Joy A Thomas. *Elements of Information Theory*. John Wiley and Sons, New York, 2006.

155. Kaidi D Huang, David Malone, and Ken R Duffy. The 802.11g 11 mb/s rate is more robust than 6 mb/s. *IEEE Transactions on Wireless Communications*, 10(4):1015–1020, 2011.

156. Karl Skretting, John Håkon Husøy, and Sven Ole Aase. Improved Huffman coding using recursive splitting. In *Proceedings of Norwegian Signal Processing*, 1999.

157. C Lawrence Zitnick, Sing Bing Kang, Matthew Uyttendaele, Simon Winder, and Richard Szeliski. High-quality video view interpolation using a layered representation. *ACM Transactions on Graphics (TOG)*, 23(3):600–608, 2004.

158. Emilie Bosc, Romuald Pépion, Patrick Le Callet, Martin Köppel, Patrick Ndjiki-Nya, Muriel Pressigout, and Luce Muriel. Towards a new quality metric for 3-d synthesized view assessment. *IEEE Journal of Selected Topics in Signal Processing*, 5(7):1332–1343, 2011.

159. Zhou Wang, Alan C Bovik, Hamid R Sheikh, and Eero P Simoncelli. Image quality assessment: from error visibility to structural similarity. *IEEE Transactions on Image Processing*, 13(4):600–612, April, 2004.

160. Ruiqin Xiong, Hangfan Liu, Siwei Ma, Xiaopeng Fan, Feng Wu, and Wen Gao. G-cast: Gradient based image softcast for perception-friendly wireless visual communication. In *2014 Data Compression Conference*, pages 133–142. IEEE, 2014.

161. Rafael C Gonzales and Richard E Woods. *Digital Image Processing, 3th edition*. Pearson Press, 2007.

162. Glen G Langdon. An introduction to arithmetic coding. *IBM Journal of Research and Development*, 28(2), 1984.

163. IEEE. Iso/iec standard for information technology - telecommunications and information exchange between systems - local and metropolitan area networks - specific requirements part 11: Wireless lan medium access control (mac) and physical layer (phy) specifications. *ISO/IEC 8802-11 IEEE Std 802.11 Second edition 2005-08-01 ISO/IEC 8802 11:2005(E) IEEE Std 802.11i-2003 Edition*, pages 1–721, 2005.

164. Nejat Kamaci, Yucel Altunbasak, and Russell M Mersereau. Frame bit allocation for the H.264/avc video coder via Cauchy-density-based rate and distortion models. *IEEE Transactions on Circuits and Systems for Video Technology*, 15(8):994–1006, 2005.

165. Jiro Katto and Mutsumi Ohta. Mathematical analysis of mpeg compression capability and its application to rate control. In *Image Processing, 1995. Proceedings., International Conference on*, volume 2, pages 555–558 vol. 2, 1995.

166. A Robert Calderbank. Multilevel codes and multistage decoding. *IEEE Transactions on Communications*, 37(3):222–229, Mar, 1989.

167. Markus Dillinger, Kambiz Madani, and Nancy Alonistioti. *Software defined radio: Architectures, systems and functions*. John Wiley & Sons, 2005.

168. Daji Qiao, Sunghyn Choi, and Kang G Shin. Goodput analysis and link adaptation for ieee 802.11 a wireless lans. *IEEE Transactions on Mobile Computing*, 1(4):278–292, 2002.

169. Joeri Barbarien, Yiannis Andreopoulos, Adrian Munteanu, Peter Schelkens, and Jan Cornelis. Motion vector coding for in-band motion compensated temporal filtering. In *Proceedings 2003 International Conference on Image Processing*, volume 2, pages II–783. IEEE, 2003.

170. Ralf Schäfer, Heiko Schwarz, Detlev Marpe, Thomas Schierl, and Thomas Wiegand. MCTF and scalability extension of h. 264/avc and its application to video transmission, storage, and surveillance. In *Visual Communications and Image Processing 2005*, volume 5960, page 596011. International Society for Optics and Photonics, 2005.

171. Szymon Jakubczak, Hariharan Rahul, and Dina Katabi. Softcast: One video to serve all wireless receivers. *MIT Technical Report, MIT-CSAIL-TR-2009–005*, 2009.

172. Tugay Eyceoz and Alexandra Duel-Hallen. Simplified block adaptive diversity equalizer for cellular mobile radio. *IEEE Communications Letters*, 1(1):15–18, 1997.

173. Lei Yu, Houqiang Li, and Weiping Li. Hybrid digital-analog scheme for video transmission over wireless. In *2013 IEEE International Symposium on Circuits and Systems (ISCAS2013)*, pages 1163–1166. IEEE, 2013.

174. Tugay Eyceoz, Alexandra Duel-Hallen, and Hans Hallen. Prediction of fast fading parameters by resolving the interference pattern. In *Conference Record of the Thirty-First Asilomar Conference on Signals, Systems and Computers*, volume 1, pages 167–171. IEEE, 1997.

175. Tugay Eyceoz, Alexandra Duel-Hallen, and Hans Hallen. Deterministic channel modeling and long range prediction of fast fading mobile radio channels. *IEEE Communications Letters*, 2(9):254–256, 1998.

176. A Du-Hallen, S Hu, and H Hallen. Long-range prediction of fading signals: enabling adaptive transmission for mobile radio channels. *IEEE Signal Process. Mag*, 17(3):62–75, 2000.

177. Tugay Eyceoz, Alexandra Duel-Hallen, and Hans D Hallen. Using the physics of the fast fading to improve performance for mobile radio channels. In *Proc. IEEE Int. Symp. Information Theory*, pages 159–159, 1998.

178. Stéphane Mallat. *A wavelet tour of signal processing*. Elsevier, 1999.

179. http://www.videolan.org/developers/x264.html.

180. John G Proakis and Masoud Salehi. *Digital communications*, volume 4. McGraw-Hill New York, 2001.

Index

Printed in the United States
by Baker & Taylor Publisher Services